WD 3/14

Pair of Golden Eagles over Ardnamurchan with the islands of Rum and Eigg in the background (with permission from artist, Donald Watson)

THE GOLDEN EAGLE

Juvenile Golden Eagle in the rain.

THE GOLDEN EAGLE

Jeff Watson

Illustrated by
Keith Brockie

With colour plate and landscapes by
Donald Watson

T & A D POYSER

London

Illustrations © Keith Brockie and Donald Watson

© T & AD Poyser 1997

ISBN 0–85661–099–2

First published in 1997 by T & AD Poyser Ltd
24–28 Oval Road, London, NW1 7DX

This book is printed on acid-free paper

Typeset by Phoenix Photosetting, Chatham, Kent
Printed and bound in Great Britain by
The Bath Press, Bath

A CIP record for this book is available from the British Library

For Vanessa and Ronan

Juvenile Golden Eagle after unsuccessful stoop at Mountain Hare in deep snow.

Studies of juvenile Golden Eagle feeding on carrion.

Contents

List of Figures

List of Tables

Acknowledgements

SO many people have contributed to the realization of this book. My mother and father, Joan and Donald Watson, gave me every encouragement to pursue an interest in birds and they have been a constant source of moral support. I owe a very special debt to the late George Dunnet for his wisdom and humanity when I was a student at Aberdeen University in the 1970s. Derek Langslow, senior ornithologist with the Nature Conservancy Council in the early 1980s, first offered me the chance to work full-time on Golden Eagles. Throughout the past 20 years I have learned an enormous amount from discussions with Ian Newton, whose understanding of raptor population ecology is unsurpassed. Since 1985, my work with the Nature Conservancy Council and then with Scottish Natural Heritage has been under the direction of Peter Tilbrook with whom it has been a privilege to work. Trevor Poyser initially suggested the idea of a book on the Golden Eagle, and Andrew Richford of Academic Press has provided constant support and advice throughout.

During my time studying eagles in various parts of western Scotland I have made many firm friends. For their kindness and warm hospitality I owe a special debt to Liz and Sandy Macdonald, Mike and Karen Macgregor, Peter and Joan Madden, Jim and Tina Rowbottom, Mike and Celia Gregory and Roy and Marina Dennis. Much of my early fieldwork on Golden Eagles was shared with Stuart Rae whose persistence, dedication and self-reliance during long hours on the hill were a constant source of inspiration. Our work was enhanced by the contribution of Alan Leitch who analysed our eagle pellets and helped confirm the identification of prey remains. Liz MacDonald did much of the recent monitoring of eagles in one of our principal study areas and I am indebted to her for this. Kate Nellist and Ken Crane generously allowed me to use information from their work on the Isle of Skye.

Among those who gave freely of their knowledge of eagles from the earliest days of our study were Dick Balharry, Morton Boyd, Geoff Bates, Roger Broad, Keith Brockie, John Buxton, Colin Crooke, Edwin Cross, Roy Dennis, Dave Dick, Pete Ellis, Mike Gregory, Art Lance, Mike MacGregor, Mick Marquiss, the late Charlie Palmer, Sandy Payne, Robert Rae, Derek Ratcliffe, Dick Roxburgh, Pat Sandeman and Adam Watson. Much of the information on Scottish Golden Eagles in this book has been enhanced through the efforts and continuing commitment of the Scottish Raptor Study Groups. Members of this dedicated band of workers gave their time unstintingly and without payment. The scale of their contribution to the conservation of our birds of prey is rarely given the public recognition it deserves. Through this book I hope that the true value of this voluntary effort will become more widely appreciated. In addition to many of the individuals mentioned above, I am indebted to the following for allowing me to use their unpublished records: Roland Ascroft, Dave Batty, Bill Brackenridge, Hugh Brown, Ewan Cameron, David Carstairs, John Carruthers, Tim Clifford, the late Philip Coxon, Alastair Duncan, Davie Duncan, Eric Duthie, Mike Everett, Pete Ewins, Keith Fairclough, Claire Geddes, Sandy Gordon, Dave Gowans, Jon Hardey, Malcolm Harvey, the late Bill Henderson, Ian Hopkins, Eric Jensen, Rose Kirk, John Love, Mike Madders, Don and Bridget Mackaskill, the late Lea MacNally, Tony Mainwood, Allan Mee, Mike Nicoll, Lorcan O'Toole, Steve Petty, Dave Pullan, Andrew Ramsey, Graham Rebecca, Adam Ritchie, Chris Rollie, Alex Scott, Ken Shaw, John Smith, Patrick Stirling-Aird, Bob Swann, Tom Talbot, Bill Taylor, Richard Thaxton, Mike Tomkies, David Walker, Mike Walker, Doug Weir, Dave Whitaker and Richard Wood.

Although work on Golden Eagles has not been part of my mainstream employment for a number of years, many of my colleagues at Scottish Natural Heritage, especially in Northwest Scotland, have been a continuing source of inspiration and encouragement. In particular, I would thank Helen Armstrong, David Balharry, Nicky Black, Barbara Bremner, Amanda Bryan, Nigel Buxton, Ray

Collier, Andrew Coupar, Lesley Cranna, Pam Chambers, Diana Gilbert, Bob Grant, Rachel Harding-Hill, George Hogg, John Lister-Kaye, Sandy Maclennan, Andrew Matheson, Ian Mitchell, Sandy Payne, Bill Ritchie, Ro Scott, Ian Strachan, Chris Sydes, Des Thompson, Paul Thompson, John Thomson, Michael Usher, Peter Tilbrook, Valerie Wilson and Peter Wortham.

Over the last five years, people have responded generously to my written requests for information and advice. Mike McGrady and Justin Grant gave regular updates on the new and exciting work they are doing in Argyll on Golden Eagles fitted with radiotransmitters. Chris Mead kindly sent me unpublished information on ringing recoveries. Ken Hunter of the Scottish Agricultural Science Agency in Edinburgh provided detailed records of post mortem analysis of Golden Eagles, as did Lois Dale from the Institute of Terrestrial Ecology at Monks Wood. Keith Morton of the Royal Society for the Protection of Birds gave me unpublished information on the instances of poison abuse in Scotland. Rhys Green made available a preliminary analysis of the 1992 national survey of Golden Eagles. Carol Warman and Kenny Grierson helped with the extraction and analysis of forestry data and Pam Chambers disentangled my most stubborn computing problems. I am grateful to Cliff Henty for his critical reappraisal of an earlier analysis that I did on an aspect of nest site selection by Golden Eagles in Scotland. John Love kindly let me use historical information he had extracted on Scottish Golden Eagle clutches from various museum collections. Keith Brockie sent me post mortem analyses of two eagles that had died from disease.

Many eagle watchers responded to my request for sightings of Golden Eagles killing prey. In particular I thank the following for offering comments and observations on this rarely witnessed aspect of eagle behaviour: Geoff Bates, Keith Brockie, John Carruthers, Ken Crane, Roy Dennis, Dave Dick, Justin Grant, Mike Gregory, Sue Holt, Kate Nellist, Liz MacDonald, Mike McGrady, Mick Marquiss, Sandy Payne, Nick Picozzi, Stuart Rae, Derek Ratcliffe, Chris Rollie, Bob Swann, Andrew Thompson, Ian Watret, Adam Watson and Donald Watson.

My correspondence with 'eagle workers' from outside Britain has been extensive and I am indebted to the many individuals who replied to my requests. Mike and Phyllis Kochert provided generous hospitality during a visit to Idaho where Mike and his colleagues introduced me to their work on birds of prey at Snake River. Miguel and Ester Ferrer were equally accommodating during a visit to Coto Doñana where I saw at first-hand some of the work on Spanish Imperial Eagles. For sending me unpublished information on Golden Eagles in various parts of the world I am especially grateful to the following: Vladimir Ivanovsky, Belorus; Tanyo Michev, Bulgaria; Peter Sherrington, Alberta, Canada; Ron Lee Kam, Ontario, Canada; Tiit Randla, Estonia; Seppo Sulkava, Finland; Štefan Danko and Miloš Majda, Slovakia; Ofer Bahat, Israel; Toru Yamazaki, Japan; Laci Kalabér, Romania; Bernardo Arroyo, Spain; Carol McIntyre and Doug Weir, Alaska, USA. Nigel Collar and Melanie Heath at BirdLife International helped with the assessment of Golden Eagle numbers in Europe. Kate Watson located a selection of invaluable papers on Golden Eagles in the culture of Native Americans and John Love allowed me to draw freely on his own researches into eagles and folklore.

One of the challenges of this book has been the need to interpret information published in so many different languages. In this respect, Rebecca Trengove kept me on the right track with Russian translations. Maggi Kaye and Anne Shalit arranged for papers to be translated from Hebrew. Many correspondents alerted me to publications on eagles in their own countries. For help in obtaining some of the less readily available texts on Golden Eagles I am indebted to Alwyn Coupe and Siobhan Marron. Phil Moors located papers on Gurney's Eagle from New Guinea and Nick Mooney sent me an important publication on the Wedge-tailed Eagle in Tasmania.

The greater part of the book was read in draft by Ian Newton and Sandy Payne who, together, suggested numerous improvements. Others who read and commented on one or more chapters were John Love, Liz MacDonald, Mike McGrady, Stuart Rae, Derek Ratcliffe, Robert Simmons, Des Thompson, Peter Tilbrook, Michael Usher, Adam Watson and Donald Watson. My thanks go to all of them.

Keith Brockie, an artist and eagle enthusiast, has drawn on first-hand knowledge of Golden Eagles to provide the bulk of the illustrations for the book. The extraordinary power of observation is an impressive feature of Keith's work and the quality and quantity of his material makes a huge contribution. The colour plate and wash drawings in Chapter 4 were done by my father, Donald Watson. To him I owe a special debt for the way he has captured so successfully the particular atmosphere of eagle country in Scotland.

During the production phase of the book I have been greatly assisted by Manjula Goonawardena of Academic Press. Manjula's endless patience and calmness in a crisis have been a constant source of inspiration. I am also grateful to Samantha Richardson at Academic Press who took on the mammoth task of sorting out the permissions so successfully.

Finally, I could not have written the book without the support of my wife Vanessa Halhead and our son Ronan. They have tolerated my prolonged absences 'in the garden shed' with exceptional patience and have never ceased to be a source of encouragement. This book is for them, and for all who enjoy the special majesty of the Golden Eagle.

CHAPTER 1

Introduction

T HE proposal to write a monograph on the Golden Eagle was first put to me
more than 5 years ago. On numerous occasions since then I have wondered
whether the task was too great. It has been a lengthy gestation, but perhaps that is
no bad thing. Year by year, new and exciting work on Golden Eagles is being carried
out and published, especially in North America but also in Europe and elsewhere.
Inevitably, statements that I make here will be challenged, tested and enhanced by
new research. That is as it should be, and I hope this book will be a catalyst in the
process as well as a source of reference for those who share my passion for this
splendid bird.

SCOPE OF THE BOOK

This account of the Golden Eagle is founded on work in Scotland where I have
studied the bird for over 15 years. I have also been privileged to observe the species

1

in several other countries in Europe and in North America. As I indicated in the Acknowledgements, I am indebted to many people, and especially to members of the Scottish Raptor Study Groups, for allowing me to use their information to extend my own work. My personal interest in the bird has been focused on two main fields: population ecology (why eagle numbers and breeding success vary from place to place) and human impact on eagles. Consequently, these themes recur regularly throughout this work. At the same time I have attempted a fairly comprehensive account of the general behaviour and ecology of the species, drawing on the extensive global literature for comparative material and to fill in gaps where work has not been done in Scotland. The end result is that I have sought to place the findings from Scotland in a wider context. I believe this to be helpful for the those who study Golden Eagles in Scotland where, in my judgement, the condition of Golden Eagle habitat is far from healthy—so serious is the degradation through overgrazing and other current land use practices. I also see benefits in this extensive approach for researchers in other countries. For these people, the results of research from another place are normally encountered only in the necessarily dry scientific literature. As such it is frequently difficult to gauge the wider context within which that research resides. For those who do not know Scotland particularly well, I have sought to define the 'sense of place' occupied by Golden Eagles in the landscape of the Scottish Highlands and Islands.

In a number of respects the role of Golden Eagles can be better understood by comparing their ecology and behaviour with that of closely allied species. To this purpose I have embraced information from research on other members of the genus *Aquila* where this seems appropriate or especially illuminating. For those who are unfamiliar with *Aquila* eagles I have included a short introduction to the other members of the genus in Appendix 1. Some readers may find it helpful to refer to that section after reading the introduction to the Golden Eagle given in Chapter 2. In several subsequent chapters I have included material reflecting on the similarities and contrasts between the Golden Eagle and its congeners. I am especially indebted here to the impressive work done by Valerie Gargett and her team on Black Eagles in Africa (Gargett 1990), and to the detailed studies of the Spanish Imperial Eagle by Miguel Ferrer (1993a) and his colleagues in southwest Spain.

PERSONAL REFLECTIONS

My interest in birds began more than 30 years ago as a young boy raised in the heart of Galloway in southwest Scotland. My father's enthusiasm for birds, both as a painter and as a studiously careful observer of bird behaviour, was an ever-present influence. Add to this the steady flow of ornithologists through our home and it was perhaps inevitable that birds would figure large in my later life. The 1960s was an exciting time for young minds whose level of environmental consciousness had been raised. I can recollect the urgency of the debate as Derek Ratcliffe began to unravel the puzzle of breeding failure among our local Peregrines, and the causal links with organochlorine pesticides. Even as the pesticide battle was being won in the late 1960s, I can recall Derek's commitment transferring to a new cause. Long before others were prepared to concede there was a serious issue at all, he had recognized the damaging ecological consequences of the uncontrolled afforestation of the uplands of Britain. This too, was very close to us in rural Galloway where month by month we watched great tracts of the hill country planted up with monocultures of exotic conifers.

My earliest memory of Golden Eagles is with my father, watching a pair as they soared effortlessly high over a nest site not far from the well-known local landmark of Murray's Monument. This was the first eagle site in the Galloway hills to be recolonized after the relaxation from human persecution brought about by the 1939–45 war. It is a sad irony that during the 1980s this territory was then the first to be abandoned. The disappearance of the pair here was almost certainly due to the growth of the conifer forests which were planted during the 1950s over huge areas of the birds' previously open range, and the consequent loss of crucial hunting grounds.

My first contact with Golden Eagles in the Scottish Highlands was in the 1970s when I studied zoology at Aberdeen University. If environmental consciousness was raised in the 1960s, by the 1970s it was positively overflowing. My interest in raptors, and in the many unanswered questions of population ecology, was encouraged by many teachers, but perhaps most of all by George Dunnet, who was then Professor of Natural History at Aberdeen. The publication of Ian Newton's *Population Ecology of Raptors* in 1979 was, for anyone interested in birds of prey at that time, an event of enormous significance. I still regularly turn to this book both for its clarity of expression, and for its unending source of reference material. It was shortly after this, in the early 1980s, that I was given the opportunity to work full-time on Golden Eagles. For nearly 5 years Stuart Rae and I had the task of trying to disentangle the various impacts of land use change on Golden Eagles in the Scottish Highlands. Although my full-time work on the Golden Eagle came to an end in 1985, I have maintained a close personal interest in the bird ever since. With my home and family now deeply rooted in the Scottish Highlands I have little doubt that Golden Eagles will, for the foreseeable future, continue to play an important part in my life.

The Highlands and Islands of Scotland have provided the inspiration for generations of eagle enthusiasts. In the first decade of this century H. B. MacPherson secured the first and quite remarkable sequence of photographs of Golden Eagles, taken at a nest in the central Highlands (MacPherson 1909). Then came the investigations of Seton Gordon, the grand old man of Scottish eagle studies, ably assisted by his wife Audrey. Their impressive observations on Golden Eagle behaviour were accumulated during more than half a century of field study and culminated in the publication of *The Golden Eagle: King of Birds* in 1955. Over 40 years later, it is a testament to the quality of observation and research which underpinned this book, that it remains today the authoritative monograph on the species. During the 1950s and 1960s a growing band of eagle watchers in Scotland was spearheaded by Adam Watson, Leslie Brown, Charlie Palmer and Pat Sandeman. Adam Watson's observations on eagles in Deeside began in the 1940s and continue to this day. His is now unquestionably the longest continuous record of nesting Golden Eagles anywhere in the world.

There are certain personal qualities that I tend to associate with eagle enthusiasts

Two of the pioneers of Golden Eagle work in Scotland, Seton Gordon (top) and Adam Watson.

and I would guess that most of the early Scottish workers had these to some degree. The first of these qualities is tenacity, and a preparedness to pursue their interest despite the frustration caused by the elusiveness of the birds they studied and the frequently inclement conditions and difficult terrain in which they work. Then there is a single-mindedness of purpose and a related tendency to be at ease with solitude. Dedicated 'eagle people' are unlikely to be the most gregarious folk on earth. From these qualities, perhaps reinforced by the daily experience of eagle field work, can emerge an understandable degree of intolerance, particularly towards man's thoughtlessness and misuse of the natural world. To an extent I probably recognize all these traits in myself. Whether these qualities are innate and therefore predispose an individual to the challenge of working on eagles, or whether they are more a product of that experience, I cannot say.

A GLOBAL PERSPECTIVE

One of the most revealing aspects of writing this book has been the opportunity to correspond and share experience with eagle workers in so many other parts of the world. Some 20 or 30 years ago it was probably true that much of the leading thinking and research on the population ecology of raptors was being done in Britain. This is no longer the case. The reason is, in part, a lamentable decline in the commitment of state funds for all types of ecological research in Britain since the late 1970s. As this process has continued, so other countries have maintained or enhanced their research investment. It is perhaps not surprising that much of the ground-breaking work on population ecology is now being done in the United States. It is my impression also that the level of commitment in Britain to ecological research, within my own particular field of interest, has now been overtaken in such diverse places as Spain, Finland and Switzerland. While I can only commend the progress which has been achieved in these places, it is a matter of regret that the opportunities for young researchers in Britain to contribute to this revitalized global effort are increasingly few.

The wealth of information from many other parts of the world makes it especially important to provide a global perspective to this book. Nevertheless, this has not been without its challenges. The sheer volume of literature on Golden Eagles and the other *Aquila* eagles was, even by the early 1980s, quite prodigious, as shown by the impressive bibliography produced by Le Franc & Clark (1983). Since that work was published, the literature has expanded rapidly. In the United States the study of Golden Eagles at Snake River Canyon in Idaho, led by my friend Mike Kochert and Karen Steenhof, has been a major contributor. I was fortunate enough to visit the Snake River project at Boise in the spring of 1991. Along with the imposing quality of the research being done there, I left with an abiding impression of the sheer number of people involved in raptor work. I was only half joking when I told friends on my return that there were more people earning a living out of raptor work in the town of Boise, Idaho than there were raptor biologists in the whole of Britain! Over the border in Canada, Gary Bortolotti has contributed important publications on Golden Eagles alongside his work on Bald Eagles and other raptors. Even as I write, new and exciting work on Golden Eagles is being carried out by Carol McIntyre

within the quite different landscape of subarctic Alaska; the findings of her research are awaited with interest.

One of the richest countries in Europe for breeding raptors is Spain. Here, there has been substantial work on the status and general ecology of Golden Eagles by Bernardo Arroyo and Carmelo Fernández, among others. Further south in Spain, Miguel Ferrer has given research into the endangered Spanish Imperial Eagle an elevated place in the scientific literature, and he has recently distilled this into an impressive monograph (Ferrer 1993a). The first international colloquium on the Golden Eagle in Europe was held at Arvieux in the French Alps in 1987 under the guidance of Samuel Michel. Out of this came an invaluable resumé of Golden Eagle status, and of contemporary research priorities across Europe (Michel 1987). For the past decade Heinrich Haller has extended the knowledge of Golden Eagles in the Swiss Alps, and he was one of the first in Europe to make use of the new technology of satellite telemetry to document Golden Eagle ranging behaviour. The major contemporary Golden Eagle research in Scotland, being done under the able direction of Mike McGrady, has also used radio-telemetry. The results from this work should appear in the near future and will undoubtedly cast further light on the pattern of range use by eagles in relation to different kinds of land use. Across the North Sea in Scandinavia, work on Golden Eagles in Norway has been carried out by Gunnar Bergo and others, while Martin Tjernberg has continued to add new insights from the work he began in Sweden in the 1970s. An exciting recent development has been the increased volume of research on raptors in Eastern Europe, much of this with the support and encouragement of the irrepressible Bernd Meyburg. Of special note are Vladimir Ivanovsky for his investigations into the Golden Eagles that nest in the wooded peatlands of Belorus, and Štefan Danko for his work in the mountains of Slovakia.

Beyond Europe there have been exciting new findings which have included the recent confirmation that Golden Eagles do indeed breed in Ethiopia (Clouet & Barrau 1993), thereby confirming a suspicion first voiced by Leslie Brown some 25 years ago (Brown 1970). In Israel, the work of Ofer Bahat has begun to reveal the ways in which Golden Eagles cope with the particular demands of life in a hot, desert environment (Bahat, 1989). In Japan, Toru Yamazuki and his colleagues have established a privately funded Society for Research into the Golden Eagle, a group which publishes its own, dedicated journal entitled *Aquila chrysaetos* (SRGE 1983). So, although I lament the lack of resources available for raptor work in Britain, it is encouraging to report that the global network of Golden Eagle enthusiasts is in pretty good shape.

Adult Golden Eagle and a distant Lammergeier above Monte Perdido, Ordesa National Park, Pyrénées.

CHAPTER 2

The Golden Eagle

Golden Eagle defecating.

To a great many people, the Golden Eagle is an exceptionally familiar bird. Much of that familiarity comes from seeing impressive paintings or photographs in books, or stunning images on the television screen. I wonder how many others can recall, as I can, the tiny picture cards of British birds painted by Charles Tunnicliffe and given away with Brooke Bond Tea in the 1950s. Somehow, the Golden Eagle card always seemed the most desirable. Although this portrait image is commonplace, first-hand experience of Golden Eagles in the wild is comparatively rare. Even among committed birdwatchers, an encounter with the Golden Eagle is often little more than a distant silhouette, glimpsed tantalizingly just before vanishing against a dark and brooding hillside.

FIELD CHARACTERISTICS

Except for the recently reintroduced and extremely rare White-tailed Sea Eagle, the Golden Eagle is the largest bird of prey in Britain. It has a wing-span of more than 2 m, approaching twice that of the much commoner Buzzard which has a span of around 1.2 m. Despite this enormous size difference, I suspect that many casual visitors to the Highlands of Scotland mistakenly identify Buzzards as Golden Eagles. Size alone can be an unreliable guide to the identification of birds in the field.

Golden Eagles are most often seen in flight. When soaring they use thermals or updraughts to gain height and often spend long periods in the air without any apparent movement of their wings. Viewed head-on in soaring flight, the wings are held in a shallow V and, when seen close to, the upturned 'splayed fingers' of the outermost primaries are sometimes visible. Seen from below, the shape of the Golden Eagle is distinctive. The tail and the head are proportionately longer than in either the Buzzard or the White-tailed Sea Eagle. The wings look broad and long, but are not normally parallel-sided. The trailing edge of the wing usually has a slight S-shaped curve caused by the shorter inner primary feathers. This is in marked contrast to the very deep, parallel-edged wings of the White-tailed Sea Eagle, giving that species the apt description of 'the flying door'.

In still, cold weather, especially when disturbed suddenly from a perching place, a Golden Eagle will sometimes use active flight. This appears laboured, and usually consists of six or eight deep and powerful wing-beats, interspersed with short glides lasting for 2–3 s. Strong, flapping flight is also a feature of the ascent phase of the Golden Eagle's classic undulating display. Flapping flight is again used when lifting and transporting heavy prey to nest sites. In general, such energetic flight is less common than simple soaring or gliding.

The adult plumage of the Golden Eagle is a predominantly uniform dark brown and, as such, birds can be difficult to locate and follow against the muted browns and greys of the Scottish hills. No doubt such pigmentation gives hunting eagles a degree of camouflage. The feathers on the upperside are generally paler, especially around the back of the head and on the wing-coverts. Indeed, it is the pale yellowish or tawny colour of the plumes at the back of the head that gives the Golden Eagle its name. The adult tail-feathers have a broad, blackish terminal band and the ground colour at the base of the tail is dark grey. In some individuals the grey base is relatively uniform and in others it is interspersed with three or more blackish bands. A recent identification guide covering North American Golden Eagles has suggested that this difference is related to sex, and that the uniform grey base to the tail is a characteristic of females (Wheeler & Clark 1995). This putative sex difference may also hold in Britain (Keith Brockie *in litt.*) and would appear to merit further investigation. To date there have been no reliable plumage criteria for sexing Golden Eagles, although there is a substantial size differences between males and females.

The juvenile plumage of Golden Eagles is quite different, being much more strikingly patterned than in the adult. The dominant feather pigmentation is a rich chocolate brown which looks almost black in some lights. In contrast the basal two-thirds or more of the tail is pure white and most juveniles also have conspicuous white patches at the base of the secondaries and the inner primaries. Adult plumage is attained after some 5 years or more and there are various intermediate immature or subadult plumage types. The plumage changes which occur during the early years of life are discussed in detail in Chapter 16.

SIZE DIMORPHISM

Virtually all birds of prey exhibit reversed size dimorphism between the sexes, that is, females are larger than males (Newton 1979). This is true for Golden Eagles, and indeed for all members of the genus *Aquila* (Table 1). In Golden Eagles, female wing-length is up to 10% greater than in males. Weight differences are greater still and female Golden Eagles can be as much as 40–50% heavier than males. In northwest Europe and North America, males weigh around 3.5 kg and females nearer 5 kg. The smallest race of all occurs in Japan where males are around 2.5 kg and females around 3.3 kg. The Golden Eagles of the Himalayas and the mountains of Central Asia are the largest of all, with males weighing more than 4 kg and females in excess of 6 kg.

The various explanations for reversed size dimorphism in raptors have been extensively reviewed by Newton (1979). The phenomenon is evidently linked to a raptorial lifestyle because it has arisen independently in several other predatory groups such as owls and skuas (Amadon 1959). Among the diurnal birds of prey there is variation in the extent of size dimorphism between species and this is related to differences in diet. Size dimorphism is greatest among species that feed on fast-moving and agile prey, such as birds, and least in those that feed on carrion. Newton (1979, 1986) proposed that the size difference between the sexes is linked to aspects of breeding as well as diet. Male raptors typically provide the bulk of the food early in the breeding season while females incubate the eggs and tend the young by brooding and sheltering the chicks. He suggested that there is a clear selective advantage in a raptor being close to the size of its prey, especially when hunting agile and fast-moving animals. Conversely, there are competing advantages in having a larger body size since this leads to more efficient accumulation of body reserves in preparation for breeding. The role of nest defence may also be a factor favouring increased body size. Reversed size dimorphism in raptors would therefore appear to be a consequence of opposing selection pressures. The greater demands of hunting have favoured smaller size in males, and the higher demands of breeding and nest defence have contributed to larger size in females. Newton (1979) further proposed that, at least in the bird-eating raptors, the size difference between the sexes is large enough to allow some separation in the diet of the two sexes. This could reduce competition for food between males and females and permit the pair to live in a smaller territory than would otherwise be possible.

As pointed out by Newton (1986), the many and various hypotheses for the evolution of size dimorphism are generally impossible to test effectively. Nevertheless, there is an extensive literature on a subject which will doubtless

Different patterns on the upper tail feathers of two adult Golden Eagles. The top bird is a female and the bottom bird a male – see text for further discussion.

continue to intrigue raptor workers in the future. Along with the review in Newton (1979), interested readers should also refer to Reynolds (1972), Snyder & Wiley (1976), Andersson & Norberg (1981), Mueller & Myer (1985) and, most recently, Bildstein (1992). Among the *Aquila* eagles there is a fairly modest size difference between the sexes and this is consistent with a general tendency to hunt comparatively slow-moving, mammalian prey. Across the genus there is a positive correlation between the amount of size dimorphism and body size (Fig. 1). Larger species tend to exhibit a greater size difference between the sexes. This pattern reflects a greater dependence on more active prey by the bigger species, and is therefore broadly consistent with Newton's overall explanation.

Size dimorphism is a useful tool for field biologists because it provides a reliable method of sexing birds for which plumage differences are unavailable. In my experience with Golden Eagles, it is almost always possible to detect an appreciable size difference between members of a mated pair when they are seen soaring together. Several workers have sought more precisely to quantify size differences as an aid to sexing birds in the hand. Using museum study skins, Bortolotti (1984a) took a range of measurements of North American Golden Eagles, including wing chord, tail length, culmen (bill) length and hallux (hind) claw length (Table 2). He found that the best measurements for separating males and females were hallux claw and culmen length. For adult and subadult eagles the discriminant function (culmen length × 0.393) + (hallux length × 0.353) − 35.142, whereby birds with positive values

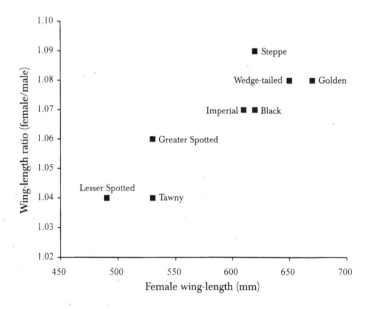

FIG. 1. *Sexual size dimorphism among eight species of the genus* Aquila. *Measurements are based on wing-length since weight data were generally less available and more variable. Across the genus there is a trend for the larger species to exhibit greater sexual size dimorphism.*

©Keith Brockie '98

were females and birds with negative values were males, correctly predicted the sex of 97% of individuals measured. Immature birds had slightly smaller bills and claws and were therefore treated separately. For these the discriminant function was (culmen length × 0.405) + (hallux length × 0.375) − 35.818 and this correctly predicted the sex of 100% of immature birds. In another North American study Edwards & Kochert (1986) used a combination of body weight and footpad length to predict the sex of individuals. In the Spanish Imperial Eagle, the best predictor of sex was found to be forearm length (Ferrer & de le Court 1992). To date, there has been no comparable work on Golden Eagles in Britain, although I have little doubt that researchers would be amenable to one or more of these approaches. Application of the Bortolotti methodology by someone with access to a collection of museum study skins would appear to offer a valuable short study.

TAXONOMY OF THE *AQUILA* EAGLES

The Golden Eagle is a member of the genus *Aquila* in the family *Accipitridae*. *Aquila* is a fairly distinct grouping of comparatively large eagles that have a cosmopolitan distribution, although no species has colonized South America. It is one of several allied genera known collectively as the 'booted' eagles. This term derives from the characteristic feathering of the legs right down to the toes. Amadon (1982) reviewed the relationships among the booted eagles and recognized five genera. In his paper, *Ictinaetus* and *Spizastur* were each represented by a single species and *Aquila*, *Hieraaetus* and *Spizaetus* comprised 10, 7 and 12 species, respectively. The essence of this classification was reinforced in a later paper although some points of detail were altered (Amadon & Bull 1988). These authors considered the booted eagles to be among the most highly evolved members of the hawk family *Accipitridae* and Amadon (1982) placed them at the apex of evolution in that family alongside the contemporary cosmopolitan genera of *Circus* (harriers), *Accipiter* (sparrowhawks and relatives) and *Buteo* (buzzards and relatives).

A dearth of fossil evidence precludes much informed speculation on the timing of separation of *Aquila* from the stem genus *Buteo*. One intriguing series of ancestral Golden Eagle fossils is available from the California tar pits at Rancho La Brea (Howard 1947). While these birds had shorter legs, longer wings and broader, heavier skulls than modern Golden Eagles, there is considerable overlap and gradation between the Pleistocene specimens and modern remains. Evidently, birds very close to contemporary Golden Eagles have been around for a very long time as Brodkorb (1964) recognized *Aquila*-like remains among fossils from as long ago as the Upper Eocene or Lower Oligocene of Europe.

The precise membership of the modern genus Aquila has been the subject of much debate. Two issues in particular have been disputed. The first is whether or not Whalberg's Eagle should be included in the genus, and the second is whether Tawny and Steppe Eagles should be considered full species or different races of a single species. Less passionate debate has centred on the taxonomic position of the Spanish race of the Imperial Eagle *Aquila heliaca adalberti* and of the Lesser Spotted Eagle subspecies *Aquila pomarina hastata* from the Indian subcontinent.

For the purposes of this book I have followed the classification and nomenclature shown in Table 1. This is similar to, but not identical to that proposed by Amadon & Bull (1988). As noted by them, there is no strong justification for regarding *A. p. hastata* as a full species and separate from the more widespread nominate *A. p. pomarina* of eastern Europe. Notwithstanding the arguments of Hiraldo *et al.* (1976), the case for attributing full species status to the Spanish Imperial Eagle *A. h. adalberti* is, I believe, unconvincing. González *et al.* (1989) sought to show that, during the nineteenth century, there was much closer geographic contact between *A. h. adalberti* and *A. h. heliaca* of Eurasia. They further proposed that the lack of evidence of interbreeding, as deduced from the absence of hybrid characters in some 248 skins examined, supported the case for full species status. This argument appears tenuous, especially since their paper gives little information on the characteristics of the skins examined, nor on the evidence they expected to find in respect of hybridization.

While Amadon (1982) included Whalberg's Eagle in *Aquila*, he later changed his opinion (Amadon & Bull 1988) and, in support of this, cited the arguments of Smeenk (1974) and Steyn (1973a). Clearly, Whalberg's Eagle shows characteristics intermediate between *Aquila* and *Hieraaetus* but several key features favour its inclusion in the latter. Smeenk highlighted similarities with the Booted Eagle *Hieraaetus pennatus* including conspicuous plumage dimorphism amongst adults, the occurrence of chocolate-brown downy plumage in some nestlings and the frequent use of high-pitched, musical vocalization particularly during the breeding period. These characteristics, along with the short erectile crest of Wahlberg's Eagle, are not typical features of *Aquila* eagles but are shared with several *Hieraaetus* species.

My only departure from Amadon & Bull (1988) is to recognize Tawny and Steppe Eagles as separate species. While acknowledging the views of Snow (1978) who favoured subspecific status, I am convinced by the argument of Brooke *et al.* (1972), eloquently restated by Liversidge (1989), who emphasized the striking differences in immature plumage between the two species. Their collective opinion has been followed by Porter *et al.* (1981), and most recently by Clark (1992). It is significant that Amadon (1982) favoured treating the two as separate species and, although he later amended this view, he was clearly still ambivalent in a more recent review (Amadon & Bull 1988). Two accounts have clarified the taxonomic position of the Wedge-tailed Eagle and Gurney's Eagle of Australia and New Guinea (Jollie 1957; Amadon 1978). As a result, both are now firmly placed in the genus *Aquila*.

On the question of phylogeny, the *Aquila* eagles which display the more primitive evolutionary traits tend to be the smaller members of the genus. As a rule, size increases across the genus, reflecting evolutionary advancement and greater ecological specialization (Table 1). There is a broad consensus that the Lesser and Greater Spotted Eagles show primitive traits with the former especially, sharing several features with Wahlberg's Eagle and thereby a link to *Hieraaetus* (Brooke *et al.*, 1972). The Tawny and Steppe Eagles were probably also the result of a

Various studies of Golden Eagle feet showing the powerful talons and the full feathering of the legs—the latter is a feature of all the 'booted' eagles.

comparatively early radiation. Jollie (1957) considered the Imperial Eagle a more recent divergence from the Golden Eagle. He suggested that Gurney's, Wedge-tailed, Golden and Black Eagles were geographic replacements of a single ancestral type, perhaps forming a 'superspecies' group (see also Brown *et al.* 1982). Few would doubt that, at least the last three species, occupy the pinnacle of Amadon's 'apex of evolution in the family *Accipitridae*'.

RACES OF THE GOLDEN EAGLE

Across the extensive global range of the Golden Eagle, six subspecies are currently recognized (Cramp & Simmons 1980). Racial separation is based mainly on small differences in size and on plumage coloration (Table 3). The general area occupied by each of the six races is indicated briefly below. A full account of the Golden Eagle's global range is given in Chapter 3.

The nominate *Aquila chrysaetos chrysaetos* breeds in northwest Europe from Scotland, through Fenno-Scandia and Eastern Europe into Russia as far east as the Yenisey River. The same race occurs in central France, the Alps, the Apennine Mountains of Italy, the Mediterranean islands of Corsica, Sardinia and Sicily and throughout the Balkans.

Golden Eagles in the Iberian peninsula and North Africa are ascribed to the smaller and darker *A. c. homeyeri* which extends east through Egypt, Crete and the Middle East to the Caucasus and Iran. There is a scattered population in Arabia extending into North Yemen (Thiollay & Duhautois 1976) and the Sultanate of Oman (Gallagher & Brown 1982). Although not yet ascribed to a particular race, the recently discovered Golden Eagles of the Balé Mountains in Ethiopia (Clouet & Barrau 1993) presumably may be attributed to this race.

Individuals of the Himalayan race *A. c. daphanea* are the largest of all the Golden Eagles. They are distributed from eastern Iran through Pakistan, north India and Nepal to western and central China (Ali & Ripley 1968). Contrary to the map by Brown & Amadon (1968) the Golden Eagle is absent from the high plateau of Tibet (Cheng 1976).

The Siberian Golden Eagle *A. c. kamtschatica* breeds from western Siberia and the Altai, where it intergrades with *A. c. chrysaetos*, through Mongolia and the heart of Siberia to the Kamchatka peninsula and the Anadyr District in northeast Russia (Allan 1905). Some authorities do not consider *A. c. kamtschatica* to be racially distinct from the North American subspecies, *A. c. canadensis* (Howard & Moore 1991), although the Siberian race does appear to be appreciably larger.

The smallest and geographically most restricted race *A. c. japonica* breeds in Japan and the Korean peninsula. Little has been published on its range in Korea (see Wolfe 1950) but for Japan the distribution is well known. In Japan it breeds on the main island of Honshū and on the southern island of Kyushu; it is a non-breeding visitor to the northern island of Hokkaido (Brazil & Hanawa 1991).

The North American race of the Golden Eagle *A. c. canadensis* is the only member of the genus in the Nearctic. It is widely distributed from Alaska across most of mainland Canada, down through the western half of the United States and into Mexico (Johnsgard 1990). In the contiguous United States the main breeding area lies west of the Great Plains, from the western Dakotas, Nebraska and Texas to the Pacific. In the eastern United States it previously bred sparingly in the Appalachian Mountains south to Tennessee (Bent 1937) but is now confined to a single pair in Maine (Todd 1989). *A. c. canadensis* occurs in central Mexico to 21°N in Hidalgo province (Mengel & Warner 1948) and in Baja California south to Vizcaíno (Rodríguez-Estrella *et al.* 1991).

GOLDEN EAGLE ECOLOGY—AN INTRODUCTION

Given the wide geographical range of the Golden Eagle, it not surprisingly occupies a great variety of habitats and displays some striking variations in diet. Nevertheless, there are a number of relatively constant features. I have sought to outline these in this brief introduction to Golden Eagle ecology.

Over most of its range the Golden Eagle is a mountain bird, hunting wide open landscapes dominated by short vegetation with restricted tree cover. Typical examples are the shrub–steppe communities of the western United States (West 1983), the open heathlands of northwest Europe, eastern Siberia, Japan, Alaska and northern Canada (Specht 1979), the maquis communities of the Mediterranean mountains (di Castri *et al.* 1981), the temperate deserts and semi-deserts of Middle Asia (Walter & Box 1983) and the high pastures of the Himalayan, Tien Shan and Alpine mountain ranges. It also occupies less typical habitats. In Siberia it breeds in relatively flat, low-lying country, nesting at the northern edge of the taiga but hunting the tundra (Labutin *et al.* 1982), and along river valleys in the taiga proper where forests are interspersed with open habitats. In the lowlands of northeast Europe it lives in a wooded-bog landscape, nesting in trees on wooded 'islands' and hunting surrounding open peatlands (Zastrov 1946). In the hot deserts of the Sahara and the Middle East it lives in arid mountains with little or no vegetation cover (Bahat 1989). The one common feature throughout is the absence of dense forest, at least in the principal hunting range. Such conditions have resulted from climatic influence— too cold, too dry or too water-logged for tree growth—or from anthropogenic influences such as burning or grazing for livestock, or a combination of these.

The majority of Golden Eagles in mountainous areas nest in cliffs but tree nests are used exclusively in flat, low-lying landscapes such as the northeast European wooded peatlands and the north Siberian taiga edge. There is a preference for Scots pine in the former and larch, but also birch and poplar, in the latter (Dementiev & Gladkov 1966; Cramp & Simmons 1980). Tree-nesting also predominates in Sweden and in parts of the northwestern United States (Bruce *et al.* 1982; Tjernberg 1983a; Menkens & Anderson 1987).

The most northerly populations of Golden Eagles are long-distance migrants. Birds from subarctic North America spend the winter in shrub-steppe and semi-desert regions of the southwestern United States (Fischer *et al.* 1984). In the eastern United States, wintering birds concentrate in wetland areas such as river valleys, estuarine marshes along the eastern seaboard and in small patches of open country on the Appalachian plateau (Millsap & Vane, 1984). Long-range migrants from northern Eurasia tend to winter in the semi-arid steppe habitats of Eastern Europe and southern Russia.

Golden Eagles are supremely aerial and search for prey on the wing using thermals to gain height for soaring, or they may quarter the ground at low levels, using the natural contours to surprise their quarry. Active prey is usually taken on, or very close to the ground following a rapid stoop, sometimes from a great height. Both members of a mated pair may sometimes hunt cooperatively (Collopy 1983b). Across the range there is some conformity in food preference, with medium-sized mammals such as hares or rabbits *Leporidae*, and marmots or ground squirrels *Sciuridae* particularly important. Young ungulates, including young domestic sheep or goats, are taken in some areas and birds such as grouse *Tetraonidae* and partridge *Phasianidae* are also favoured (Cramp & Simmons 1980; Johnsgard 1990). In the deserts of north Africa and the Middle East lizards of the genus *Uromastyx* are an important food (Bahat 1989) and tortoises *Testudinidae* are hunted in parts of southeast Europe (Grubač 1988). Carrion feeding, especially in winter, is recorded from much of the range (Arnold 1954; Cramp & Simmons 1980), although such behaviour may be less common in some eastern races (Ali & Ripley 1968).

THE GOLDEN EAGLE YEAR IN SCOTLAND

The following account briefly introduces the key elements of the Golden Eagle year in Scotland (Fig. 2). I tend to think the logical starting point of the Golden Eagle year is the autumn. This is when the young eagles from the previous nesting season have begun to move away from their parents' territory. From as early as September or October Golden Eagles may begin to refurbish their eyries, even though the nesting season is still 6 months away. During the winter months, both members of the pair spend long periods together, either soaring high over their hunting range or sitting on sheltered perches close to hilltops or ridges. Throughout the winter period Golden Eagles over much of Scotland feed substantially on carrion, mainly dead deer and sheep. Spectacular undulating display flight, which is chiefly a form of territorial behaviour, is quite common in winter and becomes especially frequent in early spring just prior to breeding. Nest-building activity tends to increase in late February.

In early March the pace of life quickens with the first signs of spring in eagle country. Most pairs lay their eggs in the second half of March and hatching occurs some 6 weeks later in the first 2 weeks of May. By this time the bulk of the diet of Golden Eagles in Scotland comprises 'live prey' rather than carrion. Across much of

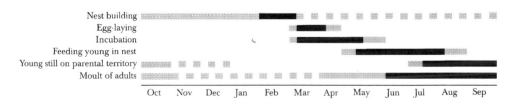

FIG. 2. *The annual cycle of the Golden Eagle in Scotland. The solid areas show the periods when a particular activity occurs most frequently.*

the range the principal prey species are Red Grouse, Ptarmigan, Mountain Hare and Rabbit. In western Scotland the summer diet is more varied and can include seabirds, various ducks and wading birds, and also mammals ranging in size from voles to young Foxes and deer calves. The eaglets spend between 10 and 12 weeks on the eyrie and most fledge in late July. Thereafter, they remain within their parents' territory for several months. At some time between about October and December, most young leave the parental territory for good. The adults begin to moult from around April and moulting reaches a peak in July or August. Moult is not completed in a single year and is normally suspended in about October, beginning again in the following spring.

CHAPTER 3

World Range

Juvenile Golden Eagle in flight over the Snake River Canyon, Idaho.

IN this chapter I describe the world distribution of the Golden Eagle by means of a biogeographical exploration of the range in both the Palearctic and the Nearctic. My intention is to give a flavour of the many and contrasting environments which together constitute the realm of the species. Many birdwatchers with a fascination for the Golden Eagle become intensely familiar with it in their own 'patch'. My purpose here is, in a small way, to raise the level of the reader's experience and appreciation of this remarkable bird.

The Golden Eagle is a widespread northern hemisphere species, adapted to a broad range of habitats, but is absent from the southern hemisphere. Its principal breeding distribution spans the latitudes from around 70°N to 20°N, with scattered populations even further south. Its tolerance of climatic extremes is remarkable, ranging from the intense cold of the arctic to the fierce heat of desert regions. The key elements of the natural environment of the Golden Eagle are open landscapes which are usually hilly or mountainous, cliffs or trees for nesting, and medium-sized birds or mammals for food. Carrion, in the form dead wild ungulates or domestic livestock, can provide an alternative source of food, especially in winter.

As a rule, Golden Eagles tend to live in places where the human population is sparse. Nevertheless, the impacts of man on Golden Eagles have been considerable, both directly through killing and indirectly as a result of various forms of extensive land use. These issues are dealt with in detail later in the book and the present chapter is chiefly about the 'natural' environment of the species.

To give structure to this exploration I have focused on a number of discernable ecological regions or zones in both the Palearctic and Nearctic. Some of the key features of these regions with respect to Golden Eagles are summarized in Table 4. Typical locations are indicated by numbers on the global distribution map in Fig. 3.

PALEARCTIC RANGE

Within the Palearctic breeding range I recognize nine zones or regions where the ecological conditions facing the bird are relatively distinct. Features of importance for Golden Eagles are described briefly, beginning in the north and progressing southwards.

1—Arctic fringe of Eurasia

All along the northern edge of the taiga from the Kola peninsula to Anadyr in eastern Siberia Golden Eagles live on the fringe of the arctic tundra, nesting in forests and hunting over nearby arctic heathland. The vegetation is a stunted, fragmented larch woodland merging into low birch–willow scrub and various heathland communities. The Golden Eagle's arctic summer is shared with a multitude of breeding waders and wildfowl, birds which, along with the eagles, migrate south for the winter. Labutin *et al.* (1982), working in the Lena River area of northeast Siberia, described a fascinating association between the scarce Little Curlew and Golden Eagles. The former apparently gains some protection from predation by crows through breeding in compact colonies close to eagle nests.

In this flat landscape where winters are intensely cold and summers short, the principal bird prey of Golden Eagles are Willow Grouse and Ptarmigan but the single most important prey animal is the Mountain Hare. Huge numbers of Reindeer, both wild herds and feral animals, migrate out of the taiga to summer on the arctic tundra where fawns are born; both Reindeer fawns and carrion provide an additional food supply for Golden Eagles.

2—Mountains of northwest Europe

In the cool, maritime countries of the British Isles and western Scandinavia the Golden Eagle is a mountain bird. It lives at elevations up to 2000 m in country

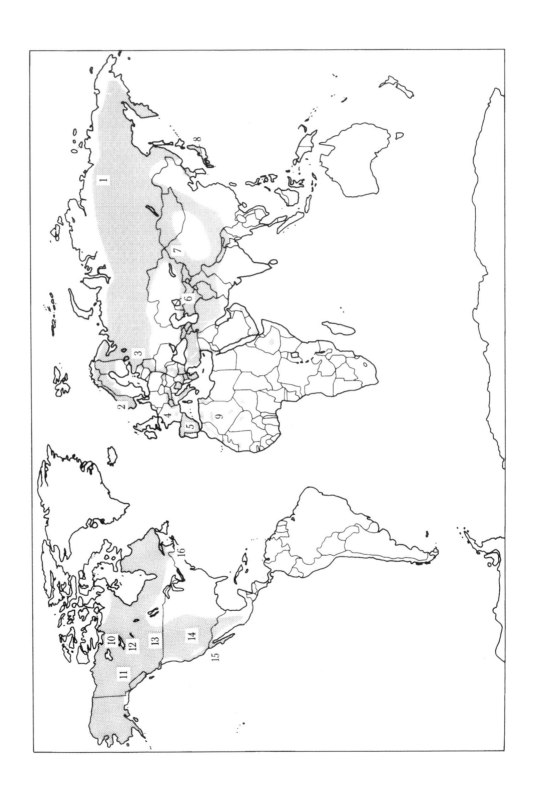

dominated by upland grassland, blanket bog and subarctic heathland, but also in areas of boreal pine–spruce–birch woodland in Scandinavia. Throughout the region it is a bird of the altitudinal and latitudinal limit of boreal forest—a creature of broken woodland or woodland edge. This is best exemplified in the mountains of Norway and Sweden where typically, Golden Eagles nest towards the upper altitudinal limit of boreal woodland and hunt both open woodland and heathland above the timberline. Most of the natural forest cover of Scotland was cleared by man long ago, and here Golden Eagles live in a mountain landscape that is now dominated by open grassland and heathland.

The Golden Eagles of the boreal mountains of northwest Europe hunt a variety of grouse species. Red Grouse in Scotland and Willow Grouse in Scandinavia occupy open heathland habitat; Ptarmigan occupy the high-level arctic heathland. Black Grouse and Capercaillie replace the other grouse species in the boreal forest zone. The Mountain Hare is the main medium-sized mammalian herbivore, except in western Scotland where rabbits are plentiful in some coastal localities. Red Deer and domestic sheep are abundant in Scotland, and in Scandinavia domestic Reindeer are numerous and widespread. All the above are important to eagles as potential sources of carrion in winter.

3—Taiga of northeast Europe and Asia

In northern Sweden the land is comparatively low-lying, generally below 500 m, and eagles here nest in extensive boreal forests where there are open peatlands and clear-cut areas that are used for hunting. They occupy a similar landscape in Finland, the Baltic States, Belorus and in the broad taiga zone across Russia to the Pacific. Conifers such as pine, larch and spruce are dominant at high latitudes and broad-leaved trees such as birch and alder are more prevalent towards the south. Much of the taiga is marginal country for Golden Eagles except where tree cover is thin, or where woodland abuts open habitat; such conditions arise where poorly drained soils have led to extensive peatland formations, especially in the Baltic States and in western Russia. Comparable conditions occur along the routes of the large river systems which flow north across Siberia to the Arctic Ocean. Generally, the distribution of Golden Eagles throughout the region is extremely patchy because forest stands in much of the taiga are too dense to permit this large raptor to hunt effectively.

Capercaillie and, to a lesser extent, Black Grouse are the principal avian prey of Golden Eagles in this region. Unlike much of the rest of the Golden Eagle's range, birds are consistently more important than mammals in the diet, at least in the western taiga. Mountain Hares are again the most numerous medium-sized mammal, with Reindeer and Elk the characteristic ungulates.

4—Alpine Mountains of Europe

Across Europe at about latitude 40°N there are several isolated ranges of very high mountains (the Pyrénées, the Alps, the Carpathians and the Caucasus). In these

FIG. 3. *The world range of the Golden Eagle. The numbers (1–16) indicate typical localities for the various ecological regions or zones described in the text.*

imposing mountain ranges where many summits exceed 2000 m, Golden Eagles nest near the timberline and hunt subalpine and alpine pastures above. The short, alpine vegetation is typically dominated by grassland communities on richer soils and heathland in chemically poorer areas. On steeper slopes there are extensive areas of bare rock and scree.

Except for a few Ptarmigan and Capercaillie the grouse of the higher latitudes are absent and, with no equivalent replacement, birds are less important in the diet than mammals. Mountain Hares occur infrequently in the Alps; Brown Hares are numerous in the west Carpathians of Slovakia. However, it is the Alpine Marmot, a colonial squirrel relative which inhabits rocky screes and burrows in alpine pastures, that is the principal mammalian prey of Golden Eagles in these high mountains. In the Carpathians, marmots are joined by the European Suslik or Ground Squirrel which also lives at lower elevations. Typical ungulates of the region are Roe Deer within forested areas and around the timberline, and Chamois at higher elevations. A variety of domestic goats, sheep and cattle also graze alpine pastures in summer.

5—Mountains of the Mediterranean

Around the shores of the Mediterranean Sea, from Iberia and the Atlas Mountains in Morocco, to Greece, Turkey and Kurdistan, Golden Eagles are widespread and numerous. Typical eagle country in these comparatively low mountains (up to 1500 m) comprises Mediterranean maquis vegetation and subtemperate open woodland in various stages of degradation. Throughout the region summers are dry and winters mild and wet but colder to the east. Dominant trees in this aromatic landscape are various pine and oak species with a huge variety of sclerophyllous shrubs adapted to withstand prolonged summer drought.

The principal gamebirds are the partridges *Alectoris* spp. which usually make up a substantial part of the eagle's diet. Other preferred prey tends to be predominantly mammals in the west Mediterranean and reptiles further east. Rabbits are widespread in southern Spain and Brown Hares are more prevalent in northern Spain and the Apennine Mountains of Italy. In the eastern Mediterranean Golden Eagles regularly hunt tortoises. Wild ungulates are now scarce in the Mediterranean region but there are large numbers of domestic and feral goats which provide a ready supply of carrion.

6—Deserts of Middle Asia

From Kurdistan and the southern Caspian Sea to the foothills of the Hindu Kush in Afghanistan Golden Eagles occupy a temperate desert landscape interspersed with mountain ranges. The region is characterized by colder, more continental winters than in the Mediterranean area. The climate is dry with precipitation, which may be

Golden Eagle on a dead Scots pine tree in a snow storm, eastern Highlands of Scotland.

rain or snow, concentrated during winter months. Vegetation cover is patchy and plant growth is largely confined to a short spring season.

In a study of Golden Eagle food in the desert region of Ust'Urt in Turkmenistan the principal prey species were Bobak Marmots, Large-toothed Susliks, Great Gerbils and tortoises, the last of these provides an ecological link with the Golden Eagles of southeast Europe (Varshavski 1968). The herds of Goitred Gazelles and Asiatic Wild Asses which occupy the lands southeast of the Caspian Sea give that region something of the character of East Africa. Wild Goats abound in the rugged mountainous terrain to the south.

7—Alpine Mountains of Central Asia

Few landscapes on earth can rival the stupendous mountain ranges that encircle Tibet and northwest China, at elevations of 3000–5000 m and more. Here, Golden Eagles extend from the Altai Mountains in the north through the Tien Shan and the Pamirs to the southern fringe of the great Himalayan massif. Once again, they are birds of the timberline and beyond, occupying the zone between 2500 and 4000 m. Almost surrounded by deserts, the mystical Tien Shan Mountains of southeast Russia show an altitudinal succession of vegetation that appears somewhat turned on its head. Here, parched desert plains encroach into the foothills where a narrow zone of desert shrub-steppe gives way to spruce forest above 1500 m. From 2500 m this passes into subalpine scrub dominated by juniper, with alpine meadows and scree slopes beyond.

Long-tailed Marmots and pikas *Ochotona* spp. occupy this country and, together with Himalayan Snowcocks and Chukar Partridges, provide food for eagles. Snowcocks are large partridge-like birds; four species are endemic to the central Asian mountains and the Caucasus, where they live between the timberline and snowline. Siberian Ibexes are the most abundant wild ungulate throughout the mountains of central Asia and 'Argalis', a species of wild sheep, graze the Tien Shan and Pamir Mountains.

8—Mountains of Japan and Korea

Geographically isolated from the rest of the Palearctic range is the population of Golden Eagles in the mountains of Korea and Japan. Its typical breeding range in Japan is at altitudes of 1000–2000 m in a mixture of open deciduous scrub woodland and carpet-like stands of *Pinus pumila* which merge into upland grassland and alpine heathland at higher elevations.

Grouse are scarce in Japan and their niche is filled by pheasants *Phasianidae* of which the Copper Pheasant is the preferred avian prey of Golden Eagles. As with most other Golden Eagle populations, however, medium-sized mammals form the bulk of the diet and nearly half of all food is accounted for by the endemic Japanese Hare. A unique feature of Japanese Golden Eagles is the high proportion of snakes, mainly of the genus *Elaphe*, in the diet. The native mountain ungulate of Japan is the Japanese Serow, a small, thickly fleeced species of goat antelope which is well-adapted to Japan's snowy winter climate.

9—Deserts of North Africa and Arabia

The southern frontier of the Golden Eagle range in the Palearctic is encountered in the hot deserts and semi-deserts of North Africa, the Middle East and the Arabian peninsula. Populations occupy various mountain areas from Atar in Mauritania, l'Aïr in Niger to Israel, North Yemen and Oman. Within the last few years a small and geographically isolated group of Golden Eagles has been discovered in the Balé Mountains of southern Ethiopia. This sub-Saharan population is located around 7°N and is therefore the most southerly breeding population of Golden Eagles anywhere in the world.

In each of these desert localities the landscape is generally treeless and largely bereft of any vegetation for long periods. Medium-sized diurnal mammals are usually lacking and the rodents that do occur are nocturnal. This gap in the prey spectrum is filled by diurnally active spiny-tailed lizards of the genus *Uromastyx*. In the remote high mountains of the Sahara desert there are Barbary Sheep; genuine Wild Goats still survive in parts of southern Arabia.

NEARCTIC RANGE

Throughout the Golden Eagle's Nearctic breeding range I recognize a further seven ecological regions and several of these are close equivalents of regions in the Palearctic.

10—Arctic fringe of North America

Golden Eagles live all along the arctic fringe from western and northern Alaska, through northern Canada to the Ungava peninsula in Quebec. The habitat is very similar to that of northern and eastern Siberia. Along the northern edge of the taiga, low deciduous shrub communities with an open canopy give way to dwarf-shrub heathland and cottongrass tussock tundra.

Willow Grouse (North American Willow Ptarmigan) and Ptarmigan (North American Rock Ptarmigan) are characteristic birds of the region. The Arctic Ground Squirrel is abundant and the main prey of Golden Eagles in the west of the region, especially Alaska. This may be so too in eastern Siberia where Arctic Ground Squirrels also occur, but there is little published information on Golden Eagle diet from that region. Further east in the North American taiga–tundra zone the bird's range narrowly overlaps that of the Arctic Hare, the largest North American lagomorph. This species and Arctic Ground Squirrels, along with a range of waterfowl, predominantly Canada Geese and eiders *Somateria* spp., are the principal prey of Golden Eagles in arctic Canada. Both Reindeer (North American Caribou) and Muskox occur within the Golden Eagle's range in the Canadian arctic.

11—Mountains of the Pacific northwest

The Golden Eagle range extends south throughout the length of the North American cordillera from Alaska to Mexico. In the high glaciated mountains, stretching from the Alaska Range to Washington and Oregon, Golden Eagles live above and around the timberline which occurs at only a few hundred metres above sea level in parts of Alaska but above 2000 m in Oregon. The greatest concentrations of Golden Eagles are found in the colder northern mountains or further south in the dry rain-shadow areas inland from the coastal ranges because tree cover is there less complete. In western Washington Golden Eagles do breed in the dense coniferous forest zone but typically only in association with very large areas of clear-cut forest. Overall, the mountains of the Pacific northwest bear comparison with the boreal mountain region of northwest Europe, although the summits are very much higher in places and topographically more like the Alps.

Arctic Ground Squirrels are abundant in the Alaska Range where they coexist with Hoary Marmots and Snowshoe Hares, the latter principally in open woodland habitat. All three species of North American grouse of the genus *Lagopus* occur here too, with Willow Grouse most abundant. Most of these species extend south along the Rocky Mountains into Canada. Columbian Ground Squirrels and Yellow-bellied Marmots replace their northern counterparts in British Columbia. In eastern Washington, where the landscape is a rich mixture of ponderosa pine, Douglas fir, sagebrush and bitterbrush communities, Yellow-bellied Marmots are the principal prey animals followed by the Blue Grouse, a large gamebird of high-altitude conifer forests. In the lower hills of southwest Alberta, Columbian Ground Squirrels are the commonest prey of Golden Eagles. Within the clear-cut forests of western Washington the main prey species are Snowshoe Hares and Mountain Beavers, a marmot relative living in wetlands within the forest zone. Both Reindeer and Dall Sheep graze the upland pastures of the Alaska Range and Bighorn Sheep replace Dall Sheep south of the Canadian border.

12—Taiga of North America

Across subarctic North America, east of the Rocky Mountains, from lowland central Alaska to the mountains of Labrador, Golden Eagles are thinly distributed through the Nearctic coniferous forest or taiga zone. This is the ecological equivalent of the Eurasian Taiga region.

Taiga forest is the principal habitat and range of the Snowshoe Hare and Spruce Grouse and these two species will almost certainly constitute the bulk of the diet. Along with Reindeer, the Elk (North American Moose) is the typical ungulate of the region.

13—Foothills east of the Rocky Mountains

South of the taiga lie the extensive plains or prairies of southwest Canada and the midwestern United States. These are essentially the ecological equivalent of the great Eurasian steppes where other species of *Aquila* replace Golden Eagles. In North America there are no other *Aquila* eagles and Golden Eagles are widespread in this largely treeless landscape, which is dominated by grassland on low rolling hills and flat plains interrupted only by cottonwood stands in river valleys and around wetlands.

Prairie Dog, Golden Eagle and Bison in the eastern foothills of the Rocky Mountains.

Here the most numerous medium-sized mammals are White-tailed Jackrabbits and Richardson's Ground Squirrels which, together with a range of ducks, are the main food found at eagle nests in Saskatchewan. The landscape is similar but at a somewhat higher elevation in eastern Montana and northern Wyoming, where typical prey animals are White-tailed Jackrabbits, Nuttall's Cottontails and Black-tailed Prairie Dogs. Wild ungulates are represented by Pronghorn Antelopes and Mule Deer; both species live in small, dispersed bands or family groups. In large parts of Montana and elsewhere in the region, huge numbers of domestic livestock, both cattle and sheep, are grazed on these rolling grasslands where the once fabulous Bison herds are now but a faint memory.

14—Deserts of the Great Basin

From southern Idaho to northern Arizona and New Mexico much of the land falls within a rain-shadow caused by the Coastal Ranges to the west and the Rocky Mountains to the east. Golden Eagles occur throughout the temperate desert and semi-desert habitats of the region. Trees are generally absent, except close to water courses, and the vegetation is dominated by sagebrush *Artemisia* and other low shrub species. This region bears comparison with the Middle Asian deserts of the Palearctic.

Black-tailed Jackrabbits, Nuttall's Cottontails and Townsend's Ground Squirrels are the principal medium-sized mammals, with the first of these being the single most important prey of Golden Eagles in Idaho (as it is in much of inland California, Nevada, Utah, Arizona, New Mexico and Texas). In the southern states Nuttall's Cottontails are replaced in the eagle's diet by various other species such as Californian Ground Squirrels in California and Desert Cottontails and Black-tailed Prairie Dogs in Arizona. Mule Deer and Pronghorn Antelopes are the native wild ungulates here. Along the eastern flank of the region, sheep ranching is an important and extensive land use.

15—Mountains of California and Mexico

The coastal regions of southern California and Baja California are characterized by hot dry summers and moist winters giving rise to classic Mediterranean sclerophyllous shrub vegetation, known locally as *chaparral*. This region is the Nearctic ecological equivalent of the Mediterranean proper. The landscape mainly comprises low rolling hills with steeper gradients on the higher peaks which rise to 1000 m or more. Vegetation is diverse and, as well as *chaparral*, includes areas of oak woodland, oak savanna and grassland.

Here, jackrabbits are comparatively scarce and Californian Ground Squirrels are the dominant mammalian prey of eagles. The diet also includes a wide variety of bird species, notably Yellow-billed Magpies; snakes are taken relatively frequently. Black-tailed Deer are the principal wild ungulate of the region.

16—Mountains of eastern North America

Golden Eagles once bred quite widely along the Appalachian plateau of the eastern

United States but have now all but gone. While remote and secure nesting sites in these mountains undoubtedly still occur, the limiting factor would now appear to be access to extensive open hunting grounds. At one time these hills were more open as a result of extensive felling, thereby perhaps explaining historical occupancy by Golden Eagles. The disappearance of Golden Eagles from Appalachia over the past 100 years or so has coincided with the recovery the great temperate forests of the region.

The high diversity of prey species taken by the one surviving pair of Golden Eagles in Maine, which includes typical animals such as Snowshoe Hare, but also atypically high numbers of wetland birds such as American Bitterns and Great Blue Herons, suggests that this is indeed somewhat marginal Golden Eagle habitat.

SUMMARY

Across their northern hemisphere range Golden Eagles occupy nearly all mountain landscapes except where, as in the Appalachians, there is a more or less complete cover of dense forest. Flat landscapes, where there are suitable trees for nesting and open areas for hunting, are also freely exploited by Golden Eagles. Food is principally medium-sized birds such as grouse, pheasants or waterfowl and similar sized mammals. The latter are especially important, and almost wherever they occur Golden Eagles are heavily dependent on one or more species of lagomorph (hares/rabbits) or squirrel (marmots/ground squirrels). In some arid regions, and especially in the hot desert landscapes of the Palearctic, reptiles are the typical prey. Across most of the range, additional food is obtained by scavenging carcasses of dead ungulates (both wild and domestic animals).

Golden Eagles avoid wooded landscapes where the trees are too dense to allow effective hunting. They are also absent from the flat, arid grassland or steppe landscapes of the Palearctic where the large avian predator niche is filled by other species of *Aquila* eagles. Golden Eagles are generally absent from areas with dense human populations and also from areas used for crop-growing and other forms of intensive agriculture.

CHAPTER 4

The Scottish Highlands—Golden Eagle Country

Golden Eagle and Hooded Crow with a backdrop of Slioch, Wester Ross.

MOST of my work with Golden Eagles has been carried out in Scotland, and mainly in the Scottish Highlands and Islands. In this chapter I describe some of the ecological variation across the range of the bird in that region. For those unfamiliar with the Scotland, and the Scottish Highlands in particular, Appendix 2 provides a short account of the ways in which the contemporary landscape of that region has been fashioned by the actions of man.

GOLDEN EAGLE COUNTRY IN SCOTLAND

Within Britain and Ireland the Golden Eagle is now confined almost exclusively to the Scottish Highlands and Islands (Figs 4 and 5). That region covers some 60% of Scotland's total land area of 79 000 km². The southeastern limit is defined by the

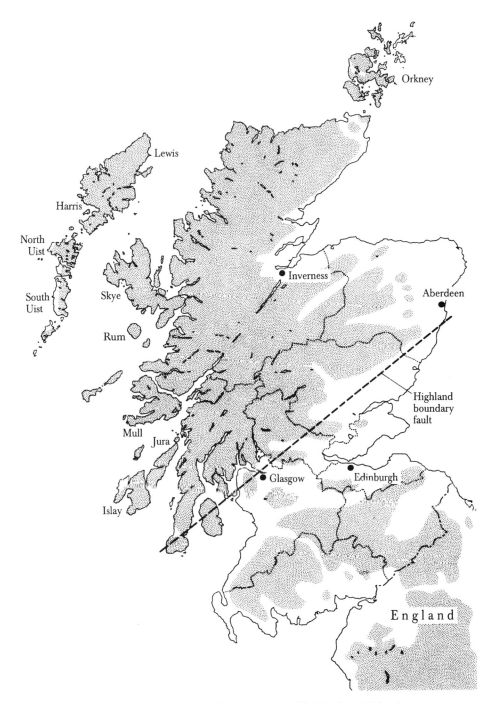

FIG. 4. *Map of Scotland showing the location of the Highlands and Islands, various islands and towns. The shading shows the distribution of upland habitats (redrawn from Ratcliffe 1990).*

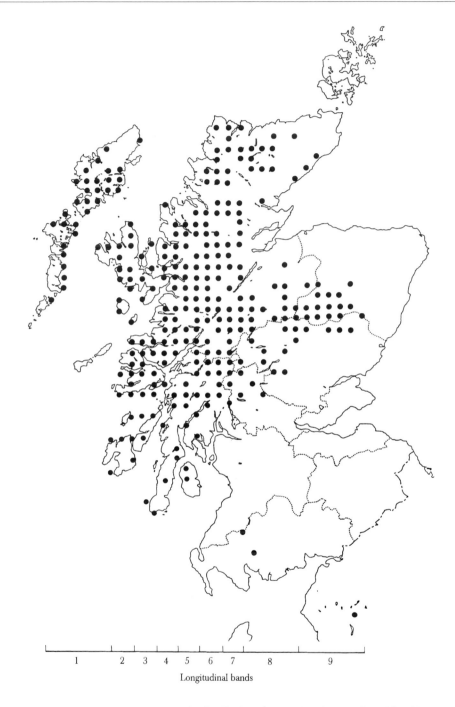

Longitudinal bands

FIG. 5.   *The distribution of the Golden Eagle in Britain based on confirmed breeding attempts in 10 × 10 km squares in 1982. For reasons of confidentiality, records for four 10 × 10 km squares have been omitted. After Watson & Dennis (1992).*

Highland Boundary Fault which runs in a northeasterly direction from near Glasgow to just south of Aberdeen. For convenience I refer throughout this book to that part of mainland Scotland northwest of the Highland Boundary Fault, along with the islands of the Inner and Outer Hebrides, as The Highlands. Much of the land is rugged and mountainous, with many summits over 900 m. The human population is sparse and concentrated on the comparatively fertile eastern fringe and, to a lesser extent, on the west coast mainland and the islands. Eagles breed more or less throughout the region, except in the moderately flat, agriculturally fertile eastern lowlands and on some of the smaller islands off the west coast. Outside the Highlands a few pairs nest in the hills of southwest Scotland and in northwest England. At various times in the past 30 years single pairs have bred in Northern Ireland and on Orkney (Sharrock 1976). Much longer ago, Golden Eagles occurred further south in England, in Wales, and throughout the west of Ireland (see Chapter 10 for a description of historical changes).

Two principal climatic gradients extend across the Highlands. These contribute to variation in the dominant vegetation communities and to other related aspects of the eagle's natural environment, notably its food supply. From south to north mean annual temperature decreases, and from west to east reducing oceanicity is reflected in reduced rainfall and lower wind speeds (Ratcliffe 1990). In summary, the west and southwest of the region are wet and comparatively mild and further north and east the climate is colder and drier.

The parent rocks over most of the Highlands have given rise to acidic, nutrient-poor soils which are predominantly podzols on better-drained sites and ombrogenous peats where water-logging occurs on gentler slopes. The whole area was under glacial influence during the Pleistocene, the ice finally retreating some 10 000 years ago, and the landscape is now studded with evidence of glacial action such as U-shaped glens and relict glacial moraines (Gordon & Sutherland 1993). Typically, the mountains to the west have sharp peaks and ridges with little in the way of montane plateaux and short, fast-flowing rivers drain the glens. East of the watershed there are broad summit plateaux, reaching their maximum extent in the Cairngorm Mountains. Rivers descend more gradually and over longer distances through wide, sweeping glens to the North Sea.

Today only small and modified fragments of the original boreal forest survive. At the maximum post-glacial climatic amelioration (7000–8000 years ago) forest covered the landscape up to 400–500 m above sea-level in Skye and the northwest and up to 700–800 m in the East Grampians. However, there was never more than a scrub woodland cover in the Western Isles and over much of Caithness and north Sutherland (Birks 1988). Today's relict woodland is principally pine-birch in the eastern and central Highlands, birch-hazel in the north and northwest and oak–birch in the southwest. Under present climatic conditions the potential timber-line is believed to be around 650–700 m in the Cairngorms and around 300 m in northwest Sutherland (Birks 1988; Ratcliffe & Thompson 1988).

The range of bog, heath and grassland communities which together comprise the semi-natural vegetation of the Highlands is described in detail by Rodwell (1991, 1992). Typical communities on peaty soils in the submontane areas of the oceanic western hills and islands are *Scirpus cespitosus–Eriophorum vaginatum* blanket bog and *Scirpus–Erica tetralix* wet heath. *Calluna vulgaris–Eriophorum vaginatum* blanket bog predominates on higher altitude ombrogenous peats in northern and eastern areas. On base-poor mineral soils where vegetation has been subject to high grazing pressure, as in parts of Skye, Mull and the southwest Highlands, anthropogenic *Festuca ovina–Agrostis capillaris–Galium saxatile* grassland is dominant. There is extensive *Nardus stricta–Galium saxatile* grassland on peaty mineral soils in the central Highlands. At moderate elevations in the east Highlands *Calluna vulgaris–Vaccinium myrtillus* and *Calluna vulgaris–Arctosaphyllus uva-ursi* dry heaths are widespread. The true montane zone lies above *c.* 750 m in the East Grampians but down to *c.* 350 m in north Sutherland. To the north and west, montane areas are characterized by bryophyte-rich prostrate dwarf *Calluna vulgaris–Racomitrium lanuginosum* moss heath, while to the southeast this tends to be replaced by a lichen-rich *Calluna vulgaris–Cladonia arbuscula* community.

Ratcliffe (1990) described the range of bird communities of the semi-natural habitats and the associated human influences which together constitute the contemporary upland landscape of Britain. The bird which best characterises the range of the Golden Eagle here is the Red Grouse. It is replaced in the montane zone by its arctic–alpine relative the Ptarmigan, in areas of scrub woodland by the Black Grouse and in the relict native pine forests by the Capercaillie. In the sheep country of the islands and the southwest Highlands, and in similar landscapes in southwest Scotland and northwest England, all the grouse species are scarce. Here, birds such as Ravens and Carrion/Hooded Crows are common. Among the upland waders the Golden Plover occurs more or less throughout submontane habitat and is especially common on land managed for Red Grouse. On the blanket bogs of the wetter northern Highlands and the Outer Hebrides, Greenshank and Dunlin are typical breeding waders and both Red and Black-throated Divers nest where suitable lochs occur. In coastal districts around the west and the islands there are scattered colonies of nesting seabirds including Puffins, Guillemots, Razorbills, Kittiwakes, Herring Gulls and Fulmars.

Alongside the ubiquitous Red Deer there are long-established herds of feral goats in localities in Wester Ross, East Inverness-shire and elsewhere. Roe Deer live in or near most areas of woodland. The Mountain Hare has a distribution similar to that of the Red Grouse, sharing its preference for feeding on young heather shoots, and is exceptionally abundant on some eastern moors. It is scarce in western Scotland except for the island of Mull where the Irish race was introduced and is now comparatively numerous (Corbet & Harris 1991). In some coastal areas, notably on the Isle of Skye where good grazing occurs on free-draining soils, Rabbits are plentiful.

The options for land use in the Highlands are constrained by the region's inherently poor fertility and cool, wet climate (McVean & Lockie 1969). Presently, there are four principal land uses; sheep grazing, plantation forestry, management for Red Deer and management for Red Grouse. Throughout most of the islands, on the southwest mainland and, to a lesser extent, in the northwest, hill sheep farming is extensive. Over much of the north, central and eastern areas Red Deer are abundant and deer stalking for sport is the principal activity. The lower hills and moors in the east and southeast are managed as sporting preserves for Red Grouse, usually in conjunction with summer grazing by sheep. In recent decades commercial forestry plantations, mainly of exotic conifers such as Sitka spruce and lodgepole pine, have been established over large areas, especially in the southwest Highlands.

Golden Eagle over the Hills of Harris, Outer Hebrides.

ECOLOGICAL REGIONS OF THE HIGHLANDS

Based on the range of plant communities, their associated birds and mammals and the prevailing human land uses, Golden Eagle country in Scotland subdivides into a number of more or less distinct ecological zones. These are shown in Fig. 6 and are the same divisions used by Watson *et al.* (1993), these in turn being an extension of the regions in Brown & Watson (1964). A short description of each Region is given below, highlighting key ecological and land use features.

Region 1: Outer Hebrides

The island of Lewis and the eastern parts of the Uists and Benbecula have a varied landscape of low rocky hills and spacious peatlands lying mainly below 200 m. There are some higher hills, especially in Harris. The climate is strongly oceanic and the vegetation is predominantly bog and wet heath with small areas of acidic grassland. On the west coast of the Uists and Benbecula natural calcareous *machair* grassland has developed on wind-blown shell sand. Red Deer are few except in Harris (densities here are <5/km²) and there are many sheep kept by crofters on common grazings, often at densities >80/km². Red Grouse are scarce except in Harris. Small numbers of Mountain Hares occur in Lewis and Harris and Rabbits are numerous in areas of *machair*. In some areas Golden Eagles have access to seabird colonies, although most of the larger colonies occur on islands some way offshore.

Region 2: Inner Hebrides (north)

The islands of the Inner Hebrides lie at the heart of the British tertiary volcanic province (Emeleus & Gyopari 1992). The principal island of the northern Inner Hebrides is Skye. Here many summits in the Cuillin exceed 900 m but otherwise much of the land is lower. The climate is again strongly oceanic with most of the Region receiving more than 200 cm annual precipitation. The vegetation is mainly wet heath and blanket bog on poorly drained soils. There are quite extensive patches of richer grassland on free-draining soils derived from richer parent rock of volcanic origin in north Skye. Red Deer are few, generally occurring at densities <5/km², but sheep densities are frequently >60/km², with flocks mainly kept by crofters on year-round common grazings. The rate of conifer afforestation has increased on Skye in recent years. Both Red Grouse and Ptarmigan are generally scarce and there are few Mountain Hares. Quite large numbers of Rabbits live on free-draining slopes on the lower ground, especially near the coast. There are mixed colonies of seabirds on the smaller islands such as Rum and Canna and Fulmars breed in considerable numbers around the west coast of Skye.

Region 3: Inner Hebrides (south)

The bulk of Golden Eagle country in this Region is on the island of Mull which, like Skye, is of volcanic origin. Much of the vegetation which comprises wet heaths and grassland on free-draining slopes is thus comparable to that on Skye. Mull has few mountains of similar stature to the Skye Cuillin and summits are typically below

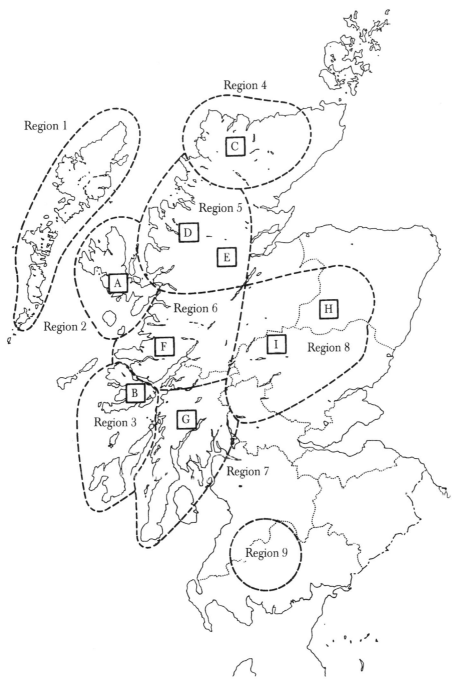

FIG. 6. *The location of the nine Ecological Regions (1–9) described in the text. Also shown are the approximate locations of the study areas (A–I) where more intensive work on Golden Eagles and land use was carried out.*

Pair of Golden Eagles and the Cuillin Hills, Isle of Skye.

900 m. On the island of Islay to the south an appreciable amount of the land is low lying and comparatively fertile compared with rest of the Highlands. On Mull, Red Deer numbers are conspicuously higher than on Skye (10/km^2) and sheep stocking densities are broadly comparable (40–60/km^2). Densities of Red Deer on Jura are exceptionally high (>20/km^2). Afforestation with exotic conifers has increased rapidly in recent years and new plantations are now extensive on Mull. Red Grouse are generally scarce and Ptarmigan virtually absent. Mountain Hares were introduced to Mull, Jura and Islay but are no longer present on Islay; they remain numerous on Mull where Rabbits are also common in coastal districts.

Region 4: North Highlands

This is an area of hills up to 900 m interspersed with wide glaciated glens to the west and lower, more rounded hills to the east. Extensive blanket peatlands or 'flows' occur over large areas east of the watershed in east Sutherland and into Caithness. Annual rainfall exceeds 200 cm on the highest ground but is more generally around 150 cm, falling to 100 cm/annum in the east. Vegetation is predominantly blanket bog and wet heath on lower ground with moss heaths at higher altitudes. Red Deer occur at densities of around 5–10/km² in the north and west and nearer 15/km² in the east. Sheep numbers are generally low (<20/km²), except in some northern and western coastal areas. Large tracts in the east of the Region have been planted with exotic conifers in the last 20 years, although the rate of planting has recently declined. Low or moderate numbers of Red Grouse occur throughout the Region and there are moderate numbers of Ptarmigan on higher hills to the west. Numbers of Mountain Hares are generally low and there are only isolated pockets of Rabbits on richer grasslands along the north coast, where there are also some seabird colonies, most notably Fulmars.

Region 5: Northwest Highlands

The northwest Highlands boast some of the grandest hill landscapes in all Scotland. Many summits reach over 1000 m and the hills are interspersed with remote glens often filled with large lochs. Rainfall is high in Wester Ross (>250 cm/annum) and lower to the east where winters are more continental and colder. The vegetation is a mixture of wet heaths and bog communities at low and moderate altitudes with moss-heaths in the montane zone. To the east of the district there are relict native pine forests. Red Deer stalking is the dominant land use and deer densities are 5–10/km² in the west and >15/km² in the east. Sheep numbers are low except in a few west coast localities and in some eastern glens during summer only. Red Grouse numbers are moderate on some hills, becoming quite numerous to the east where Black Grouse also occur. Ptarmigan occur throughout the montane zone and in considerable numbers on some hills. Mountain Hares are rare in the west but moderately common in the east. Rabbits are uncommon except in a few western coastal areas and on low ground in glens to the east.

Region 6: West-central Highlands

The hills here are commonly over 900 m, some reaching 1200 m or more, and are separated by deep narrow glens which form fjord-like sea lochs along the coast. The climate is mild and extremely wet with annual rainfall in excess of 300 cm on the highest hills but less on lower ground. Most of the steeper hill slopes are predominantly grassy with blanket bog or wet heath on gentler gradients. There are small amounts of semi-natural oak–birch woodland in coastal districts. Red Deer densities are moderate to high (15–20/km²) throughout. Sheep stocking rates are moderate on inland hills (20–40/km²) but higher in some coastal areas such as Ardnamurchan and Morvern. In some remote areas such as Knoydart most sheep have been taken off the hill within the last 20 years. There are quite extensive conifer plantations in the southwest of the Region. Red Grouse are rare throughout the Region but Ptarmigan are still quite numerous where suitable montane heathland occurs on the highest hills. Mountain Hares are virtually absent but Rabbits can be abundant on low ground around the coast.

Golden Eagle in Glen Affric, east-central Highlands.

Region 7: Southwest Highlands

South of Oban the Highland landscape is much gentler. The hills of mid and south Argyll rarely reach above 800 m and the Kintyre peninsula is lower still. Climatically, the area is comparable to Region 6. Hill vegetation tends to be grassy with wet heaths on poorly drained slopes. There are areas of heather on free-draining slopes at moderate altitudes, especially where grazing pressure has been reduced. The traditional land use of the area was extensive sheep grazing. However, over the last

50 years there has been a marked increase in conifer afforestation at the expense of sheep farming. In some parts of the district new plantations now cover more than half the hill ground. Red Deer are quite numerous to the north but southwest of Loch Etive they are almost exclusively forest animals, living in the new conifer plantations. Sheep farming still occurs but mainly on better land near the coast. Low numbers of Red Grouse survive in unplanted areas with good heather cover and there are a few Ptarmigan on the highest hills above 800 m. Mountain Hares are present in small numbers throughout the region, and Rabbits have a patchy distribution in areas of rough grazing at lower altitudes.

Region 8: East Highlands

The high hills of the East Grampians, rising above 1200 m in places, have very extensive summit plateaux interspersed with wide, gently sloping glens. To the east

Pair of Golden Eagles in Galloway, southwest Scotland.

the hills are lower with more gentle contours. The climate here is more continental than in the rest of the Highlands, with drier summers and colder winters. Dry heather moor is widespread and abundant becoming dominant on intermediate altitude ground to the east. Montane heath communities are extensive and relatively large patches of semi-natural pine woodland survive in the straths of Speyside and Deeside. On higher hills Red Deer occur at their highest densities in Scotland (>20/km^2) but sheep densities tend to be low, except in some glens during summer months (May–October) and on hills with better grazing along the southern fringe of the Region. Many lower hills to the east and southeast are managed principally for Red Grouse, which can be very numerous. Ptarmigan are common in hill corries and on montane plateaux. Small numbers of Capercaillie live in the remnants of pine forest and Black Grouse may be found in scrub woodland on lower ground. Mountain Hares occur throughout the Region and are abundant on many of the managed grouse moors. Rabbits are present in moderate numbers on lower ground in some glens.

Region 9: Southwest Scotland

Although not part of the Highlands, I should briefly mention here the hills of southwest Scotland where there is a small population of Golden Eagles, separated from the main range. The region has much in common with the southwest Highlands, especially the lower hills of south Argyll. Traditionally, this was sheep country but over the past 50 years there has been a massive shift towards plantations of exotic conifers on hill ground. There are Red Deer but these are now mostly forest-dwelling animals. Very small numbers of Red Grouse and rather more Mountain Hares still live in areas that have not been afforested. There are some Black Grouse but no Ptarmigan, which disappeared from the Galloway hills in the nineteenth century. Rabbits are quite plentiful in some lower glens and are an important food for the small population of eagles.

INTENSIVE STUDY AREAS

Some of the information presented in the following chapters is drawn widely from the efforts of a dedicated band of Golden Eagle enthusiasts working throughout Scotland. In other cases I have concentrated on work done by myself and Stuart Rae in a selection of smaller study areas where we were particularly concerned with the relationships between Golden Eagles and land use. The principal and secondary land uses of our nine study areas are summarized in Table 5. These areas were chosen to reflect both the ecological and land use variation across the bird's Scottish range. Our nine study areas were located in seven out of the nine Ecological Regions described earlier. We had no study area in the Outer Hebrides (Region 1) nor in Southwest Scotland (Region 9) but there were two separate study areas in both the Northwest Highlands (Region 5) and the East Highlands (Region 8). The approximate locations of each of the study areas are shown in Fig. 6. I have intentionally not given precise localities because to do so would be to put the birds at risk. Regrettably, Golden Eagles are still the object of much illegal persecution in parts of their range in Scotland (see Chapter 19).

SUMMARY

The natural environment of the Golden Eagle range in Scotland is briefly described. Aspects of climate, geology, land form, vegetation communities and the typical birds species which occur within the range are summarized. Reflecting differences in ecology and land use, the Golden Eagle range is subdivided into nine more or less distinct Regions which are described in greater detail. The four principal human land uses of the Highlands are sheep grazing, plantation forestry, sporting management for Red Deer and for Red Grouse. Sheep grazing predominates on the islands and in parts of the western mainland. Forestry plantations are most extensive in the southwest. Land is managed mainly for Red Deer in the north, central and east Highlands. Management for Red Grouse is largely confined to the extreme east of the range.

Studies of a juvenile Golden Eagle perched on a pine branch.

CHAPTER 5

Hunting Behaviour

Golden Eagle in pursuit of a Mountain Hare.

T HIS chapter discusses the various hunting techniques used by Golden Eagles to secure their prey. For such a well-studied bird the published literature on hunting behaviour is comparatively meagre, largely anecdotal and unquantified. Over 50 years ago Meinertzhagen (1940) observed that 'little is known about the manner in which larger raptors seize their prey' and he attributed this to the fact that 'no single person has been fortunate enough to witness more than a few instances'. The situation has changed little since then and, while there are numerous short notes on the subject (Cooper 1969; Bruns 1970; Locati 1990) these generally refer to spectacular, and less than typical attacks on large ungulates. The one exception is the work of Collopy (1983b) who observed the hunting behaviour of Golden Eagles in Idaho and saw 23 kills over a 2-year period.

The hunting strategy of a particular Golden Eagle is determined primarily by the escape response of the prey it is pursuing at the time. It may also be influenced by prevailing weather conditions, local topography and the experience of the hunting bird. Mammals such as rabbits, marmots and ground squirrels can retreat to underground burrows. They are most likely to be caught when the eagle can effect a close approach with maximum surprise. Conversely, hares attempt to escape by running, with rapid changes in direction. Alternatively, they may freeze and avoid detection through camouflage. The eagle must achieve surprise but may also need to employ considerable aerial agility. The various grouse species rely to some extent on camouflage but more typically have a rapid and explosive escape flight which depends on sheer speed to outpace an aerial predator. Certain grouse species may also gain some mutual protection by packing together into flocks at the sight of an eagle (Watson 1972).

Comparatively slow-moving animals, such as tortoises, snakes and lizards, must rely almost entirely on camouflage and low detectability, perhaps supplemented by a self-defence mechanism such as a hard shell or a venomous bite. Eagles hunting these animals need acute vision but may also require certain specialized killing techniques. Ungulates tend to use behaviour such as herding or bunching to gain mutual protection from aerial predators and some large mammals, especially carnivores, will adopt aggressive behaviour or postures to defend themselves or their offspring against attack.

From the disparate literature on the subject and through discussion and correspondence with eagle watchers, I have recognized a considerable range of hunting techniques used by Golden Eagles (Table 6). As with any aspect of animal behaviour there is inevitably a gradation between different behavioural patterns. It is therefore likely that any particular foraging attempt will involve some subtle deviation from such a necessarily arbitrary classification.

HUNTING TECHNIQUES

High soar with glide attack

Using this technique the eagle typically soars on a thermal at a height of 50 m or more, or hangs motionless against a steady breeze. When prey is detected the bird partly closes its wings and enters a long, low-angled glide which can carry it over distances of 1 km or more with speed increasing as the wings are closed further on approaching the quarry. Just prior to impact the wings are opened, the tail fanned and the feet are thrust forward to grab the prey. From under the path of such a stoop the rush of the wind through the wing feathers is impressively loud and has been likened to the sound of ripping cloth. A similar type of stoop is sometimes used by a bird launching itself from a perch on a tree or a rock into a low-angled glide attack directly towards its potential prey (Carnie 1954).

The kill, which is invariably made with the talons, can be on the ground or, in the case of bird prey, a metre or two off the ground if the quarry has detected the eagle but taken flight too late to escape. I have seen this technique used against Red Grouse on three occasions: twice the quarry escaped by fleeing just before the eagle struck and the third time the grouse was struck by the eagle just after the victim broke cover. To be used effectively the technique requires long sight-lines across comparatively open country. Prey that is dispersed and therefore not likely to benefit from the warning signals of near neighbours is particularly vulnerable, as are animals in which there is an innate conflict between 'freeze' and 'flight' behaviour. Typical targets for this technique are the various hare and grouse species.

High soar with vertical stoop

This is similar to the previous method but, when successful, it leads to a kill in flight, usually high above the ground. The eagle soars at a great height before making a sudden, rapid descent resembling the vertical stoop of a Peregrine Falcon. Comparatively slow-flying prey such as geese, herons or cranes are vulnerable and the victim is struck by the powerful talons of the plummeting eagle and is, quite literally, knocked out of the sky. This behaviour has been reported only rarely but is difficult to observe because it occurs high in the air. Cameron (1908), describing an unsuccessful attack on a flock of Canada Geese in Montana, noted that the flock scattered immediately in response to the eagle's stoop, and on re-forming subsequently rose higher in order to stay above the eagle. Clearly, the achievement of a considerable height advantage is essential for this strategy to be successful and, to gain this, the prevailing weather conditions need to be especially favourable. The grouping of prey in a flock, which offers a choice of victims, may also be important. Meinertzhagen (1940) saw a Ptarmigan taken out of a covey high above a Scottish corrie using this technique. It is likely that a variation on this method is used by Golden Eagles hunting colonial seabirds in parts of western Scotland.

Contour flight with short glide attack

This is probably the commonest of all the hunting manoeuvres used. Typically, the eagle searches for prey in low-level and sometimes flapping flight, quartering the ground at a height of 5 m or less, rarely breaking the skyline when viewed from any distance. On detecting prey the eagle enters a short, low-angled glide and strikes, sometimes returning to repeat the manoeuvre following a miss. The method depends on some variation in topography or, in flat terrain, on a vegetation structure with patches of trees interrupted by open spaces. The key to success here is again surprise and this is the usual method employed when hunting colonial, burrowing mammals when the detection distance between predator and prey must be kept to a minimum. It is also used commonly against Red Grouse, especially when the numbers of grouse in an area are high (Watson & Jenkins 1964). Bob Swann (*in litt.*) described a similar technique used by eagles hunting colonial seabirds close to a sheer sea-cliff in western Scotland. In that case, the eagle flew close to the ground on the landward side of the cliff and periodically shot out over the cliff edge where large concentrations of seabirds in flight offered abundant targets.

Unlike the 'High soar with glide attack' where a specific individual is typically the object, this method is effective against a concentration of 'colonial' prey with the selection of the individual quarry animal made late in the attack. The final stoop speed is comparatively slow and there is a greater need for agility and readjustment

when 'homing in' on the chosen victim. A number of accounts have documented tandem hunting by a pair of eagles using this hunting method: each bird may then approach the area of prey concentration from different directions or at differing heights (see Collopy 1983b for a description). One of the best descriptions of this type of attack is given by Dekker (1985) who watched migrating Golden Eagles hunting Richardson's Ground Squirrels in Alberta, Canada. Cameron (1908) also describes eagles hunting prairie dogs in this manner in Montana and I have seen the technique used successfully to hunt Rabbits in Scotland.

Glide attack with tail-chase

This technique typically involves a low-angled stoop which commences some distance from the quarry as in 'High soar with glide attack' but may also occur while contour hunting. The quarry is flushed and then pursued as the eagle closely matches the twists and turns of the prey, which may be a running hare or a grouse in flight. The key to success is the eagle's agility and the inability of the prey, to find some form of cover. When pursuing a grouse a 'tail-chasing' eagle will normally only be successful if it starts with an appreciable height advantage, from which it can then gain the necessary speed to overtake its fast-flying quarry (Watson 1972). Several accounts have documented tandem hunting using this method. Bent (1937) describes a glide attack and tail-chase by two eagles pursuing a Sage Grouse (outcome successful for the eagle), and Meinertzhagen (1940) tells of a similar attack by a pair of eagles pursuing a Mountain Hare (outcome unknown). In upland Scotland, where there is precious little cover for Mountain Hares, this method of hunting, either by individual eagles or by a pair in tandem, is quite common.

Low flight with slow descent attack

For certain types of attack, speed and aerial agility are relatively unimportant. Such is the case for eagles hunting tortoises, snakes and slow-moving mammals such as hedgehogs. The eagle typically hunts in low-level, quartering flight and, on detecting prey, may briefly hover before descending in a slow 'parachute' stoop (Grubač 1988). In the case of tortoises, once captured these are then dropped onto rocks from a height of 10 m or more in order to break open the hard protective shell (Fischer *et al.* 1975). Cameron (1905) described a Golden Eagle killing a rattlesnake where, clearly, dexterity at the moment of impact was more important than the power of the stoop. This type of attack has also been reported in the case of an eagle killing a newly born Roe Deer calf which was lying in deep heather at some distance from its mother (Ratcliffe & Rowe 1979).

The one common element in all these examples is the general absence of escape behaviour among the prey involved. In some animals such as tortoises and perhaps snakes, a specialized strategy may be required either to kill and disable dangerous prey or, as in the case of tortoises, make it eatable. A variation on this type of attack

Golden Eagle dropping a tortoise onto rocks with the purpose of cracking open the hard protective shell; the backdrop is the arid landscape of typical eagle country in Greece.

is used against carnivores such as foxes, coyotes or even wolves (Dekker 1985). In such instances the hunting eagle hangs motionless only a metre or two above the prey, sometimes for several minutes, and will only press home the attack if the victim turns its head away, thus reducing the risk of injury to the eagle from a powerful bite. Here, the actual killing technique resembles that used with larger animals, such as ungulates, which is described below.

Low flight with sustained grip attack

This is the characteristic behaviour used to catch and kill moderately large ungulates. The hunting eagle flies low over a herd of ungulates, sometimes passing near to the group on several occasions. Typically, the prey bunch together and sometimes break into a run. Several accounts have documented tandem hunting by a pair using this method and, indeed, this may be the norm. An eagle then appears to select its potential quarry which is pursued until the hunting bird lands on the victim's back or neck. The talons then grip the animal firmly and, unless the prey is knocked to the ground immediately, the eagle rides it for several minutes with wings outstretched and flapping in order to maintain balance and until the quarry eventually collapses, either as a result of exhaustion, shock or internal injury.

The success of this strategy depends on the eagle's ability to isolate a potential victim, and here tandem hunting may be advantageous; once a victim has been isolated, success will depend on the bird's strength and stamina. Prey killed in this way is generally too heavy to lift and the method is mainly of value when eagles are not breeding and can therefore consume their victim where it lies. Detailed accounts are given by Bruns (1970), who witnessed an eagle kill a 30 kg Pronghorn Antelope, and Cooper (1969) who observed the killing of a 20 kg Red Deer calf (see also: Cameron 1908; Bergo 1987b; Ewins 1987). A variation on this behaviour is reported by Nette *et al.* (1984) who recorded predation on Dall Sheep. Several of the above observations were made during periods of deep snow cover when other prey was thought to be scarce. Given the potential risk of injury to the eagle it appears likely that the technique is used mainly when alternative prey is unavailable.

Walk and grab attack

In some circumstances a Golden Eagle will attempt to secure prey by walking up to its potential victim and grabbing at it. Typically, the bird lands close to the quarry, which is usually protected from an aerial attack by an obstruction such as a bush or rock, or in the case of a young mammal, by one of its parents. Nette *et al.* (1984) recorded an eagle walking up to a ewe Dall Sheep and dragging the lamb out from under her; Locati (1990) reported a similar but unsuccessful attempt by a pair of eagles on a female Chamois with two kids; Davies (1985) watched an eagle try to pull a young Badger from underneath the legs of its parent.

Bent (1937) reported a variation on this behaviour where one eagle landed on the ground near a mesquite bush in which a jackrabbit had taken cover. The eagle then walked towards the animal which ran out the opposite side of the bush only to be captured by the eagle's mate which had been hovering overhead. I once watched an immature eagle's ungainly attempt to capture a young lamb that had become

Golden Eagle in pursuit of a cock Capercaillie in the wooded peatlands of Eastern Europe.

separated from its mother. The eagle first attempted to land on the back of the lamb which took shelter under a rock. The eagle then spent the next 10 min or so walking all round the rock, occasionally lunging at the animal with its talons, before eventually the ewe returned and the eagle flew off. A common feature of most observations of this type of attack is the slow-moving and comparatively defenceless nature of the prey involved.

CARRION FEEDING

The preceding descriptions relate to the range of active hunting behaviour used by Golden Eagles. In addition to being predatory, eagles also consume carrion, especially in winter. This is generally located from a high soaring flight, in some cases by observing the behaviour of other scavengers such as crows. The approach to carrion is broadly comparable with the 'High soar with slow descent' hunting technique, although birds will typically land several metres away from the carcass and make the final approach on foot. In a study of scavenging birds in western Scotland, Hewson (1981) found that when Golden Eagles were feeding on sheep carcasses other scavengers, such as Buzzards, Ravens and Hooded Crows, remained at a distance of several metres. Such behaviour is not surprising given that the smaller scavengers would be at risk from a 'grab attack' if they approached too close to the eagle.

DRINKING

It is generally assumed that large predatory birds such as eagles have no need to drink water and can acquire all the liquid they need from their animal prey (Brown & Amadon 1968). Recent observations from Nevada show that this is not always the case. The use of snow as a source of water in high mountain ranges in summer is reported by Johnson (1994) as are visits to high mountain bogs by Golden Eagles for the purpose of drinking, bathing and preening (Charlet & Rust 1991). Both sets of observations occurred in the arid environment of the Great Basin in Nevada, where surface water is extremely scarce. The particular 'eagle bogs' used for drinking and bathing normally shared two characteristics in addition to the presence of water. These were the presence of cover, such as trees or bushes, on three sides and at least 10 m back from the water, and a narrow opening through cover downhill from the spring, with a drop of at least 30 m in 200 m. The latter provides a safe escape route with sufficient slope for the birds to get airborne while the surrounding cover reduced the long-range detection of the eagles by ground predators. That use of such areas was a regular phenomenon was confirmed by sightings of Golden Eagles on the ground on a total of 17 days during one summer period, with up to five individuals together on three occasions. Whether Golden Eagles in other arid regions or elsewhere regularly visit drinking or bathing sites is not known.

HUNTING SUCCESS

Among predatory birds there have been few studies of hunting success—that is, the proportion of hunting forays which lead to a kill—and Golden Eagles are no exception. Brown & Amadon (1968) speculated that perhaps one in four attacks by large birds, such as eagles hunting active prey, were successful, a figure close to the ratio later reported by Collopy (1983b). Collopy witnessed 115 'pounces' by eagles where the outcome was known with certainty. Of these, 72 were by birds hunting alone and 43 involved both members of a pair hunting in tandem. Of the solo hunts 21 (29%) were successful compared with just two (5%) of the tandem hunts. He attributed this unexpected difference to the possibility that tandem hunting may be directed at larger, or more elusive prey and cited in support the work of Hector (1981), who correlated the poorer hunting success of tandem-hunting Aplomado Falcons with a higher proportion of attacks on birds, which were believed to be more difficult to capture than mammals. Whether the success rate of Collopy's Golden Eagles, which were hunting mammalian prey in Idaho, would be similar for the species in parts of Scotland or Scandinavia where more avian prey is taken, is unknown and would merit further study.

SELECTION OF DIFFERENT SEXES AMONG PREY ANIMALS

Several researchers have investigated the possibility that Golden Eagles feed selectively, in particular by taking a higher proportion of one sex of a particular prey animal than occurs in nature. This could come about, for example, if one sex is more accessible to eagles because it spends more time above ground than the other. Alternatively one sex may be more conspicuous as a result of its greater involvement in display or agonistic behaviour. In work on Golden Eagles and Rabbits in Spain, Fernández & Ceballos (1990) found that the sex ratio of Rabbits taken by eagles was skewed in favour of males and approximated closely to the sex ratio of Rabbits above ground during daylight. In contrast the sex-ratio in warrens favoured females, which tended to be above ground more at night. The unequal predation by eagles on male Rabbits was attributed to the behavioural difference between the sexes of the prey. A similar conclusion was reached by Boag (1977) who explained the higher than expected proportion of male Columbian Ground Squirrels in the diet on the basis of their greater availability above ground. Sulkava & Rajala (1966) found that male Black Grouse were taken by eagles more often than expected, based on the sex ratio in the wild which was known to favour females. This could again be attributable to the greater vulnerability of the more conspicuous and socially active males. These studies underline the importance of prey behaviour in influencing 'prey availability' to Golden Eagles.

SUMMARY

Golden Eagles have a range of hunting techniques and are equipped to catch a wide assortment of prey in a variety of different habitats. Long-range stoops, which rely on the eagle's keen eyesight and on high-speed flight, are used to catch dispersed prey in open country. In short-range stoops the flight of the eagle is slower and such attacks tend to be made in more broken country and against prey which lives in colonies. Success here depends on surprise and the ability of the eagle to make a close approach to its quarry before being detected. Various specialized hunting techniques are used to catch and kill slow-moving prey such as reptiles, and to overpower large animals such as ungulates.

CHAPTER 6

Food

A male Ptarmigan in spring plumage, crouching amongst boulders in the high Cairngorms.

ONE visit I made to a west Highland eagle eyrie in the late summer of 1982 was especially memorable. On the nest was a quite remarkable assortment of prey remains. Digging through the summer's debris I discovered bits and pieces of two Red Deer calves, a Hedgehog, several Rabbits, a Hooded Crow, two young Ravens, four Herring Gulls, a Fulmar, a Red Grouse and, most surprising of all, the remains of a Peregrine, a Merlin and a Kestrel. At the time I did not appreciate the full significance of this rich find. In time I was to learn that, to be such a food generalist did not necessarily mean that all was well for the eagle.

Of all the aspects of Golden Eagle biology, food has been the most thoroughly researched and written about. Knowledge of the diet and how it varies in time and space is the key to understanding the role of any predator. The wide geographical range of the Golden Eagle and its exploitation of many habitats are evidence of its success. With an array of hunting techniques which combine acute vision with power, speed and a surprising degree of aerial agility and dexterity, the Golden

Eagle is the pre-eminent diurnal predator of medium-sized birds and mammals in open country throughout the northern hemisphere.

SOURCES OF INFORMATION

Various techniques have been used to measure the diet of raptors, including the analysis of stomach contents, the identification of items in prey remains and regurgitated food pellets, and the direct observation of food items brought to nests. Each method has its limitations. It is now thankfully rare to encounter the large number of eagle corpses which were obtained when the bird was killed in organized campaigns such as those in Montana in the 1940s (Woodgerd 1952), and from which diet was assessed from stomach content analysis. Most recent studies have relied on assessments of prey remains and pellets or on observation of food brought to nests.

Prey remains and pellets are indirect measures of diet and are subject to various biases; consequently they tend to misrepresent the importance of certain types of food. However, long watches from hides at nest sites are time-consuming and can normally only be done at a small number of sites at any one time. The latter cannot provide information on food consumed by the adults away from the nest, or food taken outside the breeding period.

In some large raptors, such as Bald Eagles and White-tailed Sea Eagles, which feed on a range of bird, mammal and fish prey, biases can be serious, with whole categories of prey such as fish hardly represented at all among pellets or remains (Mersmann *et al.* 1992; Watson *et al.* 1992a). For Sparrowhawks, Ian Newton (1986) observed that little information of value could be obtained from pellets for that species because pellets contained only ground up feather fragments that were rarely identifiable. He was able to interpret food from remains at plucking posts but considered that even here there was a bias, with small species under-accounted for in old pluckings (Newton & Marquiss 1982). The African Marsh Harrier feeds on birds and small mammals and Simmons *et al.* (1991) found that both pellets and prey remains contained biases when compared with direct observation at nests. Birds were over-represented among remains while mammals were overstated in pellets.

In a study of Golden Eagles in Idaho, Collopy (1983a) listed prey brought in to nests and compared this with items identified in prey remains and pellets collected at the same nests. He concluded that there was no difference in the frequency of prey species recorded in prey remains and pellets combined compared with direct observation of prey delivered. However, collections of pellets and prey remains tended to underestimate the total amount of food delivered. Elsewhere, studies of Golden Eagles have depended solely on the identification of food in remains or pellets, or a combination of both (Carnie 1954; Sulkava & Rajala 1966; Tjernberg 1981; Fernández 1987).

In my work in Scotland I used pellet analysis because I wanted to compare diet both between areas and between seasons. Pellets were the only source of information that could be reliably obtained outside the breeding season (Watson *et al.* 1993). As Scottish Golden Eagles feed on both birds and mammals, my reliance on pellets alone may have tended to overstate the relative importance of mammalian prey compared with birds (Fernández 1987; Simmons *et al.* 1991).

The Golden Eagle Diet in Scotland

The range of food eaten by Golden Eagles in Scotland is described by Gordon (1955) and Brown (1976), although neither author gives much quantitative data. In my work, I was interested in measuring differences in diet across the range, and in assessing changes between summer and winter (Watson *et al.* 1993). In Scotland, ecological variation, combined with differences in contemporary and historical land use, has resulted in marked regional differences in the availability of prey for eagles. Also, the availability of different types of prey will clearly change between summer and winter, and the food needs of eagles may alter between the breeding season, when the young are reared, and the non-breeding season when prey need not be carried to nest sites.

To quantify the diet, nearly 1300 pellets were collected throughout the range in Scotland during 1981–85. From these, more than 1700 prey items were identified and these were used to assess the diet across the range in both summer (May–October) and winter (November–April). Most prey items in pellets were identifiable at least to the level of the taxonomic 'family' (Table 7). For the comparison between areas and between summer and winter, all items were placed in one of six prey categories: (1) deer; (2) sheep and goat; (3) lagomorph (Rabbit and Mountain Hare); (4) other mammals (mainly voles, mustelids and Foxes); (5) grouse (mostly Red Grouse and Ptarmigan); and (6) miscellaneous items (mainly various birds such as Fulmars, ducks, crows, waders, pipits, larks and thrushes and a few reptiles and amphibians).

Variation between areas

The numbers of pellets collected in summer were large enough to allow between-area comparisons and Fig. 7 gives a measure of diet for eagles in the nine ecological Regions (Fig. 6; eight in the Highlands and one in southwest Scotland), described in Chapter 4. Across the nine Regions six diet types were recognizable.

Type *A* diet was a feature of eagles in the Outer Hebrides and Skye (Regions 1 & 2). Three prey categories predominated (lagomorphs, sheep and miscellaneous) and the proportion of deer was low. Rabbits made up the majority of lagomorphs and Fulmars were the most numerous species in the miscellaneous category.

Type *B* diet was restricted to Mull (Region 3) and was similar to Type *A* with lagomorphs and sheep predominant, although the miscellaneous category was much less important mainly owing to the low incidence of Fulmars. A further difference was that the majority of lagomorphs were Mountain Hares.

Type *C* diet was found in the North, Northwest and West-central Highlands

Some typical and some less usual prey remains found at Golden Eagle nests in the west Highlands of Scotland.

fulmar skull

raven leg

cm

ptarmigan
primary

cuckoo (juv)
tail f. in pin

hedgehog spines

peregrine (juv) tail f's

wild cat, l. jaw

red deer calf jaw (l.)

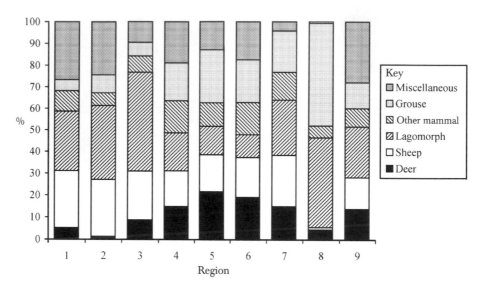

FIG. 7.   *The proportion of six main prey categories in the summer diet of Golden Eagles in nine Regions of Scotland (see text and Fig. 6). Data are from Table 8. Regions 1 and 2 had diet type A, Region 3 had type B, Regions 4–6 had type C, Region 7 had type D, Region 8 had type E and Region 9 had type F. Redrawn from Watson et al. 1993.*

(Regions 4, 5 and 6). Here prey was distributed more or less evenly across the six prey categories with appreciably more deer eaten than anywhere else. Among the miscellaneous category, Fulmars were important in Region 4, but in Regions 5 and 6 no single taxon was dominant. Most lagomorphs were Mountain Hares in Regions 4 and 5 and Rabbits in Region 6.

Type *D* diet occurred in the Southwest Highlands (Region 7) and most closely resembled Type *C*, although lagomorphs and sheep were comparatively more frequent and the miscellaneous category less so. The majority of lagomorphs were Rabbits.

Type *E* diet occurred in the East Highlands (Region 8) and was a narrow diet, being much the most distinctive of the six diet types recognized, with 90% of all prey items falling into just two of the six categories (grouse and lagomorphs). The great majority of lagomorphs were Mountain Hares.

Type *F* diet was found in Southwest Scotland (Region 9) and was a broadly based diet like others on the west mainland (Types *C* & *D*) but the miscellaneous category was predominant and included at least eight different bird families. Of the lagomorphs, Rabbits and Mountain Hares occurred in about equal proportions.

Line transect counts of numbers of grouse and lagomorphs were performed in a range of localities in seven of the nine Regions for which a measure of diet was obtained (see Appendix 4 for a description of the line transect method). The proportion of grouse (all species), and lagomorphs (Rabbits and Mountain Hares) in the diet of eagles broadly reflected the relative numbers of these animals detected on transect counts (Fig. 8). These animals are both the dominant naturally

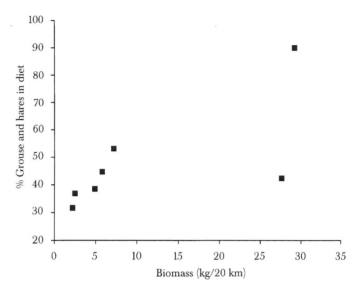

FIG. 8.   *The proportion of grouse and hares in the summer diet of Golden Eagles in seven Regions of Scotland in relation to the biomass of grouse and hares detected on line transects done on study areas within these regions. Line transect data for study areas D and E were combined. In statistical analysis* $r_s = 0.89$, $P < 0.05$.

occurring medium-sized herbivorous birds and mammals of open moorland habitat in much of northwest Europe, and the preferred prey of Golden Eagles there. When such prey are scarce then eagles must seek alternative food such as sheep, deer and a variety of birds including seabirds, crows, ducks and waders. As the proportion of grouse and lagomorphs in the overall diet declines, so the overall breadth of the diet increases (Fig. 9—for method of calculating dietary breadth see Appendix 3). Put simply, when the preferred prey species are plentiful the diet of Golden Eagles is relatively narrow and eagles are typically specialist hunters, but when favoured prey is scarce they become generalists.

Variation between seasons

Most descriptive accounts have noted that Golden Eagles feed on carrion (Gordon 1955; Johnsgard 1990), although there have been few quantitative studies of diet in the non-breeding season when such behaviour would be most likely (Lockie 1964). Comparing the six prey categories for the eight Regions in Scotland where information on diet was available in both winter and summer, I found that the frequency of deer in pellets was invariably greater in winter, and in all but one area the incidence of grouse was greater in summer (Table 8). Amongst lagomorphs there was no consistent pattern with approximately similar proportions in both seasons in all areas as was the case with sheep. Among the latter, all items in winter pellets were adult sheep, and most if not all of this would have been taken as carrion. In summer, most wool in pellets was identified as lamb. It is likely that some lamb was taken as carrion and some was live prey killed by eagles (Lockie 1964). A

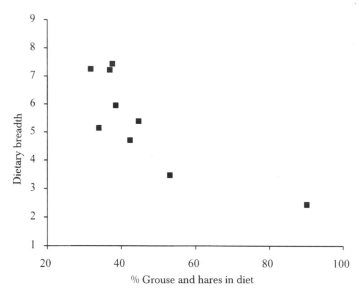

FIG. 9.   *The relationship between the breadth of the diet and the frequency of grouse and hares in the diet of Golden Eagles from nine Regions of Scotland. See Appendix 3 for method of calculating breadth of diet. Data are from Table 7.*

dependence on carrion in winter has also been reported from Spain (Fernández 1987) and North America (Knight *et al.* 1979) and is probably the norm across much of the range.

Golden Eagles appear not to feed appreciably on large items of carrion during the nestling period, although in Scotland dead adult sheep are frequently available at this time. This may be partly because of the difficulty of transporting such large items to nest sites. It may also be that carrion from large animals is deficient in certain important elements such as calcium, and, if so, it would offer poorer food value for growing nestlings.

Unusual prey

While much of the Golden Eagle's diet in Scotland is predictable, I have, over the years, come across several unexpected items. Small mammals such as Short-tailed Voles turn up quite commonly in pellets, as do Moles, Brown Rats and Water Voles. In fact, the knowledge of Water Vole distribution in the Highlands was recently extended quite appreciably from remains identified in a collection of eagle pellets (Jim & Rosemary Green, *in litt.*). It is not uncommon to find the remains of Fox cubs at nests, especially in the western Highlands. In coastal regions, and especially on the islands off western Scotland, young Otters are taken occasionally and both Stoats and Weasels are quite frequent prey throughout eagle country on the mainland. The Pine Marten, a mustelid which has greatly increased in numbers in Scotland in recent years in response to the expansion of forestry, is occasionally caught by eagles. David Balharry believes that Pine Marten behaviour in western Scotland is strongly influenced by the threat of eagle predation, with martens moving about under the cover of woodland during the day but ranging widely over open country at night.

The list of bird species killed by eagles is quite extensive. Some of the more unusual items recorded by me include Grey Heron, Manx Shearwater, Red-breasted Merganser, Buzzard, Short-eared Owl, Mistle Thrush, Meadow Pipit and Bullfinch. At one eyrie in western Scotland I have found the remains of Adders on several occasions, prompting the thought that this pair of eagles may have developed a particular ability to catch snakes. Roy Dennis once watched an eagle apparently hunting 'on foot' in a peat bog. He could only conclude that the bird was attempting to catch Frogs. Records of Golden Eagles eating fish in Scotland are rare although Gordon (1955) reports both Salmon and Pike in the diet. Fish are, of course, more frequent prey of the predominantly coastal-dwelling White-tailed Sea Eagle (Watson *et al.* 1992a).

DIET IN CONTINENTAL EUROPE AND NORTH AMERICA

Studies of the Golden Eagle diet during the breeding season have been carried out in many areas in Europe and North America (Tables 9 & 10). Whilst methods have not always been entirely comparable, these analyses reveal some consistent patterns which are sufficiently robust despite minor differences in methodology. One aspect of diet which has been of particular interest to me is the extent to which Golden Eagles are food generalists or specialists.

Breadth of the diet

Dietary breadth, derived from the proportions of prey species in different 'families' (Appendix 3), offers a quantitative measure of food specialization by eagles. This measure showed a similar range of variation across the world range to that found in Scotland, although in most other studies, values were closer to the comparatively narrow diet of the East Highlands, suggesting that the more generalized diet of eagles in western Scotland was somewhat atypical (Fig. 10). The most consistently restricted diets with the greatest dependence on prey species from just one or two families (notably rabbits and hares *Leporidae* and/or ground squirrels and marmots *Sciuridae*) occurred in North America. Dietary breadth was somewhat higher in continental Europe where, in any particular locality, preferred prey tended to come from two or three of the four principal prey families of *Leporidae*, *Sciuridae*, grouse *Tetraonidae* or pheasants and partridges *Phasianidae* (Tables 9 & 10).

Extending this finding further, Steenhof & Kochert (1988), in Idaho, found between-year differences in the breadth of the diet among Golden Eagles. They showed that diet was more varied in years when the preferred prey of Black-tailed Jackrabbits was scarce and that this resulted from most nesting pairs having a more diverse diet, rather than there being specialization on different prey by certain pairs only.

Particularly unusual diets occur on the island of Gotland in Sweden and in Macedonia (Fig. 10). In the Swedish locality, grouse are virtually absent and

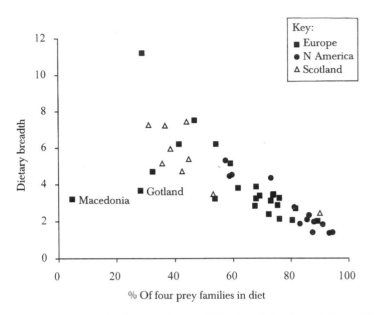

FIG. 10.   _The relationship between the overall breadth of the diet and the combined frequency of the four principal prey families (_Leporidae, Sciuridae, Tetraonidae and_ Phasianidae_) in the diet of Golden Eagles from various parts of the world. Data are from 46 accounts of the diet during the breeding season (see Tables 7, 9 and 10 for details). See Appendix 3 for the method of calculating dietary breadth. Golden Eagles in Gotland fed substantially on Hedgehogs, and eagles in Macedonia fed principally on tortoises._

lagomorphs are rare, but eagles have successfully filled this gap by an apparently unique dependence on Hedgehogs. The principal prey in Macedonia are tortoises and this may be typical over a wide area in southeast Europe and the Middle East, although precise data on diet are few for this region. The findings from these two areas are instructive. They show that Golden Eagles can have a narrow diet provided that a particular prey type is available in sufficient quantity. I believe that the key factor here is the size of this alternative prey, with both tortoises and Hedgehogs falling within the Golden Eagles' preferred size range of prey.

Selection of prey in different size classes

Another way of looking at diet is to consider the proportions taken by a predator in different size classes. From information on the proportions of different prey families I have interpreted the diet of Golden Eagles in relation to the biomass of food in eight size classes (see caption to Fig. 11). In Europe, there is a preference for food in size classes 5 and 6 (0.5–1 kg and 1–2 kg respectively; Fig. 11) with rather more prey in the smaller size classes in southern Europe and size class 7 (2–4 kg) being more important in northern and central Europe. In North America, the pattern is similar to that in northern Europe.

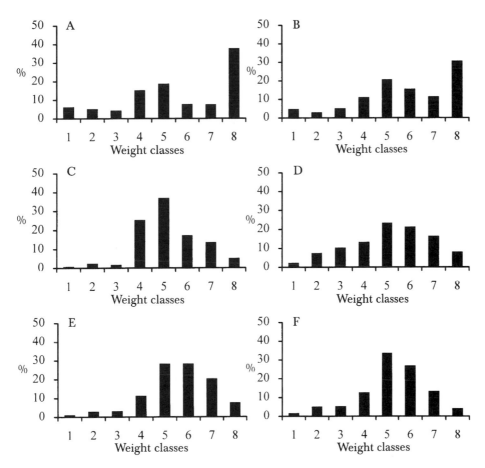

FIG. 11. *The proportion of prey in eight weight classes in the diet of Golden Eagles in Scotland (A, the Islands; B, West; C, East), continental Europe (D, North; E, South) and North America (F) during the breeding season. Prey items were allocated amongst the weight classes: 1 <63 g, 2 = 63–125 g, 3 = 125–250 g, 4 = 250–500 g, 5 = 500–1000 g, 6 = 1–2 kg, 7 = 2–4 kg, 8 >4 kg. Data on diet are from Tables 7, 9 and 10.*

Golden Eagle diet in the Scottish Islands and on the west mainland of Scotland is quite different, with the greatest number of animals in size class 8 (>4 kg). This, I believe, reflects the scarcity of medium-sized wild herbivores and the excessive numbers of large herbivores (domestic sheep and Red Deer) in these areas. The pattern of preference across size classes in the east Highlands is more like that of continental Europe and North America and reflects a better balance between medium and large herbivores in the natural environment compared with the rest of the Highlands. Nevertheless, the comparative lack of animals in size class 6 and the greater dependence on class 4 reflects the dearth of larger grouse species such as Black Grouse and Capercaillie compared with the smaller Red Grouse and Ptarmigan. The implications of these differences in dietary preference for other aspects of Golden Eagle population biology are explored in later chapters.

DIET IN OTHER *AQUILA* EAGLES

In Eurasia there are several places where the ranges of three or occasionally four species of *Aquila* eagles meet or overlap. Two examples are in southeast Europe, where the Golden Eagle range overlaps that of the Lesser Spotted and Imperial Eagle, and in the Altai region of southeast Russia, where the Greater Spotted, Imperial, Steppe and Golden Eagle all live in close proximity. While no detailed studies have been carried out on the extent of ecological separation between the species, either in terms of habitat preference or diet, it is possible to construct a general picture of the species' requirements in such zones of overlap.

There are clear differences in habitat preferences; Golden Eagles favour mountainous areas, Greater and Lesser Spotted Eagles prefer moderately dense woodland in lowland areas usually close to water, Imperial Eagles live in open woodland and semi-desert in the lowlands, and Steppe Eagles occur in grassland or semi-desert areas in flat lowlands. There is also a gradation in size from the Lesser Spotted Eagle at <2 kg to the Golden Eagle at 4–6 kg (Table 1). Allied with this are measurable differences in the diet with the smaller species such as Lesser Spotted, Greater Spotted and Steppe Eagles favouring prey items <0.25 kg (Fig. 12; Table 11). Imperial Eagles and Tawny Eagles both take prey over a comparatively wide size range although typically most is less than 2 kg (Fig. 12; Tables 11 & 12).

In comparison the two southern hemisphere species of *Aquila* (Black Eagle and Wedge-tailed Eagle), which are believed to be ecological replacements of the Golden Eagle, are of similar size and show a preference for prey in the same size range of 0.5–4 kg (Fig. 12; Tables 12 & 13). While the Black Eagle in Africa has adopted a specialist feeding strategy with a narrow feeding niche both in terms of species taken and size classes of prey, the Wedge-tailed Eagle in Australia is more of a generalist. This contrast may reflect differences in the number of competitor species of similar-sized raptors between the two continents, or perhaps in the kinds of prey available. In Africa, the Black Eagle range overlaps that of at least three potential competitors of comparable size (Tawny Eagle, Martial Eagle and Crowned Eagle) while in Australia the nearest equivalent to the Wedge-tailed Eagle is the much smaller Little Eagle.

In North America, the absence of smaller species of *Aquila* eagles has probably been a factor in the amount of ecological radiation among the *Buteo* hawks. To give just one example, in western North America the diurnal avian predator niche in open country is partitioned among at least three species of sympatric *Buteo* hawks (Red-tailed, Swainson's and Ferruginous Hawks). Ecological separation between these is achieved by subtle differences in habitat preference and nest site selection and probably not by partitioning of their shared and abundant rodent prey resource (Johnsgard 1990).

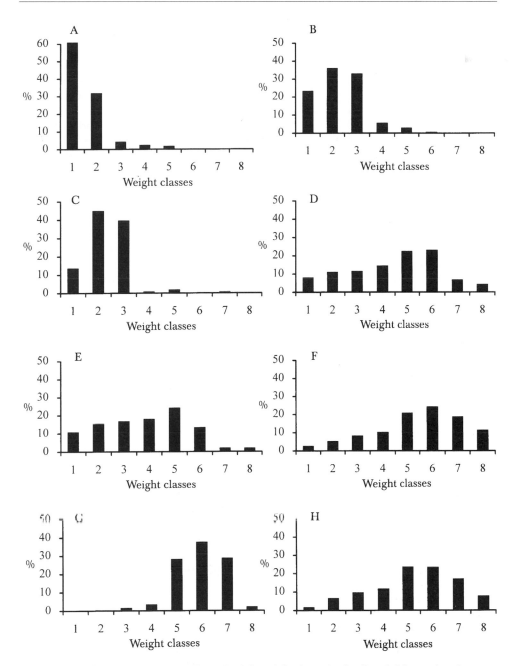

FIG. 12.   *The proportion of prey in eight weight classes in the diet of eight species of Aquila eagles during the breeding season (A, Lesser Spotted Eagle; B, Greater Spotted Eagle; C, Steppe Eagle; D, Tawny Eagle; E, Imperial Eagle; F, Wedge-tailed Eagle; G, Black Eagle; H, Golden Eagle, Northern and Southern Europe). Data for the Golden Eagle are from all studies in continental Europe. The weight classes are as described in the legend to Fig. 11. Data on diet are from Tables 9 and 11–13.*

FOOD REQUIREMENTS OF GOLDEN EAGLES

Brown & Watson (1964) calculated the food requirements of a pair of Golden Eagles during a full year. While an adult Golden Eagle could conceivably, when gorged, have consumed as much as 900 g in a day (Arnold 1954), this does not allow for the fact that, typically, in such large raptors feeding need not take place every day. Allowing for periods of gorging and fasting the average daily food intake was estimated at around 230 g of meat, or 168 kg for a pair during a year. To achieve this there will be an element of 'wastage' and this was estimated to be around 20% for kills less than 1 kg (grouse), 30% for kills of 1–4 kg (hares and rabbits) and 40% or more in larger animals such as young ungulates (Brown & Watson 1964). With such differential wastage the amount of prey that must be killed or utilized to meet the needs of the bird will vary depending on the type of prey selected.

In addition to supplying the adult pair, a Golden Eagle hunting range must also provide food to rear the young and to support a proportion of 'non-breeding' eagles. The cumulative food requirements of an average Golden Eagle hunting range for one year in the east Highlands of Scotland were estimated at 321 kg, and to comprise 50 kg carrion and 271 kg killed. This annual requirement could be met, for example, by the equivalent of two dead sheep, 70 Mountain Hares and 140 Red Grouse, or by the equivalent of one dead Red Deer stag, 110 Rabbits and 160 Ptarmigan (Brown & Watson 1964). In much of western Scotland the relative contribution from carrion would be much higher and a proportion of the hare or grouse component would be made up of lambs or deer calves.

PREDATION ON LIVESTOCK

There have been numerous studies of the interactions between Golden Eagles and livestock, particularly in Scotland and North America but also in parts of Scandinavia (Arnold 1954; Lockie & Stephen 1959; Bergo 1987b). In western Scotland and the eastern foothills of the Rockies from Montana to Texas the perceived conflict is between eagles and lambs while in northern Scandinavia predation on young domestic Reindeer is an additional concern. Work has tended to concentrate on two questions: 'do eagles kill the young of domestic livestock?' and if so, 'what is the economic impact of this predation?'.

Golden Eagles are clearly capable of killing large ungulates, exceptionally up to the size of 30 kg or more (see Chapter 5). That they are able to kill young lambs which in western Scotland weigh around 5 kg at birth and some 10 kg 6 weeks after birth (Hewson 1984) is not in doubt. Young Reindeer fawns found at Golden Eagle nests in Sweden were also around this weight (Tjernberg 1981). However, among both lambs and Reindeer fawns, many die from other causes at or around birth and some of these animals are undoubtedly scavenged by eagles with the result that only a proportion of carcasses at nests represent kills (Lockie 1964; Bolen 1975). The maximum weight of prey an eagle can carry is dictated by the size of the bird, by

Adult Golden Eagle plucking a winter plumage Ptarmigan.

wind, and by topography. Even under the most favourable conditions of orographic winds and a downhill flight path to the nest, a large female eagle (6 kg) could rarely carry prey greater than her own body weight and more typically the maximum prey lifted is less than half this (Huey 1962; Kalmbach *et al.* 1964; Snow 1973). Gordon (1955) observed that the majority of mountain hares brought to nests were partly dismembered before arrival and it is my experience in western Scotland that whole lamb carcasses are rarely seen on nests and that eagles effectively 'break in two' such items before taking them to nests.

While the ability to lift and carry large prey acts at least as a potential constraint on the levels of predation by eagles on young ungulates, this is less so for immature eagles or adults which are not breeding. Not surprisingly, some of the most persistent incidents of lamb-killing have been attributed to immature eagles or adult birds that have failed to breed (Leitch 1986; Matchett & O'Gara 1987) or to wintering eagles shortly before and during the spring migration period (Spofford 1964). In answer to my first question, Golden Eagles do sometimes kill young of domestic livestock, but the interpretation of evidence for such behaviour in any quantitative sense must be made carefully.

Predation on lambs in Scotland

Sheep farming in western Scotland is a low-intensity land use carried out over extensive semi-natural grassland and heathland communities. A convenient starting point in the annual sheep cycle is October when the previous summer's lamb stock has been sold along with the cast ewes. Lambs retained for stock replacement, typically 25% of the total ewe stock, are usually removed from the hill for the period October–March. Remaining ewes are left to over-winter on the hill, often with little or no supplementary feeding. Tupping, when the tups (rams) are released on the hill for mating, occurs in late November and lambing takes place from late April to mid-May. Sometimes lambing takes place on the hill but more often occurs on better land at lower elevations (known as 'inbye' in western Scotland) close to the farmhouse or crofthouse. Ewes and lambs which are held inbye for lambing are turned out to the hill 3–4 weeks after lambing. Lambs are gathered for marking, castration and tail-docking in June and shearing takes place in July or August, with the surplus lamb stock being put to market in September.

Stocking densities of ewes vary (see Chapter 4) with 50/km² not unusual, or as many as 1000 ewes in a typical eagle home range of 40 km² in western Scotland, with around half of that area being suitable for sheep grazing. Lamb production tends to be measured by the number of lambs surviving to marking in June per 100 ewes over-wintered. This figure for western Scotland is typically in the range 60–70% with 65% a reasonable average (Mather 1978; Hewson 1984; Leitch 1986). The frequency of barren ewes is normally around 5% and twins are exceptional (Hewson & Verkaik 1981), giving an estimated mortality rate of 30 out of 95 (31.5%) lambs born per 100 ewes up to marking in June. Several studies have sought to identify what component of this mortality is attributable to Golden Eagle kills (Lockie 1964; Hewson 1984; Leitch 1986) and estimates range from 0.5–8%. Based on these figures a sheep flock of 1000 ewes in a typical Golden Eagle range of 40 km² in western Scotland might be expected to lose something between 1 and 23 lambs to eagles in a year or 0.15–2.4% of the total potential lamb crop (see also a similar estimate by Weir (1985) for a locality in the central Highlands). Other causes of mortality include starvation, disease, and Fox or crow predation (Houston & Maddox 1974).

Does this level of eagle predation constitute an economic loss which could justify special compensation payments or control of Golden Eagles? For several reasons I believe it does not. As mentioned earlier, sheep farming in western Scotland is an extremely low-intensity activity, the economic viability of which is entirely dependent on subsidy from the tax-payer provided in the form of headage payments for breeding ewes. Such payments in the less-favoured areas of Britain such as the Scottish Highlands are higher than elsewhere and it is not unreasonable to propose that an element of this additional subsidy is intended to be set against losses such as those which occur from time to time as a result of eagle predation. Furthermore, being a low input system, the outputs in the form of lamb production are correspondingly low. As argued by Leitch (1986), it is clear that a relatively small investment in improved husbandry would lead to much improved ewe condition, and thereby increased lamb production far in excess of even the highest levels of depredation by eagles. At a much more fundamental level it must also be questioned whether the type of extensive sheep farming carried out in western Scotland now and over the past 200 years is in any sense of the word a sustainable proposition. Thus, another consequence of the system of headage payments is overstocking, leading to overgrazing and long-term decline in land productivity. I return to this question again in Chapter 20.

Predation on lambs in North America

Studies of lamb predation by nesting Golden Eagles in the United States have generally concluded, as in Scotland, that mortality caused by eagles is trivial and insignificant compared with other causes (Bolen 1975; Murphy 1975). Nevertheless, there are cases where comparatively large numbers of lambs have been killed and these have been attributed mainly to immature eagles or wintering birds, neither of which need to lift prey and carry it to nest sites (Matchett & O'Gara 1987). In such incidents the highest levels of lamb-killing occurred when populations of jackrabbits were low and/or when spring weather was cool and wet, presumably because preferred wild prey of eagles was less available at that time. Various measures were tested to try to alleviate the problem, including the trapping and translocation of over 400 eagles during nine years at a cost of more than $100 000. This approach was generally unsuccessful as it had little demonstrable effect on predation rates, was expensive, and some birds evidently returned to the capture area despite being translocated over several hundred km (Niemeyer 1977). The only tactic which had a measurable effect on predation rates was the use of human 'scarecrows' on prominent ridges, combined with harassment by people and vehicles (Matchett & O'Gara 1987). In a separate study, Phillips *et al.* (1991) trapped and relocated 14 Golden Eagles in an attempt to resolve an eagle–livestock conflict in Wyoming. All birds were transported and released at a range of sites more than 400 km away, and 12 of these eagles subsequently returned to the vicinity of their former territories— several birds returning less than 1 month after being moved.

In the final analysis, however, it would appear that the most effective deterrent against eagle predation of lambs is the retention of sufficient 'natural' prey such as jackrabbits, and this, as in the case of western Scotland, may require some fundamental readjustments of current range management practices, including reductions in sheep densities (Spofford 1964; Bolen 1975; Kochert *et al.* 1988).

Predation on Reindeer fawns and lambs in Scandinavia

In Sweden some 120 000 Reindeer fawns are born annually and it is calculated that Golden Eagles kill fewer than 500 of these (<0.4%), a figure comparable to the losses of lambs attributed to eagles in western Scotland (Tjernberg 1990). A system of economic compensation for supposed damage by large predators exists in Norway and over the 10 years up to 1987 some 10 000 claims were made with respect to sheep and Reindeer, mainly for losses said to be caused by eagles (Bergo 1987b). The validity of such claims is perhaps questionable as all losses of lambs to predators in Norway, including losses caused by large mammalian carnivores such as Wolf, Lynx and Wolverine as well as to Golden Eagles, amounted to less than 0.5% of lambs born annually (Fremming 1980). Given these low levels of predation on livestock and the comparative abundance of the eagle's natural prey over much of Scandinavia, the conflict between eagles and domestic livestock in that region would seem to be more 'apparent' than real. In effect, the sheep and Reindeer herders are being paid not to kill large predators, but this scheme shows the consequences of introducing compensation schemes that are open to widespread abuse.

Livestock predation by other Aquila eagles

Of the other *Aquila* eagles only the Black Eagle in Africa and the Wedge-tailed Eagle in Australia are large enough to pose a threat to young domestic livestock. Consistent with its specialized diet of hyraxes and the rarity of accounts of carrion feeding, it is not surprising that predation on livestock is virtually unrecorded for the Black Eagle. The tale of the Wedge-tailed Eagle is rather different. It shares much in common with the Golden Eagle and will certainly kill lambs on occasion, in addition to being a regular scavenger and feeder on carrion. Both Brooker & Ridpath (1980) in Western Australia and Leopold & Wolfe (1970) in the Canberra area concluded that, while eagles did kill some lambs when they were available, predation levels were insignificant compared with the number of neonatal deaths from all other causes. In an intriguing parallel with North America, it was recognized in the Canberra study that non-breeding Wedge-tailed Eagles may have caused higher levels of predation in lambing paddocks, although no quantitative data were available to substantiate this.

SUMMARY

The Golden Eagle diet shows marked variation across the range in Scotland. During the breeding season, eagles in western Scotland feed on a wide range of prey, including grouse, hares, rabbits, crows, various seabirds and waterfowl, mammals from the size of voles to young Otters and Fox cubs, and occasionally even snakes and frogs. Deer calves and lambs were eaten quite frequently although both were probably taken chiefly as carrion. In the east Highlands the diet was narrow and more than 90% of the food in summer comprised grouse (mainly Red Grouse and Ptarmigan) and lagomorphs (mainly Mountain Hares). Throughout the Scottish range, carrion from dead adult sheep or deer was eaten more frequently in winter than in summer.

Elsewhere in the world the principal food of Golden Eagles is medium-sized birds or mammals from the families *Leporidae* (hares and rabbits), *Sciuridae* (squirrels and marmots), *Tetraonidae* (grouse) and *Phasianidae* (pheasants and partridges). In the absence of all of these, the diet is typically diverse although some eagle populations in arid regions specialize on reptiles such as tortoises *Testudinidae,* and one population in Sweden took large numbers of Hedgehogs *Erinaceidae.* The common feature amongst all these types of prey is their size, which is typically in the range 0.5–4 kg, or the preferred weight range of prey in the Golden Eagle. A marked difference in the preferred size range of prey is one of the factors leading to ecological separation between Golden Eagles and other *Aquila* eagles.

Golden Eagle predation on young domestic livestock has been reported from Scotland, from elsewhere in Europe and from North America. Generally, the number of young ungulates killed by eagles is a fraction of those that die from other causes. Where there is a perceived conflict between Golden Eagles and livestock this is typically because of a shortage of 'natural' prey, and this in turn is probably linked to overgrazing and other aspects of poor management of livestock.

Male Red Grouse.

CHAPTER 7
Nest Sites

Adult Golden Eagle lifting a large branch during nest building in late autumn.

I CAN well remember my first visit to an eagle nest over 25 years ago. It seemed too awesome a structure to be the product of a mere bird. Perhaps it was not as massive as I now recall. But then again, it was a nest in an ancient pine tree, and eyries in trees can get very large when added to year after year.

Many things influence the choice of nesting sites by birds of prey. Some species, notably the falcons and New World vultures, do no building and therefore depend on bare ledges, holes in trees or other birds' nests in which to lay their eggs (Newton 1979). The large eagles, however, are accomplished builders and the Golden Eagle is no exception. Because of its size, and the fact that it nests early in the season, its choice is rarely constrained by competition with other species. The need for protection against predators, mainly carnivorous mammals and man, is probably the greatest single factor influencing nest site selection. Most frequently, such protection is provided by

74

a ledge on a cliff or crag, although substantial old trees are also used, and in some parts of their range exclusively so. Very occasionally, Golden Eagles nest on man-made structures such as electricity pylons.

NEST STRUCTURE

Typically, a pair possess several alternative eyries, usually two or three but sometimes a dozen or more. Nesting material is added to one or more of these sites year after year, and some eyries can become extremely large. Ellis (1986) reported a nest over 6 m tall on a basalt column in Montana; Gordon (1955) described one of nearly 5 m in a Scots pine in the Scottish Highlands. Such huge nests are the exception and 0.5–1.0 m high and around 1–1.5 m diameter are more typical dimensions; nests of around this size have a volume of 0.9–1.8 m³. The dimensions of cliff-nests from the very different environments of Scotland and Arizona are broadly similar, as are tree-nests from Sweden although the latter are probably somewhat deeper (Table 14).

The detailed morphology of a dozen Golden Eagle nests in Arizona was studied by Grubb & Eakle (1987). They were interested in the differences between these and Bald Eagle nests in the same locality. While the overall structure of nests of the two species was similar, there were some significant differences. In particular, Golden Eagles tended to use smaller sticks than Bald Eagles. For the former, the average dimensions of sample sticks were 1.2 cm (diameter), 58 cm (length) and 64 g. Equivalent figures for Bald Eagles were 1.7 cm, 86 cm and 129 g. These differences were obvious in the field and were sufficient to distinguish nests of the two species. The illustration in Eakle & Grubb (1987) shows typical cliff-nests of both species and exemplifies the frequent large, abundant medium, and frequent small sticks in the Bald Eagle nest, compared with the few large, frequent medium and abundant small sticks in the Golden Eagle nest. It will be interesting to see if comparable differences emerge between White-tailed Sea Eagle (a close relative of the Bald Eagle) and Golden Eagle nests as the former species begins to recolonize Scotland.

NEST TYPE

Details of Golden Eagle nest sites in Scotland were recorded during a national survey carried out in 1982 (Watson & Dennis 1992). Nest type was reported for 410 pairs. Of these, 392 (95.6%) used cliffs and 18 (4.4%) used trees. Of the latter, all but one were Scots pines, the other being a larch. Among eyries known about, but not used in 1982, two were in oak trees. The distribution of tree-nesting was unevenly distributed across the range with less than 1% of pairs using trees in the west Highlands but nearly 10% in the east Highlands (Table 15).

Throughout much of continental Europe fewer than 10% of Golden Eagles use tree-nests and so the Scottish 'picture' is therefore fairly typical: e.g. Bulgaria (Michev *et al.* 1989), Spain (Fernández 1989), Italy (Fasce & Fasce 1984), Switzerland (Haller 1982), France (Mathieu & Choisy 1982), Yugoslavia

(Grubač 1988). However, further east, in Sweden (Tjernberg 1983a), Finland (S. Sulkava *in litt.*) and Czechoslovakia (Voskár *et al.* 1969) tree-nests are in the majority. In Estonia and Belarus Golden Eagles are exclusively tree-nesting (T. Randla *in litt.*; V. Ivanovsky, *in litt.*). Throughout the Baltic States and eastern Fenno-Scandia Golden Eagles inhabit relatively flat wooded peatlands where, because there are no cliffs, trees provide the only secure option. Most mountain landscapes offer an abundance of cliff sites and it would appear that, wherever cliff sites are available, these are preferred (Haller 1982). The relatively high proportion of tree-nesting in eastern Scotland supports this contention, because here the rounded hills have many fewer crags than do the more rugged hills of the west. Because most of the original forest of Britain has been cleared, and given the lack of suitable cliffs in many eastern areas, a shortage of nest sites could be one factor limiting Golden Eagle density in parts of eastern and southern Scotland and northeast England today.

Tree-nesting

Martin Tjernberg, in Sweden, has carried out the most detailed study of tree-nesting Golden Eagles (Tjernberg 1983a). In Northern Sweden 167 nests were found in Scots pine and three in Norway spruce. On the island of Gotland 13 were in Scots pines, one in a downy birch and one in an ash tree. The average age of trees used in northern Sweden was 355 years (Fig. 13) and the mean trunk diameter at breast height was 53 cm (Fig. 14). While over 40% of trees used by eagles had a trunk diameter greater than 55 cm, the proportion of such

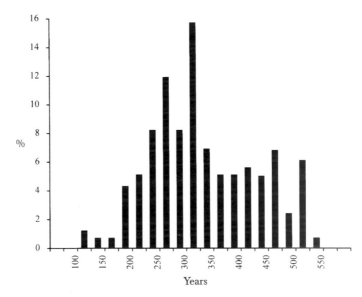

FIG. 13.   *The proportion of trees (mainly Scots pine) of different ages used by Golden Eagles for nesting in northern Sweden. Trees were placed in 25-year age classes and data are from a sample of 159 trees. Redrawn from Tjernberg (1983a).*

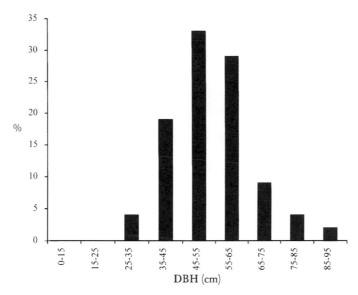

FIG. 14. *The trunk diameter at breast-height (DBH) of trees (mainly Scots pine) used by Golden Eagles for nesting in northern Sweden. Data are from a sample of 165 trees. Redrawn from Tjernberg (1983a).*

large trees in the Swedish National Forest Survey was only 0.004%. The average height of trees containing eyries was 17.2 m and the average height of the nest above ground was 11.7 m. Only 10% of all nests were placed below half the total tree height. The commonest position for the nest within the tree was on 1–4 large branches near the main or secondary trunk (Fig. 15A). Other locations were on large branches 0.5–3.0 m out from the main trunk (Fig. 15B); between the main and a secondary trunk (Fig. 15C); and on the topmost branch whorl (Fig. 15D), those in the latter position superficially resembling Osprey nests.

The great age and therefore size of the trees used in Sweden reflects the need to support the massive weight of an eagle eyrie. Kulves (1973) estimated that a White-tailed Sea Eagle nest might weigh 400 kg/m³; using this as a guide, a typical Golden Eagle nest would certainly weigh several-hundred kg. Given an estimated load-bearing for a pine-branch of 12.8 kg per centimetre in diameter (Kulves 1973), the total diameter of supporting branches would need to be at least 20 cm to hold a relatively small nest weighing 250 kg. In the taiga forests of northeast Europe the retention of very old trees is clearly crucial if Golden Eagles are to have sufficient secure nesting sites.

Tree-nesting in North America is generally less common than cliff-nesting (Johnsgard 1990). The sparse population living in the forested landscape of western Washington is one exception. Large clear-cut areas created by the logging industry have provided suitable hunting habitat which Golden Eagles have successfully colonized (Bruce *et al.* 1882). Here, nest sites are almost exclusively in Douglas firs located near the forest edge. Another predominantly tree-nesting population occurs in northeast Wyoming (Menkens & Anderson 1987). Of 170

FIG. 15.   *The four major types of nest attachment to trees used by Golden Eagles in Sweden. See text for further details. In northern Sweden the proportion of nests in different places were: A 74%, B 13%, C 4%, D 9%, based on a sample of 162 tree-nests. From information in Tjernberg (1983a).*

eyries examined there, 111 were in deciduous trees, mainly cottonwoods, 36 in ponderosa pines and 23 on the sides of buttes or river banks. The preference for tree-nesting here reflected the comparative lack of secure cliff sites in a countryside characterized by rolling, terrace-like plains. Cottonwood trees and willows grow in drainage channels and other moist areas, and scrub vegetation is dominant elsewhere. This landscape is the ecological inverse of the wooded peatlands of northeast Europe, with trees growing in places that have reasonable soil moisture but were otherwise excluded by drought conditions over the greater part of the region. The preference for deciduous trees over pines simply reflected the fact that the former were more plentiful. As in Sweden, large old trees were preferred, with an average diameter at breast height of 73 cm and an average height of 13.4 m. Nests were located at around two-thirds of the maximum tree height. Eagles selected trees that were the largest or one of the largest in any particular stand as was also the case in Sweden.

Cliff-nesting

It is comparatively easy to measure a range of variables among a sample of trees, and from these deduce whether or not eagles are favouring a particular size or structure of tree for nesting. It is less straightforward to do so for cliffs where the potential variables are much greater, and those critical to eagles may not be immediately obvious or amenable to measurement.

Two studies in Spain sought to show that Golden Eagles chose nesting cliffs with particular characteristics. They contrasted features of cliffs holding nests with those in the immediate vicinity that did not. Both studies concluded that cliffs which were relatively inaccessible and further away from human presence—specifically at greater distances from tracks, roads and villages—were preferred (Donázar *et al.* 1989; Fernández 1993b). These findings are as expected for a species which has long been the object of human persecution.

Ultimately, the choice of a cliff nest site within a particular area is dictated by the geology of that landscape. In Scotland, there are few cliffs higher than 100 m except in some coastal areas and over 60% of sites here were on cliffs less than 40 m high, and fewer than 10% on cliffs higher than 100 m (Table 16). In contrast, in the geologically much younger landscape of western Norway, some 84% of nests were on cliffs taller than 100 m, and some were more than 400 m high, with only 9% on crags of less than 50 m (Bergo 1984b). Golden Eagles generally choose cliff-nest sites on ledges large enough to support their ample nest structure, which are relatively inaccessible from above or below and which are preferably sheltered from above. If there is a superabundance of sites which meet these basic criteria, as I believe is the case over much of the Scottish Highlands, then the preferred choice may be influenced by other factors such as the proximity to hunting grounds and the degree of shelter provided.

Other types of nest sites

There are occasional records of nesting on the ground in Scotland, sometimes at the foot of a traditional nesting cliff. This may occur if a nest is blown out of a cliff late in the winter and the pair opt to build on top of the fallen structure. The records of rudimentary nests built on vegetated slopes are less easy to explain. They are perhaps emergency nests, built quickly in the late winter after an alternative site in a cliff has been covered by a late snow-fall just as the birds were about to lay. Alternatively, such nests may be built by inexperienced breeders. Whatever the explanation, at least in mainland Scotland, ground nests are rarely used for more than one season. Ian Newton (*in litt.*) knew of a nest on a gentle slope on the island of North Uist in the Outer Hebrides. The eyrie was large and had evidently been used for several years. It was in an area where there were no cliffs. The choice of such a site was probably linked to the fact that Foxes, one of the few potential predators of eagle nests in Scotland, are absent from the Uists.

Ground nests are not uncommon in the United States, especially in semi-desert areas (Camenzind 1969). These arid landscapes have little in the way of ground vegetation and the sitting bird therefore has good all round visibility; furthermore, ground predators are denied the use of ground cover to make a close approach to the nest. In Scotland, Golden Eagles have occasionally adopted man-made nests in trees (Roy Dennis *in litt.*) but otherwise the use of man-made structures is unrecorded in Europe. Nest building on artificial structures does occur in the United States, most frequently on electricity pylons in various parts of the southwest (Williams & Colson 1989). This behaviour has been used to advantage in a number of management operations involving Golden Eagles. In one case a pair nesting on the open face of an old mine-working posed a problem when federal reclamation laws required the mine face to be restored. However, regulations also prevented disturbance of Golden Eagle nests. The problem was solved by constructing an artificial nest on a 7-m high pole topped with a platform. The young eaglets from the mine-working site were moved 500 m to the artificial nest from which they were eventually reared (Fala *et al.* 1985). A similar tactic was used to relocate a pair of nesting eagles from within an area leased for coal working. This time the single eaglet was moved more than 2.5 km using four artificial nest platforms placed progressively further from the original site. The chick was fledged and in the following year the parents voluntarily nested and reared a chick on the same artificial platform at which fledging occurred in the previous year (Postovit *et al.* 1982). Perhaps sometimes we tend to think of Golden Eagle nesting behaviour as a little more 'sensitive' than it really is!

NEST SITES AND ALTITUDE

Over most of their geographical range Golden Eagles occupy mountainous or hilly terrain. Whilst people unfamiliar with the species might assume that an eagle would choose to place its nest on some remote pinnacle near the mountain summit, this is rarely the case. The severe weather conditions on most mountain ridges are a deterrent, but much more important is the location of the nest site in relation to the bird's hunting grounds. In Scotland there is a striking change in the altitude of nest sites moving from west to east across the country. Nests have a mean elevation of under 200 m close to the western seaboard rising to nearly 500 m in the eastern Highlands (Fig. 16; Table 17). Over the whole range, nests were generally located at around half the maximum elevation of the surrounding land. The relationship between the altitude of nest sites and the mean maximum elevation of the surrounding area is the product of opposing pressures. There are advantages in nesting higher to reduce predation risks and possibly also human persecution, but this has to be weighed against the disadvantages of nesting too high and thereby having to transport heavy prey 'uphill'. Given that western birds could, in theory at least, nest considerably higher, I believe that it is the need to avoid transporting prey 'uphill' that is the greater pressure. Interestingly, birds in the central Highlands nest at around 48% of the maximum surrounding elevation while those further east are at 60% of the maximum. This further supports the food transportation explanation as hills in the eastern Highlands have more extensive hunting ground on rounded summits and mountain plateaux at higher altitudes than do their neighbours immediately to the west.

The altitude of nesting sites varies widely across the species' range in Europe, and on this grander scale, differences again reflect the location of hunting grounds and food. In Norway the mean elevation is around 500–600 m (Bergo, 1984b) and this coincides closely with the natural timber-line. Here eagles hunt extensive open land above the forest and are therefore able to transport much

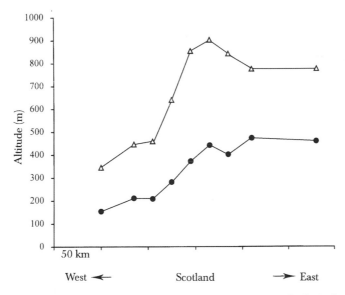

FIG. 16.   *Mean altitude (m) above sea level of nest sites of Golden Eagles in Scotland (●). Also shown is the mean maximum elevation of the surrounding land (△). Data are given separately for samples of nests in nine longitudinal bands passing from west to east across the country. See Fig. 5 for the areas falling within each of the nine longitudinal bands. After Table 2 in Watson & Dennis (1992). Data are from Table 17.*

of their prey downhill to nests, with potential energy benefits. In Spain there are populations at two distinct altitude levels, with birds nesting in some parts of the peninsula at around 600 m (Jordano 1981) and in the Pyrenees at nearer 1500 m (Fernández 1989); a similar dichotomy occurs in France (Mathieu & Choisy 1982) and Italy (Fasce & Fasce 1987; Magrini *et al.* 1987). In each case the explanation is in access to suitable hunting terrain. In the arid landscapes of the Iberian peninsula, Provence in France and the Apennines in Italy, fire combined with pastoral activity has maintained open hunting ground at lower elevations, and with it prey such as Rabbits, Brown Hares and Red-legged Partridges. In the truly alpine mountains (the Alps and Pyrenees) dense forest cover over low and intermediate slopes excludes Golden Eagles and they reappear again at around the timber-line (1500–1800 m) where they nest, transporting prey such as Alpine Marmots 'downhill' from high-level pastures. Another good example of the Golden Eagle's flexible response to altitude is found in lowland Eastern Europe where virtually the whole land mass is below 200 m. However, here again Golden Eagles occupy a 'timber-line' type habitat with patchy woodland interspersed with open peatlands (Zastrov 1946). It is the high water table in this region, rather than low temperature, or the effect of grazing, fire or drought, that prevents tree growth and thereby offers suitable hunting terrain.

ORIENTATION OF NEST SITES

Another factor influencing the choice of nest sites by eagles is weather. In cool climates bad weather can be a problem. If a site is exposed to heavy snowfall the incubating bird may desert the eggs; if nestlings are exposed to prolonged heavy rain they may die. What is less well known is that excessive exposure to the sun can also be a problem, leading to overheating and sometimes death of nestlings (Kochert 1972).

Information was collected on the orientation of over 400 occupied nests in Scotland in 1982 (Table 18). I compared this with the orientation of hill slopes (assuming this to reflect the distribution of potential nesting places) in the surrounding landscape. Figure 17 shows that the orientation of slopes in the Highlands occurs in more or less equal proportions in each of eight compass segments. Orientation of nest sites, however, was significantly different, with many more facing between northwest and east (58.3%) than in the three segments between southeast and west (21.5%). On this evidence, Golden Eagles in Scotland would appear to select nests with a northerly rather than a southerly aspect. There are several possible reasons for this. Eagles may favour north by east facing sites to gain maximum protection from inclement weather, which comes mainly from the southwest. Alternatively, they may choose north facing sites to avoid excessive exposure to sun, and thereby reduce the risks of nestlings overheating. However, it may just be that my analysis is too simplistic, as has been suggested by Cliff Henty (*in litt.*). In his opinion my comparison between the orientation of nest sites and the general orientation of hill slopes is inappropriate because it is the direction of exposure of suitable nesting crags, rather than of hill slopes, that is important. He further argues that there are

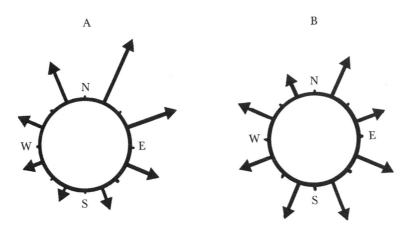

FIG. 17. *The direction of exposure of 407 Golden Eagle nests (A) and the orientation of hill slopes (B) in the Scottish Highlands (after Watson & Dennis 1992). See text and Table 18 for further details.*

strong geomorphological reasons for predicting that the direction of crags will have a north-facing bias because this is where glacial action ended most recently, and where the frost-shattering of rocks is most powerful. He goes on to show that the distribution of climber's crags in the central, western and northern Highlands is indeed predominantly north-facing, and as such is not significantly different from the distribution of exposures found for eagle nests (Table 18). Clearly, Henty's interpretation has merit and it is possible that, in Scotland at least, the orientation of Golden Eagle nest sites is unrelated to climatic factors and simply reflects the orientation of available crags.

Evidence from elsewhere in Europe does suggest a climatic influence on the choice of nest site orientation. In Norway and Sweden, where eagles nest at higher elevations (500–600 m) than in Scotland, and yet receive inclement weather on the same southwesterly airstream, the principal direction of exposure in both cases is southerly (Tjernberg 1983a; Bergo 1984b). In southern Europe, the high altitude (1500–1800 m) populations in the Alps and the Pyrénées both favour south-facing sites (Henninger *et al.* 1987; Fernández 1989) while lower-altitude populations at 600–900 m in Spain, Italy, Sicily, and Yugoslavia all avoid southerly aspects (Jordano 1981; Magrini *et al.* 1987; Seminara *et al.* 1987; Grubač 1988). Thus, populations at similar latitudes but differing altitudes show a complete shift in the orientation of nests. These findings are consistent with the view that the effects of sunshine and consequent heat stress are perhaps the most important determinant of nest site orientation. At a given latitude, birds using sites at higher elevations, where temperatures are cooler, can benefit from increased exposure to the sun by choosing a southerly aspect. It may also be that, at such heights, north facing sites are not free of snow early enough in the eagle's breeding season. Birds nesting at lower levels, where ambient summer temperature is higher, are at greater risk from overheating and can reduce this by selecting sites with a northerly aspect.

An analysis of directional exposure of nest sites among Golden Eagles in North America drew a similar conclusion. In the high latitudes and cool climate of Alaska, most nests had a southerly orientation while in the low latitudes and hot climate of Utah, nests tended to be north facing (Mosher & White 1976). In the arid regions of Israel, Bahat (1991) found that significantly fewer nest sites had a southerly than a northerly exposure. He again attributed this to the eagles avoiding sites that were exposed to the sun.

USE OF ALTERNATIVE NEST SITES

Most Golden Eagles pairs lay claim to several nest sites. In the eastern Highlands of Scotland, Watson (1957) studied 12 pairs that had over five eyries each and even this he believed to be an under-estimate. Tjernberg (1983a) believed he knew most of the nests belonging to 49 pairs and they averaged 2.4 per pair, ranging from one to six. In Idaho the number of nests ranged from one to 12 with an average of six per pair (Beecham & Kochert 1975). The national survey done in Britain in 1982 revealed nearly 1400 eyries for 411 pairs (an average of 3.4 per pair), ranging between one and 13 each (Fig. 18; Table 19). This is certainly an under-estimate because many of these pairs were poorly known and not all home ranges were thoroughly searched. In the part of western Scotland where I have worked for 15 years, and where it is now rare for me to find a new nest among the 20 pairs in the area, I know of 89 eyries (4.5 per pair), ranging between two and 10.

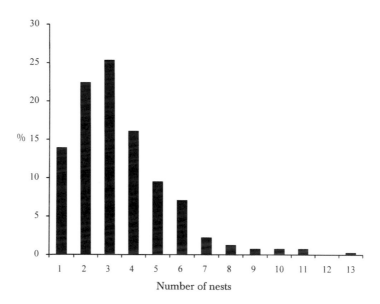

FIG. 18.   *The frequency of Golden Eagle pairs with different numbers of alternative eyries based on 411 pairs of eagles in Scotland from survey work carried out in 1982. See Table 19 for details.*

These 20 pairs fall into two types in the way in which they use their alternative sites. There were those that I class as 'stayers', having used just two or three alternatives over a 10-year sample period, but generally favouring one eyrie which was used in at least 6 out of the 10 years. The remaining pairs I consider 'movers', having used four or five alternatives and no nest more than three times in 10 breeding seasons. Of the six 'movers', five (83%) were known to suffer regular disturbance or persecution, whether from the attention of egg-collectors, from shepherds or from forestry management. Among the other 14 only four (29%) received similar levels of disturbance. In this area at least, the tactic of moving regularly between several nests may be a response to disturbance. The alternative tactic of using a favoured nest with occasional moves probably has a different cause. I have noticed that some of these 'stayers' will intermittently use a site at the opposite end of the hunting range from the favoured eyrie; one function of this could be to reinforce ownership rights. The collapse of a nest, or an unusually heavy snowfall close to the time of laying may force a pair to change its intended nesting site; the availability of an alternative eyrie offers insurance against such eventualities. Finally, periodic use of an alternative eyrie may be a means of reducing parasites, many of which over-winter in nests.

INTERACTIONS WITH OTHER SPECIES AT NEST SITES

Peregrine Falcons and Ravens share the Golden Eagle's preference for nesting on remote and inaccessible crags in the Scottish Highlands, although both will avoid cliffs with eagles in residence (Ratcliffe 1962). When Golden Eagles recolonized Galloway after 1945 Derek Ratcliffe found that two pairs of Peregrines were immediately displaced to alternative crags and another two pairs disappeared. Doug Weir also noticed that Rough-legged Buzzards and Gyrfalcons kept their distance from occupied eagle cliffs in Alaska (Weir 1982). This is presumably because of the risk of predation by eagles of nestlings, fledglings and perhaps even adult birds. I have found young Ravens as prey of eagles on several occasions, and once found a fledgling Peregrine at an eyrie, so the risk is real enough. Either of the large falcons may sometimes requisition disused Golden Eagle eyries provided that the original tenant is using an alternative site on a separate cliff several kilometres distant (Poole & Bromley 1988; Ratcliffe 1990). One of the few species reported to displace Golden Eagles from cliffs is the Griffon Vulture. While eagles could retain ownership of a nesting cliff against single pairs of Griffons, they were apparently unable to do so when faced with a Griffon colony (Verner 1909).

Occasionally, eagle nests offer a temporary home to other animals. I once knew of a disused site which was occupied by a Pine Marten. It had formed a tunnel in the side of the 2-m high structure and appeared to be living deep within the nest. David Balharry has seen Pine Martens using an occupied Golden Eagle nest and speculated that the martens may have occasionally pirated food from the young eagle. In Scotland, the tiny Wren is often a close neighbour, sometimes nesting within a few metres of an occupied eyrie. I have

never witnessed a Wren actually nesting within an eagle's eyrie although I wouldn't be surprised if this happens occasionally. Another frequent close neighbour is the Ring Ouzel, whose lonely song will, for me, always bring back memories of fresh spring days in eagle country.

NEST SITE SELECTION IN OTHER *AQUILA* EAGLES

Members of the genus *Aquila* occupy a wide range of habitats, from deserts and plains to high mountains, and from wooded parkland, temperate and boreal forests to tropical rainforest. The preferred nest site of each species is determined by the options available in a particular habitat (Table 20). Species confined to temperate and boreal woodlands such as the Greater and Lesser Spotted Eagles are invariably tree-nesters. Lesser Spotted Eagles in Latvia favour spruce and birch trees with fewer nests in oak, alder, aspen, pine and ash (Bergmanis *et al.* 1990). In the drier mountain woods of Slovakia the majority are in beech trees (Meyburg 1973). Greater Spotted Eagles also use a variety of trees including pine and oak, but also alder and willow, the last two reflecting the species close association with wetland areas (Dementiev & Gladkov 1966).

The species favouring open woodland or wooded parkland habitat are the Imperial Eagle in Eurasia, the Tawny Eagle in Africa and the Wedge-tailed Eagle in Australia. All are predominantly tree-nesting. Imperial Eagles in Spain mainly use pine trees but also oaks and eucalyptus (Calderón *et al.* 1987). Tawny Eagles favour various *Acacia* spp. or spiny *Terminalia* spp. and, uniquely among *Aquila* eagles, always place their nests on the topmost or outermost branches of the tree (Brown *et al.* 1982). This species also nests occasionally on electricity pylons (Tarboton 1978).

In the steppes and semi-deserts of central Asia the choice is severely limited for nesting Steppe and Imperial Eagles. In Kazakhstan, Steppe Eagles are mainly ground nesting, but will occasionally use buildings, low bushes or structures such as haystacks (Dementiev & Gladkov 1966). The Eastern Imperial Eagle in central Asia favours isolated trees or low bushes in these desert landscapes but will occasionally use small cliffs on the banks of dry river valleys (Lobachev 1960).

The Black Eagle, the eastern race of the Steppe Eagle, and of course the Golden Eagle throughout most of its range, are the three *Aquila* eagles of true mountain habitat. All three are predominantly cliff-nesters in such landscapes. The Black Eagle is the most exclusively cliff-nesting of all: and Gargett (1990) reported only four tree-nests in 638 nesting records from Zimbabwe. The Steppe Eagle in Mongolia and the Altai Mountains of southeast Russia usually nests in cliffs but also on the ground among stony mounds on small hills (Dementiev & Gladkov 1966).

The nest of Gurney's Eagle, which lives on New Guinea and nearby islands, has never been described. The species has been reported from a range of habitats including rainforest in the New Guinea Highlands and open savanna

Spanish Imperial Eagle at a nest site on an electricity pylon.

woodland in the southwestern rain-shadow of the island. It is more than likely that when nests are eventually found they will prove to be in trees.

Aquila eagles show a catholic choice of nest site, which reflects their success at exploiting a wide range of habitats. From the ancestral tree-nesting typified by forest-dwelling species such as Lesser and Greater Spotted Eagles, they have evolved ground nesting to breed in tree-less steppe and desert landscapes, and cliff-nesting to successfully colonize mountain regions.

SUMMARY

Golden Eagles build large nests typically in cliffs, sometimes in large trees, and very occasionally on the ground or on man-made structures such as pylons. In Scotland, as in most other parts of the world, cliff-nesting predominates. Trees are used exclusively in places where cliffs are lacking, as in the wooded peatlands of northeast Europe. Avoidance of predation by carnivorous mammals and by man is probably the major factor influencing nest site selection.

Nest sites in western Scotland are at lower elevations than in the east and this is linked to the proximity of favoured hunting grounds. Throughout the world range, nesting can occur from sea level to over 2000 m, and the choice of altitude for nesting is dictated by the availability of suitable hunting areas. The orientation of nests appears to be influenced by climatic factors, with birds in cold climates favouring south-facing sites which are snow-free earlier and offer some benefit to chicks from the sun's warmth. In hot regions, more sites face north and here nestlings may benefit from increased shade and a reduced risk of overheating. Eagles typically have several alternative eyries, usually three or four but sometimes more than 10. Some pairs use a succession of sites in different years while others favour only one or two.

Among the various species of *Aquila* eagles the choice of nest site is extremely catholic. Tree-nesting is favoured by species living in woodland habitat, ground-nesting by birds in steppe or desert landscapes and cliff-nesting by species in mountain regions.

CHAPTER 8
Ranging Behaviour

Dramatic undulating display by two Golden Eagles in early spring.

T O understand the use of a home range by an animal it is important to be able to recognize individuals—with large birds of prey like eagles this can be a problem. Rarely do they allow observers close enough to see distinguishing features, even assuming such features exist. The best information can be obtained by attaching a small radio-transmitter which allows the movement and activity of the bird to be tracked (Kenward 1978). To date, only a few studies have employed this technique with Golden Eagles. Consequently, the interpretation of ranging behaviour in Golden Eagles is in its infancy when compared with birds such as Sparrowhawks and Kestrels (Newton 1986; Village 1990). In this chapter I explore what we know about this aspect of the bird's behaviour, but it will become apparent that there are many gaps in our understanding.

HOME RANGE AND TERRITORY

Once they have entered the breeding population, most large non-migratory eagles spend their lives in a restricted area which contains their nest site and hunting range. This is the *home range*. That part of a home range which is used exclusively by a breeding pair, and is defended against others, is known as a *territory*. Leslie Brown did not believe that Golden Eagles defended their home range against neighbouring birds and he was uncomfortable about using the term territory (Brown 1976). Adam Watson thought that Golden Eagles in eastern Scotland were strongly territorial around nesting sites but, further from the nest, hunting grounds were sometimes used by several pairs at different times (Watson 1957). In western Scotland I consider that eagles use more or less exclusive hunting areas, although mutual soaring by members of neighbouring pairs at the boundary between ranges is common, especially during winter. All the studies mentioned above were hampered by the lack of individually marked birds.

In common with many of the larger raptors, Golden Eagles have a spectacular undulating display flight. This behaviour typically begins with a bird in high soaring flight. A steep dive with partly closed wings is followed by an upward swoop with three or four strong wing-beats near the top of the climb before the bird enters another dive; the procedure is repeated for anything up to twenty undulations. Collopy & Edwards (1989) closely observed ranging behaviour in four pairs of eagles in Idaho over two nesting seasons. They witnessed nearly 400 undulating flights during 700 h of observation. Traditionally, undulating flight was thought to be linked to courtship and the maintenance of the pair bond (Bent 1937; Brown & Amadon 1968). However in the Idaho study, most undulating display flight by both males (67%) and females (76%) occurred away from the immediate vicinity of mates and nest sites (Table 21). It occurred frequently near the boundary of the range or within sight of a neighbouring territorial eagle. On several occasions it was seen to be performed simultaneously by eagles from adjacent territories. These observations support the reinterpretation of the function of undulating flight by Harmata (1982) who concluded that it was an important expression of territoriality, as it is in other raptors (Newton 1979). The incidence of aggressive attacks and chases among neighbouring territorial eagles is rare, but this is not really surprising for a long-lived species in which the boundaries of home ranges are likely to remain stable over long periods. The advertisement of occupancy by means of the undulating flight display, together with high soaring flight, is probably sufficient to maintain these boundaries.

Aggressive attacks on non-breeding eagles by territorial birds are, by comparison, quite common (Haller 1982; Bergo 1987a). These typically involve a swift dive by the resident eagle followed by a chase during which the intruder seeks to defend itself by rolling over and presenting its talons. Such attacks are sometimes preceded or followed by an intense bout of undulating display by the resident eagle (Bergo 1987a). Aggressive encounters occur most frequently in autumn/winter and during the pre-laying period and are less frequent during the breeding season (Bergo 1987a; see Chapter 11).

Work on Golden Eagles fitted with radio-transmitters is currently being carried out in western Scotland (M. McGrady *in litt.*). Preliminary results support the view that resident Golden Eagles occupy mainly exclusive home ranges. Pending further findings from such studies, I believe it is reasonable to consider much of the Golden Eagle's home range as a territory, with undulating display flight, and perhaps also mutual soaring behaviour, serving to reinforce territorial boundaries between neighbours. Nevertheless, where substantial parts of the landscape provide hunting opportunities but are unsuitable for nesting, as in the high tops of the Cairngorms in the eastern Highlands of Scotland (Watson 1957), such areas are not subdivided exclusively between pairs but instead are used as 'communal' hunting grounds.

USE OF THE HOME RANGE

When watching eagles for long periods it soon becomes clear that they do not use all of their range with equal intensity, but instead tend to hunt preferentially in certain areas. These areas are often the same in different years, although different parts of the range may be used in particular seasons. Such variation results from differences in food availability. A good example is found in work on Golden Eagles in the Swiss Alps (Haller 1982). Here, during the summer, hunting was concentrated in patches of alpine pasture where there were abundant marmots. These patches generally comprised less than half the total area of the range. In winter the birds were restricted to hunting sunny slopes with thermal updraughts, and then their main food was carrion and young ungulates. Patchy use of the home range for hunting has also been detected among the small number of radio-tagged eagles studied in western Scotland (McGrady *in litt.*). It is too early to say what the precise causes are here but the explanation is almost certainly linked to food supply.

Although the principal requirements of a home range are a nesting site and an area for hunting, birds also need sheltered places for roosting at night and prominent places to perch during the day. In Scotland, Golden Eagles typically have three or four roosts which are used regularly. These are usually on or near stunted trees in cliffs, and occasionally in large trees where cliffs are scarce. Some cliff roosts are used for many years and can be conspicuous in early spring when the vegetation underneath has a richer flora than the surrounding area. This is caused by the regular addition of nutrients from the droppings of the roosting bird. During the day, eagles spend long periods on prominent perches that have excellent views over the surrounding landscape. Perches are usually well above the nest site but below the crest of a ridge. During the non-breeding season, both members of the pair may spend many hours close together on prominent perches, preferring sites with a sunny aspect in winter and rarely perching for long in windy and exposed locations.

VARIATION IN RANGE SIZE

A few studies have investigated differences in home range size between Golden Eagles in a given area. These have concluded that pairs with the smallest ranges occupy areas with the highest proportion of the best feeding habitat. Dixon (1937) estimated the size of the home range (although he used the term territory) for 27 pairs of eagles in San Diego County, California, USA, based on more than 30 years' field experience. These varied from 49 to 152 km^2 and the larger ranges invariably had a high proportion of land under plantation woodlands, orchards or other forms of permanent agriculture. Such habitats held little food for eagles compared with the natural scrub habitat of the area. Among the four pairs studied intensively in Idaho by Collopy & Edwards (1989), home ranges were between 11.6 and 49.0 km^2 (average 32.8 km^2). This variation they attributed to habitat differences. The smallest ranges comprised almost entirely greasewood, the habitat which supported the highest density of jackrabbits. The two largest ranges were dominated by habitats where densities of jackrabbits were low.

Home range size in the closely related Black Eagle in Zimbabwe has been better studied than in any population of Golden Eagles. Black Eagles feed almost exclusively on hyraxes which, in turn, are restricted to rocky outcrops known as '*kopje*' (Gargett 1990). Territory size ranged from under 6 km^2 to more than 14 km^2. The larger territories had a greater proportion of grassland habitat (where hyraxes were absent) but all ranges had roughly the same amount of *kopje* habitat—around 5 km^2 (Fig. 19). Gargett concluded that the size of Black Eagle territories was dictated by the need to maintain a minimum amount of hunting habitat. Where *kopje* habitat was widely spaced and interspersed with grassland, ranges needed to be larger to encompass enough hyrax habitat to ensure sufficient food.

A striking feature of the Black Eagles of the Matobo was the extreme stability of

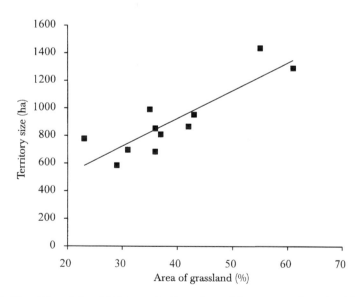

FIG. 19.   *The relationship between territory size and the amount of grassland habitat within territories of Black Eagles in the Matobo Hills, Zimbabwe. Territories with a higher proportion of grassland, where Hyraxes were scarce, were larger. In statistical analysis,* r = 0.865, P <0.001. Redrawn from Gargett (1975).

territories in different seasons and over the years. Such a highly stable dispersion pattern would be expected in a long-lived raptor living in the tropics and with a relatively stable food supply (Newton 1979). At these low latitudes the seasonal and year-on-year variation in climatic conditions is minimal. Consequently, fluctuations in food availability tend to be small when compared with higher latitudes. In many parts of North America and in northern Eurasia Golden Eagles feed on hares of the genus *Lepus* which can have huge changes in abundance between years, sometimes following approximately 10-year cycles (Kochert 1980). Such variation might be expected to be reflected in differences in home range size between years. However, no long-term study has yet been carried out on the relationship between fluctuating food supply and home range size in Golden Eagles. The radio-telemetry work in Idaho, where jackrabbit numbers fluctuate over an approximately 10-year cycle, may yet provide some answers. I return to this subject again in the next chapter when discussing variations in breeding density.

RANGING BEHAVIOUR OF NON-BREEDING BIRDS

Young Golden Eagles leave the territory of their parents 3–4 months after fledging (Walker 1987; see Chapter 14). These non-breeding eagles are not tied to a particular area by the demands of reproduction. They tend to be seen around the edges of adult territories, sometimes spending several days or weeks in a relatively small area before moving on. Non-breeders can afford to be nomadic, and indeed such a strategy may be essential if they are to survive the minimum of 4–5 years before they can expect to enter the breeding population. While the range of an individual non-breeder over a few days is probably relatively small, the accumulated range over several months tends to be very much larger.

Recent work using radio-telemetry in Switzerland has begun to reveal the nature of range use by non-breeding eagles (Haller 1994). During their first two years of life, non-breeders used accumulated home ranges of between 2000 and 15 000 km². Birds aged 2 years or older however used somewhat smaller ranges of 2–4000 km². Even the latter ranges were exceptionally large compared with the those of territorial adults in the area (75–191 km²: Haller 1982). There are probably several reasons why the ranges of non-breeders are large.

Non-breeders are rarely tolerated for long by territory holders, and are typically subject to constant harassment should they be detected by one of the residents. By ranging over large areas, non-breeding eagles will be able to monitor a number of adult territories and thus have a greater chance of detecting a gap in the breeding population. The greater accumulated range size of younger birds probably reflects their inexperience compared with birds more than 2 years old. The latter will have learned where hunting opportunities exist beyond the ranges of territorial birds. These safe havens are likely to be small, otherwise they would support a breeding pair, or they may lack a suitable nest site.

The way in which non-breeding eagles use the landscape has been closely studied by Miguel Ferrer working on Spanish Imperial Eagles (Ferrer 1993b). His observations were made on eight individuals aged between 1 and 2 years and equipped with long-life solar-powered radio-transmitters. As in the Swiss study of

Golden Eagles, he found that non-breeding Imperial Eagles used large accumulated ranges. However, these were made up of between three and eight much smaller areas (average size around 400 ha) which were visited in rotation. The areas were each about 25 km apart and were visited by young eagles for an average stay of 12 days. Such temporary settling areas were sometimes used by several different eagles in succession, and were used in successive years. Although the areas were rich in food, containing many Rabbits, they were too small to support a breeding pair and so birds using them were not subject to aggressive attacks from adults.

What intrigued Miguel Ferrer was why, having found these places, birds should not stay there indefinitely. He estimated that a single eagle would consume a maximum of six Rabbits during its 12-day stay, and yet he calculated that these areas held between 1400 and 2500 Rabbits each. The answer lay in his discovery that an eagle's hunting success dropped progressively during its stay even though it spent more and more time hunting (Fig. 20). This he interpreted as a consequence of changes in the activity of the prey in space and time, thereby leading to decreased prey availability. Changes in prey behaviour were caused by the continued and predictable presence of a large predator. So, after a while, it became necessary for the eagle to move on. These immature eagles could do so because they had no attachment to a mate or nest site. This important finding may provide a more general explanation of range use by non-breeding eagles, including Golden Eagles, and clearly merits further research. It also raises many intriguing questions about the minimum acceptable range size and the pattern of range use in territorial eagles.

In one of my Golden Eagle study areas in western Scotland I kept a record of all observations of adult and immature eagles. The pattern of sightings for part of this area over a 3-month period (January–March) in one year is shown in Fig. 21. Because none of my birds were individually marked I cannot demonstrate the nature and size of individual home ranges. However the pattern of range use by adults and immatures is revealing. Adult sightings were distributed in association with nesting sites while immature clearly were not, and tended to occur around the edges of the adult ranges. In my experience the same general locations were occupied by immature birds in successive years. I suspect that among the immature birds, different individuals were involved both between years and conceivably also during the course of a single season. There are evident parallels here with the findings of Ferrer in the Spanish Imperial Eagle.

COMPETITION WITH OTHER SPECIES

White-tailed Sea Eagles were widespread in western Scotland until the middle of the nineteenth century. They became extinct as a result of human persecution by about 1918 (Love 1983). A reintroduction programme was begun in 1975 and since 1985 a few pairs have again bred successfully in the western Highlands. John Love believed that 150 years ago Scottish Golden Eagles were scarce in western coastal areas where Sea Eagles were widespread (Fig. 22). The colonization of much of the

Two adult Golden Eagles talon grappling in flight.

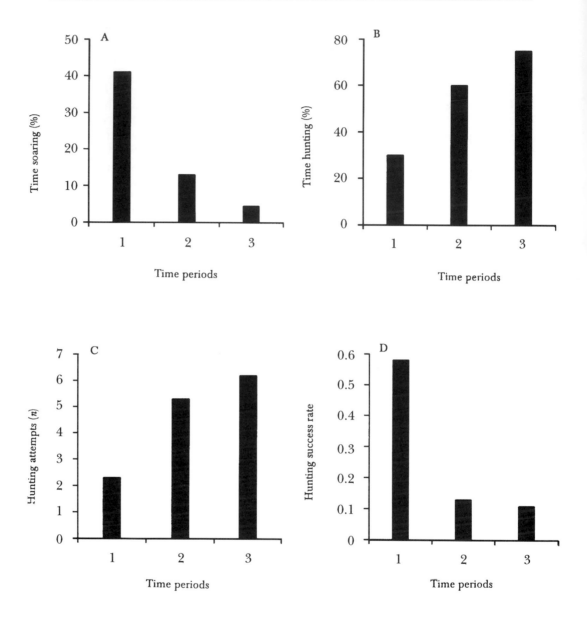

FIG. 20. *Changes in flight behaviour, and in hunting activity in relation to residence time (dividing residence time into three equal time periods) among eight immature Spanish Imperial Eagles living in defined hunting areas. In statistical analysis, (A) the percentage of soaring decreased with time ($F_{2,7} = 11.332$, $P = 0.001$); (B) the time spent actively hunting increased ($F_{2,7} = 14.733$, $P < 0.001$); (C) the number of hunting attempts increased ($F_{2,7} = 14.608$, $P < 0.001$); (D) the hunting success rate declined ($F_{2,7} = 12.262$, $P < 0.001$). After Ferrer (1993b).*

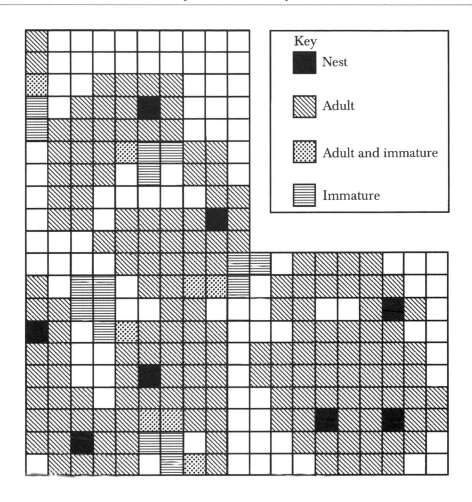

FIG. 21.   *The distribution of sightings of adult and immature Golden Eagles in an area of western Scotland during January–March. Each square represents 100 ha and squares were scored depending on whether only adults, only immatures, or both adults and immatures were seen during the 3-month period. All observations were from 1984.*

western seaboard by Golden Eagles followed the extirpation of the Sea Eagle and strongly suggests that the latter previously excluded Golden Eagles from coastal areas.

In Norway, Bergo (1987a) witnessed many aggressive interactions between the two species when a pair of Sea Eagles nested within the territory of an established pair of Golden Eagles. The Sea Eagle nest was abandoned shortly after incubation began. Such interactions are infrequent in Norway where the geographical ranges of the species overlap rather little. Golden Eagles favour inland hill areas while Sea

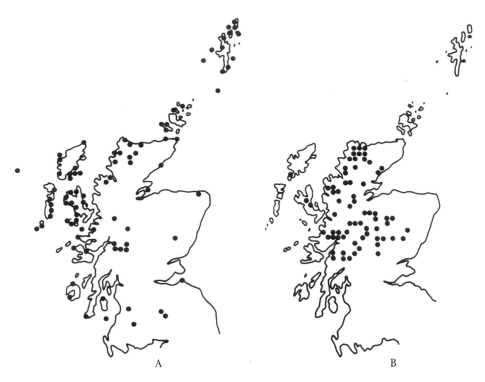

FIG. 22.   *Indicative historical distribution of White-tailed Sea Eagles (A) and Golden Eagles (B) in Scotland during the late nineteenth century. Records are far from complete but clearly indicate the predominantly inland distribution of Golden Eagles and more coastal distribution of Sea Eagles. After Love (1983).*

Eagles frequent coastal areas and freshwater lakes. To my mind it would not be surprising if, as re-establishment proceeds in Scotland, many of the coastal home ranges presently used by Golden Eagles were re-appropriated by Sea Eagles. Certainly, there are few examples anywhere of the two species sharing the same environment.

Competition for hunting ranges between Golden Eagle and Bonelli's Eagle has been reported from southern Europe and elsewhere (Cheylan 1973; Jordano 1981; Bahat 1989). Bonelli's Eagle is a comparatively large member of the genus *Hieraaetus*. There is considerable overlap in the diet of the two species with both taking large numbers of Rabbits. Bonelli's Eagle tends to take more bird prey and generally has a more varied diet (Cheylan 1977). These differences do not appear to be sufficient to permit close co-existence and where they occur together, Golden and Bonelli's Eagles hold exclusive home ranges which they defend against each other (Jordano 1981). Within a given landscape there are presumably subtle differences which increase the competitive advantage of one species over the other, although this has yet to be properly researched. There will clearly be costs in defending a territory against both conspecifics and birds of a different species but with a similar ecology. The findings of Miguel Ferrer on the loss of hunting efficiency among young Spanish Imperial Eagles when they were confined to a small hunting range (see above; Ferrer 1993b) point to one potential benefit. Given the overlap in the diet and similar hunting behaviour of Bonelli's and Golden Eagles, there could be advantages in excluding a potential competitor. By so doing the territory holder would reduce the potential contact between prey species and another large aerial predator, and therefore lessen the likelihood of any modification of prey behaviour which could reduce hunting efficiency.

RANGING BEHAVIOUR IN MIGRATORY *AQUILA* EAGLES

All the *Aquila* eagles use more or less exclusive home ranges during the breeding season (Table 22). Variation in range size and differences in dispersion during the breeding season are considered in more detail in Chapter 9. Similarly the various migratory strategies used by members of the genus are covered in Chapter 17. Here I consider briefly what is known about ranging behaviour in winter in the six species in which all or part of the population is migratory.

The Lesser Spotted, Greater Spotted and Imperial Eagles all spend the winter in small flocks or as solitary individuals (Brown *et al.* 1982). Winter ranging behaviour is poorly documented for all three. The migrant Steppe Eagle and the resident Tawny Eagle are better known in their African haunts. Both are frequently gregarious during the non-breeding season, sometimes occurring in large mixed flocks of several hundred individuals. Flocks are nomadic and move about in response to weather fronts. Rainfall associated with these fronts gives rise to temporarily superabundant food such as termites, locusts or colonies of *Quelea* (Brooke *et al.* 1972).

Many Golden Eagles from Alaska and arctic Canada move south to spend the winter in the southwestern United States. Ranging behaviour of migrants wintering in southern Idaho has recently been investigated using birds carrying radio-transmitters which were tracked by satellite (Marzluff *et al.* 1995). While the birds used fairly distinct wintering areas, these were an order of magnitude larger than areas used by the resident territorial eagles. Because of the relative imprecision of satellite tracking compared with ground observation, this finding needs to be treated with caution. As a rule, adult migrants tended to use smaller winter ranges than subadults.

Among migrant raptors in general, winter ranging behaviour tends to fall into one of two types. There are (1) those which are nomadic and range around in search of abundant but transient food sources and (2) those which return regularly to a relatively confined wintering area where food supply is more predictable (Newton 1979; Liversidge 1989). Steppe Eagles and Tawny Eagles conform well to the former while migratory Golden Eagles fit the latter. Lesser Spotted Eagles appear to be nomads, at least in Zimbabwe (Brooke *et al.* 1972). Some Greater Spotted and Imperial Eagles occupy reasonably distinct winter ranges in parts of the Middle East (Christensen 1962; Bundy 1985) but in Africa they tend to be more nomadic. These alternative strategies may reflect differences in feeding ecology, with the African birds dependent on ephemeral insect prey, and those wintering further north feeding on more predictable supplies of vertebrates.

COMMUNAL ROOSTING

Several normally solitary raptors will congregate at communal roosting sites outside the breeding season. The behaviour is especially common among the harriers *Circus* spp. (Watson, 1977). Both Steppe and Tawny Eagles, which occur in Africa during the non-breeding season, spend the night in communal roosts in trees and bushes. This behaviour is clearly allied to a gregarious feeding habit. Two species of *Aquila* that do not form feeding flocks have been found to congregate in communal winter roosts. Bundy (1985) reported communal roosting of Imperial Eagles in Saudi Arabia and northern India. In the former locality he counted up to 14 birds roosting in a 250-m strip of tamarisk trees. The eagles used the site regularly and each day went off to hunt singly in the surrounding countryside, very much in the manner of communal roosting harriers. Presumably, the trees provided protection against ground predators.

The other large concentration of roosting birds involved Golden Eagles wintering in southeastern Idaho (Craig & Craig 1984). These birds roosted on electricity pylons. On one night, eagles were seen roosting on 56 out of 85 pylons. Some 124 birds were seen altogether with as many as seven individuals on one pylon. The high number of wintering eagles in the area was explained by the exceptional jackrabbit densities. Presumably, the pylons offered a concentration of safe roosting places within potentially large foraging areas. Low overnight temperatures and the need to conserve body heat may be another reason for this communal roosting behaviour because eagles appeared to select pylons that were sheltered from the wind.

SUMMARY

Golden Eagles typically live in exclusive home ranges which are occupied all year round. Certain parts of the home range tend to be used preferentially for hunting, although little is known about this aspect of behaviour and more research is needed. Non-breeding eagles are typically nomadic and probably spend only a few days or weeks in relatively small areas before moving on. The accumulated home range size of a non-breeder is much larger than in a breeding pair. Breeding eagles defend their range against conspecifics, including non-breeders, and occasionally also against other species of eagle with similar feeding requirements.

Some northern populations of Golden Eagles are migratory. These birds occupy relatively distinct winter home ranges, which may be located several thousand kilometres south of the breeding area. Winter home ranges may or may not be defended, and occasionally in North America Golden Eagles have been found roosting in loose communal groups outside the breeding season.

Most other members of the genus *Aquila* display similar ranging behaviour to Golden Eagles during the breeding season. Dispersion behaviour in winter is much more varied and depends on the extent to which a particular species is migratory and, in turn, on the nature of its winter food supply.

CHAPTER 9
Nest Spacing and Density

Adult Black Eagle in the Matobo Hills of Zimbabwe.

A BIRD-WATCHER visiting the Highlands for the first time would more easily encounter Golden Eagles in some parts of the region than in others. I recollect Colin Crooke telling me how, on one breezy autumn day on the Isle of Skye, he saw no less than 17 different eagles. Most of his sightings were of adult pairs soaring, or performing their dramatic undulating flight display, and so the birds he saw were mainly resident territory holders. To see anything like this number in a day in the eastern Highlands would be almost unthinkable. From my own experience I can recall a walk in a lonely glen in west Inverness-shire. It was a February afternoon and the sun was shining after 36 hours of heavy rain. Within minutes my eye was drawn to a pair of eagles sky-dancing over a nearby ridge. Very soon I was watching no less than four pairs soaring simultaneously, high over their respective territories, each less than 3 km from its neighbour. No equivalent experience comes to mind from many days on the heather clad hills of Easter Ross. In this chapter I describe the variation in eagle numbers across the Highlands and explore the reasons for this.

Birds of prey which live in more or less discrete home ranges tend to use nesting

101

sites that are evenly spaced over the landscape (Newton 1979). This pattern of nesting, known as *over-dispersion*, means that when sites are plotted on a map they appear regularly distributed; in fact, much more regularly than if birds were choosing nesting places at random. Individual territorial pairs appear to choose nest sites as far from their neighbours as conditions will allow. There is probably a selective advantage in maximizing the distance from a neighbour's nest because this would reduce the prospect of territorial conflict. Choosing a nest site in the middle of the range probably also has benefits in minimizing the time and effort spent carrying food to nestlings. While avoidance of territorial conflict can explain spacing of nest sites, the intriguing unanswered question is why the average distance between neighbours (commonly known as the mean nearest-neighbour distance, NND) should vary from place to place. A useful starting point is to establish whether such variation does occur.

SPACING OF NEST SITES

The national survey of Golden Eagles in Britain in 1982 provided information on nesting dispersion for a large sample of eagles in one year. The detailed methodologies used during this survey are described by Dennis *et al.* (1984). It is sufficient to reiterate here that virtually all known and suspected nesting territories were visited and checked for occupancy in the spring and summer of 1982 with a few gaps filled during 1983. I analysed the results for sample blocks of more or less continuous eagle habitat located in each of the nine ecological regions described in Chapter 4. I used nesting territories which were occupied by a pair of eagles that made a definite breeding attempt (nests where eggs were laid or incubating birds seen). I also included pairs which probably did not lay but for which a recently refurbished nest was found. For each pair the distance to its nearest neighbour was measured on a map. A few pairs nesting on remote islands or otherwise separated from potential neighbours by stretches of unsuitable nesting habitat were excluded (see Newton *et al.* 1977). Variation in nearest-neighbour distance among the nine sample blocks is shown in Fig. 23 (see also Table 23).

Are nest sites regularly spaced?

Nest site dispersion for parts of two Regions, one from the east Highlands and one from the west-central Highlands, is plotted in Fig. 24. Clearly, the impression is one of extreme regularity. By using a mathematical computation which takes the ratio of the squares of the geometric and arithmetic means of nearest-neighbour distances (Appendix 5), it is possible to say with confidence whether nests are more evenly distributed than if sites were selected by the birds at random (Brown 1975). Values of this ratio greater than 0.65 indicate regular spacing, while lower values indicate

FIG. 23.   *Spacing of the nest sites of Golden Eagles from sample areas of continuously suitable habitat in nine Regions of Scotland in 1982. Nearest-neighbour distances were measured to the nearest kilometre. Data for the east and west of Region 4 are given separately. See Table 23 for full details.*

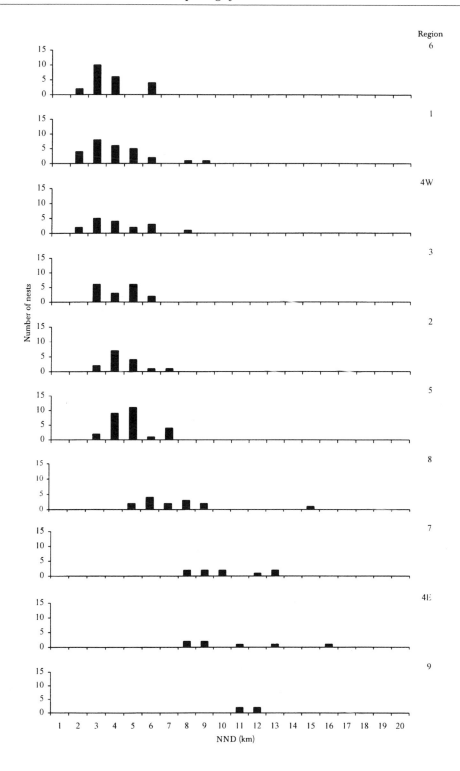

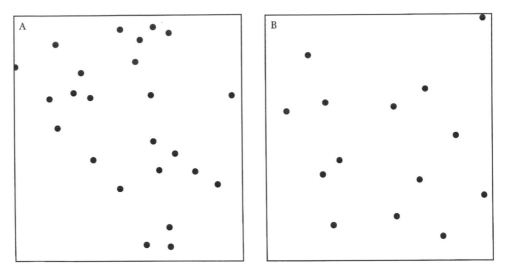

FIG. 24.   *The distribution of nest sites of Golden Eagles in parts of two Regions of Scotland. One is high density (A, Region 6) and one is low density (B, Region 8).*

randomness (Nilsson *et al.* 1982). For all nine sample blocks the value was 0.79 or higher and confirmed appreciable over-dispersion of nest sites (Table 23). For Region 9 the sample of nests was too small for this type of analysis to be meaningful. Equivalent analysis of nest spacing has been carried out in several other studies of Golden Eagles and the same tendency towards regular spacing has been detected (Table 24). Nesting dispersion has also been investigated in the east Highlands of Scotland where Golden Eagle breeding has been monitored over many years (Watson & Rothery 1986). This study examined nest spacing in three sample years between 1946 and 1978 and in each year the spacing pattern was more regular than random. This was the case even though the nesting density of eagles was different in each of the three years. Clearly, regular spacing of nest sites is the norm in Golden Eagles.

NESTING DENSITY

Across Scotland the mean nearest neighbour distance varied from under 5 km in much of the west Highlands and the islands to over 10 km in parts of the east and southwest Highlands. Nest spacing in southwest Scotland was probably higher still, although there were too few pairs there to give a meaningful sample. These distances give a theoretical maximum density of between about 10 and 60 pairs per 1000 km^2, or a sixfold difference in potential nesting density between Regions (see Appendix 5 for method of calculating maximum theoretical density). Actual densities were never as high as these theoretical maxima because each region invariably contained habitat that was unsuitable for hunting by eagles.

Golden Eagles are birds of open moorland habitat although they will also use woodland where the trees are widely spaced. They generally avoid hunting over expanses of open water, over enclosed farmland at low altitude and within plantations of closed canopy forest. In most of the Highlands such habitats are restricted in extent, or confined to larger tracts of land which eagles tend to avoid completely. Regular dispersion of nest sites is maintained even when quite large parts of the landscape are unsuitable provided that areas of suitable habitat are more or less continuous.

I measured actual nesting density for eagles in the nine study areas used in the work on Golden Eagles and land use (see Chapter 4). These areas held different proportions of land which eagles generally avoided (Table 25). There was no consistent relationship between nesting density and the proportion of the area suitable for hunting. Therefore, variation in nesting density was not simply a product of differences in the amount of unsuitable habitat in any given area: there was some other factor involved. Possible explanations were: a shortage of nest sites in some areas; a depressed breeding population in some areas resulting from human persecution; differences in food supply between areas (Newton 1979).

Density in relation to nest site availability

A number of studies in other parts of the world have concluded that the availability of nest sites can modify breeding density. When this occurs, it is often reflected in a loss of the typical regular spacing between nesting territories. A shortage of nest sites in the flat semi-desert lands of southern Idaho, and an abundance of sites along the adjacent Snake River Canyon led to a clumped distribution of eagle nests in that region (Kochert 1972). The comparatively recent habit of nesting on electricity pylons in the flat benchlands of that region is further evidence that nest sites were limiting. Clumping of nest sites was also detected in Utah where the choice of sites was restricted to isolated hills in otherwise flat desert country (Camenzind 1969). Here, several pairs nested very close together but hunting ranges radiated out in different directions from the nesting area. In Scotland, a shortage of nest sites might contribute to the lack of eagles in some localities, particularly where there are few cliffs and no old trees. Such may have been the case in parts of east Sutherland and Caithness (Region 4E) and along the eastern fringe of the Grampian Mountains (Region 8). However, over most of the range in the Highlands eagles appear to have an abundance of potential nesting places. This interpretation is supported by the fact that in each of the sample blocks taken from the 1982 survey, nest sites were regularly spaced (Table 23). In none of the blocks was there evidence of a conspicuously clumped distribution of nests.

Density modified by human persecution

Human persecution has in the past been widespread and continues to be severe in parts of the eastern Highlands which are managed for Red Grouse (see Chapter 19). In such places the incidence of single adult or subadult eagles on a breeding territory is relatively high (Dennis *et al.* 1984). This reflects human persecution of eagles, principally the killing of territorial birds. While in places persecution is intense, it cannot explain the gross differences in density that occur across the whole range.

I plotted the frequency of nesting territories containing a single eagle (assuming this to be evidence of persecution) against the average nearest-neighbour distance between nests in the sample blocks drawn from the nine Regions in the Highlands. There was no significant relationship between the two (Fig. 25) although there was a tendency for rather greater nest spacing in Regions 4E and 8 where the frequency of single eagles on territory was also highest. Persecution may therefore have been one factor modifying density in those Regions.

Density in relation to food supply

The most likely cause of variation in nesting density is food supply. A pioneering study of Golden Eagles and food supply in Scotland was carried out the early 1960s (Brown & Watson 1964). They worked in four study areas across the Highlands and concluded that there was no clear link between eagle density and food. In the early 1980s, Stuart Rae and I built on this earlier research by extending the study to six and subsequently nine areas (Watson *et al.* 1992b). We chose study areas which we believed were largely or entirely free from human persecution.

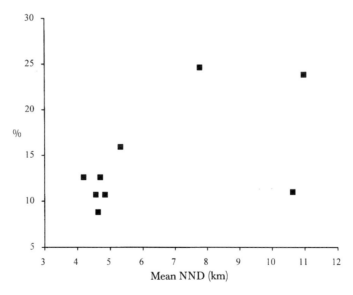

FIG. 25.   *The proportion of home ranges occupied by single eagles in eight Regions of Scotland in relation to mean nearest-neighbour distances for sample areas within each Region. Data are given separately for the east and west of Region 4, and Region 9 is excluded because the number of eagles there were too few to give a meaningful comparison. In statistical analysis the relationship is not significant (r, = 0.542, P >0.05).*

In none of our areas was there appreciable mortality of breeding eagles attributable to human action. We were able to provide a measure of food availability in eagle hunting range in each study area, and relate this to eagle density (Appendix 4). We calculated an index of abundance of the different types of prey which formed the bulk of the bird's diet. These included Red Grouse, Ptarmigan, Mountain Hare and Rabbit which are killed by eagles (live prey), as well as dead Red Deer and sheep which are eaten as carrion. Our estimates were made during the late winter and early spring (February–April). This was when eagles exhibited greatest territorial activity and was when we believed it most likely that food availability would limit the number of eagles settling to breed in an area.

With respect to food supply, our nine study areas fell into three types which broadly reflected their geographical locations (Table 26). Areas C, D and E in the north and northwest Highlands all had comparatively low amounts of total food (<30 kg/20 km) and of this more than 70% was carrion. Areas H and I in the east Highlands also had low values of total prey but less than 30% was carrion. The extreme western and southwestern areas A, B, F and G all had large amounts of total prey (>60 kg/20 km) and this comprised more than 80% carrion.

For each study area we measured the amount of land which we judged was unsuitable for hunting by eagles and subtracted this from the total before calculating eagle density (Table 26). Eagle nesting density ranged from over 30 pairs/1000 km^2 on the islands of Mull and Skye to less than 15 pairs/1000 km^2 in the two east Highland localities. In one sense, our findings confirmed those of Brown & Watson (1964) in that we found little evidence of a link between eagle density and total food supply (live prey and carrion combined). However, we did find a significant positive correlation between breeding density and the carrion index (Fig. 26). Eagle density was highest in areas where there was abundant dead sheep and/or deer.

Differences in amounts of carrion are a consequence of the numbers and management of sheep and deer in different parts of the Highlands. Golden Eagle densities over much of western Scotland are high compared with almost anywhere else where the bird has been studied (Table 27). I believe this is because of the large and predictable supply of carrion available, especially in late winter when breeding territories are reinforced. If these carrion levels were suddenly reduced as a result of changes in sheep or deer management, there would be a reduction in eagle density in these western regions. Current levels of alternative live prey could not support present west Highland eagle populations, although if there were many fewer sheep and deer, the numbers of wild prey would, in time, increase.

Our findings reinforce the conclusion of Lockie (1964) who studied Golden Eagles and Foxes in one west Highland locality. In his opinion the high density of predators in that region was a direct result of the availability of carrion during winter and spring. The findings of Watson *et al.* (1989) lend further support to our conclusion. They showed that a decline in eagle density in one east Highland area since the 1960s coincided with changes in Red Deer management. Specifically, increased culling levels resulted in reduced amounts of deer carrion available to eagles. I return to this subject again in Chapter 19 when discussing the effects of land use change on eagles in the Highlands.

A positive correlation between food supply and breeding density has been shown

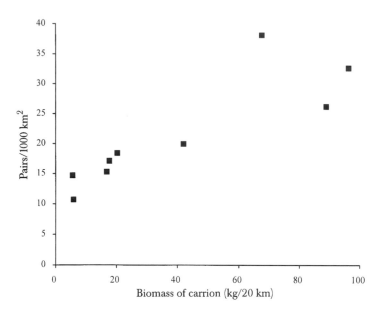

FIG. 26.   *The relationship between Golden Eagle nesting density and the index of carrion abundance (see Appendix 4 and Table 26 for details) in nine study areas in Scotland in 1985. Golden Eagles nested at higher densities where carrion was more abundant. In statistical analysis the relationship was significant ($r_s = 0.933$, $P < 0.01$). After Watson* et al. *(1992b).*

for a number of other raptors, notably Buzzards (Mebs 1964), Black Eagles (Gargett 1975) and Sparrowhawks (Newton *et al.* 1986). Generally, such findings are still rather rare because of the difficulty of measuring food availability in the field. Newton (1979) believed that food probably explained most variation in raptor densities, except where nest sites were limiting or populations were being artificially suppressed by human persecution or organochlorine pesticide use. In the Sparrowhawk he believed that the maximum breeding density was set by the number of established males which could live in an area, and that this number was geared to food supply. The territorial behaviour of these males, which occupied exclusive ranges early in the breeding season, was the proximate mechanism influencing density (Newton 1986). In Golden Eagles, the late winter territorial behaviour of established pairs probably serves a similar function, effectively preventing other pairs from settling.

Competition with other eagle species

A few studies have suggested that Golden Eagle density may be limited by competition with closely related species. The work of Ofer Bahat in Israel is one

Adult White-tailed Sea Eagle and two immature Golden Eagles above a sea cliff on an island off the west of Scotland.

example. A difference in mean nearest neighbour distance among Golden Eagles in two study areas was attributed to competition with Bonelli's Eagles (Bahat 1989). In the Negev Desert, Bonelli's Eagles were scarce and Golden Eagles nested, on average, 13 km apart. In the Judean Desert, where Bonelli's outnumbered Golden Eagles and both species maintained mutually exclusive home ranges, the mean nearest-neighbour distance between Golden Eagle pairs was 16 km. The lower Golden Eagle density in the Judean Desert was, at first sight, anomalous because that region had higher rainfall and more food than the arid Negev. It was the combined density of the two eagles, which were effectively operating as a single species by maintaining exclusive ranges, that was higher in the richer feeding area of Judea. Bahat considered that this exceptional state of affairs was possible only because of subtle topographical variation which gave Bonelli's Eagles a hunting advantage over the larger Golden Eagles in certain parts of the Judean study area. The two species were, in effect, segregated by habitat choice. When Bahat measured the actual home range size of Golden Eagles in the two areas his findings were no longer exceptional. The birds in the poor food area of the Negev hunted larger home ranges (68–81 km^2) than the birds in the richer hunting grounds of Judea (21–56 km^2). This study emphasizes the need for caution when making assumptions about home range size based on mean nearest-neighbour distance.

Breeding density outside Scotland

A large number of studies from Europe, North America and elsewhere have reported Golden Eagle nesting densities (Table 27). Methods of expressing density have varied between studies and because of this it is often difficult to make direct comparison. Some give mean nearest-neighbour distances, others have estimated breeding density and some have done both. Figure 27 shows the relationship between actual breeding density and the maximum theoretical density calculated from mean nearest-neighbour distances. These data are from studies where both sets of information were provided. The estimates for density should be considered indicative rather than precise. I also calculated the missing data for other studies where only one of the measures was available and did this using the regression equation ($y = 1.0093x^{0.7307}$) derived from Fig. 27.

Over much of continental Europe, actual densities of less than 10 pairs/1000 km^2 are usual. Densities in the United States tend to be near the continental European figure or higher (10–20 pairs/1000 km^2) except in parts of Wyoming where they are comparable to those in western Scotland (>20 pairs/1000 km^2). Densities of less than 5 pairs/1000 km^2 occurred among eagles nesting in wooded peatlands in Sweden and Belorus (Tjernberg 1985; Ivanovsky 1990). Tjernberg believed that higher eagle densities in the Swedish mountain region compared with the forest could be explained by more abundant food in the mountain region. He suggested that food in the open mountain habitat was more accessible to the eagles, which could catch prey more easily in the absence of trees and shrubs. The exceptionally low eagle density in the Apennine Mountains of Italy was again attributed to food supply (Ragni *et al.* 1986). They believed that the eagles' preferred prey—Brown Hares and partridges—were kept at very low densities as a result of shooting. Killing of adult Golden Eagles by hunters may also have depressed breeding density.

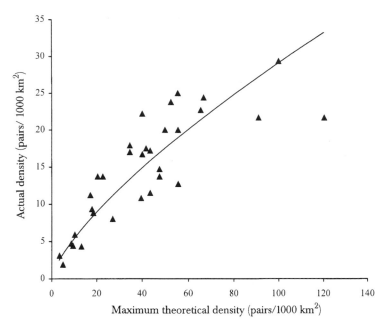

FIG. 27. *The relationship between actual nesting density of Golden Eagles and the maximum theoretical density calculated from mean nearest-neighbour distance. Data are from various studies in Scotland, continental Europe and North America. See Table 27 for full details. The equation of the regression line is* $y = 1.0093x^{0.7307}$.

Changes in breeding density over time

If there is one consistent feature of Golden Eagle breeding density over time it is stability. Change invariably occurs very slowly and nesting density is apparently not very responsive to short-term fluctuations in food. Stable breeding populations are a feature of raptors which feed on prey which fluctuates little. If fluctuations do occur in a favoured food species, then a stable breeding population may still occur provided that the raptor can then turn to alternative prey (Newton 1979).

In Scotland, between-year fluctuations in prey are modest and high stability in eagle numbers would be expected. In parts of the western United States, jackrabbits are the preferred food and these animals have large between-year fluctuations in numbers following an approximately 10-year cycle (Kochert 1980). Despite this, eagle nesting density in Idaho is no less stable than in Scotland and this is presumably because the birds are able to turn to alternative prey, such as ground squirrels, when jackrabbits are scarce.

Two long-term studies of eagles have detected small changes in breeding density over time. The work in eastern Scotland by Adam Watson was mentioned earlier (p. 107). Mike Kochert and Karen Steenhof's study in Idaho has followed the fortunes of nesting eagles since 1971. Here, there has been a gradual decline in the number of pairs of eagles in the Snake River study area. This is still not fully understood but one possible explanation involves the increase in wild fires since 1980, and increased agricultural development during the late 1960s and early 1970s (M. Kochert and K. Steenhof, *pers. comm.*). Both these changes affect the amount and quality of jackrabbit habitat, and may have reduced the numbers of jackrabbits within Golden Eagle feeding areas. Such long-term land use changes are precisely what Ian Newton predicted could lead to a gradual reduction in raptor numbers over time (Newton 1979). Although we have no information on Golden Eagle density in western Scotland from a time when carrion was much less abundant than it is today, intuitively, it seems likely that eagle densities were once less than they are now.

Further evidence of the inherently stable nature of Golden Eagle breeding density comes from populations which have recovered following intense human persecution. Heinrich Haller has reviewed the recovery of eagle numbers in the Alps (Haller 1994). At the beginning of this century numbers were seriously depleted as a result of persecution. From the 1930s until the 1980s there was a steady increase in the number of eagles in the High Alps. By 1985 the population there had stabilized and no further increase has occurred. Instead, surplus birds have begun to colonize lower altitude regions in the hilly foreland of the Alps.

NON-BREEDING BIRDS

The non-breeding component of an eagle population comprises individuals of various ages. There are birds up to about 1 year old, which I will refer to throughout this book as juveniles. For those aged between about 18 months and 4 years old I use the term immature. Some authors use the term subadult for immature birds that are clearly close to adult plumage (see Chapter 16). Eagles in their fifth summer and older have normally acquired mainly adult plumage and are then generally indistinguishable from breeding adults. Most populations probably contain a proportion of non-breeding adults. Indirect evidence for the existence of such birds comes from the rapid replacement of established breeders which have died by birds in adult plumage (Dixon 1937; Phillips *et al.* 1984; Tjernberg 1985). Where populations have been reduced below the carrying capacity of the area as a result of human persecution, such non-breeding adults are probably rare. In these circumstances gaps in the breeding population tend to be filled by birds in subadult plumage (Bergo 1984a). In a recent study in California the frequency of non-breeding birds in adult plumage (they referred to these as floaters) was high (PBRG 1995).

Our knowledge of the size of the non-breeding component of eagle populations is poor. The frequency of birds described as juvenile/immature was reported for an area in the east Highlands of Scotland by Brown & Watson (1964). Among all eagle sightings in the late summer, 34% were of juveniles/immatures and by the late winter this had dropped to 16%. The change was mainly caused by a 70% reduction in the sightings of juveniles. There were known to be a small number of non-breeding adults in that area and, including these, the non-breeding element at the

Adult Golden Eagle preening.

beginning of the nesting season was estimated to be about 20% of the total population. I recorded the ages of all eagles seen (juveniles/immatures or adult) in two west Highland areas during February–April over 4 years (Table 28). The frequency of juveniles/immatures ranged from 8 to 12% and was thus somewhat lower than in the earlier study. The difference between the east and west is probably real considering the consistently higher breeding success in the east Highlands (Chapter 15). Allowing for a small proportion of non-breeders in adult plumage, I estimate that non-breeders constitute around 15% of the total population across the whole of Scotland at the start of the breeding season. In the absence of persecution this figure would almost certainly be higher.

WINTER DENSITY IN MIGRATORY GOLDEN EAGLES

Most Golden Eagle populations are sedentary, with established pairs remaining on their breeding territories throughout the year. However, birds from high latitudes in North America and Eurasia are long-distance migrants. Many thousands of birds from Alaska and northern Canada spend the months from October to March in the southwestern United States. In New Mexico, wintering eagles were counted from a light aircraft in sample areas during three winters in the 1960s (Boeker & Bolen 1972). Estimated densities were similar in each year with high numbers between November and February (2–4 eagles/100 km²) and low numbers in April (0.2–0.4/100 km²). If the latter were mainly the resident breeders, and assuming around half of these were on nests in April and not detected during the aerial censuses, then there was an approximately fivefold increase in eagle density attributable to the winter immigrants. The same study detected much lower winter densities in nearby Texas. The relative abundance of wintering eagles (number seen/1000 km flown in the aircraft) in various western States was assessed using comparable aerial surveys in the 1970s. The highest concentrations were in Wyoming, Utah and Colorado (6.4, 3.1 and 2.1 eagles/1000 km, respectively) with 1/1000 km or less in New Mexico, Texas and Arizona and less than 0.05/1000 km in Oklahoma (Boeker 1974). Winter bird count data confirm the high concentrations of eagles from Montana south to Colorado and west to Nevada (Johnsgard 1990).

As in the case of breeding eagles, the number of migrants wintering in a particular area is probably related to the amount of food available. Because migrant birds are not tied to a nesting site they can be more responsive to spatial variations in food, and eagle numbers would be expected to fluctuate in particular localities correspondingly. There is evidence that this does occur in Idaho where the number of wintering Golden Eagles was some 16 times higher in 1981–82 compared with 1974–76. This was related to differences in jackrabbit numbers which were low in 1974–76 but exceptionally high in 1981–82 (Craig *et al.* 1984).

Little has been written about migratory Golden Eagles on their wintering grounds in Eastern Europe and on the Russian steppes. Martin Tjernberg studied wintering birds near Uppsala, well to the south of their breeding range in Sweden (Tjernberg 1977). By recognizing differences in plumage and missing flight-feathers he was able to identify and follow the behaviour of individuals. Nearly half

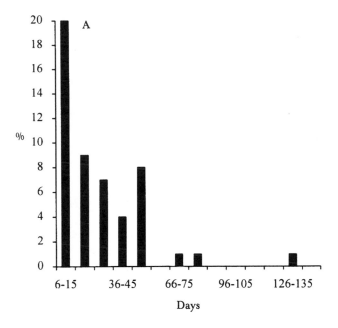

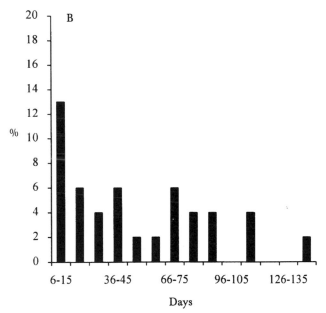

FIG. 28. *The proportion of migratory Golden Eagles resident for different lengths of time near Uppsala, Sweden during winters with and without supplementary feeding. A, No supplementary food 1966–67 and 1971–72 (n = 112); B, supplementary food 1972–73 and 1974–75 (n = 47). Among birds which remained in the area for more than 5 days, appreciably more stayed longer in years when supplementary food was provided. Redrawn from Tjernberg (1977).*

the known individuals remained in his area for less than 5 days. Many were passing through or were ranging over much larger areas than the 100 km² or so that he watched intensively. This mobility, he assumed, was a response to availability of food. He tested this by providing additional food in the form of carrion in two winters. While the proportion of birds which stayed for 5 days or less dropped only slightly in years when extra food was provided, for birds which stayed longer there was a more marked difference. Appreciably more individuals stayed in the area for more than 8 weeks in winters when birds were fed compared with winters when they were not (Fig. 28). This gives further evidence that wintering eagles are responsive to changes in food supply.

BREEDING DENSITY IN OTHER *AQUILA* EAGLES

Generally, among raptors, larger species tend to exist at lower breeding densities and in larger home ranges than do smaller species (Newton 1979). This is because larger predators typically hunt bigger prey animals which in turn live at lower densities and have lower breeding rates than smaller prey species. The expected trend is found across the range of *Aquila* eagles for which information on density is available (Fig. 29). The three biggest eagles (Golden, Wedge-tailed and Black) usually nest at densities between 5 and 20 pairs per 1000 km². The smallest species (Lesser Spotted) can nest at densities equivalent to 100 pairs per 1000 km² and the densities of middle-sized species (Tawny, Steppe and Imperial) are between these.

For any particular species very high densities can occur if food is exceptionally abundant. This was the case for Black Eagles in the Matobo Hills in Zimbabwe (Gargett 1975), for Golden Eagles in western Scotland (see earlier in this chapter), and for Steppe Eagles near Astrakhan in southwest Russia (Agafonov *et al.* 1957). In the latter study the Steppe Eagles returned from migration to their nesting grounds in the spring of 1955. Their normal food at this time is ground squirrels, which are in comparatively low numbers following hibernation. However, in that year there was an additional abundant supply of fresh carcasses of Saiga Antelope for which hunting permits had been issued in the autumn of 1954. Many antelopes were killed and many others injured and left to die. These provided a superabundant source of food for the returning eagles. The resulting densities of up to 15 pairs of Steppe Eagles in 6 km² (equivalent to 2500 pairs/1000 km²) have not been approached in any other study of *Aquila* eagles. This shows that, even in populations that are normally stable, changes can occur quickly in response to a huge increase in food supply. The fact that the Steppe Eagles were returning migrants, rather than resident birds with well-established territories, was presumably an important contributing factor.

SUMMARY

In continuously suitable habitat, the nesting territories of Golden Eagle are usually spaced at regular intervals. Spacing can be less than regular if nest sites are

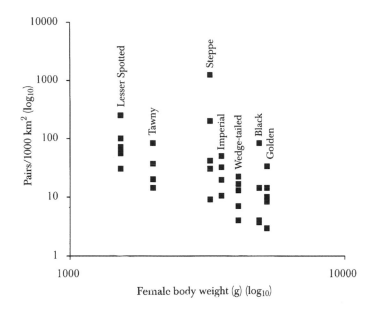

FIG. 29.   *A range of breeding densities (pairs per 1000 km²) reported for seven species of* Aquila *eagles, in relation to female body weight. Both axes are log₁₀-transformed. Data are mainly from Glutz von Blotzheim et al. (1971), Cramp & Simmons (1980), Gargett (1990), Marchant & Higgins (1993). Additional information is from Agafanov et al. (1957), Baker-Gabb (1984), Phillips et al. (1984), Król (1985), Hustler & Howells (1989), Potočný (1989).*

limiting, or if populations are depressed as a result of human persecution. In Scotland, differences in density between areas were positively correlated with differences in the amount of carrion available in late winter. Studies in other parts of the world have also shown positive relationships between breeding density and food supply. Individual breeding territories tend to be stable from year to year and in any one area overall breeding density varies little between years. Long-term changes in food supply can result in changes in eagle density, although such changes occur slowly.

Breeding densities of Golden Eagles in western Scotland are among the highest recorded for that species anywhere in the world at >20 pairs /1000 km². Densities are typically <10 pairs/1000 km² in continental Europe, and 10–20 pairs/1000 km² in North America. The densities in western Scotland are attributable to the exceptional levels of sheep and deer carrion in that region. In the eastern Highlands of Scotland, where carrion is less abundant and where eagles feed more on prey such as grouse and hares, breeding densities are close to those in continental Europe.

Migratory populations of Golden Eagles in winter, notably in the southwestern United States, can sometimes occur at much higher densities than resident eagles in the same area. Because they are not 'tied' to breeding territories, migrant eagles in winter are more immediately responsive to short-term changes and to spatial variation in food supply.

Among the *Aquila* eagles, breeding density tends to be highest in the smaller species (Lesser Spotted Eagle and Steppe), and lowest in the larger species (Black Eagle, Golden Eagle and Wedge-tailed Eagle).

CHAPTER 10

Population Estimates and Trends

Adult Golden Eagle observing a herd of Reindeer in Finnish Lapland.

I BEGIN this chapter with a short account of the known historical changes in Golden Eagle distribution in Britain and Ireland. There follows a review of the status of the species in Europe, with particular emphasis on the breeding population. This builds on a series of earlier reviews most of which were geographically incomplete (e.g. Biljfeld 1974, Génsbøl 1987, Meyburg & Meyburg 1987, Michel 1987b) and incorporates published and unpublished population estimates as available at the end of 1995. Population estimates from other parts of the world are then briefly discussed.

THE GOLDEN EAGLE IN BRITAIN AND IRELAND

Historical changes

Although the bulk of the Golden Eagle population in Britain and Ireland has always been in the Scottish Highlands, breeding was once much more extensive (Holloway

1996; Fig. 30). Until the late eighteenth century, eagles nested in the mountains of north Wales (the Welsh name for Snowdonia is Eryri, the land of the eagles; Gordon 1955). In England, breeding occurred as far south as Derbyshire in the late seventeenth century, and in the south Pennines of Yorkshire probably into the eighteenth century (Fryer 1987). Golden Eagles were still present in Lakeland until the early nineteenth century (MacPherson 1892). In the Cheviots of northern England and in the Galloway and the Moffat–Tweedsmuir Hills of southern Scotland they continued to breed until the mid-nineteenth century (Gladstone 1910; Baxter & Rintoul 1953). In Ireland Golden Eagles were widespread well into the nineteenth century when breeding was reported from a dozen or more counties especially in the north and west (Ussher and Warren 1900). The last Irish Golden Eagle was seen on the Donegal coast in 1913 (Barrington 1915). Ireland has the doubtful privilege of being the one country in the world where Golden Eagles have become extinct in recent times.

By the early years of this century, the Golden Eagle in Britain and Ireland survived as a breeding bird only within the remote hills and glens of the Highlands and Islands of Scotland (Gordon 1955). The over-riding cause of this range contraction was human persecution (Brown 1976). Since the 1940s there has been a modest recovery with recolonization of the Galloway and Carrick Hills in southwest Scotland, from one pair in 1945 to four pairs by 1963. Nesting eagles returned to Lakeland in 1969 and a pair still nests there. A second pair has also recolonized another locality in northern England. A pair nested in County Antrim from 1953 to 1960 (Deane 1962) but this was not sustained and none have bred in Ireland since.

Numbers in Britain

Max Nicholson published the first assessment of Golden Eagle numbers in Britain (Nicholson 1957). Based on the work of Pat Sandeman, Charles Palmer, Leslie Brown and Adam Watson, he estimated the population to be not less than 190 pairs. As more information became available during the 1960s Adam Watson revised the figure upwards to about 300 pairs (Everett 1971). The next important advance was the comprehensive national survey carried out in 1982 and reported by Dennis *et al.* (1984). This revealed 424 home ranges occupied by pairs, with a further 87 ranges occupied by single eagles, giving a minimum of 935 birds. Not all single eagles would have been recorded on this survey and I believe the real figure was nearer 1000 birds. Applying the figure of 15% for the proportion of non-breeding birds in the population (see Chapter 9) gives an estimated total population of just under 1000 individuals.

Most of the apparent increase compared with earlier estimates was attributed to improved coverage of poorly known areas, particularly in the Outer Hebrides and parts of the west mainland (Dennis *et al.* 1984). Intense persecution of eagles into the 1950s was probably followed by some reduction in killing in the wake of the

FIG. 30.   *Map showing the regions of Britain and Ireland where Golden Eagles occurred in the late nineteenth century. The widespread occurrence in western Ireland is evident even though extinction had already occurred in many other places. Map is after Holloway (1996).*

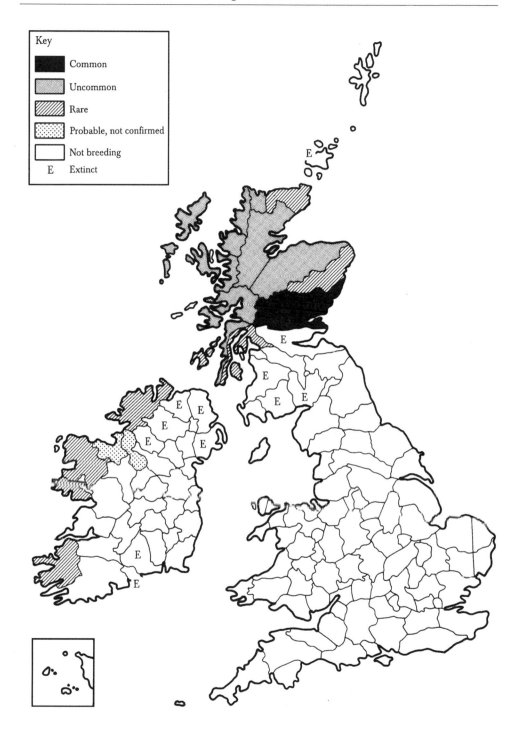

Key

Common

Uncommon

Rare

Probable, not confirmed

Not breeding

E Extinct

Protection of Birds Act (1954) and the campaigning of the Royal Society for the Protection of Birds (RSPB). This suggests to me that a genuine increase in numbers had also occurred. During 1992 a follow-up national survey was carried out and this revealed little change, with 491 ranges occupied, 422 by pairs and 69 by single birds (Rhys Green *in litt.*). In overall size, the population was apparently stable, although the consistency between the two surveys masked some quite marked localized increases and decreases. Illegal killing of eagles is probably the most important factor affecting the size of the population by preventing expansion in some areas and causing decreases in others (see Chapter 19).

THE GOLDEN EAGLE IN EUROPE

Population estimates in Europe

Europe, for my purposes, is defined as those countries north of the Mediterranean and west of the Ural mountains (Fig. 31). Turkey and the countries of the Middle East and North Africa are excluded although they fall within the Western Palearctic

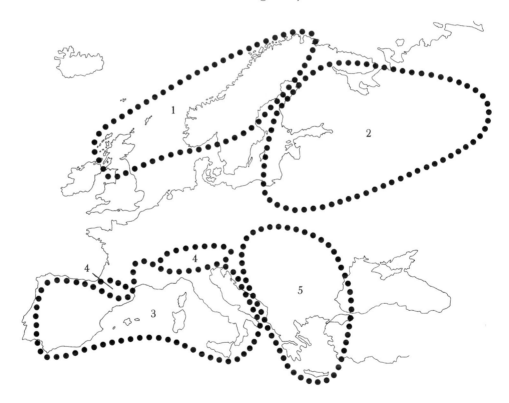

FIG. 31. *Map of Europe showing the general locations of the five biogeographic regions referred to in the text. The regions are (1) Northwest Mountains; (2) East Baltic Lowlands; (3) West Mediterranean Mountains; (4) Alpine Mountains; (5) Balkan Mountains. After Watson (1991, 1992b).*

biogeographic region. There is little knowledge of the status of Golden Eagles in places such as Turkey and North Africa.

Information on status was obtained from an extensive review of the European literature and for the majority of countries a population estimate has been published during the period 1983–1994. Where gaps were apparent I wrote to known authorities on diurnal raptors and replies were received in most cases. Full details of sources are given for each locality in Table 29 which contains an update of information published in Watson (1992b). In all cases estimates refer to the number of breeding pairs as this was the measure used by virtually all researchers. Information is presented by country except for the larger islands of the Mediterranean (Corsica, Sardinia, Sicily and Crete) which are geographically distinct from their respective geopolitical affiliations and are therefore dealt with separately (Table 29). While some figures clearly exhibit spurious accuracy I have not changed the figures given by the original authors.

The contemporary population of Golden Eagles in Europe lies within the range 5000–6000 pairs. As figures for virtually all countries with estimated populations of more than 200 pairs have now been made using complete or partial census data, it is unlikely that the actual figure will fall outside this range. The greatest uncertainty probably lies in countries with populations in the range 50–150 pairs (e.g. Albania, Croatia, Greece) where census data are few. Judging by the estimated populations in surrounding countries, the suggested figure for Romania may well be too low. In countries where partial or complete censuses have recently been made for the first time—Spain (Arroyo *et al.* 1990), Scotland (Dennis *et al.* 1984) and Sweden (Tjernberg 1990)—the result has invariably been to raise substantially the previous 'best estimate'.

The Spanish population at around 1200 pairs is the most numerous, followed by Norway and Sweden (>600 pairs each). In seven other countries (Austria, Finland, France, Italy, European Russia, Scotland and Switzerland) the number of pairs lies in the range 200–500. Together, these 10 countries support over 85% of Europe's Golden Eagles.

Numbers in biogeographic regions

Estimates of population size have invariably been derived from survey work done, and knowledge accumulated, within geopolitical units (mainly countries). However, these are essentially artificial divisions and may not be the most appropriate units within which to judge the general health and conservation needs of wide-ranging, low-density species such as Golden Eagles. Instead, such birds lend themselves to an approach based on biogeographic regions and this is particularly appropriate when information on distribution and abundance is relatively complete over an area as large as Europe. For the Golden Eagle the various country populations fall into five discernable biogeographic regions (Watson 1991). These are: the Northwest Mountains, East Baltic Lowlands, West Mediterranean Mountains, Alpine Mountains and Balkan Mountains (Table 30; Figure 31).

While the implementation of conservation policies will probably always be determined by national governments, it is helpful for the formulation of conservation priorities to view biological information in its biogeographical context. For example the Scottish population of Golden Eagles comprises some 8% of the European population but over 27% of that in the Northwest Mountains biogeographical region. This clearly places an international obligation on the British government in relation to the conservation of Golden Eagles. In contrast the population in Portugal is just 0.3% of the European and 1.2% of the West Mediterranean Mountain population. The international obligation is clearly less, although the fact that the population is apparently decreasing should be a factor in determining national priorities for bird conservation in Portugal.

Trends in Europe

For each country the trend is given in one of four categories: increasing, decreasing, stable or unknown (Table 29). The source for this is generally the same as the population estimate but has been updated by information from Tucker & Heath (1994). Information on trends is generally encouraging. Numbers are reportedly stable or increasing among 19 (57%) of the 33 population estimates. These account for over 80% of the total European population. Although the Spanish population is believed to be some 30% lower than it was 30 years ago, this decline has apparently stopped and the present numbers are stable (Arroyo *et al.* 1990).

The main areas where a continuing decline is reported are in southeast Europe (Greece, Romania) and the Baltic Lowlands (Poland and Belorus). In southeast Europe and also in Sicily and Portugal, the principal reasons are human persecution and disturbance. Habitat destruction, mainly through the loss of wooded peatlands, is a key threat in Poland and Belorus. Although reportedly stable, the Russian population may also be at risk from the drainage of wooded peatlands. It is also possible, given the trends in surrounding countries, that threats from persecution may be impinging on populations in Italy, Albania and Croatia. Neither can we afford to be complacent in Scotland, where killing of eagles, including the use of poisoned baits, still occurs (see Chapter 19; RSPB & NCC, 1991).

Across the five biogeographic regions the priorities for conservation are clear. Populations in the Northwest Mountains and the West Mediterranean Mountains are large and generally stable and that in the Alpine Mountains, although smaller, is generally increasing. The smaller populations in the East Baltic Lowlands and the Balkan Mountains are under threat, with population declines identified in several countries. The unusual lowland eagles nesting in wooded peatlands east of the Baltic are probably under the greatest pressure. While good numbers still occur in Finland, their long-term future will depend crucially on the conservation of wooded peatland habitat in European Russia. Prevention of persecution through effective legislation and conservation education will be needed if declines in the Balkans are to be reversed.

OTHER POPULATIONS IN THE PALEARCTIC

Few precise estimates are available for Golden Eagle populations in the Palearctic Region outside Europe. In the Western Palearctic several-hundred pairs nest in

Morocco and Turkey but only a few in Algeria, Tunisia and Egypt (Génsbøl 1987). Numbers in Israel appear to be increasing and there are now at least 40 pairs (Bahat 1989). There must be many thousands if not tens of thousands in the Eastern Palearctic from Kurdistan to the Himalayas and from Siberia south to Mongolia and western China. The population in Japan is comparatively well studied; the number of known pairs in 1987 was 124 and the total population was estimated to be between 370 and 500 birds in 1983 (Higuchi & Takeda 1983; SRGE 1992).

THE GOLDEN EAGLE IN NORTH AMERICA

Population Estimates

There have been several attempts to estimate the North American Golden Eagle population. Hamerstrom *et al.* (1975) thought there could be as many as 100 000 birds while Snow (1973) believed there were at least 50 000. Palmer (1988) compromised with a figure of 70 000, which seems reasonable when compared with one winter estimate of 63 000 birds in the western United States (Table 31; Olendorff *et al.* 1981). Good estimates of breeding populations are available for a few western States and these range from 500 pairs in California to nearly 3400 in Wyoming (Table 32). Extrapolating from these figures I believe a breeding population somewhere between 20 000 and 25 000 pairs is likely for the whole of North America. The proportion of non-breeders in North America appears to be appreciably higher than the 15% I estimated for Scotland (PBRG 1995). Assuming a conservative figure of around 20–30% non-breeding birds, a total population estimate of 50 000–70 000 individuals would appear reasonable.

Numbers in eastern Canada and the northeastern United States are tiny and largely irrelevant to these continent-wide estimates. Since 1987 only a single pair in

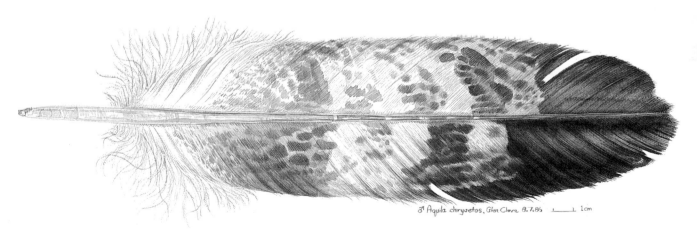

♂ *Aquila chrysaetos*, Glen Clova 8.7.85   ⊢——⊣ 1cm

Moulted and worn central tail-feather from an adult Golden Eagle.

Maine was known to breed in the eastern United States (Todd, 1989). Breeding has been proved at just two localities in northern Ontario since 1981 (Austen *et al.* 1994). Similarly sparse breeding populations probably occur in the other Canadian maritime provinces (Snyder, 1949).

Trends in North America

Most of the well-studied western populations are stable or increasing following some respite from human persecution (Table 32). There has been a pronounced decline related to land use changes and encroaching urbanization in the coastal region of southern California (Harlow & Bloom 1989). In the eastern United States there has been a steady range-contraction from early this century (Spofford 1971). This is attributed to the loss of the eagle's preferred open hunting ground as the natural woodlands of the Appalachian Mountains have recovered. Woodland recovery has been brought about by strict fire control regimes and a reversion of agricultural land to forest. It seems more than likely that the historical presence of Golden Eagles in the Appalachians was largely a product of deforestation of large areas by early settlers.

WORLD POPULATION OF GOLDEN EAGLES

The lack of information on Golden Eagles over their huge East Palearctic range makes any estimate of world population risky. Judging by the known extent of the range in this region there would hardly be fewer birds here than in North America and there could be easily double the number. I would guess that the global breeding population certainly exceeds 50 000 pairs and could be as many as 100 000. This would give an estimated world population, allowing for non-breeders, of something between 125 000 and 250 000 birds.

OTHER *AQUILA* EAGLES IN EUROPE

Population estimates and trends

Reasonably good population estimates are now available for the four other *Aquila* eagles which breed in Europe (Table 33; Tucker & Heath 1994).

Lesser Spotted Eagle numbers at 6700-9500 pairs are generally stable or increasing in the main concentrations southeast of the Baltic. All the smaller populations in southeast Europe are, however, declining. Habitat loss, including forest clearance and drainage of wet meadows, are critical threats.

Greater Spotted Eagles have a much smaller European population (860–1100 pairs) and most birds nest in Russia. This is considered a globally threatened species and is especially vulnerable to habitat loss, mainly through drainage of wet woodlands and meadows.

The Steppe Eagle has the largest population of any *Aquila* in Europe, with 15 000–25 000 pairs concentrated mainly in southwest Russia and the Ukraine.

Numbers have been reduced markedly as a result of agricultural development of virgin steppes since 1945. That decline is believed to be continuing and a new threat is posed by recently constructed electric powerlines in the tree-less landscapes where these birds breed (up to 15 dead eagles/10 km of powerline were reported from one study).

The Eastern Imperial Eagle has a population of some 320–570 pairs and is declining except in Hungary and Slovakia (Table 34). Habitat changes including the loss of nesting sites have been implicated. Following intensive conservation management action, the Spanish Imperial Eagle is now increasing (presently 150–160 pairs) but remains under threat from shooting, poisoning, electrocution at powerlines and pesticide contamination.

CONCLUDING REMARKS

The achievements of those who have worked to protect the critically endangered Spanish Imperial Eagle and the Eastern Imperial Eagle in Hungary offer encouragement to all those concerned with the conservation of large birds of prey. Sometimes it is too easy to believe that nothing can be done, or that we should be content with the depleted populations of large raptors which are now found in so many countries. I firmly believe that we in Britain and Ireland should not be complacent because we now have an apparently stable Golden Eagle population. Instead, we should look to help the species regain some of the ground it has lost over the past three centuries. Perhaps the greatest challenge would be to see the Golden Eagle restored to Ireland, and eventually to the mountains of Wales and northern England.

SUMMARY

The Golden Eagle in Britain and Ireland is now almost entirely confined to the Scottish Highlands and Islands, where some 420 pairs breed. A few pairs nest in southwest Scotland and northern England but none currently nest in Ireland. The population in Europe is estimated at 5000–6000 pairs and is generally stable, although numbers are declining in the east Baltic region and in southeast Europe.

The North American population is estimated at 20 000–25 000 breeding pairs and is generally stable except in the Appalachian Mountains where it is now virtually extinct. The world population of Golden Eagles is probably not less than 50 000 pairs and could be double this.

The numbers of all *Aquila* eagles in Europe have declined during this century, although the populations of some are probably now stable. Two are classed as globally threatened (Greater Spotted Eagle and Spanish Imperial Eagle).

CHAPTER 11
The Pre-breeding Season

Golden Eagle and Raven feeding on a dead Red Deer stag in winter.

SPEND an hour scanning the skyline of a west Highland glen on a bright and breezy day in January or February and I can almost guarantee you will see a pair of eagles soaring together. Spend half a day in the same locality in June or July and you would do well to glimpse a single bird as it slides surreptitiously out of sight behind some distant ridge. In the windy west of Scotland, winter is the season to enjoy the spectacle of eagles in apparently effortless flight.

BEHAVIOUR IN WINTER

In Scotland, the months of October to March embrace the non-breeding and pre-breeding season of the Golden Eagle. Not much has been written about the behaviour of Golden Eagles outside the nesting season. Over the years I have kept a record of all my sightings of Golden Eagles in one west Highland study area. All these observations, with records of a single bird or a mated pair together each counted as a single 'contact' or sighting, amounted to over 1000 contacts.

Individual eagles or pairs seen more than once in a particular day were included as a single record or contact for that day. Most of my sightings lasted less than 10–15 min but some were of birds watched for an hour or more.

For each sighting I kept a note of the birds' behaviour (Table 35). Specifically, I recorded whether eagles used high-level soaring flight (High Soaring), were seen in the undulating display flight which is usually directed at intruding birds (Undulating Display), were observed gathering or carrying nesting material (Nest Building), or were seen to copulate (Mating). Sometimes several of these behaviours were seen during the same contact. Figure 32 shows the changing frequency of these different behaviours over a 12-month period, from the beginning of the 'eagle year' in October. This is about the time when the young fledged in the previous July become independent from their parents, and is also when nest building activity can become more frequent.

Throughout winter in western Scotland, Golden Eagle behaviour is strongly influenced by weather. In anticyclonic conditions there is comparatively little soaring. This is probably because these large birds find difficulty gaining height in the cold, still atmosphere. Then they spend long periods perched on prominent vantage points, often with both birds sitting only a few metres apart. I have few

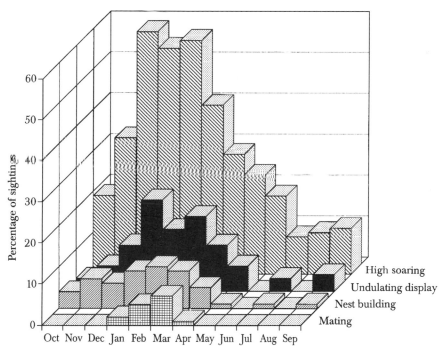

FIG. 32. *The frequency of occurrence of various types of behaviour among Golden Eagles in successive months of the year in western Scotland. All four types of behaviour, High Soaring, Undulating Display, Nest Building and Mating, occurred more frequently during the non-breeding season. Data are from Table 35.*

sightings of eagles on days of low cloud and drizzle but suspect that then they remain on sheltered perches for long spells. On two occasions, I have put up both members of a pair from an overnight roost site when I visited this to check for pellets. Each time it was near midday and there had been continuous rain since before dawn. Before my arrival the birds had probably not moved from their roosting site of the previous night.

High soaring

The bright, blustery conditions that occur after the passage of a depression provide the best opportunities for winter soaring in western Scotland. A typical high soaring flight usually lasts for several minutes (often 15 min or more). Birds gain height quickly with the help of updraughts, or thermals in summer, and then descend in a slow glide over several kilometres before circling upwards once more when they again encounter favourable conditions of lift.

In a unique observation of the high soaring flight of one Wedge-tailed Eagle in Western Australia, the bird was tracked by radar for over 30 min (Brooker 1974). During this time it moved over a horizontal distance of nearly 9 km and covered a vertical range of nearly 700 m. In the dense breeding population of Black Eagles in the Matobo Hills of Zimbabwe, a high soaring 'boundary flight' is used by the birds to delimit hunting territories (Fig. 33). These boundary flights frequently included

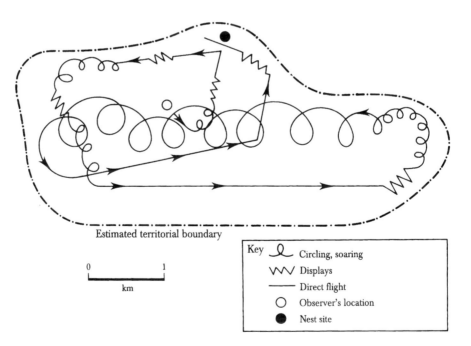

FIG. 33. *Diagram of the flight path of a pair of Black Eagles. The flight lasted less than 30 min and encompassed the entire territory. Note the association between the display flights and territorial boundaries. After Gargett (1990).*

spells of undulating display (Gargett 1990). Clearly, large eagles can use high soaring flight to cover great distances very quickly.

In the small home ranges of Golden Eagles in western Scotland the birds probably fly over the whole of their hunting range many times in a day when conditions are right. As with Black Eagles, high soaring by Golden Eagles probably demonstrates occupancy of the home range. Often, the occurrence of high soaring on one territory is mirrored by birds in a neighbouring range. The behaviour may also be associated with the feeding preference of eagles in western Scotland where carrion is especially important in winter (Chapter 6). By using high soaring flight eagles can quickly see over large parts of their range. From there they can readily detect dead animals, or the feeding behaviour of other scavengers such as Hooded Crows and Ravens that have found a carcass.

High soaring during the breeding season usually involves single eagles. Such flights are less frequent and of shorter duration than in winter. They tend to be used by birds crossing from hunting grounds on one ridge or hillside to those on another. This difference in the nature and incidence of high soaring is consistent with a greater dependence on killed prey which is hunted close to the ground during the breeding period. In Norway, Bergo (1987a) found much less aerial activity by Golden Eagles in autumn/winter compared with the pre-laying period in early spring. This apparent difference with western Scotland may have been because the Norwegian birds were less dependent on carrion and fed more on prey hunted in low-level contouring flight, even in winter. Alternatively, conditions in winter may be less conducive to soaring in the more continental climate of Norway. Aerial activity in the even more continental climate of the Alps is clearly constrained by cold weather. Here, all aerial activity by eagles in winter is restricted to 2–3 h either side of midday when the sun has warmed south-facing slopes (Haller 1982).

Undulating display and aerial chases

The undulating display flight of large eagles is primarily a function of territoriality (Chapter 8). I found that the incidence of this behaviour increased from the autumn and peaked towards the end of the pre-laying period in early spring (Figure 32). Gunnar Bergo (1987a) also found that undulating display was more frequent during the pre-laying period than at other times. In his study this was also the time when intruders appeared most often in the home ranges of established pairs. Undulating display is the most common expression of aggressive behaviour in Golden Eagles. Aggressive chases of intruding birds do also occur and, although rarely documented, these too are likely to be most frequent during the late winter period (see Haller 1982).

Whirling or cartwheeling flight, usually involving two birds locking feet together high above the ground and falling earthwards, has been reported in several large raptors (Simmons & Mendelsohn 1993). It is much more frequent in birds of the genus *Haliaeetus* (African Fish Eagle, Bald Eagle, White-tailed Sea Eagle) than in *Aquila* eagles. It was once thought to be a form of courtship behaviour involving mated pairs, but that interpretation was rejected by Simmons & Mendelsohn (1993). They showed that in over 80% of 107 well-documented cases, whirling flights were aggressive interactions between territorial birds and intruders. I have never seen cartwheeling by Golden Eagles in Scotland. However, it is easy to see that the defensive behaviour of intruders, which can involve the intruder turning over in flight and presenting its talons to the attacker, could lead to aerial cartwheeling if talons were locked.

Most of the published instances of cartwheeling by Golden Eagles have been from North America. Ellis (1979, 1992) saw two cases involving an immature and a territorial adult and another between two males attending a single female. On the latter occasion the two males joined talons and cartwheeled at least 19 times, falling 100 m before they were lost beneath a forest canopy.

Why cartwheeling should be so much less frequent among *Aquila* eagles compared with *Haliaeetus* is not clear. Given the function of the behaviour, differences in territoriality are probably involved. Certainly, some populations of African Fish Eagles and Bald Eagles nest at very high densities close to communal food sources where the frequency of intraspecific contacts, and therefore the probability of aggressive encounters, would be high (Gracelon 1990).

Nest building

Nest building behaviour can occur at any time of the year but in my area in western Scotland it was most frequent from autumn through late winter (see Fig. 32). Usually, material taken to the nest in autumn and early winter comprises the larger sticks which are important for the structure of the nest. Later, during the month or so before egg-laying, a soft lining of wood-rush, purple moor grass, sheep's wool or similar material, is brought in to form the cup.

A study in Japan, using continuous video recording, documented the behaviour of a pair of Golden Eagles at a nest site from November until the following July (Aoyama *et al.* 1988). Some 109 items of nesting material were added to the eyrie over the 95 days prior to egg-laying in mid-February, roughly half by each parent. In the 45-day incubation period 30 items were brought in, 70% by the female, and during the nestling and post-fledging period of 120 days a further 95 items added, 97% of these by the female. The possible reasons why eagles continue to add green plant material to nests during the incubation and nestling periods are discussed in Chapter 13.

Courtship

Specific evidence of courtship behaviour in Golden Eagles is poorly documented in the literature. Undulating display flight by both members of the pair simultaneously in the vicinity of the nest site may have a courtship function, as might high soaring by the pair together. The one clear instance of courtship I witnessed was in February and involved two subadult birds which were establishing themselves in a vacant breeding territory. I watched them from a distance of less than 200 m and for over half an hour. Both birds were initially perched within a few metres of each other on a small rocky hilltop. The smaller male bird then rose into the air carrying a piece of rock (*c.* 10 cm in diameter). He circled up until he was 50 m or so above the ground and then dropped the rock, entered a steep dive and proceeded to catch the rock before it struck the ground. This action was repeated three more times before the female took to the air and joined him. She carried a clod of earth which she dropped and caught in the same fashion as the male. The behaviour was continued by both birds together for about 15 min, interspersed with brief spells when they settled near each other on the ground. The pair eventually left the area when a third (immature) eagle passed overhead. The male pursued the intruder for 400 m or so and finally joined the female in an intense bout of undulating display. Copulation was not observed.

Mike MacGregor has told me of a similar sighting involving a pair of eagles, this time in January, carrying aloft small sticks which were dropped and caught. Similar behaviour involving both inanimate objects and items of prey has been described by Gordon (1955) and Glutz von Blotzheim *et al.* (1971). The use of objects, along with the aerial manoeuvres which characterize this type of behaviour, may give individuals the opportunity to gauge skills which parallel those used in catching prey.

There is a description of similar behaviour by Wedge-tailed Eagles in which one member of a pair was seen over a hill top 'falling aerobatically with closed wings, then stalling, then flying higher and repeating this' (D'Andria 1967). It is possible that the bird was dropping and catching an object that was too small for the observer to see. Both eagles subsequently settled on a hill side and picked up several objects including a stick and a tuft of dry grass, the latter taken from the male by the female in her bill. Some time after this the birds were seen to mate.

That evident courtship behaviour is infrequently seen in large eagles may be because pairs, once formed, remain together for many years. If so, there would normally be little need to assess performance except when a new bond is being formed. The whole question of faithfulness between members of a pair is, however, a poorly known aspect of Golden Eagle biology.

Mating

Copulation is one component of behaviour which may serve to reinforce the pair bond. I have only seen mating between January and April with the majority of instances in the month of March (Fig. 32). It invariably occurred on a prominent rock near the crest of a ridge. On occasions, mating followed a short flight by the male to the female who solicited copulation by adopting a horizontal body posture with wings held slightly open. I have also seen mating when a male dived steeply from a high soaring flight and landed directly on the female's back. Most copulations lasted between 10 and 20 s and were accompanied by a characteristic but quiet whistling call, which is apparently given by the female (described as *Pssa* by Ellis, 1979).

Not all instances of copulation are linked to fertilization. Mating was seen as early as 46 days before egg-laying in a study in Japan (Aoyama *et al.* 1988) and as late as 55 days after laying in a study in the United States (Ellis & Powers 1982). Indeed, in the American study only four of the 21 recorded matings occurred at a time when copulation was necessary for fertilization. These ancillary copulations probably serve a number of purposes, including the maintenance of the pair bond and displacement activity. Ellis & Powers (1982) described an instance of mating attributable to both. On one occasion a female brooding 12–15-day-old chicks

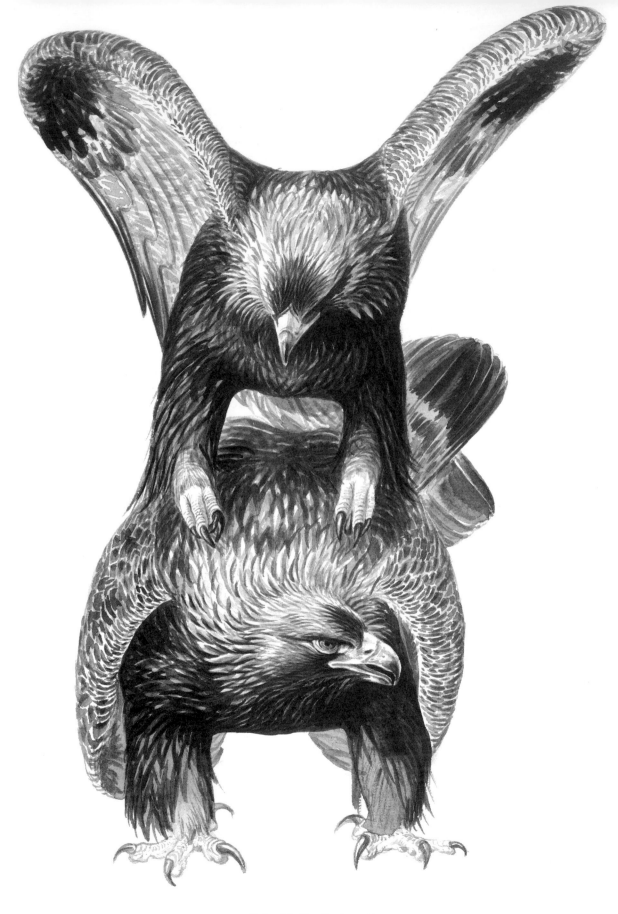

Pair of Golden Eagles mating.

successfully solicited copulation from her mate immediately after he had passed over the nest site in the company of a second large (and probably female) eagle. On another occasion, a hide was built at a nest where the chicks were 18 days old. The female appeared alarmed by the hide and would not immediately return to the nest. Eventually, after one brief nest visit she flew to a rock 400 m from the eyrie where she mated with the male.

Supplementary feeding

The principal purpose of supplementary feeding in raptors during the pre-laying period is to help the female accumulate the body reserves necessary for breeding (Newton 1979). During my studies in Scotland I have never seen male eagles carry food to females prior to egg-laying. This may be the norm as I can find little evidence of supplementary feeding among Golden Eagles anywhere in the literature. However, much of the food in the areas I watched most intensively was carrion in late winter, and this would not normally be lifted by eagles, but rather eaten *in situ*. There is little evidence of supplementary feeding by any of the *Aquila* eagles prior to incubation. It has been reported only occasionally for Black Eagles (Gargett 1990) and rarely in Wedge-tailed Eagles (Marchant & Higgins 1993).

UNUSUAL MATING SYSTEMS

Golden Eagles have generally been assumed to have exclusively monogamous mating systems (Cramp & Simmons 1980). There have, however, been a few documented cases of three eagles on one territory. In Scotland, there were three eagles in an area with two nests, each of which contained two eggs (Dennis 1983). In Swedish Lapland, three different eagles were seen delivering food to one nest (Lalstal 1966). The most closely studied instance of a 'trio' was at a site in western Norway (Bergo 1988). In none of these cases was the sex of all three birds known for certain. The first two authors believed their extra bird was female while the additional bird in Norway was probably male. Bergo knew of another 'trio' of non-breeding eagles in Norway, comprising an adult female and two smaller subadults which he thought were males.

Newton (1979) believed that the occurrence of polygamy in raptors was related to food availability. He argued that polygyny (more than one female) might sometimes occur in particularly rich feeding areas and polyandry (more than one male) in very poor food environments. The evidence from Golden Eagles is still too sparse to draw any conclusions, although Bergo speculated that the probable additional male at two sites in Norway was linked to a poor food supply. However, he was studying eagles in an area where human persecution had ceased and where recolonization of long-abandoned nesting territories had recently occurred. His findings may simply have reflected a relatively unstable period of population adjustment. Nevertheless, his observations are cautionary and argue against the assumption that Golden Eagles are automatically and invariably monogamous. The only other *Aquila* eagles in which three adults have been reported at nests are the Lesser Spotted Eagle and

Wedge-tailed Eagle, and in both species the behaviour was judged to be exceptional (Cramp & Simmons 1980; Marchant & Higgins 1993).

FAITHFULNESS TO MATES

Although convincing evidence from studies of marked birds is not available for any of the *Aquila* eagles, the prevailing view is that all species form long-term pair bonds which probably last for life (Cramp & Simmons 1980; Marchant & Higgins 1993). Such a strategy might be expected among long-lived birds which occupy year-round territories, and where there is a need to gain an intimate knowledge of the hunting range. The costs associated with changing a mate when this involved a change in nesting territory would be high in a stable population where few gaps occurred.

Among the long-distance migrants such as the Steppe Eagle and Lesser Spotted Eagle in which the bond must be re-established each spring, divorce might be expected to occur more often. There is no evidence one way or another for these species but among Ospreys, which are also long-distance migrants, 'divorce' did occur but was comparatively infrequent in a sample of ringed individuals (Poole 1989); just five out of 150 breeding attempts involved birds which had a former mate still living. This faithfulness was attributed to the strength of attachment of both members of the pair to the same site. All the Osprey divorces involved pairs which had failed the previous year, and Alan Poole (1989) believed that divorce was

triggered by females searching for new partners when they received insufficient food from their mates.

Work with radio-tagged Golden Eagles in Idaho may yet contribute information on this subject. In 1992 seven pairs of eagles had one member of the pair radio-tagged. One of the tagged females changed site and mate before the 1993 breeding season. There was a suggestion that this was linked to poor feeding opportunities in her 1992 territory, which was a site where no young had been fledged in the previous 8 years (Marzluff *et al.* 1994). Her mate remained on the original territory and secured a new partner but again failed to breed successfully. The tagged female did breed successfully with her new mate, and her ranging behaviour prior to the divorce had been somewhat unusual. This had involved periodic long-range excursions well beyond her normal hunting area, and one of these had taken her over the neighbouring territory where she finally settled. Clearly in such studies there is a risk that trapping and marking may have affected the bird's behaviour. Nevertheless, it is clear that the excursive behaviour of the tagged female during the preceding autumn and winter could have provided her with information on alternative breeding opportunities. This whole field is one in which long-held assumptions may yet have to be questioned.

SUMMARY

Little is known about Golden Eagle behaviour outside the breeding season. In western Scotland in winter, the most commonly observed behaviour is high soaring flight by members of the pair together. This may serve to advertise occupancy of territories to neighbours and potential intruders, but may also reinforce pair bonds. Eagles in western Scotland probably also use high soaring flight to locate carrion in winter.

The frequency of nest building and undulating display increases during the non-breeding season, both behaviours reaching a peak in late winter. Obvious courtship behaviour among Golden Eagles is rare. Copulation, which can occur several weeks before egg-laying, probably has a courtship function. Prior to egg-laying, no supplementary feeding of females by males was recorded among Golden Eagles in western Scotland.

Golden Eagles are typically monogamous, although there have been rare cases of three birds occupying a breeding territory. It is generally assumed that most large eagles mate for life but there is no convincing evidence for this in the Golden Eagle and more research is needed.

Adult Golden Eagle inspecting a caterpillar.

CHAPTER 12

The Breeding Cycle—Eggs and Incubation

Heavily marked clutch of three Golden Eagle eggs from a nest in a Scots pine in the eastern Highlands of Scotland.

EACH year I get a special thrill when I find my first eagle's nest with eggs. Although the experience generally coincides with the 'lambing snows' of late March or early April, it is a sure sign that warm summer days are not far away. Spring in Scotland's eagle country is a season full of extravagant expectation and unreasonable optimism!

EGGS

When spied from a distance, the off-white eggs in the typical clutch of two look surprisingly small and vulnerable. They are usually oval but sometimes more obviously pointed at one end. Average dimensions of eggs from Scotland are 75 × 59 mm and the weight of a newly laid egg is around 145 g (Table 36). In the closely related Black Eagle, second eggs are smaller and weigh some 10% less than the first

138

laid (Gargett 1990). A similar disparity probably occurs in Golden Eagle clutches. During the course of incubation eggs lose moisture and, consequently, a small amount of weight. Sumner (1929) weighed Golden Eagle eggs at the beginning and near the end of incubation and recorded weight losses of around 10%. In the warmer climate of Zimbabwe the average weight loss in Black Eagle eggs was about 15% (Gargett 1990).

The ground colour of eggs varies from dull-white to pinkish-white, although freshly laid eggs sometimes have a bluish hue which is normally lost early in incubation. (Not always though—my colleague Liz MacDonald once saw a clutch in which one specimen was almost 'duck-egg' blue even after the hen eagle had been sitting for more than a fortnight.) The extent and intensity of any surface marking is extremely variable and can give rise to remarkably beautiful eggs. Many specimens are sparsely and very faintly marked and such 'nearly white' eggs are the norm in my experience throughout much of western Scotland. Strongly marked eggs are heavily stained with amber, vinous-red or mud-brown blotches and streaks. From observations in eastern Scotland, Sandy Payne considered that, in two-egg clutches, the first laid egg was generally the more heavily pigmented.

Stuart Rae believed that heavily patterned eggs were more frequent in eastern Scotland than in the west. This may be related to differences in diet between the two regions, leading to some physiological effect on the hen eagle's ability to release pigmentation as the egg passes through the uterus. Another possible explanation is that heavily patterned eggs are associated with birds which use nest sites in trees—a more frequent occurrence in eastern Scotland. Given the relative conspicuousness of eggs in tree eyries when viewed from above, egg-markings could provide a degree of cryptic coloration and thereby enhanced protection from aerial predators. This hypothesis would presumably imply a genetic basis for the difference between east and west. The early egg-collectors firmly believed that particular females produced eggs in different years with distinctive and individually recognizable markings, so there may well be a genetic basis for egg coloration.

TIMING OF LAYING

Egg-laying occurs in Scotland from the first few days of March to the middle of April. Estimated laying dates were calculated for 111 pairs of eagles followed closely during the 1982 national survey. Known hatching or fledging dates and estimated ages of nestlings were used to calculate back to an indicative laying date placed within successive 5-day periods from 6 March (Fig. 34). This sample is clearly biased in favour of pairs that at least produced nestlings. As such, it probably under-represents the proportion of late-laying pairs which, based on experience in other raptors (Newton 1979), would be expected to fail more frequently. Nevertheless, it is clear that more than two-thirds of Golden Eagles in Scotland in 1982 commenced egg-laying between 16 March and 4 April. From observations in later years, 1982 was a fairly typical year for eagles.

Data from the 1982 survey revealed no significant differences in average laying date from south to north or east to west across the country. I assume that local factors such as differences in the altitude or the aspect of the nest site contribute to

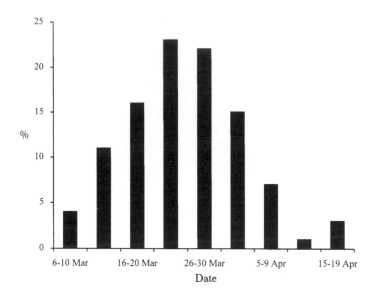

FIG. 34. *The proportion of Golden Eagle nests (n = 111) at which egg-laying began in successive 5-day periods from 6 March. Data are from nests throughout Scotland in 1982.*

variation in timing of laying between pairs in any one region. These could effectively mask any differences which might be anticipated across the country as a whole. This was the case in Sparrowhawks, where the major influence on timing of laying across Britain was altitude (Newton 1986).

For eagles in the west of Scotland I estimated the average laying date based on more than 15 pairs each year over a 10-year period (1982–91). There was a significant relationship between laying date and mean temperature in February (Fig. 35). In years when this month was coldest (1986) laying was around 10 days later than in the warmest years (1989, 1990). Such between-year differences in the average laying date point to an inherent conflict for eagles. On the one hand there is a premium on laying early to maximize the coincidence between the lengthy nestling and post-fledging periods and the availability of increased food during summer. On the other hand there is an evident disadvantage in nesting too early when cold weather could jeopardize the breeding attempt (see Chapter 15). I am aware of several cases of eggs being laid away from nests, usually at or near roost sites, especially in the cold springs of 1983 and 1986. Such behaviour was probably related to cold weather causing birds to eject eggs and abandon breeding for that year.

In their northern hemisphere range Golden Eagles are found nesting across more than 50° of latitude from the mountains of Ethiopia to the edge of the Arctic tundra. Not surprisingly, there is marked variation in the timing of egg-laying across the range (Fig. 36, Table 37). The earliest breeding reported in the published literature is for Oman (20°N) where egg-laying occurs in December. In the most

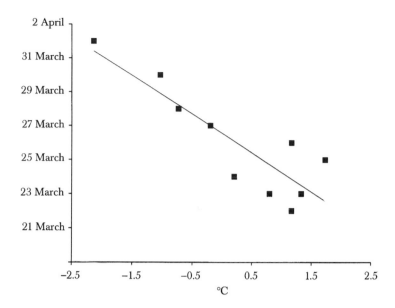

FIG. 35.   *The median laying date for Golden Eagles (n >15 for each year) over 10 years (1982–91) in western Scotland in relation to a temperature index for February. Temperature data were from three weather stations in western Scotland (Onich, Fort Augustus, Cape Wrath). The temperature index was the difference (±°C) between the mean monthly air temperature and the long-term (1951–80) mean temperature for February, averaged for the three weather stations. Laying was significantly later in years when February was colder than average (r = −0.872, P = 0.001).*

northerly populations of Alaska and Siberia (65–70°N) laying does not commence until the first 10 days of May. So, for over 6 months of the year Golden Eagles somewhere on earth will be incubating eggs.

The timing of laying has not yet been determined for the recently discovered population in the Balé Mountains of Ethiopia which are located around 7°N (Clouet & Barrau 1993). A simple projection from Fig. 36 would suggest a laying date in late November. I offer this suggestion as a challenge to some intrepid ornithologist in Africa! Across much of the species' global range the factors influencing laying date are probably similar to those for Scotland. However, in the most southerly localities, rainfall rather than temperature is probably a more important influence on prey availability, which will always be the ultimate determinant of the timing of breeding. Consequently, the relationship between laying date and latitude represented in Fig. 36 may yet break down for Golden Eagles in Ethiopia.

CLUTCH SIZE

In Scotland and continental Europe the commonest clutch size in Golden Eagles is two, with one-egg clutches quite frequent and three-egg clutches comparatively rare

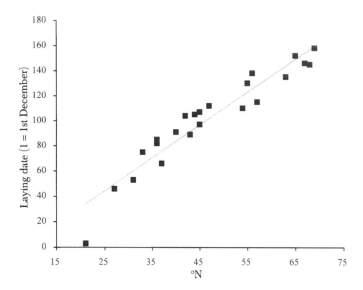

FIG. 36. *The median laying date for Golden Eagles in relation to latitude. Data are from 23 localities in Eurasia and North America. For details see Table 37. The regression equation for the relationship between laying date and latitude is* y = 2.61x − 20.88.

(Table 38). In the United States two-egg clutches are again most frequent but here the incidence of three-egg clutches (>12%) is appreciably higher than in Europe (typically <5%). There have also been exceptional cases of four-egg clutches from the United States (Ray 1928) and one case has been reported from Scotland (Gordon 1955). The tendency for eagles to lay somewhat larger clutches in the United States is almost certainly a product of more abundant food in that country.

Within Scotland the average clutch is significantly larger in the east compared with the west Highlands (Table 39). This is associated with more abundant food, notably Red Grouse and Mountain Hares, on the drier, heather-dominated hills of the east (see Chapter 15). An initially more surprising finding is an apparent reduction in clutch size in Scotland since the middle of the nineteenth century (Table 38). The evidence comes from the large number of clutches taken by egg-collectors between 1840 and 1950 and the contemporary records from Scottish Raptor Groups. Three-egg clutches are now less frequent and one-egg clutches more common. There are several possible reasons for this. It could be that past collectors tended to ignore one-egg clutches, which may have held less intrinsic appeal. However, it is difficult to believe that, having made the demanding hike to an eyrie, a collector would not have taken whatever the nest contained. Another possible explanation is that more clutches were taken from the east Highlands, where contemporary clutches are larger, leading to a biased historical sample. Evidence from the locality descriptions attached to clutches does not, however, support this view. The frequencies of clutches from east and west in the historical collections are not significantly different from the proportions in the post-1970 sample from the Scottish Raptor Group's survey work. It appears likely that there has been a genuine decline and the most probable explanation is a change in food availability.

Evidence for a widespread decline since the nineteenth century in the Golden Eagle's preferred prey, especially in western Scotland, has been well documented (see Chapter 15). In addition, there was widespread depletion of Rabbit populations following the arrival of myxomatosis in the 1950s. I consider a change in food supply as the most credible cause of the reduction in clutch size among Golden Eagles in Scotland. An independent check on this presumed decline in clutch size could be made by comparing egg-size in clutches from different periods. My prediction is that, if the decline in clutch size is genuine and is related to changes in food supply, eggs from the nineteenth century should be larger.

Interestingly a very similar and statistically significant reduction in clutch size was noted among Wedge-tailed Eagles in Australia by Olsen & Marples (1992). They compared average clutches before (pre-1954) and after (post-1953) the effective control of Rabbits by the myxoma virus. Average clutches declined from 1.98 to 1.84 with a significant increase in the frequency of one-egg clutches and a decline in three-egg clutches. They attributed this to the decline of Rabbits, which in much of Australia had become the most important food of Wedge-tailed Eagles. They also found that, in northern Australia where rabbits had always been rare and consequently much less important in the diet of eagles, there was no significant reduction in clutch size between the two periods.

REPLACEMENT CLUTCHES

There is some evidence from early egg-collectors that Golden Eagles will relay if eggs are lost early in the incubation period. Dixon (1937) reported that replacement clutches were produced in California some 28 days after the first. In a sample of over 200 breeding attempts observed in one area of western Scotland I suspected replacement clutches were laid on only two occasions. The incidence of relaying in this poor food area is evidently low but such behaviour might be higher where food is more abundant. The small second 'peak' in egg-laying observed in mid-April 1982 (Fig. 34) may possibly include one or two replacement clutches. As a general rule replacement clutches are produced only rarely by Golden Eagles. This is presumably because, unless the clutch is lost very early, there would not normally be sufficient time to relay and still rear a chick through the lengthy nestling and post-fledging period before food availability declines in late summer.

INCUBATION PERIOD

In the few documented cases in the literature the laying interval between successive eggs in a clutch was between 3 and 5 days (Gordon 1955; Aoyama *et al.* 1988). Incubation normally begins with the first egg, leading to asynchronous hatching and, subsequently, a conspicuous size difference between chicks in a brood early in the nestling period. I was able to measure the duration of incubation at just one

*Hen Golden Eagle incubating her eggs, undeterred by a sudden heavy snow fall in
late March.*

nest, and this lasted 43 days. Other published accounts give a range from 41 to 45
days (Abbott 1924; Gordon 1955; Grier 1973; references in Snow 1973; Aoyama *et al.*
1988). Early North American reports of periods as short as 28–35 days (Bent 1937)
have not been substantiated and should be disregarded.

THE ROLE OF THE ADULTS DURING INCUBATION

There have been few detailed studies of Golden Eagle behaviour during incubation.
The best account is from Idaho where Mike Collopy spent nearly 700 h at 11 nests
during incubation in 1977–79 (Collopy 1984). At 10 of these sites where young

hatched the female incubated for 83% of daylight hours against 14% by the male. Only the female incubated at night. The male relieved the female on average twice a day and for around 50 min on each occasion. The male transferred food to the female at the nest on 17 occasions during the observation period. At the one nest where the eggs did not hatch Collopy observed no food deliveries by the male. This lack of attentiveness meant that the female was frequently foraging for herself and she finally abandoned the nest in the third week of incubation.

In another study in Japan the incubation period at one nest was monitored continuously by video recorder. Here, the female incubated for more than 90% of daylight hours. The male did, however, replace her for short periods on most days (Aoyama *et al.* 1988). Incidence of food provisioning by the male was not reported. At an eyrie in the Lake District in England the incubation behaviour of both adults was documented. Once again the female did the major share, although the male relieved her on most days and accounted for some 6% of the whole incubation period. Only the female sat on the eggs during the hours of darkness (Everett 1981).

In contrast to these studies, Seton Gordon observed one pair over eight breeding seasons and believed that, for this pair at least, the incubation duties were equally shared by both adults (Gordon 1955). He also concluded that food was only rarely brought by the male to the nest during incubation. Most writers have relied on Gordon's account and reiterated that the female is only rarely fed by the male during incubation (Brown & Amadon 1968; Brown 1976; Cramp & Simmons 1980). However, in other *Aquila* eagles food delivery by males during incubation is relatively common—Black Eagle (Gargett 1990), Lesser Spotted Eagle (Meyburg 1973) and Wedge-tailed Eagle (Marchant & Higgins 1993). I believe it is probably Gordon's study that is exceptional and, across much of the Golden Eagle range, the behaviour described by Collopy (1984) is more typical. In places where food in the form of carrion can be located quickly and close by the nest, the need for food delivery by the male may well be less. Such is frequently the case in parts of western Scotland and may be the reason why Gordon witnessed few feeds during incubation. When prey must be actively hunted then either the male must bring food to the eyrie or the female must spend longer away from the nest, with a corresponding increase in the incubation duties of the male. In such circumstances food provisioning by the male would appear to be the Golden Eagle's usual strategy.

FAILURE TO LAY

Most people working on Golden Eagles recognize that an appreciable proportion of pairs do not lay eggs in a given year. It is difficult to be absolutely precise on this because of the possibility that some pairs which appear not to have laid may have lost eggs early during incubation. Nevertheless, there is a consensus that failure to lay is a relatively frequent occurrence. In one west Highland study area during the five years 1982–86 I failed to locate eggs or evidence of egg-laying for 15–35% (average 26%) of pairs each year (Table 40). The great majority of these pairs probably did fail to lay eggs. In a second area in western Scotland the equivalent figures were 17–33% (average 26%) over the same 5-year period. In contrast, suspected non-laying occurred in only 7–20% (average 12%) of pairs in a study area in the eastern Highlands. The incidence of non-laying was therefore higher in areas with poorer food supply. I return to this finding again in Chapter 15.

CLUTCH SIZE IN OTHER *AQUILA* EAGLES

There is minimal variation in clutch size across the genus *Aquila* with two-egg clutches occurring most frequently for all species for which data are available. Raptors, in common with other birds living at low latitudes, tend to have smaller clutches than congeners at higher latitudes (Newton 1979) and the Black Eagle conforms to this trend. I would expect that the clutch for Gurney's Eagle will, when it is eventually found, prove to be small (one or two eggs).

In the larger members of the genus, egg-weight in proportion to female body weight is lower than for smaller species, although in no species is the figure more than about 5% (Fig. 37). Compared with small accipiters and falcons the investment in eggs by *Aquila* eagles is relatively modest and, theoretically, these large eagles could produce more eggs. That they generally do not is principally because of the difficulty the parents would have in providing food for a large brood during the subsequent nestling period. Another limiting factor may be the rate at which females can produce eggs. For all species of *Aquila* there is a gap of some 2–5 days between successive eggs and, in captive Golden Eagles, Grier (1973) estimated that eggs took at least 3 days to pass down the uterus. This, and the commencement of

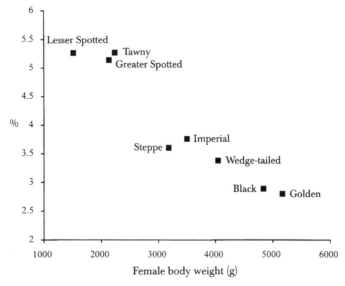

FIG. 37. *The relationship between egg weight as a percentage of femal body weight, and female body weight for eight species of* Aquila *eagles. Eggs of smaller species are larger in proportion to female body size than are eggs of larger species. Data are from Tables 1 and 36.*

incubation with the first laid egg, means that any fourth or fifth egg would produce a chick between 10 and 20 days after the first had hatched. Even with a super-abundant food supply such chicks would be severely disadvantaged in competitive encounters with their older siblings and, consequently, most unlikely to survive.

Only the Imperial Eagle regularly produces clutches of four and sometimes even fledges four chicks. Various factors probably contribute to this fecundity. They are generalized hunters, enabling them to exploit a range of alternative prey depending on availability. They live at comparatively low altitudes and in middle latitudes where equable climatic conditions in spring could allow them to make a proportionately greater investment in egg-production than in simple body maintenance. Thus, they may be able to produce eggs more rapidly than the more northerly or higher altitude nesting Golden Eagles, thereby reducing any subsequent age discrepancy between siblings. In Spain, where most four-egg clutches have been reported, adult Imperial Eagles are essentially sedentary and do not have to combine egg production with the demands of migration and a relatively truncated nesting season, as is the case for Greater and Lesser Spotted Eagles. Finally, and crucially, they live in a landscape with abundant summer food, mainly in the form of Rabbits, and unlike the Black Eagle in Africa they have few other species of diurnal raptor in direct competition for this resource. Thus, I believe they could have more time available for hunting during the nestling period as less time is required to defend their food resource against potential competitors. While field data are not generally available to confirm or deny most of these suggestions, I believe a number could be tested and perhaps ornithologists in Spain or elsewhere will do just that at some future date.

SUMMARY

The usual laying date for Golden Eagles in Scotland is the second half of March. Across the species' world range, laying date is closely related to latitude. Egg-laying occurs in December in southernmost populations and early May in the Arctic. Golden Eagles in western Scotland lay later in years when the mean temperature in February is lower.

Clutch size in Scotland is typically two, with C1 more common than C3. Contemporary clutches in eastern Scotland are larger than those in the west, and there appears to have been a decline in clutch size in western Scotland since the mid-nineteenth century. Clutch size in North America is generally larger than in Europe. All these differences are probably linked to food supply. Typical clutch size in other *Aquila* eagles is broadly similar to Golden Eagles. Large clutches in the Imperial Eagle, including occasional C4, are probably related to food supply.

In western Scotland, the proportion of pairs which fail to lay eggs is higher than in the eastern Highlands and this is consistent with gross differences in food supply between the two areas.

CHAPTER 13
The Breeding Cycle—The Nestling Period

Hen Golden Eagle brooding two chicks less than 8 days old.

THIS chapter describes the physical and behavioural development of Golden Eagle chicks and how parental behaviour changes over the 10–12 weeks of the nestling period. During this time the young eagle is transformed from a hatchling of around 100 g to a fully grown bird of between 3 and 4 kg. It must grow a complete set of feathers with which to insulate itself from the cold and to provide its means of flight. It must also develop and refine the vital behavioural skills required for tearing up prey and feeding itself.

Frequent visits to nests and long watches from hides are essential for gathering detailed information on the nestling period. The best such studies have been carried out in the United States and in continental Europe (e.g. Sumner 1929; Ellis 1979; Collopy 1984, 1986; Mathieu 1985). I have relied heavily on these studies for much of what follows. Given the essentially conservative nature of Golden Eagle breeding biology, much that has been described for the nestling period from other parts of the world will be broadly applicable to eagles in Scotland.

HATCHING

Ellis (1979) describes the complete hatching sequence for a Golden Eagle egg. The chick was first heard calling from inside the egg about 15 h before the egg was pipped. After the first chip there was no further activity by the chick for around 27 h. The eaglet's activity then increased and hatching proceeded more rapidly. The shell was broken through after 35 h, the first tiny wing emerged after 36 h and the chick became completely free from the shell some 37 h after the first chip. However, it is likely that these periods vary somewhat from egg to egg.

GENERAL PHYSICAL DEVELOPMENT OF NESTLINGS

The chronology of physical development in eaglets is shown in Fig. 38 (after Ellis 1979). After an hour or so the damp plumage of the newly hatched chick dries off under the brooding female. When they hatch, chicks are covered with short greyish-white 'pre-pennae' down and this is replaced from about 6 days old by longer, snow-white 'pre-plumulae' down (Brown & Amadon 1968). This becomes fully developed after 15 days when the first greyish down feathers are finally obscured.

The first contour feathers to appear are the primaries (from around 15 days), followed by the secondaries, tail-feathers and scapulars (around 18 days). Body feathers emerge after about 27 days and the last to appear are on the head and throat at 45–50 days. All feathers begin their development within sheaths. The dark feathers

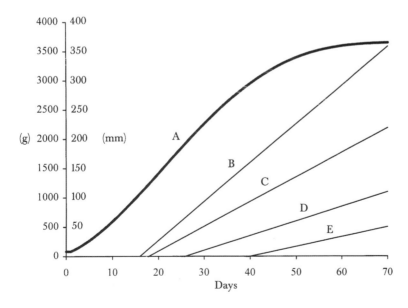

FIG. 38.   *The general chronology of physical development in nestling Golden Eagles. A, Weight; B, growth of primaries; C, growth of secondaries, rectrices and scapulars; D, body contour feathers; E, head and neck contours. Redrawn from Ellis (1979).*

only become obvious after they break out of their sheaths some 10 days after the sheaths first appear. The timing of emergence and growth of these dark feathers can give a useful guide to the age of nestlings during the 25–60 days after hatching. The reliability of plumage criteria for ageing is less certain from about 50 days onwards because plumage changes are then more subtle, and the timing of these can be modified appreciably by the bird's overall condition (Mathieu, 1985). More detail on the plumage changes that occur during the nestling period is given in Table 41.

The chick goes through three broadly distinct plumage phases. Up to about 25 days old it appears entirely down-covered and looks whitish from a distance. Between 25 and 50 days old the dark contour feathers gradually eclipse the white down and for much of this phase the bird has a piebald appearance. The brown feathers grow from the same sockets as the down, and push out the downy feathers which, for a time, adhere to the tips. The last of the down is lost from the head and neck region. From 50 days onwards the bird's body is a uniform dark brown and thereafter plumage changes are less obvious. This is the main growth period for the flight feathers of the wings and tail. Late in this period the plumes on the back of the head become fully developed. These are a beautifully rich auburn colour in nestlings and provide a stunning contrast to the blackish-brown body and flight feathers which have an almost purplish sheen when fresh.

The colour of the eaglet's talons, feet and cere changes during the nestling period. At first the talons are flesh-coloured, turning grey and then black by 4 weeks of age. The off-white or pale yellowish-flesh of the feet at hatching turns to lemon-yellow after 4 weeks and a richer and deeper yellow at 8 weeks old. The bright yellow feet, jet black talons and pale yellow cere enveloping the base of the bird's massive hooked beak, along with the intimidating stare of the bird's hazel-brown eyes, all contribute to a supremely regal appearance. The fully grown youngster is impressive standing sentinel on the edge of the eyrie.

GROWTH OF NESTLINGS AND FOOD CONSUMPTION

As young eagles grow, their weight increases following the sigmoid pattern typical of raptors and altricial birds in general (Ricklefs 1968). The form of the growth curves for male and female nestlings is shown in Fig. 39. This is based mainly on Ellis' (1979) work in the United States, but also shows comparative data for weight changes in two Scottish Golden Eagle chicks reported by Gordon (1955) and MacNally (1964). The principal period of growth in flight feathers occurs later, from around 30 days old to beyond the date of fledging (Ellis 1979).

Young of both sexes increase in weight slowly for about 10 days, then rapidly for around 30 days, then slowly again, reaching their asymptotic body weight at 45–50 days of age. Females are typically 500–600 g heavier than males at this point. Mike Collopy measured the biomass of food consumed by Golden Eagle chicks during successive weeks of the nestling period (Fig. 40; Collopy 1986). Consistent with achieving an ultimately heavier body weight, the peak daily food consumption of females (691 g/day) was appreciably higher than that of males (381 g/day). For both sexes the mean daily food consumption reached a maximum in week 8 and then declined for the final 2 weeks of the nestling period.

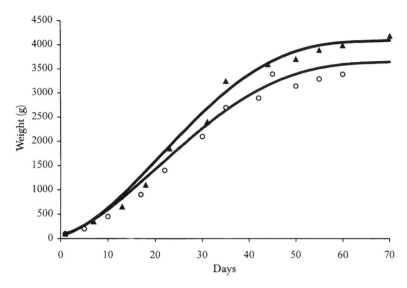

FIG. 39.   *Growth curves of male (lower) and female (upper) nestling Golden Eagles. The lines are after Ellis (1979) and the equation for males is* $y = 50.85 + 27.81x + 3.18x^2 - 0.0671x^3 + 0.0003759x^4$, *and for females is* $y = 76.83 + 17.66x + 4.530x^2 - 0.0949x^3 + 0.0005448x^4$. *Data from two Scottish birds are also shown, a probable male (○) after Gordon (1955) and a probable female (▲) after MacNally (1964).*

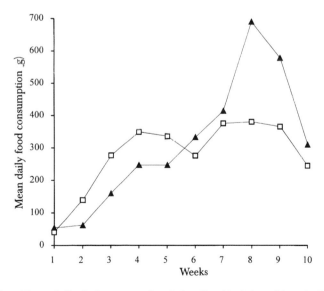

FIG. 40.   *Mean daily food consumption (g/nestling/day) by wild male (□) and female (▲) Golden Eagles (n = 6 for both sexes) during each week of the nestling period. Data are from observations at four nests over 2 years (1978 and 1979) in Idaho. After Collopy (1986).*

BEHAVIOURAL DEVELOPMENT OF NESTLINGS

Behavioural development in the Golden Eagle was studied by David Ellis who watched nestlings at eight eyries in Montana (Ellis 1979). The changing behavioural repertoire he described is summarized below and ethological terms given in quotation marks are those used by Ellis.

Posture and locomotory behaviour

Three distinct body postures, 'lie', 'sit' and 'stand', are used by nestling eagles. Changes in the amount of time spent in each of these with age are linked to the bird's developing locomotory ability. Recent hatchlings are comparatively weak and defenceless and spend almost all their time in the 'lie' position, in which the back is more or less horizontal and the crop is supported by the nest substrate. As chicks become stronger from about 10 days old, they spend more time in the 'sit' position in which the back is 45° or more above the horizontal and the crop is supported on the feet, which are usually closed. Eaglets first begin to 'stand' after about 20 days and here the back is typically 80° or more above the horizontal and the full weight of the bird is supported by the open foot-pad. After about 60 days, 'stand' is the most usual posture adopted by nestlings except during periods of sleep.

Until about 10 days of age, nestlings move rather little around the nest and to do so they 'crawl' using a paddling action with the aid of their wings and feet. 'Walk' behaviour is dependent on the bird's ability to support its weight on the open foot and typically emerges with the achievement of the 'stand' posture from 20 days old. Wing-flapping, which probably serves to strengthen the wing muscles and to develop wing coordination, develops later still. In such 'flap' behaviour the wings are widely spread and beaten up and down with the body held near horizontal and the tail fanned out. This first occurs at about 40 days of age when the flight feathers have grown appreciably. Near the point of fledging 'flap' behaviour increases in frequency and intensity. At this stage birds normally 'flap' facing into the wind and will sometimes use their feet to push themselves momentarily into the air in anticipation of true flight.

Behaviour related to food

For the first 30 days of the nestling period eaglets are entirely dependent on their parents to tear up food brought to them. Thereafter, the chicks become more proficient at standing and begin to develop the coordination and balance needed to hold prey with their talons while pulling off pieces of meat with their bill. By 50 days old food-tearing behaviour is quite accomplished. At around this time young eagles will often adopt a mantling posture in which they stand over their food with their wings partly open, their tail fanned and their head bowed low, the effect being to cover the food completely. Ellis observed 'mantle' behaviour in all but one of the nine eaglets he studied intensively and the exceptional case involved the only eaglet that was raised without a sibling. He concluded that mantling behaviour was a social display directed towards competing siblings and was specifically associated with guarding food.

Eaglets get rid of consumed waste by regurgitating undigested remains as food pellets, and by defecation. Very young birds tend not to cast pellets and this presumably reflects the fact that they receive little indigestible material from the adults. After 20 days or so they consume larger morsels containing fur, feathers and sizable bones. From then onwards chicks regularly produce one or more pellets each day.

Eaglets are strongly motivated to defecate out of the eyrie. Consequently, from day 1 they can squirt waste material several centimetres across the nest cup. Chicks less than 20 days old tend to defecate from the 'lie' or 'sit' posture and are not always successful at ejecting waste much beyond the nest rim. Consequently, nests with chicks up to 3 weeks old typically have an abundance of white splashes around the rim. Once chicks are older and able to defecate from the 'stand' position, they are normally successful at squirting their waste well beyond the nest.

Eight-day-old Golden Eagle chick attacking its younger sibling.

Maintenance behaviour and temperature regulation

From a day or two after hatching young eagles 'preen' themselves with their bill. The frequency of preening sessions increases rapidly after chicks are about 10 days old and reaches a peak at around 50 days. Thereafter, preening subsides to a lower frequency. The changing frequency of 'preen' behaviour is closely related to the emergence of contour feathers and the loss of down. Later in the nestling period body maintenance is also achieved by a characteristic 'foot-scratch' behaviour. The ability to scratch develops later than bill-preening because the former requires the bird first to be able to stand on one leg. Once this has been mastered, at around 40 days of age, the occurrence of foot-scratching increases rapidly before levelling off at around the time of fledging.

Up to 20 days old eaglets are largely dependent on their parents to help regulate their body temperature. During this early period the chicks are brooded by their mother for much of the day or shaded when ambient temperatures are unusually high (see section on *Parental behaviour*). From shortly after hatching, chicks will 'pant' when heat-stressed, and increasingly so as daily temperatures rise and as they are shaded less by their mother. Late in the nestling period the incidence of panting reduces as contour feathers grow and the chick's plumage provides a more effective aid to thermoregulation in all but the hottest weather.

Social behaviour and vocalization

Most aggressive interaction between sibling eaglets involves the use of the bill. Typically, the incidence of 'bill-stab' behaviour is relatively high from hatching until chicks are some 20 days old. In such behaviour the aggressor thrusts its head forward striking its nest-mate with its bill, sometimes with a grabbing and twisting action. Aggressive bill-stabbing by one sibling towards another is usually directed at the head, neck and back of the second, smaller chick and often leads to the death of the victim. This phenomenon, known as cainism, is widespread in large raptors such as eagles and has been the source of much debate. I return to it, and review the various explanations later in this chapter. If both youngsters survive past 20 days or so the incidence of aggressive bill-stabbing decreases and social interactions are more likely to involve non-aggressive nibbling behaviour similar to preening. On occasions they may revert to aggressive bill-stabbing late in the nestling period and particularly if food is then in short supply. In tropical eagles the period of intense sibling aggression is generally longer, being more than 40 days in Wahlberg's Eagle and as much as 70 days in the Black Eagle (R. Simmons *in litt.*; Gargett 1990).

Golden Eagles are rather silent birds, except during the nestling period when chicks call commonly and sometimes with great persistence. Most of such calling has a clear food-begging function and the typical call-note becomes progressively louder and harsher with age. For about the first 10 days chicks give a soft *'chirp'* which merges into a louder, clearly disyllabic *'seeir'* after 15 days. From 25 days the *'seeir'* call gives way to a louder and conspicuously harsher *'psaa'* call. Well-grown nestlings that are extremely hungry tend to give the *'psaa'* call, although the *'seeir'* call is still used on occasions when birds are less hungry. The *'psaa'* call is used by chicks to solicit food well beyond the age of fledging, and Ellis (1979) reported hearing this call from adult females when their mates approached the nest. Quite different from this series of food soliciting calls is the dog-like barking call of adult Golden Eagles. This is analogous to the *'skonk'* call described by Ellis and is rarely used by nestlings. It is chiefly given by adults in situations of threat and alarm, as when a potential predator approaches an occupied nest.

PARENTAL BEHAVIOUR DURING THE NESTLING PERIOD

There is a clear division of labour between adult male and female eagles during the nestling period. Males provide food for the chicks at a more or less constant rate throughout, and take virtually no part in brooding or feeding the chicks on the nest. Females spend long periods brooding or shading chicks for the first 15 days. The amount of brooding time then decreases rapidly and ceases completely at about 40 days. As brooding time by the female decreases, her rate of delivery of food steadily increases.

Brooding/shading behaviour

In Idaho, female eagles averaged around 11% of daylight hours either brooding or shading the young during the nestling period (Collopy 1984). Up to 80% of the day was spent brooding/shading chicks early in the nestling period and this then declined steeply until chicks were about 40 days old, after which they were no longer sheltered (Fig. 41). Similar findings were reported by Ellis (1979) although at one

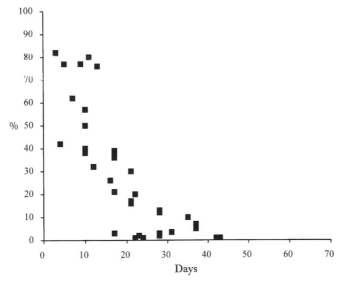

FIG. 41. *Percentage of the day spent brooding and/or shading nestlings by female Golden Eagles in Idaho in relation to the day of chick-rearing. Data are from four nests each in 1978 and 1979. After Collopy (1984). Zero values for brooding and shading after day 25 are not shown.*

of his eyries, which was exposed to the sun for the whole of the late afternoon, the female continued shading until the young were 50 days old. He found that the precise amount of time spent brooding in the early nestling period, especially when chicks were aged 10–19 days, was significantly correlated with windchill values (Fig. 42). Brooding time was longest in the coldest weather when the nestlings were at greatest risk of being chilled. In Collopy's study, female eagles brooded nestlings at night-time until chicks were, on average, 29 days old, and females continued to roost at night on the nest platform until chicks were about 40 days old.

Prey delivery by the parents

Immediately after the chicks hatch, the male increases his frequency of prey deliveries to the nest. Initially, almost all the food is provided by the male, while the rate of delivery by the female increases gradually as the requirement to brood nestlings decreases. In his study in Idaho, Collopy (1984) found that, during the first 2 weeks of brood rearing, over 80% of prey items and more than 90% of the biomass of food was delivered by the male. The contribution by the female reached a maximum during weeks 7–9, when she provided over 40% of the biomass delivered to nests (Table 42). Over the whole nestling period males brought in an average of 1.2 items of food per day and the females 0.6 items. At the peak of provisioning in week 8 the chicks received three items per day, half of these from each parent. There was no significant difference in the mean weight of prey items captured by males and females. The overall increase in biomass of food provided to

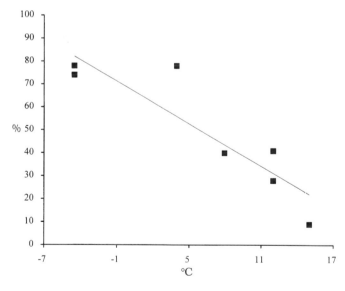

FIG. 42.   *Percentage of time spent brooding nestlings by female Golden Eagles in Montana in relation to wind-chill values (°C). Data are from observations in 1971 and 1972 and are from nests where chicks were aged 10–19 days old. After Ellis (1979). In statistical analysis,* r = −0.901, P <0.02.

the chicks peaked around week 7 to week 8 of brood rearing and was entirely attributable to the increase in the number of prey items brought by the female. During the last 2 weeks of brood rearing the amount of prey delivered to nestlings declined appreciably, a phenomenon reported elsewhere for Golden Eagles (Gordon 1927; Brown 1952, 1953). Leslie Brown speculated that this reduction in food supply, which occurs commonly in raptors, was designed to encourage the youngsters to leave the nest.

Collopy believed that the amount of prey delivered by his eagles in Idaho was comparatively high (on average, 1417 g/day) and it was certainly substantially higher than the 885 g/day delivery rate reported from Texas (Lockhart 1976). This difference resulted from both a greater rate of delivery (1.8 versus 0.9 items/day) and on average heavier prey being caught in the Idaho study (1153 g versus 947 g). Such differences would be expected to lead to measurable differences in fledging success, although no comparable productivity data from the Texas study were available to test this; neither is it clear whether differences in average brood sizes were, in part, responsible for differences in the amount of food provided by adults in the two areas.

Feeding of nestlings

Male eagles take little part in tearing up food and feeding it to nestlings. Up to 4 weeks of age this is done entirely by the female. Typically, during week 5, eaglets become more proficient at standing and are thus better able to tear up food for themselves. From then progressively more of the food consumed by eaglets is self-fed, and less is fed by the mother although she will still occasionally feed chicks as late as week 10 (Fig. 43).

Addition of green plant material to nests

The addition of sprigs of green plant material to the eyrie throughout the nestling period, and sometimes at other seasons, is a feature of many birds of prey and is common in Golden Eagles. At one nest in Japan some 95 items of plant material were brought to the nest during brood rearing (Aoyama *et al.* 1988). Why some but not all raptors do this is unclear. The reasons are probably several but the behaviour tends to occur most in those species that traditionally reuse a small number of nests. One probable explanation is that greenery placed on nests advertises occupancy of the home range or territory (Newton 1979). The fact that Golden Eagles will, at almost any time of the year place green material on several alternative eyries within the home range, tends to support the advertisement hypothesis. Greenery may also serve as an aid to sanitation, covering up debris in an occupied nest. This explanation has been taken a stage further by Wimberger (1984) who postulated that green plant material may help to repel ectoparasites which are vectors for disease. Though untested, this intriguing hypothesis is worth examining. Wimberger (1984) proposed that birds which regularly reuse nests selectively bring in green plant material which contains high levels of aromatic compounds such as mono-terpenes and isoprene. These are known to disrupt olfaction in insects and, he argued, could thereby reduce the levels of infestation by ectoparasites such as dipterans, fleas, ticks and mites.

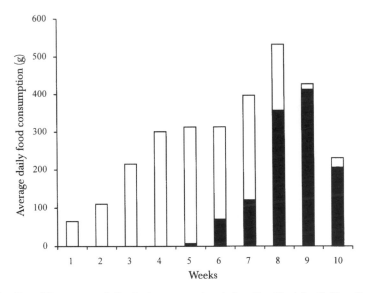

FIG. 43.   *The average daily food consumption (g/nestling/day) by Golden Eagles during successive weeks of the chick-rearing period and the proportion of this which was fed to the chicks by the female (unshaded) and self-fed (shaded) at different stages. Data are from observations in Idaho at four nests each in 1978 and 1979. After Collopy (1984).*

DURATION OF THE NESTLING PERIOD

Several factors make it difficult to be precise about the length of the Golden Eagle nestling period. The asynchronous hatching of chicks means that the precise commencement of the period is often unclear. Late in brood rearing the rate of development of individual chicks and thereby their propensity to fly, is probably quite variable. Environmental factors influencing this include prevailing weather conditions, the amount of food provided by the parents and the degree to which the nestling is subject to human or other disturbance. The sex of the nestling may also be a factor since male chicks in most raptors (and Golden Eagles are unlikely to be an exception) tend to develop more quickly than females and are therefore more likely to fledge earlier (Newton 1979). Also, unless a particular nest is under continuous observation it may not be possible to be sure precisely when a given nestling first leaves the eyrie, especially if after the first flight it then returns for food or roosting.

A range of studies have put the length of the nestling period at between 60 and 80 days (Cramp & Simmons 1980; Palmer 1988). Collopy (1984) believed all nestlings in his study fledged when they were between 66 and 75 days old. My impression from western Scotland, an area with a generally poor food supply, is that few eagles there fledge before they are 70 days old, with the majority taking their first flight between 70 and 80 days old.

Golden Eagle chicks aged 35 to 40 days old.

CAINISM AMONG *AQUILA* EAGLES

The phenomenon of cainism, in which Cain, the first-hatched and larger chick actively contributes to the death of Abel, the younger sibling, is widespread in large eagle species (Gordon 1955; Gargett 1970; Steyn 1973a; Meyburg 1974; Newton 1979). Robert Simmons reviewed cainism or siblicide in large raptors (Simmons

1988). He distinguished between siblicide which occurs as a direct result of food shortage and that which arises when there is an apparent abundance of food at the nest. The former has obvious selective advantages by reducing competition for food, and by increasing the overall condition and the probability of fledging of the surviving chick or chicks. The younger chick dies by aggression, before it otherwise would die from food shortage alone, which reduces the food wasted on a chick that is doomed anyway, and ensures that the survivor gets more food at an earlier age. The widely documented brood reductions caused by sibling aggression in response to food shortage amongst harriers, owls and various other raptors are conspicuous examples of this (Watson 1977; Newton 1979; Baker-Gabb 1982).

In the large *Aquila* eagles, sibling aggression and cainism occur frequently, and perhaps typically, even when there is a plentiful supply of food on the nest. In such cases the most intense sibling aggression, and in consequence the death of the second chick, generally occurs in the first week or two of the nestling period. Experiments with Lesser Spotted Eagles have shown that, by removing one chick from the nest for the early nestling period and then returning it after 3 weeks or so, siblicide can be avoided and the parents are then capable of rearing two chicks to fledging (Meyburg 1974). No food supplements were required to achieve this, indicating that anticipated food shortage and competition for food late in the nestling period could not be invoked as a reason for siblicide; and yet, the incidence of successful fledging of two young naturally by Lesser Spotted Eagles is exceptionally rare (Meyburg 1973). The same is true for Tawny Eagles and Black Eagles in Africa (Tarboton & Allan 1984; Gargett 1990). Despite this, all three species normally lay two eggs, even though there is little prospect of more than one young ever being reared. These eagles fall within Simmons' definition of 'obligate cainists', that is, species where brood size is reduced by 1 in >90% of cases.

Among Golden, Wedge-tailed, Imperial and Greater Spotted Eagles cainism also occurs but is less frequent (Table 43). In some populations of all these species the fledging of more than one eaglet is quite common. Following Simmons' terminology, these are all 'facultative cainists', or species where brood reduction occurs in <90% of cases.

In my view both extremes of cainism can be explained ultimately by food supply (see also Newton 1979). Among Golden Eagles in Scotland the incidence of two chick broods, and thereby the supposition that cainism is less frequent, is highest in the east Highlands where food for eagles in the breeding season is most plentiful (Chapter 15). Even in the western Highlands where Golden Eagles normally rear broods of one from a typical clutch of two, there is considerable variation between areas. For example, the incidence of two chick broods is significantly higher on the island of Skye compared with the immediately adjacent west mainland of Scotland (Table 44). This is readily explained by the much higher number of rabbits and the greater availability of seabird food on the island of Skye (Chapter 4).

The greater frequency of cainism in the poor food areas such as the west of Scotland is explainable even if food early in the nestling period appears to be sufficient to support more than one nestling at that time. It would be advantageous in evolutionary terms for one chick to prevent food reaching its sibling if the costs of doing so were less than the fitness benefits that the chick would obtain by securing a greater amount of food later, and thus fledging at a higher weight and in better condition. The asynchronous hatching of chicks gives a clear size advantage to the first nestling in the early weeks of the brood-rearing period. The greater the size disparity the lower the risk of injury to the dominant chick from any aggressive response made by its subordinate sibling. I believe this initial disparity in size between siblings is an important proximate factor influencing the likelihood of cainism in any particular brood. If this disparity is a reflection of the general condition of the female, and if this in turn is linked to the overall food supply within that eagle's territory, then there is a clear selective advantage in Cain preventing the development of Abel to a point where serious competition for food would arise during the critical growth phase of the late nestling period.

An obvious and testable prediction arising from this explanation is that cainism would be most likely to occur where the gap between hatching, or the difference in weight between eggs in a particular clutch, or both, was greatest (Edwards & Collopy 1983). Other predictions are that if broods were experimentally manipulated so that a nest contained chicks of the same age and weight, then sibling aggression should be reduced because of the potential risk of injury to both chicks. However, under such circumstances, although the parents might ultimately be able to rear both chicks, the fledglings would be lighter and in poorer condition than single chicks raised under otherwise similar conditions.

In general terms, this explanation could, I believe, apply equally to obligate cainists. In these it is rare for two chicks ever to fledge successfully. As a consequence, some authors have questioned why two eggs are laid at all (Brown *et al.* 1977). One explanation proffered is that the second egg provides an insurance against one egg failing to hatch (Meyburg 1974). This is certainly a possibility and may partly, or at least secondarily, explain the retention of the second egg. Simmons (1988) tended to doubt the insurance hypothesis and instead believed that the second egg was retained as a means of exploiting sporadic population instability. In his view obligate cainists could not normally rear more than one chick but had retained the option of rearing two by laying two eggs. The circumstances under which this option could be exercised were, he proposed, likely to arise when populations were reduced below the carrying capacity of the environment. In this case, he argued, reduced competition from conspecifics would make more time available to the parents for brood rearing. In my view this explanation, although it may tell part of the story, is probably too constraining. A depleted population is certainly one case in which breeding eagles may, by spending less time in territorial encounters with neighbours or non-breeders, be able to make the additional investment needed to raise two chicks. Ultimately, this is still the result of greater access to, and more efficient use of, food supply.

Although it was once argued that in some species (notably the Lesser Spotted Eagle) the second chick never survived naturally, this is now known not to be the case. Two-chick broods have been recorded in Slovakia by Belka *et al.* (1990). In terms of fitness, the essential requirement is that nestlings in broods of two are of sufficient quality at fledging to compete effectively with conspecifics from single-chick broods. The infrequency with which obligate cainists are able to achieve this is, I suggest, simply a reflection of greater food-stress among such species during the whole breeding season, including the post-fledging period, when compared with facultative cainists.

The facultative cainists among *Aquila* eagles (Golden, Wedge-tailed, Greater Spotted, Imperial) are all temperate or subtemperate species which are resident or relatively short-range migrants. They live in places where there are marked seasonal fluctuations in climate and hence in available food. Consequently, relative differences in food availability between the breeding and non-breeding season are greater than for species living in tropical or subtropical regions. Among the *Aquila* eagles, two of the three obligate cainists are tropical species (Black and Tawny Eagles). Both have comparatively slow nestling growth rates and long nestling periods compared with similar sized temperate species of *Aquila* (Table 36), which is consistent with the proposition that tropical species experience greater food-stress during the breeding season.

So why should the Lesser Spotted Eagle, which is a temperate breeder, exhibit obligate cainism? The explanation lies, I believe, in the fact that it is a long-distance migrant wintering in southern Africa. Unlike the more sedentary temperate species (Golden, Wedge-tailed, Imperial, and Greater Spotted Eagles) it must breed shortly after completing a migration of several-thousand kilometres (see Chapter 17). The demands of this migration will depress breeding potential, specifically reducing the prospect of rearing two chicks, except when food is unusually abundant immediately on the birds' arrival on their breeding grounds. It also means that the chick has to migrate soon after leaving the nest without the benefit of a several-month dependency period. This is another reason why the chick needs to be as well fed as possible at fledging. On the rare occasions when two chicks are reared, the proximate path leading to this should be similar to that discussed earlier. That is, the female receives sufficient food early in the breeding season to permit her to lay two large eggs comparatively close together. When these hatch the size difference between the chicks is slight, thereby reducing the intensity of sibling aggression. Assuming food resources continue to be abundant through the remainder of the breeding season, two chicks in good condition and with high competitive ability may then fledge.

SUMMARY

Young Golden Eagles spend about 70 days in the nest. They weigh around 100 g at hatching and by 40–50 days old the rate of increase in weight levels off, in males at around 3.5 kg and females at over 4 kg. Most feather growth occurs after about 30 days of age and continues beyond the time young leave the nest. Youngsters are able to stand after about 20 days and begin wing-flapping at around 40 days. For the first 10 days or so they are brooded/shaded by the mother for more than 80% of daylight hours and thereafter brooding declines and ceases after 40 days.

In a study in Idaho, the male parent provided virtually all the food initially but by about 50 days the female provided a nearly equal amount. The maximum food requirement of nestlings occurred around 50–60 days after hatching. At the peak rate of provisioning, the parents delivered an average of three items of prey to nests per day, or about 2 kg of food per day.

The phenomenon of cainism, in which the smaller chick is killed by its larger sibling, is relatively common in Golden Eagles and occurs throughout the genus *Aquila*. The various explanations for the evolution of this apparently anomalous behaviour are discussed.

CHAPTER 14
The Post-fledging Period and Independence

Juvenile Golden Eagle sheltering in a Scots pine tree in heavy rain.

AFTER leaving the nest, the life of the young Golden Eagle changes dramatically. With the achievement of flight, a whole new dimension is added to its experience. In a matter of weeks it must refine its aerial skills and thereafter begin to develop an ability to hunt and kill prey. As winter draws in the young eagle will begin to leave the familiar landscape of its parents' territory and commence a precarious, and frequently nomadic existence that will probably last for several years. Not until it is 4 or 5 years old will it have much prospect of securing a mate and entering the breeding population. I use the term 'post-fledging' to refer to the period after the young have left their nest for the first time. From this point, and during the years before the eagle enters the breeding population, little is known about the Golden Eagle's life.

LEAVING THE NEST

In the fragmented hill landscapes of western Scotland, eagles tend to nest on small crags which often have a few stunted trees close by. Most chicks here make their first move from the eyrie by jumping or hopping onto a nearby ledge, or by scrambling along the nesting cliff with the aid of small trees or bushes. In Cumbria, England, where eagle country is similar to that in western Scotland, chicks in one closely observed territory have been watched leaving the nest in a number of years. In two cases the eaglet flew a short distance from the nest and on another five occasions it jumped or fell off the eyrie (Walker 1987, 1988). Chicks reared on large, unvegetated crags, such as the sea-cliffs of western Scotland, have little option but to leave the nest by flying. In such cases the first flight probably covers several hundred metres.

THE FIRST SIX MONTHS

For the first few weeks after fledging, young eagles generally stay within about 100 m of the nest site. Having found a secure perch, they will spend long periods there and, except when food-calling, are surprisingly inconspicuous. The favoured perch is in a sheltered place such as a wooded ledge or slope and is normally inaccessible to ground predators. Food is brought there by the parents and chicks take to the wing only rarely. When they do, their flights are short and laboured because the flight feathers are still not fully grown (Walker 1987).

Learning to fly

Bahat (1992) described the development of flight behaviour in a young male and female Golden Eagle in the Negev Desert in Israel. Both birds were fitted with radio-transmitters and he was able to locate them regularly, estimating the timing of behavioural changes with some precision. Both his eaglets made only occasional and very short flights during the first 2 weeks out of the nest. The earliest soaring and gliding flight was detected 18 days after fledging. At 26 days a soaring flight lasting 5 min was observed, at 55 days a continuous flight of 14 min was recorded, and by 62 days the young were able to fly continuously for at least 30 min. From around 120 days, continuous flights typically lasted an hour or so and young were spending as much as 50% of their time on the wing. Comparable findings were reported from observations of fledged birds in Cumbria. Here, circling flight first occurred around 20 days after fledging, and young were only able to gain height as proficiently as their parents some 60 days after leaving the nest (Walker 1987).

The post-fledging behaviour of the Spanish Imperial Eagles has been studied using radio-telemetry (Ferrer 1992a). In this species the early development of flight behaviour was similar to that deduced for Golden Eagles from anecdotal information. For example the first soaring flight in young Imperial Eagles occurred, on average, 25 days (range 15–35 days) after fledging (compared with 18–20 days in Golden Eagles). Ferrer also showed that the age at which an individual made its first soaring flight was positively correlated with the physical condition of the young. Young Imperial Eagles that were in better condition made their first soaring flight earlier than did birds in poorer condition (Fig. 44; Ferrer 1993b). Whether or not a similar relationship occurs in Golden Eagles is not known, although it would be expected.

Learning to find food

Bahat (1992) saw the first hunting attempt by his young eagles 68 days after fledging and the last feeding of a juvenile by its parent was 126 days after fledging. This lengthy period of progressive decrease of dependence upon their parents for food reflects the demands on young birds to develop the difficult skills needed for catching live prey. Active hunting of large prey by juveniles in Cumbria was first seen 59 days after fledging, although in this study area carrion was commonly available (Walker 1987). Consequently, juvenile eagles here were able to feed on carcasses as

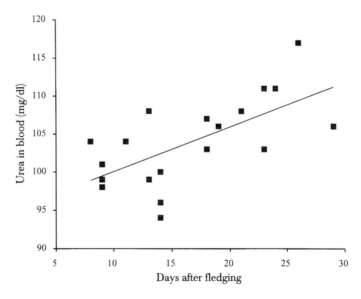

FIG. 44. *The relationship between the level of urea in the blood (mg/dl) at the end of the nestling period, and the number of days after leaving the nest when the first high soaring flight was observed. Data are for 19 Spanish Imperial Eagles fitted with radio-transmitters and followed during the post-fledging period. Birds with high blood concentrations of urea typically will have received less food and be in generally poorer condition (Ferrer* et al. *1987). The young eagles with higher urea levels were significantly later in making their first soaring flight (r = 0.617, P <0.01). After Ferrer (1993b).*

early as 35 days after fledging. In Cumbria, and also in many parts of western Scotland, eagles in their first winter typically have access to abundant supplies of carrion. They probably become independent of their parents for food earlier than in areas where food must be obtained wholly by catching live animals. Consistent with this, Walker (1987) considered that his eagles were largely independent of their parents for food by 75–85 days after fledging.

Development of dispersal behaviour

In Bahat's study in Israel, three distinct stages in the development of dispersal behaviour in post-fledging Golden Eagles were recognizable (Fig. 45; Bahat 1992). Until 60–70 days after fledging the juveniles remained close to their nest sites, they tended to roost in the vicinity of the eyrie and they were then almost entirely dependent on their parents for food. The next stage lasted until 120 days or so post-fledging. In this the youngsters moved 4–5 km away from the nest and spent progressively less time in contact with their parents. Hunting attempts by the young were begun during this period, although for most of this time some food was still provided by the parents. During the third stage, which lasted until 160–180 days post-fledging, the young moved progressively further from the nesting territory and no feeding by the parents was recorded. After this dispersal phase, the young male settled some 12 km and the young female some 28 km from the nest site. Both birds then spent their first winter in these newly adopted home ranges. Reflecting on the

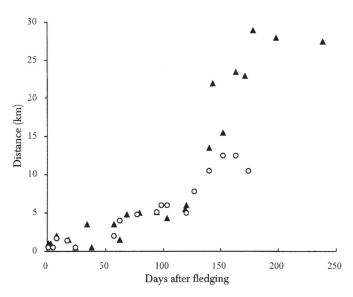

FIG. 45. *Maximum recorded distances (km) of two young Golden Eagles—one male (○), one female (▲)—from the nest site on different days during the post-fledging period. Data are from birds fitted with radio-transmitters in the Negev Desert, Israel. After Bahat (1992).*

comments made earlier on the availability of carrion in Cumbria, the observations of Walker (1987) point to a somewhat earlier dispersal phase in that region compared with the Negev.

Factors affecting the timing of dispersal

In my experience there is little evidence of aggression between adult Golden Eagles and their own young. Young appear not to be driven out by their parents but may be encouraged to leave as parental feeding rates decline (see also Walker 1987). What factors then trigger the dispersal of the young? Walker (1988) explained the unusually early departure of one chick from the parental territory in 1986 on the grounds that food supply that year was poor. In his view, early dispersal was linked to food shortage and the need for the chick to hunt for itself. The fact that the juvenile eagle in 1986 was seen feeding on carrion much earlier and for longer periods than in previous years was, he believed, further support for this hypothesis. It is possible, however, that the opportunity to feed on a ready source of carrion may have enhanced the condition of this chick. If indeed this was the case such improved condition could have encouraged an earlier departure date.

The conclusions from work on the Spanish Imperial Eagle would suggest that the latter interpretation is the more likely. Using radio-telemetry, Miguel Ferrer was able to follow the dispersal of young Imperial Eagles and to correlate the timing of this with the condition of the birds at fledging. He found that the better the condition at fledging the sooner birds were likely to leave the parental territory (Ferrer 1992b). The driving force behind this was, he suggested, the intense competition which would be experienced by independent young for the best feeding areas, placing a premium on early dispersal. According to this hypothesis, dominant chicks should disperse as soon as possible, giving them access to the best feeding areas before these become occupied. Birds in poorer condition should, in contrast, stay longer in the natal area to improve their condition because they would be likely to end up in poorer quality habitat after dispersal. Whether or not a similar situation exists for the Golden Eagle is unknown.

FROM SIX MONTHS TO ADULTHOOD

The life of the Golden Eagle from its first winter to its fourth or fifth summer is still largely a mystery. Some work has been carried out in Switzerland using eagles fitted with radio-transmitters (Haller 1994). Between 6 months and 2 years of age these birds showed widespread dispersal, with some individuals ranging over 12–16 000 km^2. Amongst older immature birds (2+ years) the ranges were much smaller, at around 2–4000 km^2 (Fig. 46). The existence of these two phases of dispersal is further supported by the recoveries of Golden Eagles ringed as nestlings in Switzerland. Here, the birds found dead when aged less than 2 years ranged between 200 and 1000 km from their place of birth, whilst all recoveries of birds more than 2 years old were within 120 km of the natal territory (Haller 1994).

Immature Golden Eagle in flight over the Quiraing on the Island of Skye.

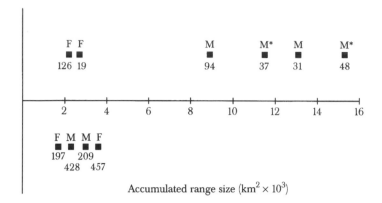

FIG. 46. *The accumulated ranges (minimum area polygon) of non-territorial Golden Eagles monitored by radio-tracking in Switzerland. Birds above the line were aged between 9 months and 2 years and birds below the line were more than 2 years old. Numbers refer to the number of days when radio contact was made and stars refer to birds monitored by satellite telemetry. M = male, F = female. After Haller (1994).*

Steenhof *et al.* (1984) reported dispersal distances for juvenile and immature eagles ringed in Idaho. Here, most birds moved less than 100 km from their place of birth, although occasional birds travelled more than 1000 km. In this study a few marked birds were subsequently found breeding 4 years or more after marking. The known distances between hatching site and subsequent breeding area ranged from 7 to 65 km, again revealing a tendency for older birds to return to the vicinity of their natal area. In the Wedge-tailed Eagle in Australia a similar dispersal pattern has been recorded involving comparatively long-range movements, followed by return to the natal area as birds approach breeding age (Ridpath & Brooker 1986b).

The post-fledging period in the Golden Eagle, and probably in other non-migratory populations of *Aquila* eagles, is characterized by an initial exploratory and nomadic phase followed by a return to the vicinity of the natal territory. In the earlier part of this period the bird's behaviour is driven more by the need to locate reliable sources of food and less by the requirement to secure a mate and enter the breeding population. As the bird matures it will, assuming it survives the early years, become a more proficient hunter and a more effective competitor for a space in the breeding population. By returning to an area close to its place of birth the eagle presumably enhances its prospects of securing a mate and a breeding territory.

PLUMAGE DEVELOPMENT AND AGE OF FIRST BREEDING

The juvenile plumage of the Golden Eagle is quite distinct from that of the adult. The tail feathers are white for about two-thirds of their length and this contrasts sharply with a broad blackish terminal band. In many juveniles the bases of the inner primaries and the outer secondaries are also white, giving a conspicuous white crescent mark on the centre of the wing, especially when viewed from below. During the first moult, which begins in the spring of the year after birth, some of the juvenile feathers are replaced. This next set of 'immature' wing and tail feathers may have less white than the juvenile feathers but the tail in particular still retains a substantial amount. Only after immature Golden Eagles have completed a further moult, and this is not normally achieved before the fifth or sixth summer, is the full adult plumage attained (for a more comprehensive account of moult see Chapter 16).

Delayed acquisition of adult plumage is typically associated with deferred breeding in birds (see Newton 1979 for examples among raptors). Golden Eagles conform to this, with the incidence of breeding by birds in subadult plumage being exceptional (Watson 1957; Teresa 1980). In most cases the age of first breeding in Golden Eagles is probably at least 4 years or older. Steenhof *et al.* (1984) knew of six eagles which were marked as nestlings and were subsequently found in the breeding population. The average age of these birds when first detected as breeders was not less than 4.7 years (range 4–7 years).

The function of distinctive subadult plumage in Golden Eagles is discussed by Steenhof *et al.* (1983). The characteristic plumage of juvenile Golden Eagles may act as a signal to adult territorial eagles. To the adults it identifies the intruder as an inexperienced bird unlikely to compete for a mate or a breeding site. Furthermore, by mimicking juveniles through the retention of distinctive white markings in the plumage, older immature birds may reduce the level of aggressiveness displayed to them by territorial adults.

Occasionally, eagles in immature plumage do attempt to breed, and they can sometimes nest successfully (Bates 1973; Teresa 1980). Golden Eagles are evidently physiologically capable of breeding earlier than the age at which they normally enter the breeding population. Newton (1979) proposed that subadult breeding could occur either when food was especially abundant, or when the adult population was artificially depleted by human persecution. In Scotland, the incidence of breeding by subadult Golden Eagles is frequent only in areas where human persecution is severe (Watson *et al.* 1989). This is consistent with the view that subadults are normally excluded from breeding by territorial adults.

Further support for this explanation was provided by Steenhof *et al.* (1983). They found that the incidence of subadult breeding varied between 0 and 13% during a 12-year study in Idaho (Table 45). The frequency of subadult nesting was not correlated with food abundance, nor with the density of subadult eagles in the previous winter. However, it was related to the density of adult eagles in the preceding winter, the incidence of subadult breeding being highest in years following winters with low densities of adults. Steenhof *et al.* concluded that territorial vacancies were most often filled by subadults when non-territorial adults were not available. Conversely, when adult populations were high, then birds in adult plumage were more likely to fill slots than were subadults. They also found that subadults occurred in certain territories significantly more often than in others. These were typically sites where human activity was greatest. They concluded that higher turnover rates, due to either increased emigration or mortality, and attributable to human disturbance, were resulting in increased mate replacement and thereby a greater opportunity for subadult nesting.

SUMMARY

Rather little information is available on the life of the Golden Eagle after it leaves the nest. Flight skills develop after several weeks but hunting skills take longer to master, and it may be several months before birds are able to catch and kill sufficient prey to feed themselves. When available, carrion may be an important source of food at this time. Most young eagles are probably independent of their parents by 4 months old. The factors influencing the nature and timing of dispersal in Golden Eagles are unknown. In a study of Spanish Imperial Eagles, the individuals which left their natal territory first were those birds that were in best condition at the point of fledging.

Golden Eagles do not breed until they are at least 4 or 5 years old. During the early non-breeding years they range widely but later probably return nearer to their place of birth. Breeding by birds in subadult plumage does occur, principally when the adult population is depressed as a result of human persecution.

CHAPTER 15
Breeding Performance

Golden Eagle nestlings aged about 20 days old.

THIS chapter deals with the reproductive success of Golden Eagles and explores the reasons why some pairs breed consistently more successfully than others. The classic evolutionary imperative facing all species is the need to contribute as many offspring as possible to the next generation of breeders. For birds such as large eagles which do not normally breed until they are several years old, it is all but impossible to know just how many offspring produced by a particular pair survive long enough to breed. The most widely used and attainable measure of productivity is therefore the average number of young fledged per territorial pair per year. In this context I use the term fledging to mean the point at which young leave the nest.

In collecting such information for comparison between years or between different study areas there are several sources of potential bias. It is especially important that observations cover the whole of the breeding season so as not to miss those pairs that fail early or do not nest at all. In most areas Golden Eagle

173

populations are quite stable and numbers of territorial pairs do not fluctuate appreciably between years. By getting to know all the traditional breeding territories in a given area, and by checking these sufficiently frequently and on a consistent basis, the potential bias resulting from incomplete recording of non-breeding or of breeding failure should be minimized (Postupalsky 1974; Steenhof 1987).

My own systematic work on Golden Eagle breeding performance in Scotland began in the early 1980s and continues today. During the early years, work was done jointly with Stuart Rae. Our findings have been greatly enhanced by access to information gathered over the years by members of the Scottish Raptor Study Groups. Because of the widely dispersed nature of Golden Eagle breeding pairs and the rugged terrain in which they live, it would be almost impossible to gather statistically adequate data on breeding performance without the help of these immensely dedicated, voluntary fieldworkers. I am greatly indebted to all the members of the Raptor Groups for allowing me to use their hard-won information in the various analyses which follow. While aircraft or helicopters have been used to facilitate the monitoring of the breeding of Golden Eagles in the United States (Boeker 1970; Hickman 1972), in Scotland we will probably always be dependent on people who are prepared to make 'the long walk in'.

Newton (1979) provided powerful evidence that, in the absence of human factors, the breeding rate of most raptors varies in response to food supply. Human influences which can depress breeding rate independent of food supply may operate indirectly as in the case of pesticides, or directly through the killing of adults or the destruction of the nest contents. The effects of pesticides and persecution on Golden Eagles are dealt with in Chapter 19.

INFLUENCE OF FOOD ON BREEDING PERFORMANCE

Although generally convincing, most of the evidence linking breeding performance with food supply in raptors tends to be circumstantial. It has relied typically on correlations between annual fluctuations in breeding success and food supply, or on area differences in breeding performance related to area differences in prey. Both types of study require the use of a standardized and repeatable measure of food availability. A number of published accounts have reported Golden Eagle breeding success in different parts of Scotland (Sandeman 1957; Brown 1969; Everett 1971; Watson *et al.* 1989). Because no information on food was collected, in none of these was it possible to relate variations in breeding success, from year to year or from area to area, to annual and spatial variations in food supply. Seeking to fill this gap, Stuart Rae and I measured breeding success across a variety of study areas in which we also obtained a measure of the relative abundance of food. The study areas were the same as those used for the work on nesting density (Chapter 9) and the assessment of food was made by counting prey along line transects (see Appendix 4).

Between-area differences in food and breeding success

The measure of breeding success we used was the number of young fledged per occupied breeding territory per year. These data were gathered for six study areas

(A–F, Fig. 6) over 4 years (1982–85) and for a further three areas (G–I, Fig. 6) in 1985 only. Line transects were walked to obtain an index of food abundance for each area (Appendix 4).

There was a significant positive correlation between breeding success and gross differences in the amounts of the principal summer prey species (live prey) which are usually killed and not scavenged by eagles (Table 46; Fig. 47). The highest breeding success occurred in the east Highlands where heather moorland is still abundant, and where both Red Grouse and Mountain Hares are plentiful. The geologically and biologically richer parts of the western Highlands (the Inner Hebrides and the southwest Highlands) still have quite good numbers of Rabbits and/or Mountain Hares. Breeding success here was broadly comparable with the east Highlands. The poorest success consistently occurred in the wet, acid and overgrazed parts of the west-central and northwest Highlands where heather moorland is scarce. Here Red Grouse and Mountain Hares are scarce and alternative live prey are few.

Our study identified the east Highlands as the area with much the highest numbers of live prey, specifically Red Grouse and Mountain Hares. And yet the breeding performance of eagles here was not conspicuously better than in the best western areas, even though food in the latter was apparently less plentiful. There are several possible explanations for this. The breeding performance in the east Highlands may have been somewhat suppressed by human persecution (Sandeman 1957; Watson *et al.* 1989). Although we tried to select areas where we believed illicit persecution was

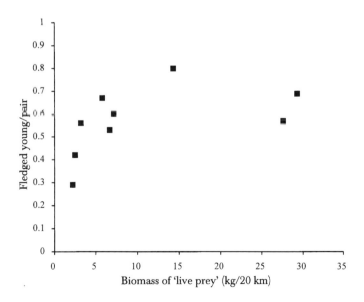

FIG. 47.   *Relationship between Golden Eagle breeding success and the live prey index (see Appendix 4 for details) for nine study areas in Scotland in 1985. Breeding success was higher where more live prey such as grouse and hares were detected on line transects. In statistical analysis, r,= 0.767, P <0.05. After Watson et al. (1992b).*

low, it is still likely that some deliberate destruction of nests by people occurred within our east Highland study areas where much of the land is managed as grouse moor (see Chapter 19). It is possible that there is an upper limit beyond which increased food supply has little effect on eagle breeding performance. The latter seems unlikely in the context of our Scottish study since the breeding performance of Golden Eagles in parts of the western United States is frequently appreciably better than that achieved in eastern Scotland (McGahan 1968; Kochert 1980).

For three areas in Scotland, comparable data on breeding performance are available for an 8- or 10-year period from 1982 (Table 47). These were collected from the east Highland study area (H), the island of Skye (A) and the west Highland mainland (F). They represent, respectively, an eastern region with a rich food supply, a western locality with a moderately rich food supply, and a western area with a poor food supply. The average breeding success (around 0.8 young fledged/pair/year) was highest in the east Highlands, intermediate in Skye (0.6 young/pair/year) and lowest in the west Highland mainland area (0.3 young/pair/year). Fledging success was low in the latter area, partly because more pairs did not even attempt to breed, but also because more breeding attempts failed completely in the poor food area (Fig. 48). The average brood size in successful nests was also lower in the poor western food area, with significantly fewer broods of two fledged in this area than in Skye (Table 44).

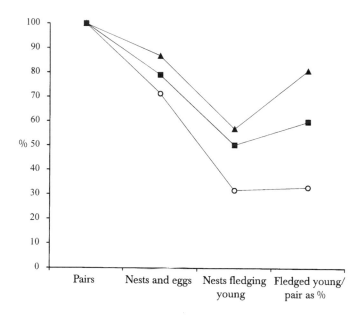

FIG. 48. *Three measures of breeding success (percentage of pairs laying eggs, percentage of pairs fledging young and mean young/territorial pair converted to per cent) for Golden Eagles in three study areas in Scotland. Data for areas A (■) and F (○) were averaged over a 10-year period (1982–91) and for area H (▲) over an 8-year period (1982–89). For details see Table 47. Food in summer was most abundant in area H, intermediate in area A and least abundant in area F.*

Few other studies of Golden Eagles have measured variation in breeding performance in different areas while at the same time providing a measure of food supply. However, in the closely related Black Eagle, Gargett (1977) found that breeding success was significantly higher (0.56 young/pair/year versus 0.28 young/pair.year) in areas where the bird's favoured food of hyrax was more plentiful. In her study the difference in performance between areas was mainly attributable to the higher incidence of non-breeding among pairs in the poor food area (66%) compared with the better food area (24%). Rather more studies, including several involving Golden Eagles, have investigated the relationship between breeding performance and between-year variations in food supply. These are discussed next.

Between-year differences in food and breeding success

In our Scottish study, the run of consecutive years for which a measure of food supply was obtained was too few to permit an assessment of any relationship between breeding success and food supply over time. Such a relationship has been found in Sweden and in the United States. Martin Tjernberg recorded Golden Eagle breeding success in two Swedish regions over six years (1975-80). He related this to an index of food abundance derived from hunting bag statistics supplied by the Swedish Sportsmen's Association (Tjernberg 1983b). In his northern study area a significant positive correlation was found between eagle breeding performance and the total hunting bag (Fig. 49). In southern Sweden, except for one year

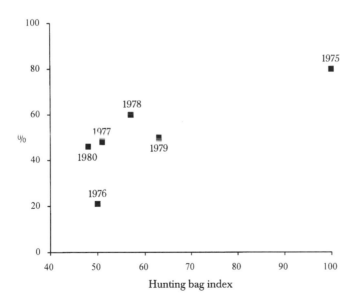

FIG. 49.   *The relationship between the proportion of Golden Eagle pairs that bred successfully (fledged at least one young) and the total hunting bag (grouse spp. and Mountain Hares) in the previous winter in northern Sweden. The hunting bag figure for 1974–75 was set to 100. In statistical analysis the relationship is significant ($r_s = 0.886$, P <0.05). After Tjernberg (1983b).*

(1977), the relationship was similar (Fig. 50). In 1977 his eagles were more successful than the hunting bag statistic would have predicted. He pointed out that weather in the spring of 1977 was unusually mild, leading to reduced snow depth and greater accessibility of prey. The milder weather may also have lessened the daily energy demands on female eagles, making it easier for them to put on weight and to produce eggs.

The best example of a link between Golden Eagle breeding performance and food supply in different years appears in work from the western United States. Here, eagles feed predominantly on the Black-tailed Jackrabbit, a species which follows an approximately 10-year cycle of abundance. Murphy (1975) provided anecdotal evidence of a link between performance and jackrabbit numbers over the period 1967–73 in central Utah. The average number of young reared by 16 pairs of eagles rose from 0.56 in 1967 to a peak of 1.06 in 1969, and declined to 0.31 by 1973 (Table 48). Although there were no quantitative data on jackrabbit numbers, Murphy's subjective assessment was that numbers were moderate in 1967, reached a peak in 1969 and fell to exceptionally low levels by 1973.

A long-term study of Golden Eagles at Snake River, Idaho, has recorded breeding success through two complete 10-year jackrabbit cycles (M. Kochert and K. Steenhof *pers. comm.*). During the period of peak jackrabbit numbers in the late 1970s and early 1980s eagle success was high, with up to 100% of pairs attempting to breed and a successful fledging rate in excess of one chick per pair per year. As jackrabbit

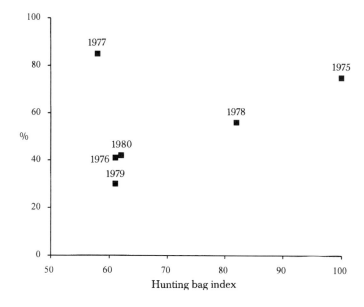

FIG. 50.   *The relationship between the proportion of Golden Eagle pairs that bred successfully (fledged at least one young) and the total hunting bag (grouse* spp. *and Mountain Hares) in the previous winter in southern Sweden. The hunting bag figure for 1974/75 was set to 100. The relationship is not significant and breeding success in 1977 was higher than would have been predicted by the food available (as indicated by the hunting bag index). See text for discussion. After Tjernberg (1983b).*

numbers crashed in the mid-1980s, eagle fledging success dropped to around 0.2 chicks per pair. By 1990 jackrabbit numbers had recovered and so too did Golden Eagle productivity.

The peak in jackrabbit numbers detected in Idaho in the early 1980s evidently occurred quite widely elsewhere in the western United States. Jenkins & Joseph (1984) believed that this was the reason for the unusually high frequency of 'triplets', or eagle nests fledging three chicks, in various western states in 1981. Their analysis also revealed a second case of an unusually high incidence of three-chick broods in 1971, which coincided with the previous peak in jackrabbit abundance in that region (Arnell 1971). Golden Eagle breeding performance in the western United States is clearly closely related to the fluctuating numbers of its principal prey species.

Breeding success in response to major changes in prey numbers

One further piece of evidence linking breeding success with food supply comes from Spain. Here, the disease viral haemorrhagic pneumonia (VHP) has recently arrived from China and is causing large-scale mortality in Rabbit populations in Mediterranean regions (Fernández 1993a). Rabbits are a staple food of Golden Eagles throughout much of Spain. Carmelo Fernández has documented eagle breeding success in Navarra, northern Spain since 1982. VHP reached his study area in late 1989, with a consequent widespread reduction in the Rabbit population. Between 1982 and 1989 the average breeding success in his Golden Eagles was 0.77 chicks per pair, and during 1990 to 1992 it was 0.38 chicks per pair (Table 49; Fig. 51). The breeding parameter most affected by the reduction in Rabbit numbers was the proportion of pairs that failed to lay eggs. The average number of chicks reared from successful nests did not decline and this Fernández attributed to the greater availability of sick Rabbits in spring when the VHP virus is most virulent. The long-term consequences of these changes in food supply for Golden Eagles in the Mediterranean region remain to be seen.

Another extreme example of changing food supply affecting breeding is the case of the Steppe Eagle reported by Agafanov *et al.* (1957). This has already been referred to on p. 116 as it related to effects on breeding density. When migrating Steppe Eagles returned to their nesting grounds on the Russian steppes in spring 1955, they encountered exceptional amounts of food in the form of dead and dying Saiga Antelopes which had been shot by hunters. As well as settling to breed at higher than usual densities, the Steppe Eagles laid unusually large clutches (Table 50). Of 101 clutches recorded, ten were of four eggs and two were of five. This is the only case I know of 5-egg clutches being laid by an *Aquila* eagle. Undoubtedly, the birds were responding to the extraordinary abundance of food. Although the subsequent breeding performance of the birds that year was not precisely documented, there was widespread breeding failure during the nestling stage. This was because the abundant food supply of early spring was not sustained as Saiga Antelopes were no longer being killed. Furthermore, the Steppe Eagles' usual prey of ground squirrels were not especially plentiful later in the season and the eagles were therefore unable to rear the very large broods which the early food glut had triggered.

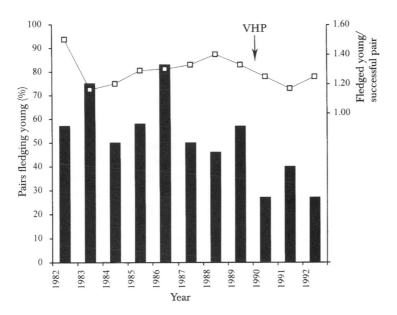

FIG. 51.   *Two measures of breeding success (percentage of pairs that bred successfully, and mean number of young/successful pair) of Golden Eagles over an 11-year period in Navarra, northern Spain. The proportion of pairs breeding successfully dropped appreciably in the years following the arrival of the VHP virus in 1989 (see text for further details). The virus killed large numbers of rabbits, the eagles' preferred prey in that region. Data are from Table 49, and after Fernández (1993a).*

WEATHER EFFECTS ON BREEDING SUCCESS

Extreme weather conditions can occasionally affect breeding success in Golden Eagles independent of food supply. In Scotland, exceptionally late and heavy snowfalls probably cause a few pairs to abandon nests with eggs in some years. An exceptional case of breeding failure caused by bad weather was reported from a study in Montana (Phillips *et al.* 1990). In that instance 71% (10 out of 14) of nests containing chicks failed shortly after a 3-day blizzard in late April 1984. At the other climatic extreme the deaths of a number of eaglets in Idaho were attributed to overheating (Beecham & Kochert 1975). Here, the young that died from heat-stress were in nests most exposed to the sun at the hottest time of day. Such reductions in breeding success directly attributable to weather are comparatively rare in Golden Eagles. Rather more frequent are examples of the indirect effect of weather acting through its effect on food supply.

In western Scotland, at least part of the between-year variation in breeding success is probably linked to weather, and the influence of weather on food and the eagles' hunting ability; weather conditions just before breeding are especially

Adult Golden Eagle landing on a nest with a chick.

important. One initially surprising finding from my own work is that breeding success in two different study areas tended to fluctuate in parallel (Fig. 52). Breeding success on the island of Skye (area A) was invariably better than on the adjacent mainland of western Scotland (area F), reflecting consistent differences in overall food supply. In addition to this, however, years with good breeding success on Skye also tended to be relatively good breeding years on the mainland (Fig. 53). This was despite the fact that the diet of the eagles in the two areas was different (see Chapter 7). Because the areas are close together and therefore likely to be subject to similar weather, I believe that weather factors may have contributed to the synchrony in breeding success between the two areas. This is supported by an analysis of breeding success in relation to mean temperature over the month just prior to breeding. In western Scotland, in years when the average temperature in February was colder, breeding performance was poorer than in years with milder weather at that time (Fig. 54).

Isolating the effects of different weather conditions on breeding success is difficult because of the number of potential weather variables involved (temperature, snow-cover, rainfall, wind, etc.). Furthermore, several of these variables are not independent of one another. By monitoring the breeding performance of a large number of pairs over many years it should be possible to identify the more important correlations between weather and breeding performance. The causal factors behind the relationship between cold weather and breeding performance in western Scotland are not known but there are probably several. In cold weather the energy demands on females will be higher, leading

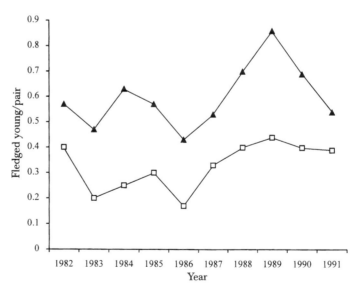

FIG. 52.   *Fluctuations in the average number of young fledged/territorial pair of Golden Eagles in two study areas—A (▲) and F (□)—in western Scotland over a 10-year period (1982–1991). Data are from Table 47. Although breeding success in area F was consistently poorer than area A, fluctuations between years occurred in parallel (see Fig. 53).*

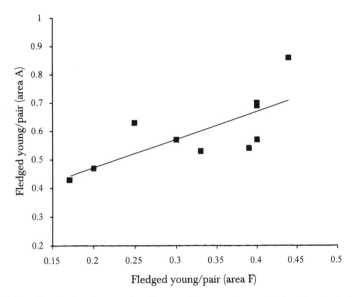

FIG. 53. *Correlation between breeding performance (young fledged/territorial pair) in two study areas in western Scotland over a 10-year period (1982–1991). The correlation is significant (r = 0.737, P <0.02). Data are from Table 47.*

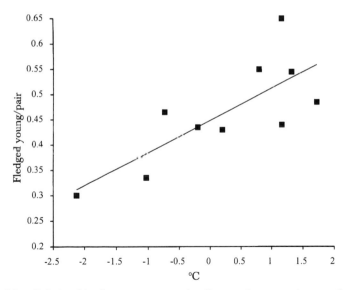

FIG. 54. *Relationship between average breeding performance (young fledged/ territorial pair/year) in two study areas (A and F) in western Scotland over 10 years (1982–91), and the temperature index for February. Temperature data were from three weather stations in western Scotland (Onich, Fort Augustus, Cape Wrath). The temperature index was the difference (±°C) between the mean monthly air temperature and the long-term (1951–80) mean temperature for February, averaged for the three weather stations. Breeding success was significantly less in years when the temperature in February was lower than the long-term average (r = 0.771, P <0.01).*

potentially to greater investment in simple body maintenance at the expense of egg production, or the accumulation of reserves in advance of the lengthy incubation period. Prey may also be less abundant directly as a result of lower temperatures, or prey may be less available if hunting conditions are then poorer for eagles. Some evidence for weather conditions reducing hunting efficiency is found in a study of Golden Eagles during the nestling period in Japan (Aoyama *et al.* 1988). Here, adult eagles feeding nestlings at one closely monitored site brought in significantly fewer prey items on days of rain and snow than on fine days (Table 51).

Several other studies have identified a link between weather and breeding success in Golden Eagles. K. Steenhof & M. N. Kochert (*in litt.*) believed that winter weather in Idaho had a modifying influence on the underlying effect of jackrabbit numbers on breeding success. Specifically, in years with cold winter temperatures and above average snowfall, the subsequent eagle breeding performance was less than would be predicted simply by jackrabbit densities. In years with mild winter weather the reverse was true. A comparable finding was made by Clouet (1981) who studied Golden Eagles in the French Pyrénées. In his study, breeding success was poorest when weather in April was worst, his measure of bad weather being the number of days of snow, rain and strong winds (Clouet 1981). In both these studies, poor weather probably affected the eagle's hunting efficiency and may also have increased the energy demands for simple body maintenance, leaving less available for breeding.

A rather different example comes from Israel where rainfall rather than temperature is the most important climatic variable influencing the eagle's food supply. Bahat & Mendelssohn (1996) found that, in the dry landscapes of the Judean and Negev deserts, rainfall in the year prior to nesting was positively correlated with the number of young fledged by eagles. The mechanism they proposed was as follows. In these arid regions the quantity of rainfall had a direct effect on plant growth, which subsequently resulted in increased breeding among herbivores such as Brown Hares and Chukars; these are the principal prey of eagles. The effect on eagle breeding success occurred in the year immediately following a year of above average rainfall. An exception to this occurred in the Eilat Mountains of southern Israel where the eagle's breeding success was not correlated with the preceding year's rainfall. This was as expected, however, because the main food of eagles at Eilat is the Spiny-tailed Lizard, the numbers of which are much less affected by the previous year's rain than are the numbers of bird and mammalian herbivores.

Another case of weather affecting breeding has been reported for the Spanish Imperial Eagle in the Coto Doñana, Spain (Calderón *et al.* 1987). They showed that hatching success of eggs was positively correlated with the average minimum temperature in March. In the coldest years hatching success was as low as 30% and in the warmest years it was over 60% (Fig. 55). The precise causal link is not clear, but again, in cold springs the energy demands on the female would be greater, possibly resulting in her having to hunt more and consequently spend less time incubating the eggs. As a result, the risk of desertion of eggs or of chilling and subsequent mortality of the eggs would be greater. This is, I believe, another instance of weather influencing breeding through its effect on food.

In the tropics, rainfall is a more important climatic variable than temperature.

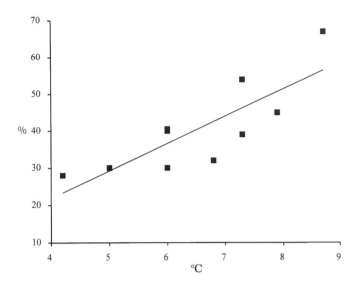

FIG. 55.   *Relationship between the hatching rate of eggs of Spanish Imperial Eagles at Coto Doñana and the average minimum temperature in the month of March. Data are for a 10-year period. Hatching rate was significantly lower when March temperatures were colder (r = 0.816, P <0.005). After Calderón et al. (1987).*

Not surprisingly, there is evidence for an effect of rainfall on breeding in both the *Aquila* eagles which breed in central and southern Africa. Gargett (1977) found that the proportion of Black Eagles that attempted to breed was negatively correlated with total annual rainfall: in the wetter years the frequency of breeding attempts was lower (Fig. 56). The link is probably again through the effect of rainfall on food supply, although direct evidence from her study was lacking. Extrapolating from Gargett's work, Newton (1979) proposed that the above average rainfall would have resulted in greater growth of plants, leading to improved cover for the hyraxes, which were the eagle's favoured prey. As a result hunting would be more difficult for the eagles and breeding success thus reduced.

A not dissimilar but rather more complicated finding was made by Hustler & Howells (1986) working on Tawny Eagles in Zimbabwe. They looked at breeding over the 11 years from 1973 to 1984. This coincided with a comparatively dry period from 1973–78 and a much wetter period from 1979–84. During the wet period breeding success was lower in years with higher rainfall, but in the dry period breeding success increased with increasing rainfall (Fig. 57). They had no measure of food abundance which might have clarified this relationship. One likely explanation is that, in a generally dry period, increasing rainfall would tend to result in more abundant prey, and hence better breeding in eagles. However, over a sequence of wetter years, increasing rainfall could ultimately result in the growth of vegetation leading to reduced availability of prey as cover increased and, consequently, to poorer breeding performance among eagles.

In summary, Golden Eagle breeding performance varies considerably between areas, and between years in the same area. Much of this variation can be accounted

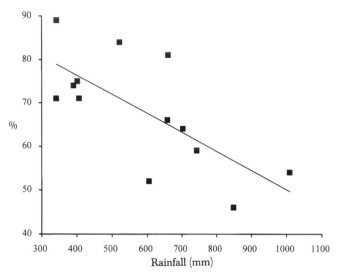

FIG. 56.   *Relationship between the proportion of Black Eagles breeding in a study area in Zimbabwe and the annual rainfall in the previous 12 months. Data are for 13 years. More pairs attempted breeding after years when rainfall was below average (r = −0.707, P <0.01). After Gargett (1977).*

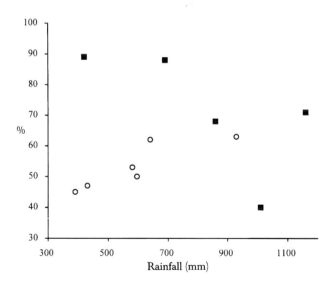

FIG. 57.   *Relationship between the proportion of Tawny Eagles breeding in a study in Zimbabwe, and the annual rainfall in the previous year. Over a series of years with above average rainfall (■, 1973–78) the relationship was negative but not significant (r$_s$ =−0.700, NS); over a series of years when rainfall was below average (○, 1979–84) the relationship was positive and significant (r$_s$ = 0.943, P <0.01). See text for discussion. After Hustler & Howells (1986).*

for by differences in food supply. Weather conditions early in the breeding season or in the previous winter can have an additional effect on breeding performance, moderating the direct link between breeding success and food supply.

DISEASE AND PARASITISM AMONG NESTLINGS

There is little published information on disease or parasitism leading to death in Golden Eagle chicks. This is probably, in part, because affected individuals rarely survive for long and are quickly removed from the nest or eaten by siblings after death. As pointed out by Newton (1979), parasites or disease probably act mainly as contributory factors in the death of chicks which have already been weakened by starvation. In other words, food shortage is usually the ultimate cause even where the proximate cause of death can be attributed to disease.

From autopsies of 10 recently dead fledgling eagles, Beecham & Kochert (1975) found that four had died of trichomoniasis, a disease caused by parasitic protozoa. Keith Brockie (*in litt.*) found an emaciated 9-week old eaglet at an eyrie in the east Highlands of Scotland. This bird subsequently died and post mortem analysis ascribed death to capillariasis, a disease caused by an infestation of nematode worms. In this case the chick may have ingested prey infected with capillaria eggs which were then released into the eaglet's gut. There was an apparent abundance of food on the eyrie at the time the chick was discovered, although this may have accumulated after the nestling became too ill to feed itself.

Ellis (1979) reported weight-loss and retarded growth in two eaglets at a nest which was heavily infested with larvae of the dermestid beetle *Dermestes* spp. Both chicks ultimately regained weight after the infestation ended but fledged at substantially lower than the normal weight for their sex. Among infectious diseases, there have been occasional records of Golden Eagles with avian pox, tuberculosis and the fungal disease aspergillosis (Waterston 1959; Kochert 1972; Moffat 1972).

Cases of abnormal development in young Golden Eagles have been described by Bouche (1989) from the French Alps and mentioned by Walker (1988). In the latter, two young eagles which fledged in Cumbria during the 1980s had deformed bills and these birds presumably had little prospect of surviving beyond independence. The French eagle failed to develop any contour feathers on its body and wings. The juvenile feathers of the head did emerge but the rest of the body remained covered in white down even when the chick was, by mid-August, at least 10 weeks old. The causes of such abnormalities are unknown but genetic factors may have been involved.

NATURAL PREDATION AS A CAUSE OF BREEDING FAILURE

Their large size, predatory habits and secure nesting places ensure that Golden Eagles are not usually subject to natural predation at nest sites. A few clutches may be taken by corvids, but this probably occurs mainly after the eggs have been abandoned. The likelihood of predation during incubation will be greater if food is scarce and the female has to spend periods off the nest hunting for herself.

Similarly, any predation of small nestlings would tend to occur only if the nest was left unattended for long periods. So, as with disease, mortality caused by predation would normally be linked ultimately to food shortage. While most Golden Eagle eyries are inaccessible to the majority of mammalian predators, many in Scotland are potentially vulnerable to predation by Pine Martens and Wild Cats, and some could be visited by Foxes. Having said this, I am unaware of any convincing evidence of predation of eggs or nestlings of Golden Eagles by any of these species in Scotland. In northern Eurasia and North America there are other potential mammalian predators; because of its size and climbing ability, the Wolverine probably poses the greatest threat to nesting eagles.

Among some of the other *Aquila* eagles, natural predation of the nest contents is possibly more frequent. Meyburg *et al.* (1995b) reported the killing by an Eagle Owl of a juvenile Greater Spotted Eagle at or near the eyrie. Tropical eagle species may also be more vulnerable to natural predation, notably by monkeys and large snakes. Gargett (1990) attributed the death of at least one Black Eagle chick to Baboons, and suspected that Rock Pythons may have taken the occasional nestling from other sites. However, it appears likely that natural predation of nests amongst all *Aquila* eagles is an extremely rare event.

SOCIAL BEHAVIOUR AND BREEDING PERFORMANCE

It has been suggested that social interactions between neighbouring territorial eagles, or between the nesting pair and non-breeding birds, can lead to reduced breeding success. Haller (1982) used this argument to explain variation in Golden Eagle breeding success in the Swiss Alps. He reported that contemporary breeding success in the High Alps was appreciably less than in the early part of this century. The principal difference between these two periods was the density of eagles, with many fewer territorial pairs and non-breeders in the past as a result of human persecution. He went on to propose that the lower breeding success which occurred now was a consequence of the greater frequency of territorial encounters between eagles, leaving less time available for the demands of nesting. He also observed that breeding success in recently recolonized areas of the Low Alps was better than in the High Alps. He argued that breeding density, and consequently territorial activity, in the Low Alps was again less than in the High Alps. This was partly because not all suitable nesting habitat in the Low Alps had yet been occupied by eagles.

While Haller's (1982) findings appear consistent with the hypothesis that territorial interference can reduce breeding success, he has not discounted another possible explanation. The same result could have arisen if, historically, the eagles that 'hung on' in the High Alps had done so on the best quality feeding areas and were therefore a biased historical sample in terms of breeding success. This would seem intuitively likely. Furthermore, the rather better success amongst birds which have recolonized the Low Alps could again be related to food supply rather than reduced territorial interference. It appears at least possible that food supply could be better in the lower alpine region where climatic conditions would be more favourable. The extirpation of the Golden Eagle from this part of the Alps is known to have been a direct consequence of human persecution. These areas, being closest to human habitation, would have lost their eagles first, independent of the fact that they may have provided a better food supply. Just such a situation occurred with Red Kites in Britain, where the species survived in Wales following extinction elsewhere as a result of human persecution. This was despite the fact that the bird's food supply in Wales is much poorer than in many parts of its previous range (Davis & Newton 1981; Evans & Pienkowski 1991).

Work on the Spanish Imperial Eagle further stresses the need for caution in interpreting the effects of social behaviour on breeding success (Ferrer 1993a). In the Coto Doñana there has been a marked decline in mean breeding performance as the population of Imperial Eagles has recovered following the cessation of human persecution. Initially, this appeared to support the hypothesis that a denser population of birds, leading to more frequent social interactions, was depressing breeding success. On closer inspection this proved not to be the case. The reason why overall breeding success declined was because new colonists were settling in poorer quality areas and consequently breeding less successfully. There was no significant decline in breeding success in territories that were occupied from the start of the period of population recovery. Even more powerful evidence rejecting the 'territorial interference' hypothesis comes from observations on the frequency of intrusions by immatures into adult territories. In Doñana it was found that most intrusions occurred in the territories with the highest average productivity (Fig. 58). This is precisely the opposite of what would be expected on the 'territorial interference' hypothesis. It is, however, consistent with an explanation based on food supply. Both breeding success among territorial eagles and the attractiveness

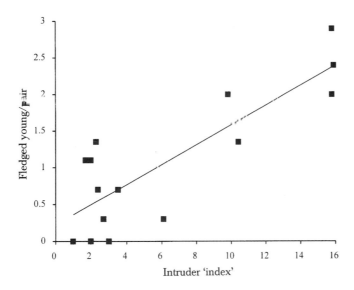

FIG. 58. *Relationship between the average breeding success (young fledged/pair) of Spanish Imperial Eagles at Coto Doñana and the frequency of intrusions by non-breeding eagles recorded at each territory. Breeding success was highest at territories where the frequency of intrusions was also highest (r = 0.836, P <0.001). After Ferrer (1993a).*

of an area to non-breeding eagles, leading to more frequent intrusions into adult territories, would be expected to be highest where food was most abundant.

Evidence in support of territorial activity affecting breeding success in eagles would seem, at best, to be equivocal. In natural selection terms there is no particular reason why it should not occur, especially where breeding density is close to the carrying capacity of the environment and when the number of non-breeding eagles in a population is high. Both these conditions would be more likely in the tropics where food supply typically fluctuates less than in temperate regions. Gargett (1975) believed that in the Black Eagles of the Matobo Hills, persistent intrusions by an unmated adult into an established territory had an adverse effect on breeding success. African Fish Eagles in Uganda also had reduced breeding success in places where nesting density was highest (Thiollay & Meyer 1978).

BREEDING SUCCESS IN GOLDEN EAGLES IN DIFFERENT PARTS OF THE WORLD

One of the problems of trying to understand the reasons for differences in breeding performance in Golden Eagles in various parts of the world is the lack of comparable information on food supply from different localities. Although many studies around the globe have reported breeding success, comparative data on food availability was not generally collected. Nevertheless, there are some general trends which would appear to merit further consideration. For example, evidence in the literature suggests that Golden Eagles in the United States typically breed more successfully than in Scotland (Table 52). Is this a reflection of a rather better food supply in much of the bird's range in the United States?

My examination of the literature has revealed a large amount of information on the diet of Golden Eagles from a range of studies in North America and continental Europe (see Chapter 6). In some of these, data were also available for breeding success. One of the few parameters which can be used to describe the food of eagles from many different parts of the world is the breadth of the feeding niche (see Appendix 3). Given that this measure is available from a large number of eagle studies, it would be instructive to pose the question 'do Golden Eagles breed more successfully when their diet is broad and generalized or narrow and specialized?' My prediction is that they should be more successful where they can concentrate on hunting one or two prey species which lie in the bird's optimal size range. Where such animals are abundant, then the breadth of the diet should be relatively narrow and breeding success correspondingly higher.

In Chapter 6 I showed that feeding niche breadth was typically narrow in North America, broader over much of continental Europe and broader still in much of Scotland, especially in the west. Across the world range of the Golden Eagle there are four 'families' of prey animals which tend to be favoured, at least during the breeding season. These are the rabbits and hares *Leporidae*, squirrels and marmots *Sciuridae*, grouse *Tetraonidae*, and pheasants *Phasianidae*. Where the proportion of one or more of these families in the diet is high then dietary breadth tends to be low and, conversely, where these families comprise little of the diet, then feeding niche

Immature Golden Eagle (aged about 24 months) mantling a recently killed Mountain Hare.

breadth is broad (Fig. 9; Chapter 6). The implication is that, when these prey are available and abundant, they are eaten in preference; otherwise Golden Eagles subsist on anything they can get.

Data on breeding success were available for some 24 studies for which information on diet was also available (Table 52). Among these, there was a significant negative correlation between breeding success and trophic diversity. Where Golden Eagles had a narrow feeding niche comprising suitable-sized items, they tended to breed more successfully than where the feeding niche was broad (Fig. 59). This finding is consistent with my earlier prediction.

The need for an individual eagle constantly to modify and adapt its hunting behaviour in order to catch a diverse range of prey may result in reduced hunting efficiency. This could be one reason why eagles which exhibit a broader feeding niche tend to breed less successfully than those with a narrow diet. Also, if eagles are forced to generalize across taxa it appears likely that they would have to catch food in a wider range of size classes. This would again lead to hunting inefficiencies, particularly if many very small or very large items had to be taken to nestlings. The evidence would appear to suggest that where eagles can specialize on one or two types of prey in the optimal size range, then breeding success is likely to be high. I do not propose that feeding niche breadth *per se* is necessarily a measure of the quality of food resources available to Golden Eagles in any particular area.

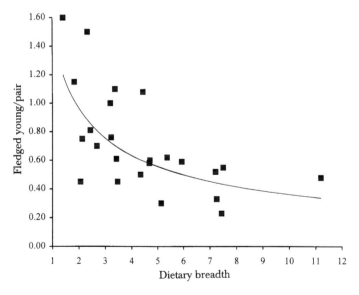

FIG. 59.   *Relationships between breeding success (fledged young/territorial pair) of Golden Eagles from 24 studies in various parts of the world, and breadth of the feeding niche (see Appendix 3) for eagles in the same studies. Data are from Table 52. Where the feeding niche is narrow and Golden Eagles are specialist hunters they breed more successfully than where they are food generalists (equation:* $y = 1.472x^{-0.606}$, $r = -0.660$, $P < 0.001$).

Nevertheless it does appear to offer a useful approximation of 'habitat quality' and, as such, a potentially valuable way of contrasting the overall condition of eagle habitats in widely differing parts of the world.

SUMMARY

Golden Eagles in the east Highlands of Scotland fledge more chicks per pair per year than on the west mainland. This is related to differences in food supply, and specifically to the higher densities of Red Grouse and Mountain Hares in the east. Fledging rate on the island of Skye is intermediate and is substantially higher than on the adjacent west mainland. This is attributable to the high numbers of Rabbits on Skye. Breeding performance in the east Highlands is probably below its full potential because of illicit persecution. In the absence of persecution, food supply (especially the numbers of grouse and lagomorphs which are the preferred source of live prey among eagles in Scotland) is the primary factor influencing breeding performance. Similar relationships between eagle breeding performance and food supply have been found in several studies in continental Europe and the United States.

Poor weather, especially in late winter/early spring can have a secondary effect on breeding performance. In western Scotland, breeding success is lower in years when weather was colder in February, the month just prior to egg-laying. Mortality factors such as disease, parasitism and natural predation have been found only rarely in nestling eagles. Evidence that social interactions between territorial eagles and intruders can depress breeding success is equivocal. In one study of Spanish Imperial Eagles there was clearly no such effect.

CHAPTER 16
Moult

Close-up of worn and fresh feathers in the wing-coverts of an adult Golden Eagle.

AMONG the general clutter of eagle memorabilia in my 'garden shed' where this book is being written, I have a box full of moulted flight feathers. These have been gathered over the years, mainly during late-summer searches of roosting sites or from the debris of abandoned nests. The size and strength of the larger primary and tail-feathers never ceases to impress me. They are certainly a source of great wonder for children, who have never experienced Golden Eagles at close quarters. For many of these young people, my box of feathers is often the only actual contact they are likely to have with this impressive bird of prey.

Close examination of a large primary feather, which may be half a metre or more in length, confirms the sheer investment in feather growth by eagles. As in most large birds of prey, Golden Eagles do not have a complete annual moult. Instead, they shed and replace a proportion of feathers each year, and some of the larger flight feathers can be retained for up to 3 years. Because of their less than straightforward and lengthy moulting arrangement, this aspect of Golden Eagle biology has been difficult to study. The first detailed description was given by Jollie (1947) and this is still the most complete work on the subject. For much of what follows I have relied heavily on Jollie's paper. The birds he studied were from the North American race *canadensis* and some of his conclusions may not apply to the nominate *chrysaetos* of western Europe. However, many of his general findings probably hold true.

Some deductions on moult, specifically on the changing pattern of plumage with age, have been made by Tjernberg (1988) working in Sweden on the nominate *chrysaetos.* His conclusions on the age determination of Golden Eagles using plumage characteristics are rather different from those of Jollie. I suspect that this is unconnected with the fact that different races of Golden Eagles were involved in the two studies. Rather, I believe that Tjernberg's study benefited from a larger sample of eagles than was available to Jollie.

TIMING OF MOULT

The period of moult in Golden Eagles begins in March or April each year and continues through to September or October. Moulting normally ceases during the winter. Presumably, the energy demands on the bird in cold winter weather, as well as the need to retain a more or less complete set of flight feathers for hunting in this difficult season, are the reasons why this happens.

Malcolm Jollie observed the moult of a captive eagle during the second and third summer of its life. In the second summer, the moult began in early March and stopped at the end of August. In the third summer it occurred a little later, commencing in late March and continuing through to September. From examination of museum specimens of adult eagles, which typically would have had to combine moult with breeding duties, Jollie concluded that these birds began moulting somewhat later still, and continued moulting even later in the season. From his captive eagle, Jollie collected all the moulted feathers and these amounted to about 1850 in the second summer and 2600 in the third summer. In both years the bulk of feathers were shed between May and July, with peak numbers in the latter month. The suspension of moult for the winter period occurred in the captive individual and the same phenomenon was evident among museum specimens of birds of various different ages (Jollie 1947). He examined 24 eagles collected during the period November to February and none showed evidence of active moult.

The timing of moult in Scotland appears to be broadly similar to that found by Jollie in the United States. I have found freshly moulted flight feathers at roost sites most often between June and September, although a few feathers were collected in most months throughout the winter (Fig. 60). Therefore, in some individual eagles in Scotland, moult may continue through the winter period. Perhaps the abundance of carrion available to these birds at this time, and their reduced dependence on hunting active prey, means that they do not invariably suspend moult in winter.

PATTERN OF FEATHER MOULT

The complete replacement of plumage in Golden Eagles is achieved in not less than two seasons and may often take longer. Moult of the contour feathers begins on the head and neck region, and proceeds along feather tracts in a general anterior–posterior direction. In the first moulting season most feather tracts on the dorsal surface are replaced and there is patchy replacement of contour feathers in ventral regions. In the second season these ventral tracts are moulted but feathers of the head, neck, back and scapulars may be moulted again and are perhaps replaced annually. In any particular feather tract, individual plumes are sometimes missed and if so, these are then picked up in the next moulting season.

The pattern of moult of the large feathers of the wings and tail (the remiges and rectrices) either follows an ordered, linear sequence or commences in several places at once (Fig. 61). In the primaries, moult in the first season begins with the innermost feather and proceeds outwards in a relatively straightforward manner known as 'descendant' moult. Three or four of the outermost primaries are not lost

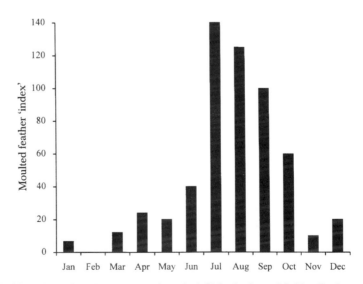

FIG. 60.   *An index of occurrence of moulted flight feathers of Golden Eagles at roost sites in Scotland in different months of the year. The index is the ratio of the number of flight feathers located at roost sites divided by the number of visits to roost sites made each month. Data are from accumulated roost visits over an 8-year period in the 1980s.*

until the second moulting season when some of the innermost primaries may again be replaced. Consequently, some primaries are replaced each year and others every two years.

In the secondaries, the pattern of moult is more complicated and usually begins in several different places at once. In Jollie's captive bird there were three recognizable centres where moult began during the first season. In the second moulting season, moult of the secondaries typically continued from where it stopped in the previous year, but even by the end of the second season not all secondaries were replaced. Eagles from their second moulting season onwards normally have at least three ages of secondary feathers. The tail-feathers are shed with no clearly discernible pattern, although the two central feathers are normally the first to be replaced. In any one season as many as two-thirds of the 12 tail feathers are replaced, leading to some being moulted annually and others every 2 years.

Compared with the secondaries, the primary and tail-feathers are replaced more frequently. Jollie surmised that this was because the latter were more prone to damage or wear and that, for the purpose of flight, maintaining the condition of the primary and tail-feathers was more important. The patterns of moult he described for the remiges and rectrices in the first and second season, based on observations on a single captive individual, were comparatively straightforward. He noted, however, that in adult eagles the picture tended to become progressively more confused. This is especially so when individual feathers in a particular series are missed from time to time.

PLUMAGE CHANGES WITH AGE

This is a subject over which there has been some confusion in the literature. One view was given by Jollie (1947), based on detailed observations of plumage changes in a captive individual, and supported by examination of museum specimens of known aged birds. A different view was given by Martin Tjernberg from work on known individual eagles which were observed over a number of years in Sweden (Tjernberg 1988).

Jollie believed that there was a general decrease in the extent of white, at least on the tail feathers, in individual birds during successive moults. In his captive individual this appeared to be the case; his view that tail feathers became gradually darker with age was also reinforced by evidence from museum skins. From these he again detected variation in the extent of white in the feathers with age. He concluded that, for a selection of individual eagles of different ages, typical tail feathers had the greatest extent of white in the juvenile plumage (<12 months old), reduced amounts of white in immatures (1–2 years old), and less still in subadults (2–3 years old). The first adult plumage was, he believed, achieved during the third season of moult (birds >4 years old). Because he did not follow the moult of his captive bird through the complete third season of moult this final assertion remains conjecture. Jollie believed that the key feature of adult plumage was the attainment of adult-like tail feathers. Such tail feathers have a broad, dark terminal band, three or four indistinct

mottled-grey bands across the inner portion of the feather, and very little if any white at the base.

However, Jollie did recognize that, even within a particular age group, there was considerable variation between individuals in the amount of white on the tail. Variation among juvenile tail feathers taken from several different eagles in Scotland is illustrated in Fig. 62. In some of these the dark terminal band is less than 10% of the length of the plume while in others it is substantially greater.

Tjernberg emphasized the considerable individual variation in the amount of white on the tail in different birds of the same age, and also incidentally in the amount of white at the base of the primaries and secondaries. Because of this, he argued that the use of these characters for ageing individual Golden Eagles was unreliable. In his opinion the changes in the amount of white on the wings and tail of an individual eagle were not very substantial between the first, second and third plumages. He believed that the change between the first and third plumages within a particular individual was less than the amount of variation that occurred between different eagles of the same age. Like Jollie, however, he recognized the attainment of distinctive adult feathers in the tail in the fourth plumage.

Given Tjernberg's findings, it appears that Golden Eagles cannot be confidently aged based on the amount of white on the wings and tail. Tjernberg was nevertheless able to offer an alternative means of ageing birds, at least until birds were in their fourth (near-adult) plumage. The features he used require closer scrutiny than is often possible with birds in the field, and can probably only be used when birds can be closely observed through a telescope or with birds in captivity. He recognized the following plumage stages.

First plumage

This is retained for about 9 months, or until the spring of the second year of life. Birds typically have uniformly dark brown upper wing-coverts. Usually, the tail is predominantly white with a sharply defined blackish-brown terminal band which varies in width between individuals. The white patches on the upper- and under-wing are extremely variable in size and some juveniles have almost no white visible at all. The extent of white on both the wings and the tail remains relatively unchanged for a particular individual during its first, second and third plumages.

Second plumage

This is attained during the moult of the second summer of life. In this plumage the median and lesser upper-wing coverts are light in colour and uniformly worn. The under-wing coverts are replaced in this plumage and have a characteristic rusty-brown colour. The pattern of the tail is virtually the same as in the first plumage.

FIG. 61.   *The upperside and underside of the wing of an adult Golden Eagle showing the typically 'jumbled' pattern of moult in the primaries and secondaries. There are at least three ages of feathers among the larger flight feathers.*

Third plumage

This is achieved during the third summer of life. In this plumage the upper-wing coverts are largely replaced by dark feathers. However, some feathers remain unmoulted giving light patches here or there in the wing-coverts. Typically, the border between the dark band and the white base to the tail is more diffuse and jagged than in younger plumages. Some individuals may have a few dark, adult-type feathers in the remiges and rectrices.

Fourth plumage

This is attained during the fourth summer of life. In this plumage the upper-wing coverts appear predominantly pale but are interspersed with groups of dark feathers. The tail has a typically, dark central pillar where the adult-type central tail feathers have grown. Usually, at least some of the tail feathers still have the extensive white base characteristic of the third plumage. Any white patterning on the underwing is broken up by dark, adult-type primaries and secondaries.

Both Jollie and Tjernberg recognized that individual variation in moult increased with age. This makes the determination of age after the fourth plumage much less certain. Tjernberg (1988) described some of the subtle changes which can occur in later plumages. He considered that the complete adult plumage was not normally achieved until after the fifth or sixth moult, that is at an age of about 5.5–6.5 years. By this stage normally all vestige of white in the wings and tail has been lost. However, a few individuals may retain a greyish-white base to the tail for the remainder of their lives.

MOULT IN OTHER *AQUILA* EAGLES

Little has been written about the moult of other members of the genus *Aquila*. In general, the pattern of moult appears to be broadly similar to that in Golden Eagles and all the species studied to date take more than one season to complete the moult. There are, however, differences in the time taken to achieve adult plumage. The large and moderately large species (Wedge-tailed, Imperial, Steppe and Tawny Eagle) go through at least two complete plumage changes before acquiring full adult dress. Consequently, like the Golden Eagle, they achieve adult plumage in the fifth or sixth year of life. This is probably also true for the Black Eagle. The smaller Lesser Spotted Eagle appears to attain full adult plumage a little earlier at 4 or 5 years old (Brooke *et al.* 1972) and the same may be true for the Greater Spotted Eagle. Possibly, these species go through one less intermediate plumage than the larger *Aquila* and, if so, this may reflect a tendency to breed at an earlier age.

Several of the *Aquila* eagles differ in the timing of periods when moult is suspended. I speculated earlier that the incidence of the suspension of moult

FIG. 62. *One-half of a juvenile Golden Eagle's upper tail with the 4th from outer-feather separate alongside. Below shows the variation in pattern on the same numbered tail feather from fine museum specimens.*

during winter in Golden Eagles might vary between areas, possibly linked to food supply. A different strategy has been adopted by the Steppe Eagle which breeds in eastern Europe and winters in Africa. Up to 4 years of age Steppe Eagles typically arrest their moult before migrating and do not begin again until the following spring. In contrast, older Steppe Eagles ($\geqslant$5 years) apparently continue to moult when on their wintering grounds in Africa (Brooke *et al.* 1972). This is presumably because such birds will normally have bred during the previous summer and then the opportunity to moult would have been more constrained than in the younger, non-breeding eagles. Because of their long migration they do not have as much time as Golden Eagles for moulting on their breeding grounds in the autumn. Consequently, they have little option but to moult on their winter quarters in Africa.

The Wedge-tailed Eagle in Australia has a different strategy again. It suspends moult during the breeding season but otherwise has an extended moult throughout the year (Marchant & Higgins 1993). These various moulting strategies are probably ultimately linked to food supply. In raptors, timing of moult should typically be geared to periods of the year when food is sufficient to sustain the demands of feather replacement, but when individuals are otherwise free from competing demands such as breeding (Newton 1979).

SUMMARY

Among Golden Eagles in Scotland, moulting takes place between April and October with a peak in July/August. Some birds may continue to moult during winter. Typically, in Golden Eagles, a complete change of feathers takes at least two moulting seasons and some feathers can be retained for up to 3 years. Among the larger flight feathers, the primaries and tail feathers are moulted more frequently than the secondaries.

In Golden Eagles the juvenile plumage is retained for about 9 months. Thereafter, birds go through two further plumage changes in which they retain variable amounts of white on the feathers of the wings and tail. The extent of white on these feathers is not a reliable means of determining the age of Golden Eagles because individual variation in the amount of white is probably greater than between-year changes within a particular bird. The first adult feathers are grown during the fourth summer of life and complete adult dress is probably not usually achieved until after the sixth or seventh summer of life (birds 5.5–6.5 years old).

Across the genus *Aquila* the timing of moult varies between species. In some species it occurs mainly in late summer and is typically suspended during winter. In adults of the two long-range migrants, Lesser Spotted Eagle and Steppe Eagle, moulting occurs when birds are in Africa during the northern winter.

CHAPTER 17
Movements and Migration

*Adult (left) and immature Steppe Eagle, Black Stork and Black Kite catching a
thermal on migration through Israel.*

IN the comparatively mild maritime climate of Scotland, where food is available all
year round, Golden Eagles have no need to migrate. Once an adult has acquired
a breeding territory it is unlikely to move more than a few kilometres for the
remainder of its life. However non-breeding juvenile and immature eagles do
disperse widely from their place of birth. Over much of the Golden Eagles'
temperate range, whether in North America or Eurasia, strictly sedentary behaviour
in adult breeders and short-range dispersal movements by non-breeders are the
norm. Only at the highest latitudes (above about 65°N) in the more continental
regions of North America and Eurasia are Golden Eagles genuine long-distance
migrants. In some northern populations only the young and non-territorial birds
migrate, and the adults remain on their breeding territories all year. In the most

203

northerly breeding localities of all, the entire population vacates the breeding range during winter.

In this chapter I begin with a short discussion of dispersal movements by non-breeding eagles in Scotland and elsewhere. This is followed by a section on the true migration which occurs in subarctic populations. Across the genus *Aquila* there is a great variety of migratory behaviour and these large eagles contribute to some of the most spectacular of all visible bird migrations. In the final part of the chapter I explore the various migration strategies adopted by other members of the genus.

Historically, most information on movements has been gathered from ringed birds which have been found dead or caught in traps. In recent years there have been a few studies of long-range migration in *Aquila* eagles using radio-transmitters attached to birds. As technology has improved, so the size of these transmitters has become smaller. There are now exciting developments using transmitters (technically called platform transmitter terminals or PTTs) which emit signals that may be detected by satellites (Meyburg *et al.* 1993). With this emerging technology it has become possible to plot the long-range movements of individual birds, such as migrating eagles, at frequent intervals and with remarkable precision.

DISPERSAL MOVEMENTS IN SCOTLAND

Up to 1994 more than 850 Golden Eagles had been ringed in Scotland, nearly all as nestlings, and 35 had been recovered (C. Mead *in litt.*; J. Grant *in litt.*). Most were found dead, although six birds were caught in crow traps and reportedly released alive. Given that these birds were probably caught on land managed as grouse moor, I suspect that most were in fact killed. The direction of movement of the 32 birds that moved more than 10 km from the natal area is shown in Fig. 63. Some 26 recoveries were of birds less than 18 months old and nine were older than this. The oldest recovery was a bird of 5 years and 8 months.

For all recoveries the average distance between ringing and recovery sites was 57 km. Birds which were less than 18 months old tended to range more widely than older individuals. The average recovery distance for the younger age group was 63 km and for older birds it was 36 km (Table 54). This suggests a tendency for birds to have a relatively wide-ranging, excursive phase during the early non-breeding period, followed by a return towards the natal area as they mature. Similar findings were reported by Haller (1994) for Golden Eagles in the Alps (see Chapter 14). Young eagles in Scotland showed no strong propensity to disperse in any particular direction. Among the small number of recoveries there was a slight tendency for more birds to move in an easterly rather than a westerly direction (Fig. 63).

Because information derived from ringing recoveries gives only a single record of movement, it cannot reveal much about the nature of dispersal in individual eagles. The difference in average dispersal distances between the two age classes of Golden Eagles would suggest that younger birds (<2 years old) range more widely than do older immatures. One way in which this difference could arise is if, among the

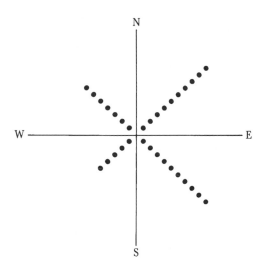

FIG. 63.   *The pattern of dispersal movement among Scottish Golden Eagles based on ringing recoveries. Each dot refers to an individual bird recovered in one of four compass segments indicating the direction moved from the natal area. Birds recovered less than 10 km from the natal area have been excluded.*

younger eagles, the early 'dispersive' phase included more frequent long-range exploratory movements. The maximum distance travelled in these early 'dispersive' movements, as indicated by ringing recoveries, was around 100–150 km. This upper limit is probably a function of the extent of continuously suitable eagle habitat in Britain. For the great majority of eagles reared in Scotland, dispersal movements in excess of 150–200 km would take the birds beyond the limits of suitable habitat. More research is needed if we are to gain a better understanding of the nature of dispersal behaviour among non-breeding eagles in Scotland. A study of non-breeding eagles fitted with long-life radio-transmitters is clearly both feasible and desirable.

DISPERSAL MOVEMENTS ELSEWHERE IN EUROPE

Ringing recoveries from eagles in Norway and Switzerland showed patterns of dispersal akin to that in Scotland (Fremming 1980; Haller 1994). In both these countries young eagles tended to disperse with no very strong directional bias, although in Norway rather more birds moved in a south or southwesterly direction (Fig. 64). The maximum dispersal distances of the birds was greater than in Scotland, with some individuals from Norway travelling over 1000 km and from Switzerland in excess of 800 km. This is, I believe, a reflection of the greater extent of continuously suitable eagle habitat in these countries. In neither country do territorial adults appear to make long-range movements, and this is as expected since in both places food is available all year round.

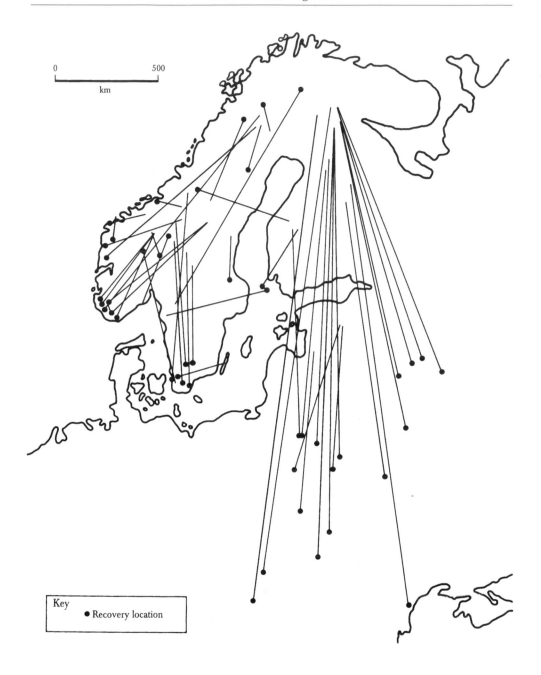

0 _____ 500
km

Key
● Recovery location

FIG. 64.   *Movements of juvenile Golden Eagles ringed in Scandinavia. Most records refer to birds ringed as nestlings and recovered in their first year of life. Birds from Norway and Sweden tend to disperse over relatively short distances in various directions, and birds from Finland are relatively long-range migrants, moving in a predominantly southerly direction. Redrawn from Fremming (1980).*

DISPERSAL MOVEMENTS IN THE UNITED STATES

Steenhof *et al.* (1984) reported the dispersal movements of non-breeding Golden Eagles which had been ringed or wing-tagged in southern Idaho. Once again the general direction of movement was more or less at random, except that few birds here were recovered or sighted in the coniferous forest zone of northern Idaho where the predominant habitat was unsuitable for hunting by Golden Eagles. Although one individual moved more than 1400 km from its nesting area, this was exceptional. Some 78% out of a total of 200 recoveries and sightings were within 100 kms of the place of birth (Table 54). The fact that most young eagles in Idaho remained comparatively close to the natal area was attributed to the availability of a year-round food supply in the form of jackrabbits.

TRUE MIGRATION OF GOLDEN EAGLES

Migration involves the twice-yearly movement of many or most individuals of a species between traditional breeding grounds and wintering areas. Typically, migration occurs in response to, or in anticipation of, food shortages at the end of the breeding season and during the winter ahead. Compared with summer, winter food stocks will be lower for all Golden Eagles throughout the species' holarctic range. For most populations the availability of food in the form of carrion is probably important in sustaining the birds through the winter period. This is especially true when alternative food is less available, either as a result of seasonal prey decline or because food is less accessible as a consequence of deep snow cover. Only in the extreme north of the breeding range, above about 65°N, are winter conditions severe enough for Golden Eagles to undertake long-distance migration.

Two different migration strategies are used by Golden Eagles. One strategy is demonstrated by the birds from northern Finland (Fig. 64). Here, virtually all the juveniles and probably some of the older, non-breeding eagles migrate south in winter. From ringing returns it appears that most of these birds move between 1000 and 2000 km more or less due south. Whether these birds return north in their second summer, or remain for a year or two on their winter territories, is not known. Territorial adults in the same population do not migrate but instead remain on their breeding grounds throughout the winter. Presumably, for these experienced individuals, the balance of advantage is to remain on the breeding territory rather than to undertake a lengthy and potentially hazardous migration. By not migrating they ensure that ownership of the breeding site is retained between successive nesting seasons. Again, by staying on the breeding territory they are able to begin the next breeding attempt as early as prevailing spring conditions allow, and without the added demands of a lengthy return migration. Non-territorial birds do not normally breed until they are at least 4 years old. Consequently, for them, the balance of advantage is in favour of a long-distance migration to areas where the winter climate is less severe, and where there is presumably less competition for food in winter.

Further east into Eurasia, winter conditions in the extreme north of the Golden Eagle's range are too severe to allow even the territorial adults to remain on the breeding grounds after about September/October. In the northern taiga forest zone on the fringe of the arctic tundra, from the Kola peninsula to Anadyr in eastern Russia, the entire Golden Eagle population moves out for the winter. These birds presumably migrate on a fairly broad front. They spend the winter on the Russian steppes, in Mongolia, or in northern China (Dementiev & Gladkov 1966). Most of these eagles probably winter in relatively flat, open landscapes where there are few resident Golden Eagles, possibly because of a lack of suitable nest sites. Such habitat may also hold more food for Golden Eagles in winter as a result of the migration of prey animals from further north, and because of concentrations of winter food in the form of carrion. Little else is known about the migration and wintering behaviour of these eagles from northern Siberia. Rather more is known about the equivalent population in subarctic North America.

Throughout northern and central Alaska, and in northern Canada, the entire population of Golden Eagles migrates south for the winter (Palmer 1988). Birds from Alaska and northwestern Canada leap-frog over more sedentary populations in British Columbia and Alberta to spend the winter in the southwestern United States. Relatively low numbers of Golden Eagles from north-central and eastern Canada spend the winter in the eastern United States. Some of these birds pass down the eastern seaboard as far south as Florida and winter in coastal wetland areas, and others move southwards along the Appalachian Mountains to Tennessee (Millsap & Vana 1984).

Until recently it was believed that the main migration of Golden Eagles in western North America occurred across a broad front down the Rocky Mountains. It is now known that large numbers of Golden Eagles pass through the Mount Lorette area of Alberta in western Canada in a relatively narrow corridor (Sherrington 1993). In the autumn of 1992, Golden Eagles were observed crossing Mount Lorette from mid-September until early November (Fig. 65) with a peak daily count of 476 birds on 6 October. Golden Eagles were seen returning north along the same route in the

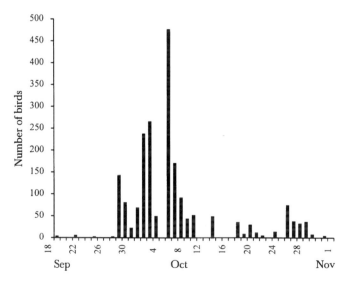

FIG. 65.　*The numbers of Golden Eagles seen migrating each day over the Mount Lorette area in Alberta, Canada in the autumn of 1992. After Sherrington (1993).*

spring of 1993 when a maximum number of 845 birds were seen on 25 March (Fig. 66). This is now known to be a regular migration route; around 4000 Golden Eagles were recorded each spring and autumn between 1993 and 1995 (Table 55). Sherrington believed that, at least in this part of Alberta, migrating eagles were concentrated in just one or two narrow corridors in the Rocky Mountain Front Ranges. He proposed that the principal reason for such concentrations was that the mountains along the migration corridor are all of moderate and relatively uniform elevation, thus providing reliable conditions for thermals and updraughts. Also, the various valleys which cut across the northwest–southeast orientation of the mountain ranges in this area are generally narrow, and short enough for birds to cross in a single glide. He also judged that the mountains in the Mount Lorette and Fisher Range area were cloud-free more often than neighbouring ranges to the east or west, thereby providing consistently more favourable conditions for raptor migration.

A small number of migrant Golden Eagles from Alaska and northern Canada have recently been studied on their wintering grounds in Idaho. Birds were trapped and fitted with radio-transmitters and their subsequent locations and movements detected by satellite (Marzluff *et al.* 1995). For three adults, the average date of departure for the northward migration was 14 March. Two of these adults made the journey from Idaho to Alaska (a distance of about 3000 km) in around 20 days. These birds all tended to have relatively small and well-defined winter home ranges, and individuals probably returned to the same winter range in successive years. Two radio-tagged subadult eagles wintering in southern Idaho were also followed and they ranged more widely than the adults. Their radios stopped

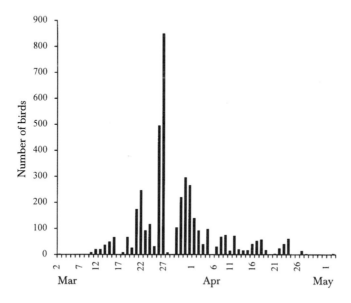

FIG. 66.   *The number of Golden Eagles seen migrating over the Mount Lorette area of Alberta, Canada in the spring of 1993. After Sherrington (1993).*

functioning in March and it was therefore not possible to say whether they too returned north for the summer. At least some of the younger, non-breeding Steppe Eagles do make the return migration to central Asia from their winter quarters in Africa (Christensen & Sorensen 1989). Whether migrant non-breeding Golden Eagles in North America also return to their natal area before they have reached breeding age, or alternatively stay for several years on their wintering grounds, remains unknown.

MIGRATION OF OTHER *AQUILA* EAGLES

Among other members of the genus *Aquila*, the range of migratory behaviour falls broadly into three types (Table 56). In some species the adults are resident but younger birds have short dispersal movements, not unlike the situation that occurs with most Golden Eagles. Others are partial migrants in which the more northerly part of the population migrates south in winter. At the other extreme are the true intercontinental migrants in which the entire population vacates the breeding range in winter.

Resident species

The Black Eagle in Africa, the Wedge-tailed Eagle in Australia and the Spanish Imperial Eagle are all strictly resident once they have secured a breeding territory. In all three species, young eagles undertake relatively short-range dispersal movements during the early, non-breeding years (Gargett 1990; Ridpath & Brooker 1986b; Ferrer 1993a). The sedentary nature of the adult birds would be expected, given the comparatively low latitudes and equable climate in which they live. In each case, the reduction of food supply during the non-breeding season would be less than that experienced by related species at higher latitudes. Even under the extremes of seasonal drought in Western Australia, adult Wedge-tailed Eagles were apparently resident (Ridpath & Brooker 1986b). This species and the Spanish Imperial Eagle have generalized diets and feed readily on carrion. This mean that these eagles are less vulnerable to seasonal fluctuations in their principal food sources.

Partial migrants

Two members of the genus exhibit partial migration. The Greater Spotted Eagle leaves much of its extensive breeding range in Russia and migrates southwards to winter in the Middle East, India and southern China (see example in Fig. 67). Similar migratory behaviour occurs in the eastern race of the Imperial Eagle *heliaca*. Individuals of both species can migrate over quite long distances (several thousand kilometres), but normally nothing like as far as the true intercontinental migrants (see below). Both species breed in wooded or semi-wooded landscapes in eastern

Three juvenile Golden Eagles in flight showing individual variation in the extent of white in the plumage.

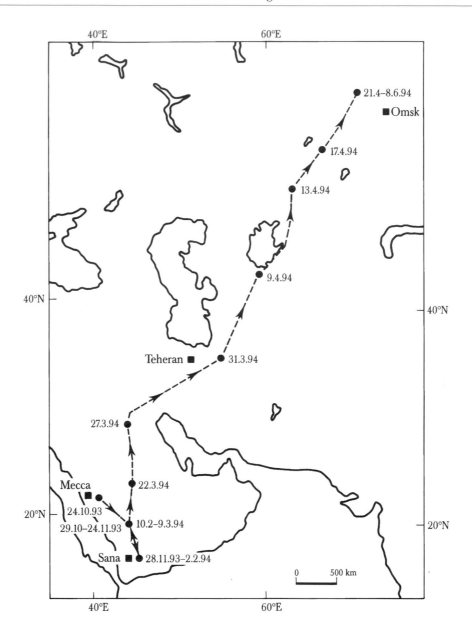

FIG. 67.   *The movement of an adult Greater Spotted Eagle, as indicated by satellite tracking. The bird was trapped and fitted with a transmitter in western Saudi Arabia in October 1993 from where it continued to move south until late November 1993. It then spent the winter in the southern Arabian peninsula before returning northwards, arriving on its nesting ground near Omsk in Russia in late April 1994. After Meyburg et al. (1995a).*

Europe and central Asia. In the harsh winter weather of central Siberia, much of their prey either migrates south (waterfowl) or becomes unavailable because of hibernation (mammals). Both eagles have quite generalized diets during the breeding season. As such, they are well equipped to adjust to a range of food sources and hunting strategies in their wintering quarters. While some individuals winter in arid regions such as Saudi Arabia (Meyburg *et al.* 1995a), most probably favour localities where there are wetlands with large concentrations of waterfowl (Christensen 1962; Prakash 1989; Naoroji 1990).

Intercontinental migrants

Two species of *Aquila* are long-range, intercontinental migrants. The Lesser Spotted Eagle breeds in eastern Europe and migrates to Africa for the winter. The western race of the Steppe Eagle *orientalis* breeds in west and central Asia and virtually the whole of that subspecies winters in Africa. What happens to the eastern race of the Steppe Eagle *nipalensis* in winter is less clear. A large east–west migration of Steppe Eagles that was observed in the Himalayas during October (Fleming 1988) may have been that race, and these birds may have been destined for India where some at least winter (Ali & Ripley 1968). Further east still, *nipalensis* has been recorded as a regular visitor to eastern China in October (Davis & Glass 1951) and small numbers have recently been reported on a northerly migration through the Malaysian peninsula in March (Helbig & Wells 1990).

Large birds of prey such as eagles use thermals to gain height in order to move over long distances by energy efficient gliding flight. Thermals are absent over the sea and consequently eagles must avoid long sea crossings because of the enormous energy costs involved in flapping flight. For the two intercontinental migrants this has led to the funnelling of huge numbers birds across the Sinai land bridge into Africa. Because of this, the timing of migration in both species is well documented. The dramatic migration of tens of thousands of *Aquila* eagles through Israel over a few weeks each spring and autumn must surely be one of the finest spectacles in all ornithology.

Lesser Spotted Eagles leave their nesting grounds in eastern Europe in late August—many cross the Bosphorus and a few pass to the east of the Black Sea (Porter & Beaman 1983). In the course of about a month from mid-September virtually the entire world population passes over northern Israel and enters Africa through Suez (Table 57, Fig. 68; Christensen & Sorensen 1989). Lesser Spotted Eagles winter almost exclusively in southern Africa where they are gregarious and somewhat nomadic (see Chapter 9). During the northern winter they are probably largely insectivorous. The return migration occurs through Israel between mid-March and early May with the peak numbers occurring in late March and early April. In spring, very small numbers have also been seen migrating over Cap Bon in Tunisia, presumably on a flight path north through Italy (Dejonghe 1980).

Steppe Eagles have a more eastern breeding range and thus further to migrate between their nesting grounds and Africa. Consequently, peak numbers reach Suez via Eilat in southern Israel in late October (Fig. 68). This is about 1 month later than Lesser Spotted Eagles. Evidently, not all Steppe Eagles enter Africa at Suez—

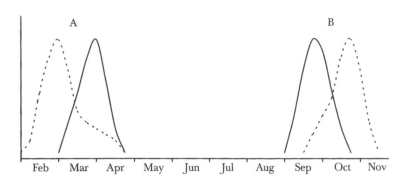

FIG. 68. *Diagrammatic representation of the pattern of peak migration of Lesser Spotted Eagles (———) and Steppe Eagles (– – – –) over Suez in spring (A) and autumn (B). The vertical scale is arbitrary and does not reflect absolute numbers, but simply shows the difference in the timing of migration in the two species in each season. Redrawn from Christensen & Sorensen (1989).*

over 60 000 have been seen crossing the Bab-el-Mandeb Straits at the southern end of the Red Sea (Table 57; Welch & Welch 1989). Steppe Eagles winter throughout most of eastern Africa from Sudan southwards. Juvenile and immature Steppe Eagles tend to winter further south than do adults. Like Lesser Spotted Eagles they are gregarious and somewhat nomadic, feeding on abundant, and sometimes transient food such as emerging flocks of termites and nesting colonies of *Quelea*. Steppe Eagles return through Suez comparatively early, reflecting the longer migration ahead of them, with peak numbers occurring in late February and early March.

During the breeding season, both the intercontinental migrants have comparatively specialized diets, chiefly comprising small mammals such as voles or ground squirrels. Such prey is either unavailable or extremely scarce on the eagles' breeding grounds in winter and so some kind of migration is essential. Compared with other *Aquila* eagles, Lesser Spotted and Steppe Eagles are weaker predators. By leaving the Palearctic region in winter they avoid competition with the other *Aquila* species. The fact that neither species is constrained by breeding duties at this time allows them to exploit temporarily abundant but unpredictable sources of food in Africa.

Other species

The last two *Aquila* eagles both have tropical or subtropical breeding distributions. Gurney's Eagle in New Guinea is essentially unknown. It is a bird of tropical rainforest, a habitat in which the seasonal fluctuations in food availability are usually small. Consequently, territorial adults are almost certainly sedentary, although short-range dispersal movements may be a feature of non-breeders. In a study of the Tawny Eagle in Zimbabwe, territorial adults were resident while non-breeders had regular seasonal movements (Hustler & Howells 1989). The pattern of migration and dispersal in Tawny Eagles across the species' whole range in Africa is, however, more complex and is a subject that needs further investigation (Liversidge 1989).

SUMMARY

Territorial adult Golden Eagles in Scotland are sedentary, although non-breeding juveniles and immatures disperse for distances up to 100–150 km from their natal area. Ringing recoveries of non-breeders <2 years old average 63 km from their place of birth, and older immatures average 36 km. In more northern and more continental populations many young Golden Eagles migrate several thousand kilometres south each winter. In subarctic populations in Eurasia and North America, virtually all Golden Eagles, including territorial adults, are long-range migrants.

Such migration in Eurasia probably occurs over a broad front. In western North America, many Golden Eagles migrate along a narrow corridor along the Front Range of the Rocky Mountains, and up to 1000 birds per day have been seen crossing Mount Lorette in Alberta during the peak autumn migration. Some individual eagles are known to make the 3000-km journey from Idaho to Alaska in around 20 days. Adult migrant eagles in Idaho have quite small and well-defined winter home ranges, and individual eagles may return to the same winter range in successive years.

Across the genus *Aquila* there is a range of migratory behaviour. The strategy adopted by a particular species, or population of a species, is determined by food availability on the breeding grounds during the non-breeding season and, to some extent, by the particular eagle's predatory behaviour.

CHAPTER 18
Mortality

Portrait of a nestling Golden Eagle aged 50 to 60 days old.

THE question I am most often asked about Golden Eagles is 'how long do they live?' Behind this lies the assumption that such large and impressive creatures must surely live for a long time. The simple answer is that, as birds go, Golden Eagles are comparatively long-lived. The oldest Golden Eagles recorded in the wild are one which was ringed as a nestling in France and found dead at the age of 25 years 8 months (Jacquat 1977), and another ringed in Sweden in its fourth year and recovered dead when more than 32 years old (Staav 1990). Although interesting, these longevity records do not tell us anything about the average life expectancy in the population as a whole. Also of interest, but of little relevance to studies of birds in the wild, are the various records of Golden Eagles in captivity living to a great age. Discounting one unbelievable record from a zoo in Vienna of an eagle of more than

216

100 years old, the oldest captive individual quoted by Gordon (1955) lived for 46 years.

As a general rule, among raptors, large species live longer than smaller ones (Newton 1979). Annual adult mortality rates have been estimated at 30–50% in small falcons and accipiters, 15–25% in medium-sized hawks such as buzzards and kites, and 5% or less in the larger eagles. As a rough guide, these mortality rates translate to average life expectancy among adults of 1–2 years in the smaller raptors, 4–5 years in medium-sized species and 20 years or more in the large eagles.

The full picture is still more complicated. In all birds, mortality rates prior to breeding age are normally substantially higher than for adult breeders. Among raptors for which data are available, pre-adult mortality has been shown to be at least 50% and frequently higher (Newton 1979). Because of the low adult mortality and, consequently, the intense competition for the few vacancies that occur in the adult population, breeding in large eagles is normally deferred for several years. For such species, pre-adult mortality will be especially high and as many as 80% or 90% of the young which leave the nest probably die before reaching the age at which they would normally gain their first breeding territory.

In this chapter I attempt to piece together the fragmentary information that is available on Golden Eagle mortality rates. Because precise data for Golden Eagles are rare, I have also drawn on studies of other large eagles where better information exists. Later in the chapter I discuss the causes of death in Golden Eagles with particular emphasis on causes that can be attributed directly or indirectly to man.

ESTIMATING MORTALITY

The commonest method of estimating annual mortality rates is to use information from ringing recoveries. For a given sample of ringed nestlings the number recovered during each year after ringing can sometimes be used to estimate mortality rates. Such estimates are reasonably reliable if the number of recoveries is large, if the mortality of ringed birds is broadly typical of all deaths in the population, and if rings stay on for the full life-span of the birds. For Golden Eagles in Scotland none of these conditions is met. Not enough birds have been recovered (only 35 up to 1994) to provide a statistically useful sample. Furthermore, it is strongly suspected by raptor workers in Scotland that the type of rings used on eagles up to at least the early 1980s were capable of being removed by some birds. As rings become progressively more worn with age the possibility of ring removal increases and this would lead, in turn, to an unaccountable bias in mortality estimates among older individuals.

Another way of estimating mortality is to catch and mark large numbers of individuals breeding in an area and then establish what proportion of these is present in succeeding years. No such study with a large enough sample of eagles has yet been made in Scotland, nor indeed in any other population of Golden Eagles. However, some researchers have been able to recognize individual Golden Eagles using plumage differences and follow these birds over several breeding seasons (K. Nellist & K. Crane *in litt.*). Assuming that the loss of a known individual means that it has died and not simply moved to another territory, then the rate of loss of these birds can give a measure of mortality.

Yet another method of estimating adult mortality has been used in other large eagles, notably Bateleurs, and African Fish Eagles (Brown & Cade 1972; Brown & Hopcroft 1973). In these studies the proportion of birds in different age-classes up to about the fifth year was assessed. This technique depends on the existence of distinctive plumage amongst birds in the subadult age-class just prior to breeding. Annual turnover in the adult breeding population is then assumed to equate to the proportion of birds in the subadult class just prior to breeding. This technique has been tried with Golden Eagles but is probably not very dependable given the unreliability of plumage characteristics used to age birds in such studies (see Chapter 16). Also, some birds do not become breeders until they have been in adult plumage for several years.

MORTALITY ESTIMATES IN GOLDEN EAGLES

Adult mortality

The breeding population of Golden Eagles on the island of Skye in western Scotland has been monitored by Kate Nellist and Ken Crane for a number of years. They have closely observed the breeding adults at around 30 sites each year for over 10 years. From this they have been able to recognize individuals based on plumage characteristics that remain consistent between seasons.

During the most recent 10 years of their study they have detected changes of one, or occasionally both members of the pair, with the replacement birds normally exhibiting some sign of subadult plumage such as white feathers in the tail. In 30 pairs over 10 years (giving a total of 600 eagle-years) they have seen a minimum of 15 changes and suspected changes. This gives a rough estimate of annual adult survival of 97.5% and average adult life expectancy of over 39 years (Perrins & Birkhead 1983; Table 58). Some deaths may have been overlooked if individuals were replaced by birds with similar plumage characteristics and it is possible that some birds which were presumed dead had merely moved to another nesting territory. Nevertheless, the estimated survival rate is not dissimilar to that found in other large eagles (Table 58). Using the same technique of recording the disappearance of known individuals, researchers in Germany estimated appreciably lower annual adult survival of 92.5% for Golden Eagles (Bezzel & Fünfstück 1994). This gives an estimate of average adult life expectancy of just under 13 years.

These two estimates are at either end of the range of adult survival rates estimated for various large eagles (Table 58). Using a variety of techniques, adult survival was estimated for the Spanish Imperial Eagle in the Coto Doñana (Ferrer 1993a). The four methods used gave annual adult survival estimates between 93% and 97%. Adult survival of 95% was estimated for Bald Eagles in the Aleutian Islands based on the frequency of birds in the oldest subadult plumage-class (Sherrod *et al.* 1977). In another study of Bald Eagles in Saskatchewan using the same technique, survival was around 92–94% (Gerrard *et al.* 1992). The adult survival rate for Bald Eagles in Prince William Sound, Alaska was somewhat lower at 88% (Bowman *et al.* 1995). It is possible that the results from this study, which was carried out in the wake of the Exxon Valdez oil spill, were somewhat atypical. Survival estimates for adult Bateleurs and African Fish Eagles were believed to be in the range 96–97% (Brown & Cade 1972; Brown & Hopcroft 1973). Given this range of figures it would appear that an adult survival rate of 95% or more (giving an average adult life expectancy in excess of 20 years) is a not unreasonable estimate for an unpersecuted Golden Eagle population.

While the difference in adult survival between 92% and 97% appears relatively small, such variation translates into substantial differences in average adult life expectancy—around 12 years at 92% and over 32 years at 97%. Consequently, quite a small reduction in adult survival, or an equivalently small error in estimating adult survival, will have serious implications for the population dynamics of such a long-lived species. Because of this there is a powerful case for future research to be geared towards obtaining better estimates of adult survival rates than are presently available for both persecuted and unpersecuted populations of Golden Eagles.

Pre-adult mortality

While some empirical estimates of adult survival are available for Golden Eagles, very little indeed is known about pre-adult survival rates. That they will be substantially lower than adult survival is very likely. Initial survival estimates among non-breeders in California suggest that around 70% of fledglings probably died before they reached 5 years old (PBRG 1995). Among Bald Eagles in Alaska, pre-adult survival was estimated to be substantially lower, at around 5% (Sherrod *et al.* 1977). As an approximation, a typical figure for pre-adult survival may be around 15%. However, the actual figure probably varies considerably, both between populations and between different time periods in the same population. This is because in most eagle populations the adult breeding density is relatively constant and both between-year and between-area productivity is extremely variable (Chapter 15). In the absence of immigration/emigration, the maintenance of a stable breeding population over time will be achieved through the combined effects of adult mortality, and pre-adult mortality. The length of the pre-adult period will also vary between populations, with younger birds recruited into some populations earlier than in others.

The theoretical relationship between these three population parameters (adult survival, pre-adult survival and breeding success) is shown in Fig. 69, assuming a stable breeding population. This shows that for Golden Eagle populations with productivity figures characteristic of better areas in the United States (0.8–1.0 young reared per pair per year), the predictions for adult (95%) and pre-adult (15%) survival indicated above are credible. For the island of Skye in western Scotland where long-term productivity is around 0.6 young per pair (Chapter 15), one estimate put adult survival at 97.5%; the population would therefore require pre-adult survival of less than 10% to maintain itself. In an adjacent area on the mainland of western Scotland, breeding success was 0.3 young per pair per year. Assuming a similar adult survival to that on Skye, pre-adult survival of around 15% would be sufficient to maintain a stable breeding population. In a Bavarian study by Bezzel & Fünfstück (1994), adult survival was estimated at 92.5% and productivity

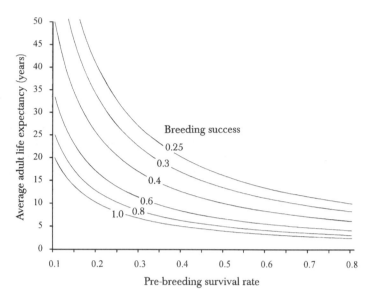

FIG. 69.   *The theoretical relationship between average life expectancy of adults (years) and pre-adult survival rate (as a fraction of unity) for a range of breeding success figures (young fledged/pair/year). Data are for populations which are stable (no increase or decrease) and in which there is no immigration or emigration. So, for example, in a stable population with average adult life expectancy of 15 years and breeding success of 0.6 young/pair/year, pre-adult survival would be around 28%.*

was 0.25 young per pair per year. The authors believed the eagles were living in a region of very poor food supply and that the apparently stable breeding population could only be maintained by immigration from elsewhere in the Alps. The pre-adult survival (>75%) that would be required to maintain this population without immigration would certainly appear to be exceptional, and therefore unlikely for a large raptor.

CAUSES OF DEATH

Many different causes of mortality have been reported for Golden Eagles in Scotland. In most cases where the cause was known these were attributable either directly or indirectly to man (Table 59). These include deaths by shooting, trapping and poisoning, and collisions with wires. Reasons for death probably unconnected with man include starvation, disease, killing by another predator (including other eagles), and even oiling by Fulmars. No sample of dead eagles found by people will be truly representative of deaths in the wild. Certain kinds of 'natural' mortality such as starvation or disease are likely to be under-recorded compared with poisoning, trapping and shooting which would tend to occur more often in places visited by people. It is therefore difficult to attribute relative importance to the various mortality factors. Nevertheless, it is clear that, despite the fact that Golden

Eagles in Britain have had statutory protection since 1954, the majority of birds still die as a result of the actions of man.

Shooting and trapping

Shooting and trapping of Golden Eagles in Britain is much less frequent than it was during the nineteenth and first half of the twentieth century. The Protection of Birds Act (1954) made it an offence to kill birds such as Golden Eagles. This, combined with a growing tide of public opinion in favour of conservation, has reduced the more overt methods of destruction of birds of prey. Nevertheless, there are still cases of eagles being shot or trapped and 13 such incidents were recorded during the period 1979–89 (RSPB & NCC 1991). This was probably a fraction of those that occurred.

In several other European countries the number of eagles shot in recent decades has declined as protective legislation has been brought in (see Haller, 1982 for Switzerland). However, in some countries shooting or trapping still remain important causes of death in Golden Eagles. For example, during the period 1980–90 in Spain, nearly 60% of 266 eagles found dead had been shot and a further 8% were killed in traps (Table 60; Arroyo *et al.* 1990).

Poisoning

In Britain the most common cause of death in eagles directly attributable to man is now poisoning (Table 59). Because Golden Eagles will readily feed on carrion they are especially vulnerable to carcasses laced with poison. Such baits, which are illegal in Britain, are usually laid in places calculated to be visited by predatory and scavenging mammals. A wide range of poisons have been used, with the most common types identified in bird of prey incidents being alphachloralose, followed by mevinphos and then strychnine (RSPB & NCC 1990). While the principal target is usually the Fox, such baits are indiscriminate and annually account for many deaths of birds of prey, including Buzzards, Red Kites and Golden Eagles. During the period 1979–89 some 27 Golden Eagles were known to have been poisoned. This is probably a small proportion of the total numbers killed by poisoning and I suspect that the actual figure could be many times greater then this. Within the Golden Eagle range in Scotland, the use of poisoned baits is most frequent in the eastern Highlands where land is managed for Red Grouse (see Chapter 19). In these areas, the effect on Golden Eagles is acute and a major factor inhibiting the establishment of breeding territories and any expansion of the population. Where poisoning is endemic, adult birds are typically absent and ranges are consistently occupied by subadults. In the worst-affected areas, a succession of non-breeding eagles is poisoned annually and, as such these poisoning black-spots act as mortality sinks for Golden Eagles.

Appreciable numbers of Golden Eagles are killed by poisoning in the United States, where carcasses laced with strychnine and intended for Wolves, Coyotes and Foxes are the principal source (Bortolotti 1984b; Table 60). Golden Eagles are also apparently vulnerable to the effects of secondary poisoning through the consumption of target animals killed in legitimate pest control schemes. In a recent

case in California several eagles apparently died after eating Californian Ground Squirrels which had in turn been poisoned by the anticoagulant rodenticide chlorophacinone (Peeters 1994). The squirrels were perceived as agricultural pests by cattle ranchers and numbers were being controlled by spreading poison-coated grain.

Electrocution and collisions with wires and wind turbines

Mortality caused by electrocution at power poles or by collision with power lines has not generally been considered a serious problem for Golden Eagles in Britain. It may, however, be one that is underestimated as, among the small number of ringed birds recovered, no less than six were reported dead following collisions with wires (Table 59). This is a matter on which further research is clearly needed in Scotland. In the United States and in Spain, electrocution in particular has been a major cause of mortality (see Chapter 19). The risk of electrocution varies for different designs of power pole. For poles where perching eagles can easily touch two wires at once, deaths by electrocution are most frequent. Also, in relatively flat landscapes where alternative perching places are few, many more eagles can be killed at power poles. Deaths resulting from collisions with wires have been less well studied. These are likely to be greatest in places where transmission lines coincide with favoured hunting grounds, or cut across important migration routes. A recent study in California has found an appreciable level of mortality among Golden Eagles and other raptors resulting from collisions with the blades of wind turbines (PBRG, 1995). In that study, many Golden Eagle deaths occurred in the 189 km² wind farm site which contained over 6500 turbines. Several other raptor species were similarly killed, including Red-tailed Hawks, American Kestrels and Turkey Vultures.

Pesticides

The implications of pesticides and other pollutants for Golden Eagles are discussed in more detail in the next chapter. Where effects have been identified, they have tended to be linked to changes in breeding performance. Newton & Galbraith (1991) believed that adult survival of Golden Eagles in Scotland was probably not affected by current levels of organochlorines. They expressed some concern over the potential for contamination among eagles in western coastal areas where eagles fed heavily on seabirds such as Fulmars. One eagle from the island of Lewis, where it was known to have fed on Fulmars, had quite exceptional levels of pollutants (Table 61). They described this bird as 'the most contaminated raptor they had ever examined'. It is conceivable that the high concentrations of pollutants may have contributed to the death of this individual.

Other mortality related to man

Reports of other types of Golden Eagle mortality, directly or indirectly attributable to man, are relatively few. A Golden Eagle died after attacking a glider in Argyll,

Bald Eagle perched on a dead Douglas fir, northwestern United States.

western Scotland (Gregory 1985). The eagle fell to the ground and Mike Gregory subsequently recovered the corpse which proved to be an adult male. He believed that the attack on the glider may have been an aggressive act by a territorial eagle which perceived the glider as an intruder. There has been at least one incident of a Golden Eagle killed in a collision with a low-flying jet in Scotland (Love 1989). The eagle died, the jet crashed but the pilot bailed out.

Mortality due to 'natural' causes

Mortality among nestling Golden Eagles is discussed in Chapter 15. Reports of death as a result of 'natural' causes in free-flying eagles are few and mainly anecdotal. Most deaths are undoubtedly overlooked because corpses quickly disappear in the wild. It is likely that a great many of these undiscovered deaths are attributable to 'natural' causes, which certainly include starvation, disease and death by other predators.

Evidence for starvation as a cause of death in Golden Eagles is difficult to find. One small piece of evidence consistent with this type of mortality is revealed in the pattern of ringing recoveries of Scottish Golden Eagles over the first 12 months of life (Fig. 70). This shows a small peak in recovery rate during the second summer of life, after the young birds were about 9 months old. By then, the amount of easily obtainable carrion which would have sustained these birds over the winter would

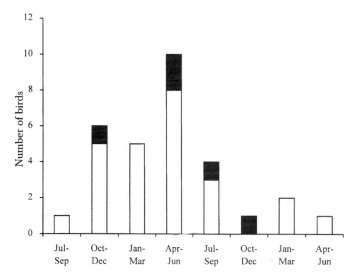

FIG. 70.   *The number of Golden Eagles ringed as nestlings and recovered in Scotland in successive 3-month periods after fledging. Shading indicates birds caught in crow traps, otherwise birds were found dead. The small peak in recoveries in the spring of the second year of life may reflect the reduced availability of winter carrion and greater demands on the birds to hunt active prey which are more difficult to catch. Alternatively, the spring peak may reflect an increase in illegal poisoning and predator destruction prior to the gamebird breeding season.*

have declined. The young eagles must then begin to hunt live prey, which is more difficult to secure, and consequently an increase in death by starvation would be expected at this time. Any influence on these figures resulting from differential ring loss with age would tend reduce the observed peak in second summer recoveries and so I believe the pattern is probably real.

There have been a few confirmed cases of death by disease in free-flying Golden Eagles. Kochert (1972) reported three cases of the bacterial disease trichomoniasis as a cause of death among eagles in Idaho. Keith Brockie (*in litt.*) found a 10-month-old bird in a weak condition attempting to feed on a dead Red Deer stag. On examination by a vet the bird was found to have an osteosarcoma on the humerus. Further cases of disease leading to death in both wild and captive Golden Eagles are listed by Ikeda & Yamazaki (1988).

Physical injury and even death of non-breeding eagles as a result of attacks by territorial adults have been reported from Switzerland (Haller 1982). In one case in Scotland and another in California, a territorial eagles was apparently killed by an intruder which probably then took over the breeding territory (M. McGrady *in litt.*;

PBRG 1995). There have been one or two cases in Scotland where the death or injury of a Golden Eagle was attributable to an aggressive attack by a White-tailed Sea Eagle. In one of these, Mike MacGregor watched an immature Golden Eagle being repeatedly dived at by an adult Sea Eagle when both birds were flying over the sea. Eventually, the Golden Eagle landed on the water and 'swam' back to the shore. Although the Golden Eagle was rescued and subsequently rehabilitated, if not for Mike's intervention it would surely have died.

There have been several cases of Golden Eagle deaths or serious injuries caused by the prey they were attempting to catch. Seton Gordon (1971) saw an eagle which was covered in oil, and which subsequently died. Although he considered the source of the oil to be a mystery, he did not rule out the possibility that this eagle had been contaminated by Fulmar oil. White-tailed Sea Eagles hunting nestling Fulmars have sometimes been known to become covered in Fulmar oil to the point that they were no longer able to fly (Love 1983). Another unusual type of death was recorded by Love (1989) from the island of Rum. Here, on two different occasions, Golden Eagles were found apparently trampled to death by Red Deer. John Love speculated that these were birds which had been gorging on deer calves and had been too slow to get airborne and thus avoid a fatal kick from the returning deer hind. Seton Gordon (1955) recounted a dramatic encounter between a Golden Eagle and a Scottish Wildcat that was ultimately fatal for both animals. Another improbable death involving an encounter with a potentially dangerous prey animal was reported from the United States where a Golden Eagle was apparently killed by porcupine quills (Lano 1922).

SUMMARY

The longevity record for a Golden Eagle in the wild is for a ringed Swedish bird that was 32 years old. Annual adult survival in Golden Eagles is probably in the range 92–97% and average adult life expectancy in unpersecuted populations is probably 20–30 years or more. Typical pre-adult survival rates, up to the age of first breeding at about 5 years old, probably lie within the range 5–30%. Pre-adult survival and the age of first breeding are likely to vary considerably between populations, although few data are available on this subject.

In most published accounts of death in Golden Eagles the majority of mortality is attributable directly or indirectly to man. In Scotland, many deaths are still caused by illegal poisoning, and in Spain the principal cause of mortality among free-flying eagles is shooting. In the recent past in the western United States, large numbers of Golden Eagles were electrocuted at power poles. Exceptional causes of deaths include collisions with wind turbines, trampling to death by deer, death caused by porcupine quills and collisions with aircraft. There have been a few cases of Golden Eagles killed in territorial encounters with other eagles.

CHAPTER 19
Threats

Portrait of a Golden Eagle with wind-ruffled feathers.

THE demands of late twentieth-century man on the natural environment of the planet are immense. Few populations of birds of prey are immune from these pressures, and virtually throughout their global range Golden Eagles are no exception. To many people, the fact that eagle populations are at risk because of man's actions is cause in itself for concern. To biologists, predators such as birds of prey that sit at the top of terrestrial food chains have a value far beyond their intrinsic right to exist. Their continuing health is one of the most powerful indicators of the well-being of the natural systems which support all life on earth.

Man's effects on Golden Eagle populations have shifted dramatically over the past two centuries. Few of these influences have been beneficial. What has happened to Golden Eagles in Scotland is, in many ways, quite typical. In this chapter I discuss the historical and contemporary human impacts on Golden Eagles in Scotland and draw parallels with other countries as appropriate. In many traditional human societies the relationship between man and Golden Eagles was one in which this impressive bird was celebrated, or even venerated (Nelson & Nelson 1977). This phenomenon is discussed in more detail in Chapter 21. Systematic persecution of Golden Eagles in Scotland by shooting, trapping, egg-collecting and destruction of nests became widespread during the nineteenth century. It continued largely unabated during the first half of the twentieth century. Eagles were killed because they were perceived as a threat to the numbers of game animals, especially Red Grouse. They were also persecuted by sheep farmers who believed eagles were responsible for killing large numbers of lambs. While some direct persecution still continues, the nature of human impacts on Golden Eagles has shifted over the last 50 years.

Impacts are now less deliberate and are more a consequence of man's actions on the eagle's natural environment. These include the effects of pesticides and other pollutants, various forms of development such as electricity generation and transmission, increased recreational use of the countryside, and land use changes in forestry and agriculture. Although the timing has been different in various countries, the shift in impacts, from direct persecution to the negative consequences of environmental change, has occurred over much of the eagles' range in continental Europe and in North America.

PERSECUTION

Killing of adults in Scotland and elsewhere

During the nineteenth century many estate owners in Scotland required their game-keepers to destroy birds of prey which were invariably considered to be 'vermin'. Sometimes landowners went further, offering a financial inducement for each bird killed or egg destroyed. Love (1983) recounts the numbers of both Golden and White-tailed Eagles allegedly killed on various estates. While some figures appear far-fetched, for example there is a report of 295 eagles (of both species) killed on an estate in Caithness between 1820 and 1826, there is little doubt that persecution was intense. By the late nineteenth century eagles came under added pressure from Victorian collectors of eggs and skins for museums and private collections. The end result was that, by the early 1900s, Golden Eagles in Britain were entirely confined to the more remote and inaccessible parts of the Scottish Highlands (see Chapter 10). The intervention of two world wars ensured that the number of game-keepers on estates was, for short spells at least, greatly reduced. This, and the statutory protection of Golden Eagles in 1954, prevented the species being lost as a breeding bird in Scotland as had already happened in England, Wales and on the island of Ireland.

Even after 40 years of protection, Golden Eagles are still killed illegally each year in Britain. While the numbers involved are now probably only a fraction of those killed in the late nineteenth century, the fact that persecution occurs at all is reprehensible. As I indicated in the last chapter, the commonest method of deliberate destruction of eagles today is by poisoning. In upland areas of Scotland the pattern of confirmed poisoning incidents is clear (Fig. 71). This shows the

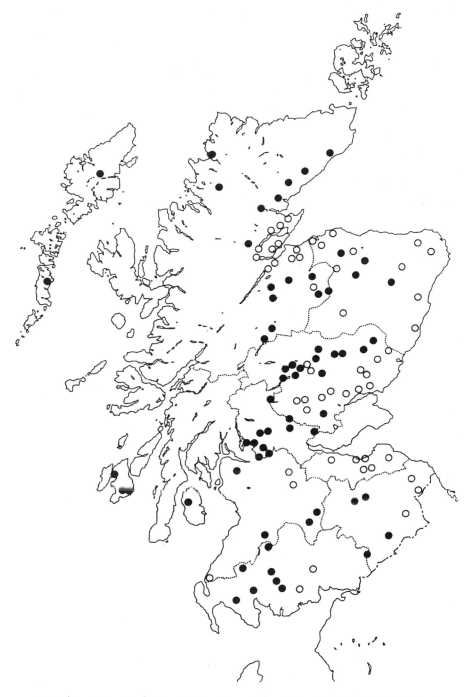

FIG. 71. *The distribution of all confirmed illegal poisoning incidents in Scotland during the 7-year period 1989–95. Golden Eagles would be especially vulnerable to abuse of poisons in upland areas and these are shown with solid symbols. Data are from the RSPB investigations department (K. Morton in litt.).*

distribution of all confirmed cases involving the illegal use of poisons in moorland areas, and not just cases where eagles were found dead. I have included all poisoning incidents because, whenever poisoned baits are used in moorland areas, eagles are potentially vulnerable. There have been relatively few cases recently of poisoning in northwestern Scotland and the vast majority have been in the eastern and southern Highlands and in the Southern Uplands. Poisoning intensity is greatest on land managed as grouse moor. The effect of this is to constrain the recovery of the Golden Eagle population in Britain, preventing recolonization of areas in the southern and eastern Highlands and in parts of the Southern Uplands. Although Fig. 71 only depicts poisoning incidents from Scotland, the situation in the uplands of northern England is broadly similar. Until illegal poisoning is brought under control throughout northern Britain, there is no prospect of an appreciable number of Golden Eagles returning to nest in northern England.

The continued illegal use of poisoned baits is a product of both ignorance and arrogance. While the gradual process of education can hope to address the former, it is the latter which is the more worrying. I am reminded of a piece written by my father nearly 20 years ago in his monograph on the Hen Harrier (Watson 1977). Reflecting on the attitude of some people who manage upland shooting preserves he was forced to conclude that, to them, 'the law is somehow an impertinence on the moorlands of Britain'. Regrettably, that attitude is all too prevalent today and Fig. 71 is clear evidence of this. Part of the solution must be to ensure that those who carry out or condone the illegal killing of predators are made aware that their habit is totally unacceptable to society at large. Increasingly, there are landowners who are prepared to say this in public, and I trust they also do so in private. I am encouraged by a tactic used by Roy Dennis when he is challenged to defend the continued protection of our birds of prey. His retort is that land managers need to recognize that there is more prospect of the Red Grouse being made a protected species than there is of Golden Eagles, Peregrines or other birds of prey ever being taken off the protected list. I think he is right.

The past practice of deliberately killing large numbers of Golden Eagles was not confined to Britain (see references in Bijleveld 1974, for other countries in Europe). In Switzerland, more than 100 Golden Eagles were shot each decade in the late nineteenth century, and killing continued largely unchecked until the species was legally protected in 1953 (Haller 1982). The population in Norway declined as a consequence of human persecution and only began to recover once legal protection was afforded in 1968 (Hagen 1976). Golden Eagles were afforded legal protection in Spain in 1980 although killing is still prevalent today (Arroyo *et al.* 1990).

The most prolific destruction of Golden Eagles anywhere occurred in the United States from the mid-1930s into the 1960s. For example, in Carter County, Montana some 286 Golden Eagles were killed in the month of March, 1948 (Woodgerd 1952). A bounty of five dollars was paid by the Montana Fish and Game Department for each eagle killed. The killing was initiated by pressure from sportsmen and ranchers who believed that eagles were killing large numbers of antelopes. Stomach analysis of the dead eagles failed to support this contention.

In the southwestern United States very large numbers of Golden Eagles were killed in a sustained campaign lasting 20 years or so from the early 1940s (Spofford 1964). Most of the estimated 20 000 eagles killed during this period were shot from light aircraft (Table 62 lists the numbers killed from an aircraft by a single operator in a 6-year period). These winter shoot-offs were triggered by an increase in sheep rearing in the area from the 1930s onwards, and by the perception that eagles were serious predators of lambs. The population of eagles in the southwestern United States is swollen each winter by immigrants from Alaska and western Canada. The sheer numbers killed over so many years must certainly have depleted populations in northern breeding areas (Newton 1979). Killing eagles from aircraft was eventually banned and Golden Eagles were given full federal protection in 1963. Nevertheless, widespread killing still continued at least in some regions into the 1970s. Over 800 Golden Eagles were allegedly shot from aircraft in Wyoming and Colorado during the winter of 1970–71 (Palmer 1988).

The only other *Aquila* eagle of which officially sanctioned killing has occurred on a scale comparable to that of Golden Eagles was the Wedge-tailed Eagle in Australia. Again, the justification for killing, which involved the inducement of bounties, was alleged predation on lambs (Fig. 72; Ridpath & Brooker 1986b). In the State of Queensland, bounties were paid on up to 10 000 Wedge-tailed Eagles a year until payments were stopped in 1974. Bounties were paid in Western Australia until 1968, prior to which some 2000 eagles had been killed annually in sheep-rearing areas. Now, small numbers of permits to kill this species are issued annually by most Australian States and illegal killing is still quite widespread in sheep country (Marchant & Higgins 1993).

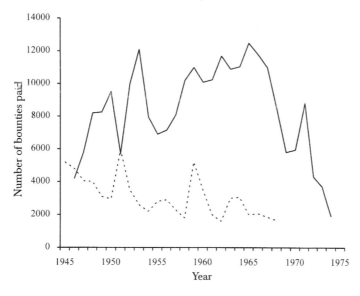

FIG. 72. *The numbers of Wedge-tailed Eagles for which bounties were paid in two Australian states. Bounties were paid in Queensland (———) until 1974 and in Western Australia (– – – –) until 1968. Redrawn from Ridpath & Brooker (1986b).*

Destruction of nests in Scotland

In addition to killing adult eagles, some game managers in Scotland deliberately destroy the contents of eagle nests in spring. Nests with eggs are also vulnerable to the small number of egg collectors who are still active in Britain. It is difficult to gauge how many nesting attempts are destroyed deliberately in Scotland each year, but some measure of this was gathered during the national survey in 1982 (Watson & Dennis 1992). We analysed breeding success in relation to the level of disturbance experienced at over 300 nests. Disturbance was classified as low, moderate or severe by fieldworkers (see Table 63 for definitions). Nesting eagles affected by severe and moderate levels of disturbance failed to rear nestlings in 93% and 74% of occasions, and breeding failure was significantly more frequent than at nests where disturbance was low (46%). The occurrence of different levels of disturbance varied across Scotland (Table 64). In particular, sites affected by severe disturbance were significantly more frequent (16%) in the east than in the west (2%).

This analysis allows an estimate of the number of young which could have been reared in 1982 in the absence of moderate or severe disturbance. Assuming that the 99 pairs that experienced moderate or severe disturbance would, in the absence of such disturbance, produce at least as many young as the pairs experiencing low disturbance, then the figure for young fledged per pair should match the 0.62 per pair from little-disturbed nests. This suggests that a minimum of 22 chicks failed to fledge from 70 nests that received moderate disturbance, and a further 16 chicks failed to fledge from the 29 severely disturbed sites. Therefore, an estimated 38 chicks were lost through disturbance, which is around 18% of the potential production of 209 chicks from the 335 nests for which disturbance levels were assessed. This is probably an underestimate since a higher proportion of severely disturbed sites occurred in the eastern half of the range, where breeding success in the absence of persecution was generally higher than in the west (Chapter 15). As with the killing of adults, the major human impact on nests of eagles occurred in the east Highlands, and specifically in areas where land is managed for grouse shooting. Some nesting attempts in western Scotland are probably destroyed each year by sheep farmers and egg-collectors but the impact on eagles is small compared with that in the east of the range.

UNINTENTIONAL HUMAN DISTURBANCE

The consequences of unintentional human disturbance on birds of prey such as Golden Eagles are difficult to quantify. Disturbance implied here is that resulting from human activity in the nesting or hunting area. Among the activities that could give rise to unintentional disturbance are recreation, forest management and development projects such as road construction, mining or power generation. The principal effect on Golden Eagles would be to depress breeding success. This can occur directly as a result of disturbance close to nesting sites leading to failure to breed, or indirectly by preventing birds from hunting over part of their feeding range. Chronic disturbance of a home range could lead ultimately to its

Wedge-tailed Eagle at a nest site in a eucalyptus.

abandonment and, consequently, to a permanent reduction in the number of pairs living in an area.

Evidence that unintentional disturbance has affected Golden Eagles in Scotland is largely anecdotal. I am aware of several nest sites located close to roads and regularly used in the 1950s that have not been occupied for the past 20 years or more. In the Cairngorm Mountains the number of hill-walkers has increased substantially over the past 30 years, especially during summer. At the same time, several pairs of Golden Eagles are known to have abandoned nest sites in those parts of the Cairngorms most frequently visited by people, and some territories may have been completely lost.

Using data from the 1982 survey we analysed Golden Eagle fledging success in relation the accessibility of nest sites by people (see Table 65 for definitions) (Watson & Dennis 1992). Pairs of eagles using nest sites that were most inaccessible fledged young on 50% of occasions, and were significantly more likely to be successful than pairs nesting in the most accessible sites (31%) (Table 65). While a number of factors probably contributed to this difference, the vulnerability of easily accessible sites to unintentional human disturbance is probably an important contributor.

Elsewhere in Europe there is circumstantial evidence for a link between human disturbance and breeding failure. In Norway the incidence of failure among Golden Eagles was greater in years when the Easter holidays were early (Fremming 1980). This was attributed to the presence of more skiing tourists in eagle territories at a time when the birds were egg-laying and therefore particularly prone to desertion. In Italy, several types of disturbance, including increased numbers of tourists in remote mountain areas, construction of new roads and mining activities, have each contributed to nesting failure by Golden Eagles (Allavena 1985).

More systematic work on the impact of disturbance on birds of prey has been done in the United States. Evidence for the effects of recreational disturbance in particular has been reviewed by Knight & Skagen (1988). The selection of nest sites by Bald Eagles appeared to be influenced by the proximity of human activities, notably recreation and logging (Anthony & Isaacs 1989). Recently used nests were further from recreational facilities, and from roads, than were older, disused nests. The same study found that breeding success was poorer in territories where logging activity was greatest. In Bald Eagles again, the effects of human activity on feeding behaviour were studied by McGarigal *et al.* (1991). Using an experimental approach, they found that eagles avoided foraging in areas within about 400 m of a stationary boat. They concluded that the presence of a boat could change the way in which Bald Eagles used an area for feeding. If boating activity coincided with particularly rich feeding places then the hunting success and subsequently the breeding performance of Bald Eagles could be reduced.

Another study examined the effects of military activity on home range use by Red-tailed Hawks, Swainson's Hawks, Ferruginous Hawks and Golden Eagles in Colorado (Anderson *et al.* 1990). Birds living in an area where military training occurred showed several changes in home range activity compared with birds in a control area nearby where there was no such activity. Compared with controls, birds in the military training area shifted the centres of their home ranges, made more frequent long-range movements outside their usual home range, and increased the size of their hunting ranges. All these changes were believed to be a consequence of birds actively avoiding areas of human activity. The costs of these behavioural changes in terms of productivity and overall fitness were not measured in this study. One likely effect would have been to reduce the hunting efficiency of birds in the disturbed compared with the undisturbed area. If disturbance was sustained over time its effects on productivity would become appreciable and could eventually lead to the area being abandoned.

PESTICIDES AND POLLUTANTS

DDT and other insecticides

The harmful effects of organochlorine compounds on birds of prey have been the subject of detailed study over the past 30 years (Cooke 1973; Ratcliffe 1980; Newton 1986). The insecticides which have caused the greatest damage to raptor populations are DDT, and the cyclodienes such as aldrin, dieldrin, endrin and heptachlor (Newton 1979). They are all toxic in their own right, but have several other properties that make them especially harmful to raptors. They tend to last in the environment for a long time so that the effects can be very persistent. They are soluble in fat and can therefore accumulate in animals and become concentrated at successive levels in food chains. Consequently, birds of prey at the top of food chains tend to accumulate the largest concentrations of these chemicals. Organochlorines can also be dispersed over wide areas, either in the bodies of migrant animals or by wind and water movement. At high concentrations they can be lethal but even at comparatively low levels they are known to increase breeding failure sufficiently to induce population declines.

DDT gives rise to the metabolite DDE which is the chemical consistently associated with egg-shell thinning in raptors, leading to egg-breakage and widespread breeding failure (Newton 1979). The cyclodienes, aldrin and dieldrin, break down to the chemical HEOD which is much more toxic in its own right than is DDE. In Sparrowhawks at least, the effects of HEOD have been mainly to increase adult mortality, although deaths of embryos may also be involved (Newton 1986).

Among birds of prey the greatest effects of pesticides have been on bird and fish-eating species, including Peregrines, Sparrowhawks, Merlins, Ospreys, Bald Eagles and White-tailed Sea Eagles (review by Newton 1979). Generally speaking, birds such as Golden Eagles, which feed more on mammals, have been less seriously affected. This is largely because the mammals they eat tend to be herbivorous, resulting in a food chain with only two steps. In raptors that feed on birds and fish, many of the prey species are themselves carnivorous or insectivorous leading to at least three steps in the food chain.

Golden Eagles and pesticides in Scotland

Work was done on the effects of organochlorine pesticides on Golden Eagles in Scotland during the 1950s and 1960s (Lockie & Ratcliffe 1964; Lockie *et al.* 1969; Ratcliffe 1970). In these studies, the organochlorines implicated were DDT and dieldrin. From 1947 until the mid-1950s DDT was used as an insecticide in sheep dips in Britain. It was then replaced by the more effective dieldrin until that was stopped in 1966 following concern over HEOD contamination of mutton samples. The tendency for Golden Eagles to feed on sheep carrion, especially in western Scotland, meant that they were likely to ingest and accumulate organochlorines.

Findings from this work pointed to organochlorines as a cause of increased breeding failure in eagles at that time. Ratcliffe (1970) showed that, in western Scotland, eggs laid during the period 1951–65 were around 10% thinner than those collected before 1947 (pre-DDT). Marquiss *et al.* (1985) reported comparable eggshell thinning among eagles in Galloway during the same period. Lockie & Ratcliffe (1964) detected an appreciable increase in the frequency of egg breakage at eyries in western Scotland between 1951 and 1963. Later, Lockie *et al.* (1969) showed a marked improvement in breeding success in western Scotland following the banning of dieldrin as a sheep-dip in 1966. During 1963–65, young were successfully fledged from 31% of 39 nests while during 1966–68 some 69% of 45 nesting attempts were successful (Table 66). They linked this change to a significant reduction in the mean level of HEOD in unhatched eagle eggs between the two periods. The source of the dieldrin was assumed to be sheep carrion which was an important source of food for eagles in western Scotland. That conclusion was supported by the finding that HEOD residues in eagle eggs from the period 1963–68 from eastern Scotland, where little or no sheep carrion was eaten by eagles, were significantly lower than concentrations in eggs from western Scotland during 1963–65.

Further work was carried out on organochlorines in Scottish Golden Eagle eggs by Newton & Galbraith (1991). They found that post-1970, eggs from western Scotland had significantly thicker shells than those from 1951–65, and this coincided with reductions in both DDE and HEOD levels (Table 67). For all organochlorine compounds they found that levels were highest in western coastal areas, lower in western inland areas and lowest in eastern inland areas. This regional trend was attributed to differences in the diet between the three areas. Greater accumulations in western, and especially coastal eagles, were attributed to greater amounts of sheep carrion and also seabirds in the diet. The latter are known often to be heavily contaminated with organochlorines and other pollutants, such as mercury (Bourne 1976; Newton *et al.* 1989). Newton & Galbraith (1991) believed that the current levels of organochlorines and other pollutants in Scottish Golden Eagles, even in western coastal areas, were generally too low to affect breeding success. Precisely how organochlorines affected Golden Eagle breeding success in the 1950s and 1960s will never be known. Circumstantial evidence that some decline in breeding performance did occur is quite strong. Any effect of HEOD on eagle survival at that time is unknown. Compared with Peregrines and Sparrowhawks, the longer life expectancy of Golden Eagles may have ensured that eagles did not suffer an equivalent reduction in breeding numbers; and the banning of dieldrin as a sheep dip may also have been timely.

Golden Eagles and pesticides in other parts of the world

No studies from other parts of the world have shown a link between organochlorines and Golden Eagle breeding success. Typically, the concentrations of pesticides have been below levels at which effects would have been expected (Kochert 1972; Hernández *et al.* 1988; Kropil & Kornan 1990). In the closely related Spanish Imperial Eagle, recently collected eggs were around 12% thinner than those collected pre-1907 (González & Hiraldo 1988). This change did not appear to have had a detrimental effect on overall reproductive success.

Golden Eagles and other pollutants

Other pollutants that have been found at appreciable concentrations in Golden Eagles are the polychlorinated biphenyls (PCBs) and heavy metals such as mercury

(Hg) and lead (Pb). PCBs are used in various industrial processes and tend to enter the environment through leakage into river systems. The most toxic sources of mercury are the 'alkyl-mercury' compounds which were used up to the 1970s as fungicides and seed dressings. Both pollutants can reach especially high concentrations in aquatic and especially marine ecosystems. The main potential source of lead poisoning is from lead shot ingested by raptors feeding on injured or dead waterfowl.

In Scotland, levels of PCBs and mercury are currently highest among eagles living in western coastal districts and the source of these chemicals is probably seabirds (Table 67; Furness *et al.* 1989; Newton & Galbraith 1991). Unlike HEOD and DDE, the levels of PCBs in Scottish Golden Eagles have not declined in recent years and this presumably reflects both high persistence and the continued input of PCBs to the environment. In general, the levels of both PCBs and mercury detected in Golden Eagles are probably not high enough to have affected breeding success appreciably. However, a study of eagles on the island of Rum in western Scotland did suggest that high levels of both compounds may have contributed to very low breeding success there (Furness *et al.* 1989). Golden Eagles on Rum feed substantially on seabirds such as Fulmars, Manx Shearwaters and large gulls (Corkhill 1980). Clearly, further work is needed on the impact of pollutants at various levels of contamination, and the effects of these pollutants on coastal Golden Eagles in Scotland.

Deaths caused by lead poisoning in several raptor species have been reported from North America, and especially in Bald Eagles feeding on dead and injured waterfowl (Bloom *et al.* 1989; Elliott *et al.* 1992). In southern Idaho, 10 out of 17 Golden Eagles examined were found to have had some exposure to lead (Craig *et al.* 1990). At least five of these birds had died from lead poisoning. Two eagles were found to have lead in their intestinal tracts and this probably came from jackrabbits that had been shot by hunters but were subsequently consumed by the eagles. The extent to which lead poisoning is a cause of mortality elsewhere among Golden Eagles is not known and merits further study.

GOLDEN EAGLES AND POWER POLES

Golden Eagle deaths by electrocution at power poles in Scotland appear to be rare. In the United States, large numbers of eagles were found dead under power poles during the 1960s and early 1970s (Table 68; Boeker & Nickerson 1975; Nelson & Nelson 1977; Benson 1981). Around that time, it is estimated that between 300 and 2000 Golden Eagles were killed annually in this way in the United States. The majority died from electrocution although a few died as a result of collisions with power lines. A proportion were shot illegally by hunters who found that eagles perched on power poles were an easy target.

The great majority of the eagles that suffered electrocution were young birds just learning to fly (Benson 1981). Electrocutions occurred most frequently in relatively flat landscapes where alternative perches were few. They were especially common in winter when young eagles from mountain areas moved to foothills, valleys and open grassland areas to hunt. Within a given area most electrocutions were confined to a small number of poles that were typically located on small hills or ridges where there were good updraughts, and therefore ideal conditions for take-off and landing. Deaths were largely confined to power lines carrying relatively low voltages (around 12–24 kV). These lines were generally on wooden poles around 8–10 m high with three wires positioned at the same height on a single cross-arm, and each wire was spaced less than 1 m apart (Nelson & Nelson 1977). In addition, such poles typically had lightning conductor wires extending from near the top of the pole to the ground. The much larger, high-voltage transmission lines (69 kV) were not a problem because the phase conductors were spaced 3 m or more apart.

With a wing span of more than 2 m, eagles using perches on power poles were at risk in a number of ways. Electrocution occurred when a bird made simultaneous contact between the ground wire and one of the phase conductors, or between two of the phase conductors. The critical factor was the minimum distance between each phase conductor and the separation distance to the ground wire. Once the nature of the eagle electrocution problem had been identified, work was done to modify the design of power poles (Anderson 1975). Some of the successful modifications made to power poles are described in Chapter 20. Electrocution of Golden Eagles is now much less of a problem in the United States than it was 20 years ago.

Outside the United States, electrocution of large birds of prey at power poles has been, and continues to be, a serious problem in several countries, including Spain and Russia. Large numbers of raptors, including the globally threatened Spanish Imperial Eagle, are still electrocuted each year at power lines in southwestern Spain (Ferrer & de le Court 1988; Ferrer *et al.* 1991). Here, the main threat is from 16–45 kV power lines on metal pylons. In a 12-month survey done along a 100-km length of transmission line in 1982–83, over 140 dead raptors were located. Less than 3% died from collisions and the principal cause of death was electrocution. Mortality was significantly greater at pylons with erect insulators, in which wires were positioned above the cross-arms, than at those with suspended insulators. Among the pylons with erect insulators, much the most dangerous design was that with an exposed loop of wire above the insulator. The fact that these Spanish pylons were made of metal meant that birds were at risk from electrocution not only by touching two cables at once, but also by touching one wire and the metal pylon.

One unexpected revelation from the study of electrocutions in Spain was the higher mortality rate among females than males in several raptor species (Ferrer & Hiraldo 1992). In the Spanish Imperial Eagle significantly more females (78%) than males (22%) were electrocuted (Table 69). This was despite the fact that the sex ratio of birds leaving the nest was nearly equal, and that females were no more likely to use pylons as perches than were males. The suggested explanation was that the larger female, with a greater wingspan, was more likely to make a fatal contact between wires. Whatever the cause, Ferrer & Hiraldo considered that the development of a potentially serious bias in the sex ratio in the breeding population of Spanish Imperial Eagles posed a major risk to this endangered raptor.

A serious electrocution problem has recently been detected among Steppe Eagles in Russia (Tucker & Heath 1994). In the past few years hundreds of kilometres of power lines have been constructed in the tree-less landscapes of the Russian steppes, where power poles have been adopted as perching places by Steppe Eagles.

One survey reported an average of 15 dead eagles for each 10 km of power line. Clearly, there is a need for further work to establish the extent and nature of this threat. Given the experience of the United States and Spain, it should be possible to reduce these mortality rates substantially by modifying power pole design.

GOLDEN EAGLES AND LAND USE CHANGE

Throughout their world range Golden Eagles tend to live in landscapes where the dominant vegetation comprises mainly naturally occurring species, although the actual composition of vegetation communities may be greatly modified by the actions of man. Human land uses in eagle habitat are chiefly extensive, involving management for grazing by both domestic animals and game species, and management for forestry. Changes in such land uses tend to occur comparatively slowly and, consequently, any effects on eagles can be difficult to measure, and key causal factors hard to identify. In general, land use changes which cause a reduction in food available to eagles would be expected to lead to poorer breeding success, or to lower nesting densities, or perhaps to both. In Scotland the biggest single change in recent years within the upland areas where eagles live has been large-scale afforestation.

Afforestation and Golden Eagles in Scotland

Since 1945 huge tracts of land in upland Britain have been converted from sheep walk to forestry. In Scotland, the largest amounts of upland afforestation have occurred in southwest Scotland, and in Argyll in the southwest Highlands. Over large parts of both these regions more than 50% of the land between 200 m and 600 m altitude has now been planted. Afforestation involves the removal of sheep and either fencing out or control of deer by shooting. The land is normally ploughed and trees are planted in the upturned ribbon of earth at densities in excess of 2500 seedlings per hectare. Until recently most planting in the uplands has been with exotic conifers, mainly Sitka spruce with lodgepole pine on wetter sites. In the first few years after planting the original ground vegetation recovers following release from the previously heavy grazing pressure. Then, after about 10 years, the woodland canopy closes and the ground vegetation dies back. From then until harvesting in 40 or 50 years these monoculture forests remain dark and gloomy places. Ground vegetation is lost almost completely except along forest rides and there is little structural or biological diversity over very large areas. While this description of forestry is accurate for many of the plantings of the 1960s and 1970s, it is fair to say that over the past 10 years forestry practice in Scotland has become a little more imaginative. Especially encouraging has been the trend towards planting more native broad-leaved trees and Scots pine, as well as the greater consideration given to forest design.

From the Golden Eagle's perspective, afforestation of large parts of its hunting range presents several problems. Sheep, and to an extent deer, are removed with a consequent loss of food supply (especially carrion in winter). In the early years after planting, the rapid growth of ground vegetation can lead to an increase in the

numbers of smaller herbivores and, if these include grouse and ha...
should benefit. Once the canopy closes, these forests hold little f...
eagles and that which does occur is generally unavailable under th...
trees. Given these changes, what evidence is there for any long-te...
afforestation on Golden Eagles in Scotland?

Two studies have demonstrated reduced breeding success in Go...
linked to increased afforestation. In Galloway, Marquiss *et al.* (1985)
large-scale afforestation in the 1970s coincided with reduced breedi...
among three of the four pairs of eagles nesting in that region (Table
confirmed that eagles did not feed appreciably on animals living in...
plantations, and they concluded that afforestation of open country had...
much of the most productive foraging areas. The second piece of evidenc...
from Argyll, where extensive areas have been afforested since the 1950s...
breeding success was recorded for 15 pairs over 10 years from 1980...
compared with the amount of plantation forestry in a 75 km² the surroundin...
nesting territory (Watson 1992a). I found that mean breeding success was
correlated with the amount of forestry planted in the 10 years prior to...
(Fig 79). There was, however, a significant negative relationship between breed...
success and the amount of forestry >10 years old when the breeding study beg...
(Fig 74) I believe that the lack of any effect of younger forestry was because any f...

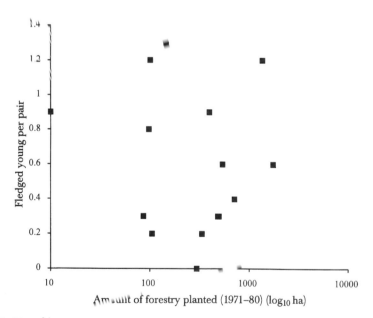

FIG 79. *Mean breeding success (young fledged/pair/year) for each of 15 pairs of Golden Eagles in Argyll, Scotland over the 10-year period 1980–89 shown in relation to the amount of plantation forestry (log₁₀ha) in the potential hunting range. The forestry figures include all planting done between 1971 and 1980. The regression of breeding success on forestry planted between 1971 and 1980 was not significant ($b = -0.47 \pm 0.47$, $t_{13} = 0.38$).*

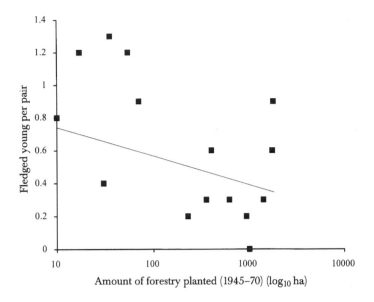

FIG. 74. *Mean breeding success (young fledged/pair/year for each of 15 pairs of Golden Eagles in Argyll, Scotland over the 10-year period 1980–89 shown in relation to the amount of plantation forestry (log$_{10}$ha) in the potential hunting range. The forestry figure includes all plantings between 1945 and 1970. The slope of the regression line was significantly different from zero (b = −0.34± 0.27, t$_{13}$ = 2.65, P <0.05).*

of food resulting from the removal of sheep was compensated by increases in the numbers of grouse and hares as a result of the recovery of ground vegetation. After about 10 years this secondary benefit was lost as the forest canopy closed and such habitat no longer provided suitable feeding habitat for eagles. This, I suggest, is the reason why eagles in ranges containing large amounts of >10-year-old forest had significantly reduced breeding success.

Evidence for the effects of afforestation on eagle breeding density is less clear cut. This is partly because changes may take a long time to occur in such a long-lived bird. It is quite possible that ranges containing large amounts of forestry could still hold sufficient food to sustain an adult pair of eagles for many years, even after breeding success was substantially reduced. Loss of breeding adults and any realignment of nesting density may therefore take many years. Nevertheless, there is now some evidence that such changes have occurred in Argyll, notably on the Kintyre peninsula south of Lochgilphead (Fig. 75). Here, the historical information on Golden Eagle breeding density is relatively complete as far back as the early 1960s owing to the work of Mike Gregory and Sandy Gordon. Prior to 1950 less than 5% of land at altitudes above 200 m on the Kintyre peninsula was afforested; by the middle of the 1980s this had increased to over 60%. In the 1960s, at least eight and perhaps as many as 10 pairs of eagles nested there. By 1995 this had dropped to four pairs—a decline of at least 50% in 30 years. Although increases in afforestation equivalent to those in Kintyre have occurred further north in Argyll, these have not yet resulted in such large reductions in Golden Eagle density. Work by Mike

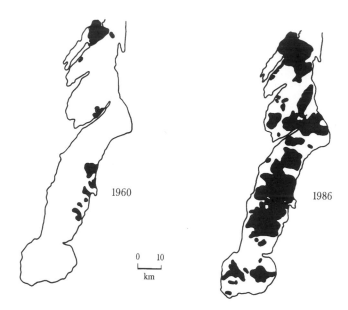

FIG. 75.   *Changes in the extent of plantation forestry in the Kintyre peninsula, Argyll, Scotland between 1960 and 1986. The number of pairs of Golden Eagles on breeding territories in this area declined by at least 50% (from eight or ten pairs to four pairs) between the early 1960s and the late 1980s.*

McGrady using radio-tagged eagles is currently being carried out in Argyll. This should provide a better understanding of the effects of forestry on the behaviour of individual eagles, and indicate ways in which the worst effects of plantation forestry might be mitigated.

The existence of detrimental effects on Golden Eagles as a result of blanket afforestation are likely given the wholesale structural change this land use has on large areas of previously open hunting ground. Empirical evidence is now beginning to confirm that such effects do occur, and to identify how they operate. Researchers in several other parts of the world have suspected that insensitive afforestation programmes can be detrimental to Golden Eagles: e.g. Portugal (Palma 1985), France (Simeon & Cheylan 1985), and Japan (SRGE 1991). It would be wrong to end this section on a wholly negative note. I acknowledge that, in many parts of the world, Golden Eagles live in comparatively wooded landscapes, most notably in many parts of Scandinavia (Tjernberg 1983a). These woodlands are essentially natural in origin and tend to be much more open and structurally diverse than the exotic conifer plantations established in upland Scotland over the past 50 years. I will return to this subject again in Chapter 20.

Golden Eagles and grazing animals

One of the most intractable questions for land managers interested in Golden Eagles concerns the bird's relationship with large grazing animals, both wild and domestic ungulates. I have discussed the question of eagle predation on livestock in Chapter 6. Here, I consider briefly the effects of grazing by large herbivores on Golden Eagle habitat, especially in western Scotland. Across much of Europe, Golden Eagles live in areas where the predominant land use is low-intensity pastoral agriculture (Watson 1991). This is also true in much of the rest of the world range, including the United States (Chapter 3). What evidence is there that management for grazing animals has had a detrimental effect on Golden Eagle habitat?

Jim Lockie was the first to propose that the very high density of Golden Eagles in western Scotland was attributable to the large numbers of dead sheep and deer in that region (Lockie 1964). The amount of carrion was a consequence of the numbers of grazing animals exacerbated, at least in the case of sheep, by poor husbandry. At first sight, such an abundant and predictable source of food would seem to be entirely beneficial to eagles. Certainly, the breeding density of Golden Eagles in much of western Scotland is now as high if not higher than that described by Lockie over 30 years ago. However, breeding density is only one measure of condition and in the case of Golden Eagles in Scotland I believe it may mask a deeper problem.

I indicated earlier (Chapter 12) that the average clutch size of Scottish Golden Eagles appeared to have declined significantly since the middle of the nineteenth century. This was, I suggested, related to a long-term change in the eagles' food supply, especially the numbers of grouse and hares. That numbers of these animals have declined substantially over much of western Scotland since the nineteenth century is generally accepted (see Table 71 for evidence from game book records for a typical estate in western Scotland). For over 150 years the semi-natural moorlands and grasslands of this region have been grazed by large numbers of sheep, and in recent decades by greatly increased numbers of Red Deer (Chapter 4).

One of the key changes resulting from this long period of heavy grazing pressure has been the loss of ericaceous plants, such as heather, and their replacement by grasses (McVean & Lockie 1969). This loss is partly a direct result of grazing but is also attributable to repeated and extensive burning of moorland done traditionally to 'improve grazing' for sheep and deer in the spring. Loss of heather and a reduction in its nutritional quality have contributed to the decline of grouse and hares in western Scotland.

So, whereas eagles have apparently benefited from large amounts of carrion to the extent that they can live at very high densities, their natural prey has been decimated. As a result, they breed very poorly when compared with unpersecuted populations in eastern Scotland where there are few sheep and where heather is still abundant and grouse and hares are still plentiful. The situation for eagles in western Scotland is, in my view, evidence of fundamentally unsustainable land management. Put simply, populations of naturally occurring small herbivores have been almost completely displaced as a result of grazing by excessive numbers of large herbivores such as sheep and deer.

A not dissimilar problem has been identified in the very different semi-desert region of the southwestern United States (Kochert & Pellant 1986; Kochert *et al.* 1988). Here, increased grazing pressure, sometimes also associated with an increased frequency of wildfires, has had a marked effect on natural vegetation

communities. Intensive grazing has led to an increase in annual plant species at the expense of perennial species, and to an overall reduction in vegetation height. An important consequence has been the reduction in the numbers of many small and medium-sized herbivores. For Golden Eagles the key prey species here is the Black-tailed Jackrabbit. While jackrabbits appear tolerant to light or moderate grazing they are likely to decline where grazing is heavy or wildfires abundant. Evidence that such declines have occurred and have affected Golden Eagle numbers in one area in Idaho is given in Chapter 9.

It is the interrelationship between large grazing animals and the smaller, naturally occurring herbivores that provides the key to understanding the effects of changes in grazing management on Golden Eagles. In general, very high numbers of domestic grazing animals such as sheep will tend to result in reduced numbers of smaller herbivores. Such a change will not benefit Golden Eagles in the long term.

SUMMARY

Historically, the greatest threat to Golden Eagles was direct killing by people, involving shooting and trapping of adults and destruction of nests. This was the case in Scotland, in many other parts of Europe and in the United States. Since the middle of this century Golden Eagles have been legally protected in most of these places. Illegal killing remains a threat in many parts of the world, and killing of eagles by poisoned baits is probably the principal cause of mortality among eagles in Scotland. Poisoning is concentrated in the east Highlands, especially where land is managed for grouse. Unintentional disturbance of eagles by hill-walkers and other recreationalists is less of a problem, although rather little information is available on this.

In the 1960s Golden Eagles in Scotland showed a decline in breeding success and this was linked to contamination with organochlorine pesticides. By eating sheep carrion, Golden Eagles ingested DDT and dieldrin, both of which were used for a time in sheep-dips. This is no longer a problem because organochlorines are not now used in dips. The effects of contamination with PCBs, ingested by eagles feeding on seabirds, are poorly understood and require further research.

In the United States, large numbers of eagles were killed in the 1960s and 1970s by electrocution on power poles. Changes in power pole design have largely removed this threat. Large eagles in other countries are still electrocuted in considerable numbers, and the lessons from the United States need to be employed elsewhere. New threats, from lead poisoning as a result ingesting carcasses containing lead shot, and from mortality caused by collisions with wind turbines, have been identified in the United States.

This young eagle was ringed at a nest in the southern Scottish Highlands in June 1995 and died of starvation in a crow trap in January 1996. The resident keeper had apparently failed to check the trap for months. The case was especially tragic because a large number of birdwatchers had provided round-the-clock protection at the nest site during the previous summer, and had thereby ensured that young were fledged there for the first time in many years.

Other than poisoned baits, the main threat to Golden Eagles in Scotland is now from change of land use. Inappropriate afforestation of large areas of open hunting ground in the uplands has had an impact on Golden Eagles, both in terms of breeding success and nesting density. Some of the long-term effects of afforestation are probably yet to be felt. Overgrazing and other inappropriate grazing management, such as excessive burning, have contributed to a decline in the Golden Eagle's wild prey in much of western Scotland. The resulting paucity of summer food in much of that region is the principal reason for very low breeding success among eagles.

CHAPTER 20
Conservation

VARIOUS protection measures and conservation management techniques have been used to mitigate the damaging effects of human actions on birds of prey. In this chapter I review the approaches to conservation used to date, with particular emphasis on Golden Eagles in Scotland. I also consider what further steps are needed if we are to retain healthy populations of Golden Eagles in circumstances where human pressures can only increase.

The range of human impacts that impinge on various of the *Aquila* eagles are summarized in Table 72. The Golden Eagle and the Spanish Imperial Eagle are probably subject to the greatest range of threats, although this may be in part because these are the most intensively studied and best known members of the genus. Habitat change is the one impact that currently affects every species in at least some part of its range. Sustained human persecution, involving various forms of deliberate killing, has been a serious threat to all except perhaps the two predominantly African species, the Tawny Eagle and the Black Eagle.

To be effective, the conservation of large eagles will always depend on a blend of different approaches. Decisions will be dictated by the nature of a particular threat or combination of threats. The options available include: conservation education; statutory protection of the species and its habitat; policy protection through various types of land use incentive and constraint; and, intervention through appropriate directed management. In addition, any management option needs to be underpinned by good quality applied research in order to further inform the choice of options. Fig. 76 summarizes what I believe to be the most appropriate conservation options for Golden Eagles in Scotland.

Problem	Solution				
	Conservation education	*Legislation/ enforcement*	*Policy protection*	*Provision of incentives*	*Directed management*
Persecution	**	**	*	–	*
Unintentional disturbance	*	*	*	–	*
Pesticides and pollutants	*	*	*	–	*
Afforestation	*	–	**	*	–
Grazing management	*	–	**	*	–

FIG. 76.   *Summary of the recommended conservation management options/actions required in order to maintain and enhance the Golden Eagle population in Britain. The options/actions are prioritized (high **, medium *, low −) with respect to the principal conservation problems facing Golden Eagles now.*

COUNTERING THE EFFECTS OF PERSECUTION

The driving force behind the killing of birds of prey such as the large eagles is the perception that such predators are in competition with man for some economic resource such as wild game or livestock. In Scotland, there is little evidence for the view that Golden Eagles cause serious economic hardship as a result of predation on livestock (Chapter 6). With respect to managed game, Golden Eagles in Scotland are not perceived to be a serious problem on grouse moors because they kill some grouse. Rather, as large aerial predators, they are unwelcome because their appearance on a moor can disrupt the behaviour of driven grouse. So, instead of flying over the guns, grouse will typically scatter in all directions at the sight of an eagle. In my judgement, neither the small numbers of lambs killed nor the irritation which eagles may occasionally cause some grouse shooters, are justification for persecution.

Various conservation measures can help reduce the level of illegal killing of eagles. Principal among these are conservation education and statutory protection. Killing of Golden Eagles in Britain was made illegal under the Protection of Birds

Act (1954). The contemporary legislative protection is the Wildlife and Countryside Act (1981), which includes special penalties for the killing and intentional disturbance of Golden Eagles and other birds of prey (RSPB & NCC 1991). Deterrent legislation can only be effective up to a point, and the continued illegal killing of birds of prey necessitates a parallel and sustained campaign of education. Such work is ably done in Britain by the Royal Society for the Protection of Birds, the principal non-government organization committed to the protection and conservation of wild birds in Britain. Given the continuing illegal persecution of birds of prey, there is a case for government agencies to take a higher profile on this issue.

Gamekeepers and hill farmers need to be made aware constantly that the killing of birds of prey is illegal. There is a special need for education on the inherent dangers arising from the abuse of poisoned baits for the control of predators. Awareness of the extent of poison abuse, and especially the risks to children and dogs, needs to be raised in the minds of the general public. All forms of the media should be used to get these messages across. The ultimate objective must be to reinforce in the minds of the perpetrators that their behaviour is selfish, dangerous and deeply objectionable to society.

While not strictly persecution, there is in Scotland some illegal theft of young Golden Eagles from nests for the purposes of falconry. The extent to which this occurs is unclear. One obvious way of reducing this illegal trade and transfer of birds would be to develop a register of legally held birds and to compile information on individual birds using the technique of genetic finger-printing. There is an equally strong case for falconers to develop a captive breeding programme, as has already happened with Peregrine Falcons, and from this provide birds for the legitimate falconry market.

MANAGING THE EFFECTS OF UNINTENTIONAL DISTURBANCE

Because unintentional disturbance is, by definition, not intended deliberately to destroy or otherwise damage birds of prey, the effects are generally easier to manage and mitigate than are the effects of persecution. Where disturbance occurs it is usually through lack of knowledge about the location, habits and sensitivities of vulnerable species. Increased education and heightened awareness among sympathetic land users and 'recreationalists' in the countryside can go a long way to mitigating the effects of disturbance. For example, potential conflicts between rock climbers and nesting Golden Eagles, should they occur, could be largely avoided through the adoption of a voluntary code of practice. This might include agreement on spatial zoning and the avoidance of climbing on or near the small number of crags used by nesting eagles, or on temporal zoning so that climbing in sensitive areas was restricted to seasons when eagle nests were not in use. A more formal approach might be needed where the demand for a particular human activity exceeded the capacity of the resource. This could happen, for example, with photographers who have a legitimate wish to use photographic hides at nests of rare or sensitive species. In Scotland this demand is managed by Scottish Natural Heritage which can issue a restricted number of photographic licences each year, using powers embodied in the Wildlife and Countryside Act. As a rule, the need for these restrictions is understood and accepted by most reasonable people.

Certain kinds of infrastructure development carry a risk of disturbance to birds such as Golden Eagles, especially if done during the nesting season. Most such developments in Scotland would require planning permission under the Town and Country Planning Act (1972). Through a process of consultation that follows any application for planning consent there is an opportunity for Scottish Natural Heritage, and others, to draw attention to the potential damage which may result from a development proposal. In general, planning authorities are sympathetic to such concerns. These authorities have the power to attach to a consent conditions which could help to mitigate impacts. For example a condition might restrict the time of year when construction work could be done, thereby avoiding or reducing disturbance to birds such as eagles during the breeding season.

Some developments may be so large or potentially damaging as to require full Environmental Assessment before a planning application is even considered. In a hypothetical case which could conceivably affect Golden Eagles, such as a new hydro-electric power plant, quarry or recreational development in an otherwise undeveloped part of the Scottish Highlands, Scottish Natural Heritage would advise the developer on matters to be considered within the assessment. Such an assessment must identify ways of mitigating impacts, although mitigation may not

Golden Eagle in flight with a California wind farm in the background.

always be possible. When the latter occurs, the environmental costs need to be identified and weighed against the socio-economic benefits that the development will bring. Initially, this judgement will be made by the planning authority but in certain circumstances the final decision can be referred to the Secretary of State for Scotland. A key purpose of this apparently bureaucratic procedure is to ensure that, where environmental damage is anticipated, it is not done in a climate of ignorance. In some cases the development may be deemed to be completely inappropriate and so refused. In others approval may be granted with conditions to minimize impact.

Most developers are now aware of the widespread public support for conservation and have accepted the need to minimize the environmental impact of their proposals. Nevertheless, the attitudes of developers in Scotland are not yet as advanced as those in the United States. In that country, acknowledgement of the legitimacy of environmental concerns has ensured that developers are often prepared to use their own funds to help understand and mitigate environmental impact. In effect, this is an extension of 'the polluter pays' principle. A good example is the detailed study of the impact of reconstruction activities related to the Swan Falls hydro-electric power plant on nesting raptors in southern Idaho (Holthuijzen 1989). This cooperative venture was funded by the Idaho Power Company, Pacific Gas and Electric Company and the US government's Bureau of Land Management. In another case in Wyoming, funding from a mining company (Arch Mineral Corporation) was used to test and successfully implement a technique for relocating the nesting sites of Golden Eagles (Fala *et al.* 1985). In another case in California, KENETECH Windpower and the National Renewable Energy Laboratory have made a substantial research commitment into the effects of wind turbines on Golden Eagles (PBRG 1995). That study set out to quantify impacts and to indicate modifications needed to reduce eagle mortality caused by wind turbines. Following these examples, I believe that in Britain there is a powerful case for more research investment on environmental impacts by private sector development companies and by the government agencies charged with promoting economic development.

REDUCING THE EFFECTS OF PESTICIDES AND OTHER POLLUTANTS

Compared with several of the bird and fish-eating raptors, Golden Eagles have been much less affected by pesticides (Chapter 19; Newton 1979). This is no cause for complacency and there continues to be a need to reduce the level of pesticide contamination in the environment as a whole. Avoidance of the most toxic and long-lasting compounds must be a priority, and continued vigilance is needed to ensure that dosages used are kept to a minimum. The potentially harmful effects of newly developed compounds must also be identified in advance wherever possible, and the subsequent levels monitored closely in the natural environment. Although many of the most persistent and toxic substances are no longer used in many northern countries, some, such as DDT, are still quite widely applied in tropical areas (Newton 1979). There is a continuing need to identify the effects of these chemicals on vulnerable populations of raptors in these areas, and to find ways of minimizing their use.

The problems associated with lead poisoning were mentioned in the previous chapter. Here the priority must be to develop non-toxic substitutes for lead shot and to ensure these are used, even if replacements are more costly. While voluntary bans can be effective, legislative action might eventually be needed against the use of lead shot in cartridges. This is a case where environmental protection cannot be secured solely by the workings of the market place. In the United States and in several countries in continental Europe a complete legislative ban on the use of lead shot for hunting waterfowl is already in place (Fawcett & van Vessem 1995).

MINIMIZING THE RISKS FROM ELECTROCUTION

One of the great successes of directed management involving Golden Eagles has been to reduce deaths by electrocution at power poles, principally in the United States. Working with the Idaho Power Company in the early 1970s, Morlan Nelson used a trained eagle to help identify the electrocution risks posed by various types of pole construction (Nelson & Nelson 1977). His captive bird was trained to perch on dummy power poles where the risks from electrocution were simulated. From these experiments, Nelson identified the changes needed in power pole design in order to reduce electrocution risks; following his study power poles were modified in several ways. Where possible, the central insulator was raised more than 1 m above the level of the cross-arm and the position of the groundwire was lowered on the pole. Both changes reduced the chances of an eagle making a fatal contact between the wires as it spread its wings at take-off or on landing. Another modification was to surround a length of the central cable with an insulated tube for about 1.2 m either side of the pole attachment. Where these modifications were not possible the best solution was to build an elevated perch positioned well above the insulators and such perches were readily adopted by eagles. From field research Nelson showed that modifications were only necessary on a small number of existing power poles because eagles were selective in their choice of poles for perching. He estimated that some 95% of all electrocutions could be prevented by changing the design on only 2% of poles. These were poles mostly located on crests or small hills where wind conditions were especially suitable for landing and take-off by eagles.

Electrocution problems in Spain are rather different, and have proved more intractable because the pylons are made of metal and the risks of electrocution are much greater (Chapter 19; Ferrer 1993a). The only sure way of eliminating deaths by electrocution was by covering the wires with insulation for a distance of 1.2 m on each side of the pylon (Ferrer *et al.* 1991). In Britain, Golden Eagle mortality due to electrocution has occurred only rarely. This is probably because there are few transmission lines over large parts of the eagle's range, and where lines do occur, there are usually plenty of alternative perches on nearby crags. Nevertheless, this is a matter about which we in Britain are largely ignorant and, as I indicated in the Chapter 18, the proportion of ringed birds found dead under wires might indicate an as yet unrecognized problem. I believe there is a case for further research here, perhaps funded by the newly privatized electricity companies.

MODERATING THE EFFECTS OF LAND USE CHANGE

The principal land uses in the uplands of Scotland where Golden Eagles live are sustained by economic or social subsidies or incentives. Hill sheep farming is only viable because of the substantial 'headage' payments from government based on the numbers of breeding ewes on individual land holdings. Similarly, afforestation of bare land is only made economically attractive by large government grants which substantially underwrite the capital costs of establishing new woodland.

While various government departments have an obligation to take into account the impact on nature conservation of their land use policies, the way that this is actually done is often far from transparent. The one part of the countryside in Britain where nature conservation obligations are largely fulfilled in practice is where land use change is being proposed within designated Sites of Special Scientific Interest (SSSIs). In Scotland, change of land use within these special areas requires prior consultation with Scottish Natural Heritage because of the acknowledged high nature conservation value of SSSIs. In the event that a proposed change is judged to be damaging to the nature conservation interest in an SSSI, then Scottish Natural Heritage can enter into a management agreement with the owner or occupier of the land in order to prevent damage taking place. Outside designated SSSIs, nature conservation considerations receive little attention when land use policies and programmes are being drawn up and implemented.

Most SSSIs are comparatively small and few are large enough to contain the territorial needs of more than one or two pairs of Golden Eagles. Also, the total area of SSSIs is only around 10% of the Golden Eagle range in upland Scotland. As a consequence, the SSSI designation system does not on its own offer a satisfactory mechanism for ensuring the long-term conservation of such a low density and wide-ranging species. However, the British government has committed itself to the conservation of its Golden Eagles, as well as many other wild bird species, by adopting the European Union's Directive on the Conservation of Wild Birds (79/409/EEC) (Stroud *et al.* 1990). There is a need for changes in government policies for land use in the uplands if the obligations under this Directive are to be met. Until these changes are made and implemented, there is a risk that the government will be found to be in breach of the Directive.

Government policy on land use in the uplands could be improved with respect to Golden Eagles in a number of ways. Such changes would equally benefit several other wide-ranging species which depend on a high-quality upland environment in Britain. The first need is for comprehensive strategic environmental assessment of the current policies designed to support and encourage hill sheep farming, afforestation and management for game (notably Red Deer stalking and grouse shooting). This assessment should quantify the environmental costs and benefits of existing policies and incentives, and place these in a social and economic context. Clearly, such an assessment should identify policy changes required to maintain or enhance the commitment of government to the fragile human communities of the uplands. Equally importantly, it should identify changes in the level and targeting of incentives so as to ensure that upland land

uses are designed in ways that maintain and enhance the high-quality upland environment.

With the work that has been done on Golden Eagles, it is already possible to anticipate some of the advantageous policy changes which such an assessment might identify. For hill sheep farming the system of 'headage' payments for breeding ewes must be questioned. The current system favours excessive stocking levels and fails to reward good husbandry of the sheep stock. The traditional practice of muirburn, in which extensive areas of upland sheep country are burned each spring, should be reviewed. While muirburn is believed to provide improved grazing for sheep, the uncontrolled nature of burning in western Scotland is ecologically, and in some cases economically very damaging. There is a powerful case for a fundamental change in government policy towards muirburn over large parts of the upland landscape.

Bare-ground afforestation in much of the Scottish Highlands is generally achieved by fencing out grazing animals. The present commitment of landowners (who receive grants for woodland establishment) to make parallel reductions in grazing animals, especially Red Deer, has to be questioned. Afforestation policies and incentives need to be revised to ensure that grazing pressure in the uplands is reduced and perhaps ultimately to allow woodland to regenerate naturally without the need for fencing. A much larger differential is needed in the level of incentive offered for environmentally sensitive woodland (comprising native species established with a more natural structure) compared with monoculture plantations of exotic species.

While it is now widely accepted that the numbers of Red Deer in large parts of the Scottish Highlands are far too high, there remains resistance to tackling the problem. Much of this results from the shared nature of deer populations between different ownership units, and the innate distrust between owners of adjacent properties. Culling rarely reaches the recommended level because each owner believes that his/her neighbour is shooting too many animals, despite all the evidence to the contrary. There is also a widespread misconception that retaining high hind numbers will somehow increase future stag levels, and thereby increase land values and stalking income. Comprehensive management plans covering whole deer-management units are now needed, and just such an approach is now being pursued by the government's advisers, the Red Deer Commission. Implementation of the culling levels advocated in these plans will be essential. Only then will benefits to the natural environment, and to the overall condition of the Red Deer herd, become apparent. Government might yet need to use leverage through various fiscal measures to ensure that reductions in deer numbers are achieved. The recent relief from payment of rates for sporting land in Scotland is one such fiscal incentive, and its potential for securing environmentally sensitive management practices on sporting land needs to be kept under constant review.

Adult Golden Eagle sitting on a specially constructed raised perch above power lines; such modifications have dramatically reduced eagle deaths by electrocution in the western United States.

CONCLUDING REMARKS

The principal damaging effects of current land use practices on Golden Eagles in the uplands of Scotland have occurred through changes to the bird's food supply. Specifically, over-grazing and poor management of sheep and deer have caused a major reduction in the bird's natural prey, notably grouse and hares. The establishment of large areas of closed canopy commercial forestry has had a similar, if more localized effect. Each of the land use policy changes outlined above would, if enacted, contribute to the recovery of the eagle's natural prey, and indeed to an overall improvement in biodiversity in the Scottish uplands. The full suite of recommendations proposed could be implemented with minimal short-term economic cost and would offer enormous long-term economic and environmental benefits.

CHAPTER 21
History and Tradition

Falconer's hood used on Golden Eagles by the Kirghiz tribesmen of the Tien Shan Mountains in central Asia.

THE marked improvement in the technology of firearms which occurred from the early nineteenth century was a key turning point in man's relationship with birds of prey such as Golden Eagles. With these weapons there came a greatly enhanced ability to kill wild game for food and later also for sport. Eagles were soon perceived as unwelcome competitors in the chase. Men with guns quickly lost their ancestor's reverence for these noble creatures. Instead, they chose to label all birds of prey as unwanted vermin, to be hunted ruthlessly, sometimes to the very edge of extinction. It was not always thus. In this chapter I reflect on man's relationship with Golden Eagles at an earlier period in human history. This whole subject could offer enough material for a book in itself and so my treatment must inevitably be superficial. This short account is given in recognition and appreciation of those

257

traditional societies whose attitudes to nature offer profound lessons for many of us today.

My account is drawn from three very different regions of the world. These are Europe (including North Africa), North America and Central Asia. In each case the nature of the testimony supporting a once closer bond between man and eagles is quite different. From Europe the evidence is fragmentary and is mainly to be found in a smattering of ancient myths and fables. In North America the cultural link between Golden Eagles and man is much more recent. Inevitably though, many of the traditions and beliefs of the indigenous peoples of that continent have fallen silent along with their ancestors. Only in the mountains of Central Asia is there a people whose culture is still intimately bound up with the Golden Eagle. Here, in the fabulous Tien Shan mountain range which straddles the borders of Russia, China and Mongolia, trained Golden Eagles are still used by man to hunt foxes, gazelles and even occasionally animals as large as wolves.

EUROPE—GOLDEN EAGLES IN MYTH AND LEGEND

The attitude of early Europeans to the Golden Eagle appears to have been largely one of reverence. The bird was certainly admired for its mastery of the skies and for its impressive power as a predator. Both the ancient Greeks and Romans identified the eagle as a messenger of the gods. Through the ages, a plethora of myths and legends have celebrated the eagle as the link between terrestrial mankind and celestial deities (Armstrong 1958). When a Roman emperor died, his body was burned in a funeral pyre and an eagle was ceremonially released into the flames. The bird's intended purpose was to carry the emperor's soul to the heavens. Some tales of transcendency went further still, endowing eagles with supernatural powers of rejuvenation. According to medieval scholars, an eagle could restore its youth by diving into the sea. Perhaps ignorance of the whereabouts of eagle nesting places, which were tucked away on remote and inaccessible mountain ledges, contributed to these mythical tales of reincarnation.

Throughout Europe and elsewhere, the power and majesty of the Golden Eagle has led to its widespread use in symbolism. One of the earliest examples is in the picture writing of the early Egyptians (Johnston 1966). While initially the eagle picture probably meant just the bird itself, over time this symbolic image came to incorporate other meanings. As with the Greeks and Romans, the Egyptians too attached religious significance to the bird and, in their writings, began to use an elaborate eagle picture to represent the 'soul' after death. As picture writing developed, so these symbols came to mean word sounds. In the case of the eagle this was the letter 'a'. It was in fact the two eagle pictures on the Rosetta Stone, and the recognition that these represented the letter 'a' in the name 'Cleopatra', that helped unlock the mystery of Egyptian hieroglyphic writing (Love 1989). Subsequently, the Phoenicians refined the Egyptian picture writing into a formal alphabet, with stylized images representing letter sounds; the shape of the letter 'a', which we still use today, reflects the stylized outline of a perching eagle.

Eagle symbolism has been used to depict the power of armies and empires for thousands of years. Roman legions always marched behind the emblem of an eagle,

The perching eagle shape was the origin of the letter 'a' in modern writing—see text.

and a choice of camp site close to an eagle nest was believed to be especially propitious. The double-headed eagle was adopted as the emblem of Emperor Charlemagne who united Europe under his rule in 800 AD. By so doing he incorporated the eagle of Rome which faced to the right and the German eagle which faced to the left. Alongside such symbolism came superstition, and the belief that eagles could foretell momentous events such as war. Perhaps this belief was rooted in the eagle's propensity for carrion, and its likely occurrence at the scenes of bloody battles. In ancient times, the Golden Eagle of Snowdon was believed to anticipate war by perching on 'the fatal stone', there sharpening her beak in anticipation of the bodies of the dead (Love 1989).

The elevated status of the Golden Eagle is now perpetuated through the bird's name which, in so many European languages has regal connotations (Table 73). Names such as King or Royal Eagle in part reflect the bird's intrinsic majesty, but probably also relate to the ancient sport of falconry. The Golden Eagle, the largest and most spectacular of the birds traditionally used in falconry, was strictly the preserve of kings and emperors. In Gaelic, the original language of the people of the Scottish Highlands, the Golden Eagle is known as *Iolaire*. The etymology of the word is uncertain, but it is probably descriptive of the bird itself rather than derived from any human association. Although Gaelic is now generally spoken only in the far west of Scotland, and principally on the islands, the legacy of the Gaels remains in many place names. Many crags and hills in the Highlands go by the name of *Craig na h-iolaire,* or crag of the eagle, and some at least are occupied by Golden Eagles even today.

NORTH AMERICA—GOLDEN EAGLES IN NATIVE AMERICAN CULTURE

For countless generations, Golden Eagles played a vital part in the culture of native Americans, especially in those tribes living south and west of the Great Plains

(Palmer 1988). There were many rituals surrounding the capture of Golden Eagles whose feathers, and especially the tail-feathers of juvenile birds, were of great ceremonial value. A method of pit-trapping for catching wild eagles was clearly widespread and was practised by many tribes including the Apache, Arapaho, Blackfoot, Cherokee, Cheyenne, Dakota, Gros Ventre, Havasupai, Hidatsa, Hopi, Mandan, Navajo, Nez Percé, Pawnee and Seneca. In some tribes, notably in the southwest of the continent, young eagles were also taken from nests and subsequently kept captive in cages until their feathers were fully grown.

Across the region, the actual method of pit-trapping was essentially similar. A hole was dug, typically on a bluff or an escarpment, and the catcher sat, kneeled or lay in the pit which was covered over. A bait such as a dead jackrabbit was placed on the surface next to a small hole through which the catcher was able to pass his hand. When an eagle landed on the bait, the catcher grabbed the bird's legs and drew the eagle inside the pit. There were many important rituals surrounding the catching of eagles and these varied greatly between tribes. In the Hidatsa tribe of the Upper Missouri the ceremonies associated with pit-trapping were many and complex (Wilson 1928). These included rituals surrounding the construction of hunting lodges, the offering up of prayers and burning of incense, and strict customs related to the selection and preparation of baits, among many others. The purpose of all these was to placate the eagle spirit, and presumably to increase the chance of a successful hunt.

In contrast, the Hopi tribe usually collected young eagles directly from nests; only one young was taken from broods of two, and single eaglets were never taken (Fewkes 1900). In this tribe, ceremonies were mainly associated with the captive bird. Following collection the young eagle was taken to the village where it was ritually anointed in watery white clay and given its own name. It was then tethered to the roof of a hut, fed fresh meat such as jackrabbits, talked to by members of the tribe, presented with gifts by children and finally sacrificed when fully fledged. The precious feathers were then removed and the body of the bird ceremonially buried in an eagle cemetery.

The most conspicuous use of eagle feathers by Plains tribes was in their spectacular war bonnets. For these, the dramatic black and white tail-feathers of a juvenile eagle were essential. A complete headdress typically contained as many as 60 feathers, requiring the tail-feathers of at least five eagles. However, all eagle feathers were precious and even the small body feathers were used, being tied to bushes to ward off evil spirits. Other feathers were used to adorn friendship pipes, shields, spears and as a component of fans (Palmer 1988; Ducey 1992).

The reason for the supreme veneration of Golden Eagles by native Americans is to be found in their deep spiritualism, which is closely tuned to their natural environment. A good example comes from a study of the ornithology of Cheyenne religionists (Moore 1986). In Cheyenne cosmology, vertical space is divided into a series of concentric spheres. Birds are considered to occupy the three outermost of these spheres which are called *Otatavoom*, the Blue Sky-space, *Setovoom*, the Nearer Sky-space, and *Taxtavoom*, the Atmosphere. Birds associated with the outermost sphere are the sacred birds or *maheonevekseo*, those in the middle sphere are the great birds or *maxevekseo*, and those in the Atmosphere the ordinary birds or *xamaevekseo*. In the Cheyenne religion, sacred birds are the property of priests, great

Juvenile Golden Eagle feathers as used in native American Indian war bonnets.

birds are used by war doctors and ordinary birds by healers to treat disease and injury. Golden Eagles occur twice in this taxonomy. They are the highest of the sacred birds, also known as 'thunderbird' or 'bird father'. They are also placed at the head of the list of great birds under various names such as 'war eagle', 'striped eagle' and 'prairie eagle'. So, because flying creatures are the most revered animals in the eyes of the Cheyenne, and since Golden Eagles represent the zenith of this life form, it is not surprising that this splendid bird has a special place in the life of the tribe. On this I would readily share their judgement, but perhaps I am a little biased.

CENTRAL ASIA—GOLDEN EAGLES WORKING WITH MAN

For centuries the people of the high mountains of Central Asia have kept and trained Golden Eagles for falconry. This practice has been richly described and illustrated by Georges Dementiev for the Kirghiz tribesmen who live in the Tien Shan mountains of southeast Russia (Dementiev 1936, 1937). It occurs too across the border in Mongolia and also in Chinese Turkestan from where Ludlow & Kinnear (1933) tell of a Colonel Schomberg's colourful encounter with a man and his donkey. The donkey was weighed down with two panniers, each containing five Golden Eagles for which the man intended to receive a handsome remuneration from local tribesmen. Although the practice of falconry in Central Asia is undoubtedly much less common than in the past, there are still today eagle hunters in various parts of the Tien Shan range (Severin 1991; Miller Mundy 1996).

Traditionally, the eagles are collected as half-grown young birds from carefully guarded nests in the spring. Once fully fledged the birds are trained for falconry in about a month. In contrast with western falconers who use the left hand, the Kirghiz carry their birds on a glove on the right hand. Where the terrain permits, they usually hunt with their eagles from horseback, although some hunts are conducted on foot. Because of the great weight of the bird (more than 4 kg), the horseman's wrist is typically supported by a short wooden prop attached to the saddle or the knee. On occasions the hunters fly eagles in conjunction with dogs, which are used to flush the potential prey. Once trained, individual eagles are highly valued possessions and can be kept as working animals for 15 years or more.

Most eagle hunting in the high tablelands of the Tien Shan takes place in the crisp days of autumn and early winter, before the arrival of the deep winter snows. Certainly in the past, and to some extent even today, eagles play a vital part in the economy of the people of this rugged landscape. The usual quarry of the Kirghiz huntsmen is the Corsac Fox which is hunted for its fur, the pelts being sold or bartered for other goods. A good eagle is reported to catch between 30 and 50 foxes during a single hunting season. Eagles are also flown successfully at Roe Deer and Goitred Gazelle, both of which are hunted for their meat. Perhaps the most remarkable quarry of all is the Steppe or Asiatic Wolf, except that the race in question is a comparatively small one. Although some of the stories seem a little far-fetched (one eagle in 1923 was said to have dispatched 14 wolves on a single hunting excursion), there seems little doubt that wolves are occasionally killed by the trained eagles of the Kirghiz.

Kirghiz falconer on horseback with a hooded Golden Eagle.

MORE GOLDEN EAGLE TALES

During my research for this book I have encountered many eagle tales for which there is no space here. But two in particular appealed to me greatly, and I recount them briefly here. The first is the story of the Greek poet and dramatist Aeschylus who lived in the fifth century BC (Love 1989). One day he was advised by an old witch that his death would be caused by a house falling on his head. The witch could name the day of the year, but not the actual year when this would happen. Being a wise and cautious man, Aeschylus took care each year always to be out in open country on the day in question. But then, one year on the appointed day, he was working in the fields feeling secure in the open countryside when an eagle passed overhead. The bird was carrying a tortoise which it proceeded to drop from a great height onto the bald pate of the unfortunate Aeschylus. The poor man died and, consistent with the witch's prophesy, his death was caused by the tortoise's shell which is none other than that animal's house. As pointed out by John Love, this little fable illustrates that the habit of eagles dropping tortoises onto rocks to crack open their shells was well known to the ancient Greeks. Only comparatively recently has this piece of natural history been 'rediscovered' by ornithologists in parts of southeast Europe and the Middle East.

A more contemporary story involving a trained Golden Eagle has emerged from the dark days of the Soviet prison camps of Siberia (Ramovski 1979). Many years after the event, Simiyon Ramovski, who had been imprisoned in a Siberian labour camp in the 1940s because he was a Jew, told how his life was saved by an eagle. One day, early in his confinement, one of the prison guards gave him an eagle chick. Because of his knowledge of birds and some previous falconry experience, Ramovski was able to raise and train the bird, but eventually he had to liberate her for lack of food. He assumed he would never see the eagle again, but later that same day she returned 'carrying a fat Russian Rabbit' (this was probably a Mountain Hare given the location). Then, for the next 2 years, which were among the harshest for Ramovski and his fellow prisoners, the eagle regularly flew from the camp and returned with prey including hares, sables and martens. This was all too good to last though, and the eagle was eventually shot by one of the prison guards when the bird attacked a pet dog. Ramovski was eventually released in 1956 after which he emigrated to Oregon, USA. From his account he was clearly convinced that, but for the intervention of the eagle and the food she provided, he would never have survived his Siberian incarceration. Could this tale be true ? I think it just might be.

CONCLUDING REMARKS

Contemporary attitudes to Golden Eagles have been greatly influenced by the exploitationist philosophy perpetrated on nature by mankind in Western Europe and North America during the late nineteenth and early twentieth centuries. Since the 1960s and 1970s attitudes have been changing and the outlook for birds like the Golden Eagle is now much more positive (Nelson 1982). Perhaps it is even possible in the years ahead, that some of the empathy for the natural world which was implicit in so many traditional societies, will be rekindled and embraced again by people in the so-called 'developed' world.

CHAPTER 22

Further research

Golden Eagle nestling sunning itself, aged 50 to 60 days old.

IN the 40 years since the publication of Seton Gordon's *The Golden Eagle: King of Birds* much has been learned about Golden Eagle biology and ecology. I have, in this book, attempted to cover some of that ground, especially by bringing together findings from many different parts of the world. However, there remain many unanswered questions and in this short concluding chapter I explore some of the opportunities and challenges for future research on the species.

Throughout its northern hemisphere range the status and distribution of the Golden Eagle is comparatively well known in places, and hardly at all in others. Knowledge is especially sparce over large parts of the eastern Palearctic, notably in

265

eastern Siberia and south into Mongolia, western China and the Himalayas. Perhaps more surprisingly there is a dearth of information for much of Canada east of the Rocky Mountains. In North Africa and the Arabian peninsula there have been several recent discoveries that have extended the known range and it is likely that further isolated populations may be found in suitable mountain areas in those regions.

The racial distinctiveness of the east Siberian subspecies *Aquila c. kamtschatica* remains a subject of debate. Recent accounts have not distinguished this subspecies from the North American race *A. c. canadensis* and evidently there are few morphological differences between Golden Eagles of the two regions. This leads to the intriguing prospect that colonization of eastern Siberia by Golden Eagles may have arisen from North American birds that crossed the Bering Strait towards the end of the Pleistocene glaciation. The technique of DNA finger-printing could perhaps throw some light on the extent to which there is currently, or has been in the recent past, gene flow between populations in Alaska and eastern Siberia.

Work in North America has provided a reliable technique for separating male and female Golden Eagles based on size differences using such features as bill length and hind claw length. There is an abundance of study-skin material available in museum collections in Britain and elsewhere in Europe, and this could be used for an equivalent study here. Field biologists would benefit from such an analysis, and especially if this could be extended to enable the sexing of well-grown nestlings at the age when they are ringed.

There has been comparatively little work done on Golden Eagles in the non-breeding season compared with the breeding season. It is only quite recently that comprehensive studies of Golden Eagles fitted with radio-transmitters have been carried out and much of this work has not yet been published. With the rapidly improving transmitter technology it is now possible to use this technique to help understand the nature of range use by territorial adults during different seasons and over several years. Such work could reveal how much of the home range is used for hunting, the relative importance of different habitats, and whether there are seasonal variations in range use linked to such factors as changing climatic conditions. Not all such work is dependent on the potentially costly technique of radio-telemetry. Given time and an intimate knowledge of one or two pairs of eagles, much could undoubtedly be learned through careful field study on the pattern of range use in relation to day-to-day changes in weather variables such as wind-direction.

The consequences of different weather conditions on Golden Eagle breeding success are still far from clear. Reliable long-term data on breeding success are now becoming available, often as a result of voluntary monitoring initiatives. From these it may soon be possible to identify some of the most striking relationships between breeding performance and weather factors. More focused research will be needed if precise causal links are to be identified, and if the interplay between weather, food supply and the condition of the territorial eagles are to be better understood.

One of the least known aspects of eagle biology is the behaviour of young birds after they leave the nest and before they enter the breeding population some 5 years or so later. Only long-term studies with comparatively large numbers of birds fitted with radio-transmitters would begin to address this question. In time, such studies would provide estimates of pre-breeding survival and demonstrate the nature of dispersal behaviour. In Scotland, this kind of work is urgently needed if conservation policies are to be tailored effectively to meet the complete needs of the species. Radio-telemetry work is also needed in order to understand more about the long-range migrations of subarctic populations of Golden Eagles in North America and Eurasia.

Portrait of a chick aged 45 to 50 days old.

As in virtually all long-lived raptors, the information available on adult mortality in Golden Eagles is minimal. Probably the only way to plug this knowledge gap would be to mark a substantial number of adults and measure the rate of disappearance of such birds from the population. Radio-telemetry again, is probably the best available technique although the capture of sufficient adults to provide a statistically useful sample is rarely going to be achievable. At some point in the future it may become possible to use moulted feathers for DNA finger-printing purposes, and thus identify individual birds from feathers collected at roost sites. This could ultimately give an indirect measure of the rate of turnover among territorial adults, and perhaps even an indication of mortality rates.

There are clearly opportunities to use the spatial analysis and information sieving techniques of Geographical Information Systems (GIS) to understand more about land use and Golden Eagle population ecology. With the increased availability of more sophisticated data sets, there are exciting opportunities for combining these with hard data from range use drawn from telemetry studies of eagles. Ultimately, it should be possible to use GIS to make predictions for the consequences of land use change on populations of Golden Eagles in the future. For those charged with the implementation of conservation management of wide-ranging species like the Golden Eagle, the need for such studies is pressing.

One of the most critical problems facing Golden Eagle populations in Scotland and elsewhere is the mismanagement of land for grazing by large herbivores, and the consequent loss of smaller wild herbivores on which eagles depend for food. There is a powerful case for applied research into the restructuring of grazing management in order to test whether or not, and how quickly, the smaller wild herbivore populations can recover. Elsewhere in this book I have argued that such an approach will have benefits not only for top predators such as Golden Eagles, but also for land managers and others whose long-term livelihood depends on the adoption of more sustainable land management practices.

These are just some of the needs and opportunities for research on Golden Eagles in the years ahead. How much progress is made will crucially depend on the extent to which long-term funding commitments can be secured. Given the vital role that top predators play in natural ecosystems, the value of birds of prey as biological indicators and the symbolic importance of the Golden Eagle in the minds of so many people, I believe that, in Scotland at least, such commitments cannot be avoided.

APPENDIX 1
The Genus Aquila—*Distribution and Ecology*

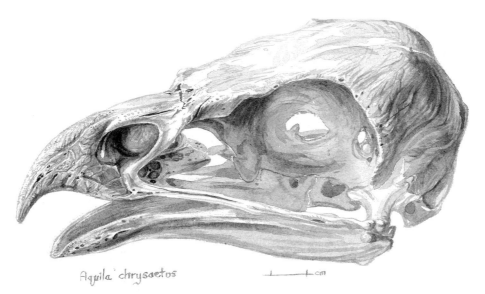

Aquila chrysaetos

Golden Eagle skull.

THE genus *Aquila* comprises nine species of comparatively large eagles. All are superbly adapted for soaring with long, broad wings and moderately long tails which are either rounded or wedge-shaped. They are typically robust predators with large, arched beaks and powerful feet. The adult plumage in all species is predominantly brown or blackish-brown although some, such as the Black and Imperial Eagles, have conspicuous white patches on the wings, back or rump. In the two smaller species, the Lesser and Greater Spotted Eagles, adults occur in distinctive light and dark colour phases although in both species the light morph is very rare (del Hoyo *et al.* 1994). All have distinctive juvenile and immature plumages and the full adult dress is not normally attained until 5 years of age or older. Full descriptions of all species are given by Brown & Amadon (1968). For the five *Aquila* eagles which occur in Europe the diagnostic identification features are described in detail by Porter *et al.* (1981). Clark (1992) lists a range criteria for separating Tawny and Steppe Eagles which occur together in Africa during the northern winter.

The following accounts summarize the contemporary breeding and wintering ranges and the key ecological requirements of the Golden Eagle's eight close relatives. Distributional information is mainly after Brown & Amadon (1968), updated with more recent information where this has come available.

269

LESSER SPOTTED EAGLE *AQUILA POMARINA*

Distribution

Two subspecies of the Lesser Spotted Eagle are recognized, *A. p. pomarina* and *A. p. hastata.* The nominate race breeds in eastern Europe from the Baltic to the Black Sea with its population stronghold in eastern Germany, Poland, the Baltic States and European Russia; smaller numbers nest south to Greece and east through Turkey to the southern edge of the Caspian Sea (Meyburg 1973; Génsbøl 1987). Birds of this race are intercontinental migrants wintering in southern Africa from Tanzania south to the Transvaal (Christensen & Sorensen 1989). Virtually the entire world population migrates through Israel in spring and autumn, entering Africa at Suez (Lesham 1985). In some years small numbers winter west to Cameroon and Chad (Thiollay 1989) and these may be the birds recorded leaving Africa at Cap Bon in Tunisia (Dejonghe 1980).

The Indian race *A. p. hastata* is, in contrast, strictly sedentary. It nests across most of India, although it is apparently absent from the southwest of the subcontinent. It is reportedly uncommon except in the Ganges Plain and eastwards into Bangladesh (Ali & Ripley 1968).

Ecology

In Europe, the Lesser Spotted Eagle occupies a range of open temperate woodland habitats, including swamp woodland bordering wet meadows in the lowlands of Poland and dry mountain woodland at 300–800 m in the Balkans (Meyburg 1973). Nests are in large deciduous trees such as beech or oak, less commonly in pines, and usually within 1 km of the woodland edge. It hunts by quartering open areas adjacent to woodland or by dropping on prey from a perch; it may also stalk prey on the ground in the manner of a crow (Brown & Amadon 1968). Its main food is the Common Vole but other similar-sized rodents and frogs are sometimes important in the diet; carrion is rarely eaten (Meyburg 1973). In Africa in winter it favours areas of moist forest–savanna where it tends to be gregarious, feeding on termite alates and nestlings of the colonial Red-billed Quelea (Brown *et al.* 1982).

The Indian race inhabits relatively dry wooded country next to open ground. It is probably the least 'predatory' of all the *Aquila* eagles, capturing frogs, young birds and rodents while walking on the ground and regularly pirating food from Black Kites. In Bengal it takes silkworm pupae from which habit it gets the Bengali name of *Gūtimār* or 'Cocoon Destroyer' (Ali & Ripley 1968). Nests are built at a height of 10–20 m in large trees such as mango or fig.

GREATER SPOTTED EAGLE *AQUILA CLANGA*

Distribution

The Greater Spotted Eagle breeds in a wide band from the Baltic States, European Russia and the Ukraine eastwards to the Pacific Ocean with outliers in Poland and Romania (Génsbøl 1987). Ali & Ripley (1968) report breeding in Pakistan (see also

Eates 1937) and in northwest India eastwards to Nepal and Bangladesh. This
disjunct population apparently extends west into Afghanistan and Iran (Nielsen
1969; Smith 1974). It is a comparatively short-range migrant, some individuals
wintering in northeast Africa, principally from the Nile Valley south to Kenya
(Brown *et al.* 1982). Many of the western breeders winter in southeast Europe and
the Middle East (Christensen 1962). More eastern populations winter from Pakistan
through north India to Cambodia and southeast China (Dementiev & Gladkov
1966).

Ecology

This species favours forested landscapes and shows a strong preference for
woodland in river valleys or close to marshes. It is typically a lowland species rarely
nesting above 300 m (Dementiev & Gladkov 1966). Nests are normally built at
8–10 m in trees such as oak, alder or willow but in the west Siberian steppe nests can
be as low as 3 m in willow thickets. Hunting behaviour is similar to the previous
species but the Greater Spotted Eagle tends to be more aerial, with frequent soaring
high over river valleys in search of prey (Brown & Amadon 1968). The diet reflects
the bird's association with wetland habitats and several Russian studies have shown
a preference for water voles and wetland birds, frogs and toads and occasionally
even fish (Glutz von Blotzheim *et al.* 1971). It feeds on carrion quite frequently
(Dementiev & Gladkov 1966). In the winter quarters in northeast Africa Greater
Spotted Eagles occur in semi-arid acacia grasslands where they feed on insects,
mainly locusts, termites and grasshoppers. In India it is again strongly associated
with wooded areas near rivers, canals, swamps and 'jheels' and the staple diet is
frogs but also includes a wide range of wetland birds such as coots and moorhens
(Ali & Ripley 1968). Here, nests are at or near the top of trees some 10–15 m
above ground.

STEPPE EAGLE *AQUILA NIPALENSIS*

Distribution

Two races of Steppe Eagles are recognized with the nominate Eastern Steppe Eagle
A. n. nipalensis occurring from the Altai Mountains eastwards through Mongolia and
north and central China (Flint *et al.* 1984). This race migrates south to India and
Nepal for the winter (Singh 1961; Fleming 1988) and occasional individuals go as
far as northeast Africa (Brown *et al.* 1982).

The Western Steppe Eagle *A. n. orientalis* breeds from the Ukraine, where it is now
very rare, eastwards through the Russian steppe to Kazakhstan where it intergrades
with the previous race near the Chinese/Mongolian border (Dementiev & Gladkov
1966; Génsbøl 1987). This race is a long-distance migrant, entering Africa in large
numbers at Suez and across the Bab-el-Mendab Straits at the southern end of the
Red Sea (Lesham 1985; Welch & Welch 1989). It exhibits apparently separate
wintering areas for adults, mainly in east and northeast Africa, with immatures,
mainly in southern Africa south to Namibia (Brooke *et al.* 1972). This separation is

not complete as Jensen (1972) reported adults and immatures together in flocks in Namibia.

Ecology

This is a breeding bird of flat, wide open plains or steppes and semi-desert or desert landscapes. The western race avoids mountains but the eastern race occurs on dry, rocky hillsides and valleys with low vegetation cover, nesting at elevations over 1600 m in Mongolia (Dementiev & Gladkov 1966). Birds of the western race usually nest on or very close to the ground and occasionally on man-made structures such as haystacks. Eastern birds sometimes nest in cliffs but also among stones on small hills or mounds. Birds of the western race feed mainly on Pygmy Ground Squirrels (Tyurekhodzhaev 1973; Varshavski 1973) although they will also feed on carrion and other prey if they arrive on the breeding grounds before the ground squirrels emerge from hibernation (Agafonov *et al.* 1957). In eastern birds the diet tends to be more varied with a preference for Daurian Ground Squirrels, Daurian Pikas and the young of Siberian Marmots or 'tarbagan', giving the bird its local name of *Tarbazhin* in Transbaikalia. Both races search for prey from soaring flight, catching animals on the ground after a short stoop. They also 'ambush' prey by perching next to burrows and pouncing on emerging animals.

The Steppe Eagle in winter is largely insectivorous, at least in Africa where it occurs in dry woodland and grassland, but also up to 4500 m in Ethiopia where it feeds on Mole-rats; it is gregarious in the lowlands and closely follows major weather fronts to ensure a ready supply of its preferred food of emerging termites (Brooke *et al.* 1972). The eastern race occupies more thickly wooded terrain in its wintering grounds, although the recent, and first recorded sightings in peninsular Malaysia were attributed to the increased availability of open habitat in that region following deforestation and the extension of rice-growing areas (Helbig & Wells 1990). Ali & Ripley (1968) record that in India in winter it lives by piracy and carrion-eating.

TAWNY EAGLE *AQUILA RAPAX*

Distribution

Three races of Tawny Eagles are recognized, two breed in Africa and one in the Indian subcontinent. The nominate *A. r. rapax* is largely resident and breeds from South Africa north to Kenya and southern Ethiopia, although it is absent from the equatorial forest zone (Brown *et al.* 1982). There is also a small breeding population in the south of the Arabian peninsula (Thiollay & Duhautois 1976). In northeast Africa it intergrades with the second resident African subspecies *A. r. belisarius* which extends from Ethiopia and Sudan in a broad band across the Sahel west to Senegambia. In west Africa this race makes fairly predictable movements southwards into moist woodlands in October–November, returning north to drier areas in April. Liversidge (1989) describes a frequent but non-annual influx of migrant Tawny Eagles into the Kalahari region of southern Africa and attributes these, by virtue of some very pale plumaged immatures in the flocks, to *A. r. belisarius* from north and west Africa. That race would therefore seem to be, at least in some years, a true intra-African migrant.

There is a disjunct breeding population of *belisarius* in northwest Africa where it previously bred from Morocco to Tunisia (Etchécopar & Hüe 1964) but is now scarce and largely confined to Morocco south of the High Atlas (Thévenot *et al.* 1985; Gaultier 1985). The third race *A. r. vindhiana* is widespread and sedentary, breeding in Pakistan, most of India except the extreme southwest and eastwards into northern Burma (Ali & Ripley 1968).

Ecology

In east and southern Africa Tawny Eagles occupy dry acacia grasslands and a range of open, semi-desert landscapes (Hustler & Howells 1989). In west Africa they breed in moist forest–savanna moving out into dry woodland and semi-desert in the non-breeding season (Thiollay 1977). Nests are invariably placed conspicuously on the tops of trees with a preference for thorny Acacia trees at heights of 6–15 m in east Africa (Steyn 1973b). The Tawny Eagle hunts mainly by stooping from perches but does sometimes take birds up to the size of flamingoes in flight. During the breeding season it feeds on a wide range of mammals, birds and reptiles with the most important species in Kenya being the African Hare, Kirk's Dikdik, Yellow-necked Francolin and Crested Bustard (Smeenk 1974) and in Zimbabwe, the Scrub Hare and Helmeted Guineafowl (Steyn 1973b, 1980). Some of this prey is probably taken as carrion, particularly road-kills. Outside the breeding season it is more insectivorous but also regularly feeds on carrion up to the size of elephant, and also pirates food from other raptors and storks. In northwest Africa it is commensal with man, feeding on offal around villages (Brown *et al.* 1982).

The Indian race occupies dry woodland, plains and semi-desert landscapes and frequently associates with villages and human cultivation. It nests in the tops of trees such as *Acacia arabica*. It is only weakly predatory, collecting much of its food by pirating other raptors or as carrion (Ali & Ripley 1968).

IMPERIAL EAGLE *AQUILA HELIACA*

Distribution

The nominate race *A. h. heliaca* breeds in southeast Europe where it is now very scarce; pockets occur in Slovakia, Hungary, Romania, Bulgaria and Greece, with a more extensive range in Turkey (Génsbøl 1987). The principal population is in Russia from the Black Sea eastwards in a band north of the Caspian and Aral Seas to northwest China and Mongolia and around Lake Baikal (Flint *et al.* 1984). There is a second eastwards extension around the south of the Caspian through Afghanistan to Pakistan and northwest India. It is a medium to short-range migrant wintering in northeast Africa (the Nile Valley south to Kenya; Brown *et al.* 1982) and the Arabian peninsula (Bundy 1985), and from the Middle East through south-central Asia to India and east to the Pacific coast of China (Cheng 1976). Wintering birds have been reported as far north as Mongolia and east to Korea and Japan (Dementiev & Gladkov 1966; Brazil & Hanawa 1991).

The Spanish Imperial Eagle *A. h. adalberti* is now confined to the southwestern part of the Iberian peninsula (González *et al.* 1987, 1990) but previously bred in northwest Africa (Heim de Balsac & Mayaud 1964) and further north in Spain (González *et al.* 1989). Breeding adults are essentially sedentary while immatures undertake short-range dispersal movements (González *et al.* 1989) with small numbers crossing the Mediterranean at Gibraltar to winter in north Africa (Pineau & Giraud-Audine 1977; Calderón *et al.* 1988).

Ecology

Much more is known about the ecological requirements of the endangered Spanish race (Ferrer 1993a) than the Eastern Imperial Eagle which in Russia occupies a band of forest–steppe, typically open woodland of either deciduous trees or pines (Dementiev & Gladkov 1966). It also extends into semi-desert lands in Turkestan and up to 1300 m in the Altai Mountains. Nests are almost invariably in trees (pine, oak, poplar), typically in or close to the crown and 10–20 m above ground. Hunting is usually by a stoop to the ground from a low perch or knoll; in Russia it is called *Mogil'nik* or 'Burial-ground Eagle' from its habit of perching on burial mounds in the steppe (Dementiev & Gladkov 1966). Its principal food in the breeding season is small and medium-sized mammals, particularly various ground squirrels and Great Gerbils (Lobachev 1967; Varshavski 1973), with smaller numbers of birds and occasionally snakes.

In winter in India it occupies open semi-deserts and is predominantly a carrion feeder, sometimes pirating food from other birds of prey (Ali & Ripley 1968). Little is known about its winter habits in northeast Africa where it is confined to lowland semi-arid grasslands. The Spanish race occupies low hills or plains with dry oak or pine woodland and mediterranean scrub, and tends to avoid areas of human habitation and activity (González *et al.* 1992). Nest sites are typically in the crowns of trees (pine, oak or eucalyptus) some 10–20 m above ground (Calderón *et al.* 1987). The favoured prey is the Rabbit and in marshy areas such as Coto Doñana, ducks, coots and other wetland birds (Delibes 1978). Carrion is taken quite frequently in winter (Hiraldo *et al.* 1991).

GURNEY'S EAGLE *AQUILA GURNEYI*

Distribution

Without question this is the least known of all the *Aquila* eagles. It occurs on the large island of New Guinea, on the Western Papuan Islands of Waigeo, Salawati and Misool, on Yapen Island in Geelvink Bay, on the Aru Islands to the southwest of the main island, and on the Eastern Papuan Islands of Goodenough and Normanby (Beehler *et al.* 1986). It is also reported from Morotai, Halamahera, Ternate and Bacan Islands in the Northern Moluccas (Brown & Amadon 1968). Garnett (1987) saw this species on Boigu Island which is, politically, part of

Australia but biogeographically linked with Papua New Guinea. He also reported a hitherto unpublished record from nearby Daru Island. It is likely that this list of localities is far from complete, although any new records would almost certainly come from islands near to New Guinea and the Northern Moluccas. Beehler *et al.* (1986) considered it was largely coastal in New Guinea, occurring within 10–15 km of the sea and generally below 1000 m altitude. However, Mackay (1988) drew attention to a number of records from the highlands in Papua New Guinea; further information on range on the main island of New Guinea is clearly desirable. The species is almost certainly entirely sedentary, at least as far as breeding birds are concerned.

Ecology

From the relatively few sightings of this species it would appear to occupy a range of thickly forested and more open woodland habitats. Among the latter are the swamp–forest and forest–savanna areas of the Trans-Fly lowlands. It also occurs in forested mountainous regions at 2000–3000 m (Mackay 1988) and it is tempting to speculate whether Gurney's Eagle might indeed hunt over the high level alpine heaths and deschampsia grasslands above the timberline at around 3700 m (Beehler *et al.* 1986). Use of such habitat would provide a neat ecological link with its holarctic relative the Golden Eagle, but for now this must remain speculation. It shows some morphological adaptation to hunting in wooded areas by virtue of its comparatively short wings and long tail (Amadon 1982). No nest has ever been reported, although it would presumably be in a tree. If the birds reported from the many smaller offshore islands are breeders then presumably, given the relative accessibility of such places, this is where a nest is most likely to be discovered; there is, however, the prospect that such records merely refer to wandering non-breeders. The only recorded food is a cuscus which is a mainly arboreal marsupial (Mackay 1988).

WEDGE-TAILED EAGLE *AQUILA AUDAX*

Distribution

This Australian species is separated into two races. The nominate *A. a. audax* breeds throughout mainland Australia, is less frequent on the coast than inland, is rare in rainforest and probably avoids the driest parts of the continent such as the Gibson Desert (Blakers *et al.* 1984). It also occurs and probably breeds in the Trans-Fly region of southern Papua New Guinea (Amadon 1978). Eagles of breeding age are essentially sedentary while juveniles and immatures disperse quite widely from their natal area (Ridpath & Brooker 1986b).

The second race *A. a. fleayi* is endemic to Tasmania where it is distributed throughout the island at relatively low densities (Mooney & Holdsworth 1991) with breeding also reported from Flinders Island in the Bass Strait (Blakers *et al.* 1984). Once again the race is sedentary.

Ecology

Wedge-tailed Eagles favour dry woodland, mediterranean-type shrubland and semi-desert habitats throughout mainland Australia and Tasmania, tending to avoid only the dense rainforest and perhaps the most arid desert landscapes (Blakers *et al.* 1984; Mooney & Holdsworth 1991; Marchant & Higgins 1993). In New Guinea it occurs in forest-savanna (Beehler *et al.* 1986). Nest sites are nearly always in trees, at heights of 2–6 m in arid regions and but up to 20 m elsewhere. Typical trees are *Acacia* spp. in dry landscapes and in *Eucalyptus* spp. in more moist areas, including Tasmania (Leopold & Wolfe 1970; Ridpath & Booker 1987; Mooney & Holdsworth 1991). There are occasional records of nesting on cliffs or on the ground (Marchant & Higgins 1993).

Wedge-tailed Eagles hunt from high soaring flight but also from perches on trees or other prominent features. Active prey is caught following a low-angled stoop, sometimes followed by a chase (Marchant & Higgins 1993). Over large parts of the range much of the diet now comprises Rabbits and hares—both introduced species in Australia. The principal indigenous species taken in Western Australia are young kangaroos (Brooker & Ridpath 1980). A variety of medium-sized birds and lizards are also taken (Leopold & Wolfe 1970) and both this and the previous study reported lambs, a proportion of which are taken as carrion, in the diet. Carrion feeding is common and 'congregations' of 15 or more birds have been reported, presumably feeding on large carcasses (Blakers *et al.* 1984).

BLACK EAGLE *AQUILA VERREAUXII*

Distribution

The Black Eagle breeds from South Africa and Namibia through the mountains of east Africa to the Red Sea, and around the borders of Chad and Sudan (Brown *et al.* 1982). A handful of pairs nest outside subsaharan Africa in Sinai (Génsbøl 1987) and North Yemen (Thiollay & Duhautois 1976). Breeding adults are sedentary and, based on information from a small number of ringing recoveries, juveniles appear to move relatively short distances from their natal area (Gargett 1990).

Ecology

This is a bird of mountainous terrain and isolated rocky hills in Africa, ranging from sea-level to over 4000 m; it favours dry landscapes from forest-savanna to semi-desert and even desert, and avoids areas of dense forest (Gargett 1990; Brown *et al.* 1982). Nest sites are almost invariably in cliffs with very occasional use of trees or man-made structures.

Prey is chiefly caught following a rapid, sometimes twisting dive from low-level flight or from a perch to the ground; as with Golden Eagles, the ground's natural contours are used to increase the element of surprise. The Black Eagle diet is the most conservative of all the *Aquila* eagles with all studies showing a strong preferences for hyraxes *Procaviidae*, especially in Zimbabwe (Gargett 1990; Tarboton & Allan 1984). Hyraxes are an exclusively African and Middle Eastern family of medium-sized (*c.* 3 kg) mammals which live in colonies. Although they look superficially like rodents, hyraxes are in fact very distant relatives of the elephant. In South Africa the diet is more varied with a selection of other medium-sized mammals and some birds taken. In some parts of the population carrion is taken fairly regularly (Steyn 1982) but in others hardly at all (Gargett 1990).

APPENDIX 2
The Shaping of the Highland Landscape

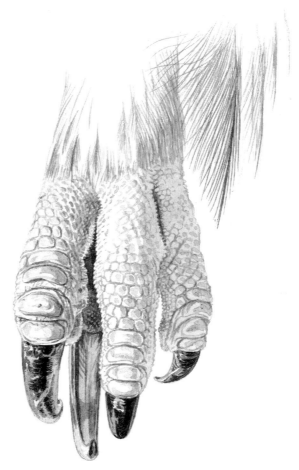

Golden Eagle talon.

THE landscape of the Scottish Highlands has been created by many forces. The last major event of the Pleistocene glaciation, the Loch Lomond re-advance, ended some 10 000 years ago when a rapid warming of the climate led to the development of forest cover over much of Scotland. Around 7000 years ago the climate became wetter and during the past 2000 years, gradually cooler. The

278

replacement of forests by blanket bog in some areas, and the lowering of the timberline were essentially natural processes. There is early evidence of forest clearance by Neolithic man from around 4000 years ago and a continuing steady loss of woodland up to the sixteenth century. There was then a rapid acceleration in deforestation during the seventeenth and eighteenth centuries as the remaining Highland forests were 'discovered' by people from the south, culminating in wholesale destruction as huge areas of woodland were felled for iron-smelting purposes and charcoal (Darling & Boyd 1964). The loss of important elements of the Highland fauna can also be attributed to the hand of man. The Northern Lynx was an early casualty, probably caused by Neolithic man but Reindeer, Elk (North American Moose) and Beaver all survived much longer, the Beaver still living in the Highlands until the sixteenth century. The Wolf survived a little later still and the last one was killed in 1743 (Darling & Boyd 1964).

During the eighteenth century the rate of change in the landscape gathered pace. This was a period of great turmoil in Scottish history, beginning with the Act of Union with England in 1707, followed by the Jacobite risings in 1715 and 1745, and the crushing defeat of Charles Edward Stewart (Bonnie Prince Charlie) and his Highland army by the Duke of Cumberland at the battle of Culloden in 1746. After this, the Highland Clan system, a feudal society based on militarism and close kinship, never again functioned in the way it had done for many centuries previously. Military defeat was quickly followed by the power of legislation which banned the carrying of firearms by Highlanders, outlawed the wearing of Highland dress and prohibited the playing of bagpipes. Meanwhile, Highland chiefs and chieftains began to adopt the attitudes and actions of Lowland lairds, and a society with a powerful egalitarian streak was rapidly transformed into one where the privileges of birthright were carefully protected (Smout 1969).

Throughout this period sturdy black Highland cattle were the principal livestock and virtually the only realizable asset of the region. Transhumance was widely practised and whole families moved to summer habitations or 'sheilings' with their stock. This was the century of the great drove roads through the Highlands. Down these roads the cattle were taken on long and frequently hazardous journeys to fairs or markets in the south and east. The introduction of the potato, followed by the discovery that Cheviot and Blackface sheep could survive, and indeed thrive in the Highlands, laid the foundation for the momentous events of the first half of the nineteenth century. This was the period of the infamous Highland clearances when a whole generation of people was, at first forcibly and later by more subtle persuasion, evicted from huge areas. Some were 're-settled' in coastal districts and on the islands but many left Scotland, never to return. The driving forces were the realization by Highland landlords that sheep were much more profitable than people in the glens, and also the failure in 1846 and 1847 of potato crops. The failures led to widespread famine and bankrupted or seriously depleted the wealth of many lairds as some at least sought to relieve their tenants' abject poverty with charity. The surviving remnants of the once great Caledonian forest were further depleted at this time as the land was over-run with sheep.

During the late nineteenth century royal patronage made popular the field sports of grouse shooting and Red Deer stalking and there was an influx from the south of new landlords whose wealth was founded on the fruits of the industrial revolution.

Wholesale and merciless destruction of any predator, especially birds of prey, which might conceivably be in competition with man for grouse or other game, was the order of the day. Scotland lost its nesting White-tailed Sea Eagles and Ospreys by the early decades of the twentieth century and numbers of many other raptors were sorely depleted. As the Highlands became the playground of the rich, so too was the wider British public made aware of the extent of social depravation among the crofting people who had tenaciously clung on in scattered communities around the west coast and on the islands. Finally, in 1886 the Crofters Act was passed into law and no longer could crofters be evicted from their land. The tradition of part-time agriculture that is 'crofting' continues today.

The War of 1914–18 signalled the decline of many of the major sporting estates of the Highlands, especially in the western part of the region. The reasons are several, including the reduction in numbers of game-keepers as men left the land to fight another enemy but also a widespread decline in numbers of Red Grouse, Black Grouse and other animals. There are many accounts which show that Red Grouse, Black Grouse and Mountain Hares were shot on estates in the west Highlands in the early years of the twentieth century in numbers that are inconceivable today (Mackenzie 1928; Gaskell 1980; Hudson 1992). While the precise cause of this change will probably never be known with certainty, it seems very likely that the previous century of excessive grazing pressure by sheep, and a consequent loss of overall fertility in the region, was a significant factor (McVean & Lockie 1969).

The pattern of private land ownership in the Highlands has changed little over recent centuries, with a comparatively small number of large units or 'estates' dominating the region. Throughout the mainland part of Highland Region in 1976, over 94% of private land was owned in 176 units of 2000 ha or more with the remaining 6% divided amongst 1178 units of less than 2000 ha (Armstrong & Mather 1983). A change which did occur in the twentieth century, but one which is now being reversed, was the increase in public ownership, which had reached nearly 20% by 1976. Most of this land was purchased by the Forestry Commission, established in 1919 following the First World War and the realization that the nation's timber resources were hopelessly depleted, and by the Department of Agriculture for Scotland (DAFS). Land purchased by DAFS in the 1920s and 1930s was mainly in the west and on the islands and was used for the purpose of land settlement by crofters. This undoubtedly contributed to some extent to the revitalization of human communities around the western seaboard, although much of the central and eastern Highlands remained little changed from 100 years earlier. A substantial increase in forest cover has been achieved since the inception of the Forestry Commission with a doubling of the total wooded area of Britain over the past 60 years, and much of this in the uplands of Scotland, northwest England and Wales. However, precious little of this woodland has been planted using indigenous species or sympathetic establishment techniques and most is doubtfully sustainable in an ecological sense (NCC 1986).

For much of the present century the sporting interests of Highland estates have increasingly centred on management for Red Deer. In Scotland the Red Deer population, which very largely occurs within the Highlands, was estimated at around 150 000 in 1900, dropping to 139 000 in 1939 as a result of increased shooting and poaching. Thereafter, there was a recovery to around 150 000 by 1960 and a doubling of the population to 300 000 over the next 30 years (SNH 1994). Among the causes of this increase were the removal of sheep from large parts of the range in the central, north and west Highlands, successive mild winters and consequent low winter mortality and underculling of hinds (Clutton-Brock & Albon 1989). The consequences of this increase for the natural environment of the Highlands are considerable, ranging from loss of heather and its replacement by grasses, lack of regeneration of natural woodlands and, in the worst affected areas, erosion of soils. Clearly, a radical overhaul of deer management in Scotland is both essential and long overdue (Callander & Mackenzie 1991; SNH 1994). Without a very substantial reduction in Red Deer numbers the ecological condition of the Highlands will continue to deteriorate.

In 1949 the British government established the Nature Conservancy to provide independent advice on nature conservation and related issues. Since the 1950s there has been a steady growth in, and more recently rapid acceleration in public concern for, the environment. This concern was heightened by the large and conspicuous pollution incidents of the 1960s and by the unravelling of the more insidious but equally alarming effects of pesticide contamination. Ratcliffe (1980) gives an eloquent account of the science, and the power of vested interests which constantly sought to undermine the case against the damaging consequences of organochlorine pesticides on birds of prey.

A conspicuous change in the Highlands in the past 20 years has been the growth of interest in outdoor recreation, both mechanized and formal in sports such as downhill skiing, and informal hill-walking and mountaineering. The politics of public access to the hills of Scotland are complex and way beyond the scope of this book. Nevertheless, the debate is intense and will continue as pressure for recreational use builds in an increasingly affluent, mobile and exercise-conscious society.

This then is a very brief account of the contemporary context within which the population of Golden Eagles in the Scottish Highlands now sits. It is abundantly clear that much is wrong with the land and with the forces that now drive its management. Perhaps in the years ahead, steps will at last be taken to restore the ecological capital of this precious region.

APPENDIX 3

Dietary Breadth

Golden Eagle pellet.

THE extent to which Golden Eagles and the other *Aquila* eagles have narrow or broad diets varies considerably. Birds in some populations are food specialists, and in these the great majority of the prey is from just one or two prey families. At the other extreme, eagles are food generalists in which no single prey family is dominant and the diet comprises prey from a dozen or more families in more equal proportions. In order to compare diet between populations, and between species, I calculated dietary breadth using the approach of Steenhof & Kochert (1985).

In that study, population dietary breadth was calculated using the formula of Levins (1968):

$$B = 1/\sum p_i^2$$

where p_i represents the proportion of the diet contributed by the ith taxon. Values for this index range from 1 to n. To be consistent, prey taxa were grouped by family for all birds and mammals, and by order for reptiles. Amphibians and fish were each treated as a single taxon, as were birds in the few cases where identification was not given to the level of the taxonomic family.

A typically narrow diet might comprise 85% of prey in one taxon, 5% in two further taxa, and 1% in each of 10 further taxa. This would give a measure of dietary breadth (*B*) of 1/0.7285, or 1.37. A generalized diet might comprise five prey taxa at 12% each, three taxa at 10% each and a further five taxa at 2% each. This would give a measure of dietary breadth (*B*) of 1/0.104 or 9.62. Note that, although the number of taxa (13) is the same in both examples, the measure of dietary breadth is quite different.

282

APPENDIX 4

Assessment of Food Supply

Nape feathers.

FOR the study of Golden Eagles in Scotland an index of food abundance was obtained using a series of line transect counts made between 1982 and 1985. All transects were covered on foot and were carried out each year between late February and the end of April. Transects were stratified across each of the study areas (A–I) using the 10 × 10 km national grid. Line transects were walked in eight or more of the 10 × 10 km squares in areas C–H and in four or five squares in areas A, B and I. Routes were selected at random within each square and, where possible, each transect totalled around 20 km in the form of a 5 × 5 km square. Some adjustments were made in transect routes to avoid open water, forestry plantations and precipitous slopes; because of these modifications the average length of individual transects was 19 km (range 14–25 km). The following prey were recorded on line transects:

1. *Mountain Hares and Rabbits.* The total number of each species was recorded and, as with grouse, all animals more than 200 m from the transect line were ignored.
2. *Red Grouse and Ptarmigan.* The total numbers of Red grouse and Ptarmigan were recorded although birds seen at distances of more than 200 m from the transect line were ignored.
3. *Red Deer.* All dead Red Deer within 50 m of the transect line were recorded and, where possible the sex (stag or hind) and age (calf or >1 year old) was assessed.

Each carcass was placed in one of two categories which differentiated between 'recent' deaths and 'others'. Carcasses which contained some flesh or dried skin were considered 'recent' deaths. Based on observations of individual carcasses over time, 'recent' deaths were assumed to refer to animals that had died up to 1 month prior to discovery.

4. *Sheep.* Dead sheep were recorded using similar methods ascribed to dead deer counts. Once again, animals more than 50 m from the transect line were ignored, and 'recent' deaths and 'others' were distinguished as for dead deer.

To compare indices of food abundance between areas, the counts of prey on transects were converted to biomass and calculated to a standard measure of kg/20 km of line transect. For carrion, only 'recent' deaths were included in the analysis. For each transect the number of prey items was converted to biomass using average weight data and figures for 'wastage' (defined as the proportion of an item which had no food value for the predator) given in Brown & Watson (1964) and Hewson (1984), and summarized below. A total of 2778 km of line transects were walked during the study, divided between four areas (C, D, F and H) in 1982, six areas (C–H) in 1983 and 1984, and all nine study areas (A–I) in 1985.

All transect data were separated into 'live prey' (comprising Red Grouse, Ptarmigan, Mountain Hare and Rabbit) and 'carrion' (both sheep and deer carrion). Confidence limits (± SE) for indices of prey abundance in each year were calculated by averaging individual transect data which were converted to a standard n kg/20 km walked.

The average weight data and the proportions of each type of prey which comprised 'wastage' were as follows:

Mountain Hare   Weight = 2.6 kg, % wastage = 30
Ptarmigan   Weight = 0.55 kg, % wastage = 20
Rabbit   Weight = 1.6 kg, % wastage = 25
Red Deer   Weight = 60.00 kg, % wastage = 50
Red Grouse   Weight = 0.65 kg, % wastage = 20
Sheep (Cheviot)   Weight = 52.00 kg, % wastage = 50
Sheep (Blackface)   Weight = 45.00 kg, % wastage = 50.

APPENDIX 5

Nearest-neighbour Distance
and Density

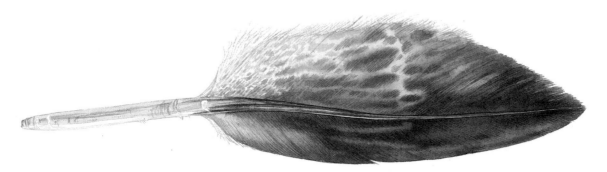

Golden Eagle alula or 'bastard' wing feather.

THE spacing of nest sites among Golden Eagles in various studies was assessed using an analysis of nearest-neighbour distance. In the study of nest spacing in different parts of Scotland the nest sites used by different pairs of eagles in one year (1982) were plotted on a map and the distance to the nearest neighbour was measured to the nearest kilometre. In some other studies (e.g. Tjernberg 1985) distances were measured between neighbouring nesting territories, with the nesting territory being defined as the arithmetic centre between the known alternative nest sites of a particular pair.

To test for regular nest spacing the G-statistic (GMASD) was used as recommended by Brown (1975). GMASD is calculated as the geometric mean of nearest-neighbour distances^2 divided by the arithmetic mean of nearest-neighbour distances^2. Values for GMASD range from 0 to 1. Larger values indicate greater regularity of spacing and values less than about 0.65 indicate that nest sites are randomly spaced (Nilsson *et al.* 1982).

Mean nearest-neighbour distances were used to compare nesting density in various studies of Golden Eagle in Scotland and elsewhere. The maximum theoretical nesting density in continuously suitable nesting habitat was calculated using the equation:

$$N = 1000/2\sqrt{3}b^2$$

in which N is the number of pairs per 1000 km^2 and b is equal to half the average nearest neighbour distance (km). This equation assumes that spacing is completely regular and that the maximum possible packing of nesting territories is achieved

285

(each territory is therefore assumed to be a regular hexagon with six equal sides). Such completely regular spacing is never achieved in nature, principally because in any one area not all habitat is continuously suitable. Actual nesting densities are therefore invariably less than the theoretical maximum nesting density (see Newton *et al.* (1976) for comparable data for Sparrowhawks). The relationship between these two measures of nesting density for a wide range of Golden Eagle studies is shown in Fig. 27.

Scientific Names of Animals and Plants

Worn greater-covert.

SCIENTIFIC names for birds are after Howard & Moore (1991) and for mammals are after Macdonald (1984a,b).

Birds

African Fish Eagle *Haliaeetus vocifer*
African Marsh Harrier *Circus ranivorus*
American Bittern *Botaurus lentiginosus*
American Kestrel *Falco sparverius*
Aplomado Falcon *Falco femoralis*
Bald Eagle *Haliaeetus leucocephalus*
Bateleur *Terathopius ecaudatus*
Black Eagle *Aquila verreauxii*
Black Grouse *Lyrurus tetrix*
Black Kite *Milvus migrans*
Black Stork *Ciconia nigra*
Black-throated Diver *Gavia arctica*

Blue Grouse *Dendragapus obscurus*
Bonelli's Eagle *Hieraaetus bonelli*
Booted Eagle *Hieraaetus pennatus*
Bullfinch *Pyrrhula pyrrhula*
Buzzard *Buteo buteo*
Canada Goose *Branta canadensis*
Capercaillie *Tetrao urogallus*
Carrion Crow *Corvus corone corone*
Chukar Partridge *Alectoris chukar*
Coot *Fulica atra*
Copper Pheasant *Syrmaticus soemmerringi*
Crested Bustard *Eupodotis ruficrista*
Crowned Eagle *Spizaetus coronatus*

Cuckoo *Cuculus canorus*
Dotterel *Eudromias morinellus*
Dunlin *Calidris alpina*
Eastern Imperial Eagle *Aquila heliaca heliaca*
Ferruginous Hawk *Buteo regalis*
Flamingo (E Africa) *Phoeniconaias minor*
Fulmar *Fulmarus glacialis*
Golden Eagle *Aquila chrysaetos*
Golden Plover *Pluvialis apricaria*
Great Blue Heron *Ardea herodias*
Greater Spotted Eagle *Aquila clanga*
Greenshank *Tringa nebularia*
Griffon Vulture *Gyps fulvus*
Guillemot *Uria aalge*
Gurney's Eagle *Aquila gurneyi*
Gyr Falcon *Falco rusticolus*
Helmeted Guineafowl *Numida meleagris*
Hen Harrier *Circus cyaneus*
Heron *Ardea cinerea*
Herring Gull *Larus argentatus*
Himalayan Snowcock *Tetraogallus himalayensis*
Hooded Crow *Corvus corone cornix*
Imperial Eagle *Aquila heliaca*
Kestrel *Falco tinnunculus*
Kittiwake *Rissa tridactyla*
Lammergeier *Gypaetus barbatus*
Lesser Spotted Eagle *Aquila pomarina*
Little Curlew *Numenius minutus*
Little Eagle *Hieraaetus morphnoides*
Manx Shearwater *Puffinus puffinus*
Martial Eagle *Hieraaetus bellicosus*
Meadow Pipit *Anthus pratensis*
Merlin *Falco columbarius*
Mistle Thrush *Turdus viscivorus*
Moorhen *Gallinula chloropus*
Osprey *Pandion haliaetus*
Peregrine Falcon *Falco peregrinus*
Ptarmigan (Eurasia) *Lagopus mutus*
Puffin *Fratercula arctica*
Raven *Corvus corax*
Razorbill *Alca torda*
Red-billed Quelea *Quelea quelea*
Red-breasted Merganser *Mergus serrator*
Red Grouse (Scotland) *Lagopus lagopus scoticus*

Red Kite *Milvus milvus*
Red-legged Partridge *Alectoris rufa*
Red-tailed Hawk *Buteo jamaicensis*
Red-throated Diver *Gavia stellata*
Ring Ouzel *Turdus torquatus*
Rock Ptarmigan (North America) *Lagopus mutus*
Rough-legged Buzzard *Buteo lagopus*
Short-eared Owl *Asio flammeus*
Spanish Imperial Eagle *Aquila heliaca adalberti*
Sparrowhawk *Accipiter nisus*
Spruce Grouse *Dendragapus canadensis*
Steppe Eagle *Aquila nipalensis*
Swainson's Hawk *Buteo swainsonii*
Tawny Eagle *Aquila rapax*
Turkey Vulture *Cathartes aura*
Wahlberg's Eagle *Hieraaetus wahlbergi*
Wedge-tailed Eagle *Aquila audax*
White-tailed Sea Eagle *Haliaeetus albicilla*
Willow Grouse (Eurasia) *Lagopus lagopus lagopus*
Willow Ptarmigan (North America) *Lagopus lagopus*
Wren *Troglodytes troglodytes*
Yellow-billed Magpie *Pica nuttalli*
Yellow-necked Francolin *Francolinus leucoscepus*

Mammals
African Hare *Lepus capensis*
Alpine Marmot *Marmota alpina*
Arctic Ground Squirrel *Spermophilus parryii*
Arctic Hare *Lepus arcticus*
Argali *Ovis ammon*
Asiatic Wild Ass *Equus hemionus*
Asiatic Wolf *Canis lupus campestris*
Baboon *Papio* spp.
Badger (Europe) *Meles meles*
Beaver (Europe) *Castor fiber*
Barbary Sheep *Ammotragus lervia*
Bighorn Sheep *Ovis canadensis*
Bison *Bison bison*
Black-tailed Deer *Odocoileus hemionus*
Black-tailed Jackrabbit *Lepus californicus*

Black-tailed Prairie Dog *Cynomys ludovicianus*
Bobak Marmot *Marmota bobac*
Brown Hare *Lepus europaeus*
Brown Rat *Rattus norvegicus*
Californian Ground Squirrel *Spermophilus beecheyi*
Caribou (North America) *Rangifer tarandus*
Chamois *Rupicapra rupicapra*
Columbian Ground Squirrel *Spermophilus columbianus*
Common Vole *Microtis arvalis*
Corsac Fox *Vulpes corsac*
Coyote *Canis latrans*
Cuscus *Phalanger* spp.
Dall Sheep *Ovis dalli*
Daurian Ground Squirrel *Spermophilus dauricus*
Daurian Pika *Ochotona daurica*
Desert Cottontail *Sylvilagus audubonii*
Elephant (Africa) *Loxodonta africana*
Elk (Eurasia) *Alces alces*
Elk (North America) *Cervus (elaphus) canadensis*
European Suslik *Spermophilus citellus*
Fox *Vulpes vulpes*
Goitred Gazelle *Gazella subgutturosa*
Great Gerbil *Rhombomys opimus*
Hedgehog *Erinaceus europaous*
Hoary Marmot *Marmota caligata*
Hyrax *Procaviidae* (family)
Japanese Hare *Lepus brachyurus*
Japanese Serow *Carpricornis crispus*
Kirk's Dikdik *Madoqua kirkii*
Large-toothed Suslik *Spermophilus fulvus*
Long-tailed Marmot *Marmota caudata*
Mole *Talpa europaea*
Mole-rat (Ethiopia) *Heterocephalus glaber*
Moose (N America) *Alces alces*
Mountain Beaver *Aplodontia rufa*
Mountain Hare *Lepus timidus*
Mule Deer *Odocoileus hemionus*
Muskox *Ovibos moschatus*
Northern Lynx *Felis lynx*
Nuttall's Cottontail *Sylvilagus nuttallii*
Otter *Lutra lutra*

Pine Marten *Martes martes*
Porcupine (North America) *Erethizon dorsatum*
Pronghorn Antelope *Antilocarpa americana*
Pygmy Ground Squirrel *Spermophilus pygmaeus*
Rabbit *Oryctolagus cuniculus*
Red Deer *Cervus elaphus*
Reindeer (Eurasia) *Rangifer tarandus*
Richardson's Ground Squirrel *Spermophilus richadrsonii*
Roe Deer *Capreolus capreolus*
Saiga Antelope *Saiga tartarica*
Scrub Hare *Lepus saxatilis*
Short-tailed Vole *Microtus agrestis*
Siberian Ibex *Capra ibex sibirica*
Siberian Marmot *Marmota sibirica*
Snowshoe Hare *Lepus americanus*
Stoat *Mustela erminea*
Townsend's Ground Squirrel *Spermophilus townsendii*
Water Vole *Arvicola terrestris*
Weasel *Mustela nivalis*
White-tailed Deer *Odocoileus virginianus*
White-tailed Jackrabbit *Lepus townsendii*
Wild Cat *Felis sylvestris*
Wild Goat *Capra aegagrus*
Wolf *Canis lupus*
Wolverine *Gulo gulo*
Yellow-bellied Marmot *Marmota flaviventris*

Reptiles
Adder *Vipera berus*
Rattlesnake *Crotalus* spp.
Rock Python *Python sebae*
Spiney-tailed Lizard *Uromastyx* spp.
Tortoise *Testudo* spp.

Amphibians
Frog *Rana temporaria*

Fish
Pike *Esox lucius*
Salmon *Salmo salar*

Invertebrates (Order)
Beetles *Coleoptera*
Fleas *Siphonaptera*
Flies *Diptera*
Grasshoppers/Locusts *Orthoptera*
Mites/Ticks *Acari*
Silkworm Moths *Lepidoptera*
Termites *Isoptera*

Plants
Acacia *Acacia* spp.
Alder *Alnus* spp.
Ash *Fraxinus excelsior*
Aspen *Populus tremula*
Beech *Fagus sylvatica*
Birch *Betula* spp.
Bitterbrush *Purshia* spp.
Cotton-grass *Eriophorum* spp.
Cottonwood *Populus* spp.
Douglas fir *Pseudotsuga menziesii*
Downy birch *Betula pubescens*
Eucalyptus *Ecucalyptus* spp.

Fig *Ficus* spp.
Greasewood *Sarcobatus* spp.
Hazel *Corylus avellana*
Heather *Calluna vulgaris*
Juniper *Juniperus* spp.
Larch *Larix* spp.
Lodgepole pine *Pinus contorta*
Mango *Mangifera* spp.
Norway spruce *Picea abies*
Oak *Quercus* spp.
Pine *Pinus* spp.
Ponderosa pine *Pinus ponderosa*
Poplar *Populus* spp.
Purple moor grass *Molinia caerulea*
Rowan *Sorbus aucuparia*
Sagebrush *Artemisia* spp.
Scots pine *Pinus sylvestris*
Sitka spruce *Picea sitchensis*
Spruce *Picea* spp.
Tamarisk *Tamarix* spp.
Willow *Salix* spp.
Woodrush *Luzula sylvatica*

Bibliography

ABBOTT, C. G. 1924. Period of incubation of the Golden Eagle. *Condor*, 26: 194.

AGAFANOV, A. V., REZINKO, D. S., ROZHKOV, A. A. & SEMENEOV, N. M. 1957. Ecology of the Steppe Eagle (in Russian). *Bull. MOIP Otd. Biology*, 62: 174–181.

ALI, S. & RIPLEY, S. D. 1968. *Handbook of the Birds of India and Pakistan*, Vol. 1. Oxford University Press, Bombay.

ALLAVENA, S. 1985. Preliminary results of research on the Golden Eagle *Aquila chrysaetos* in the central-southern region of the Appennines in Italy. *WWGBP Bulletin*, 2: 79–81.

ALLEN, J. A. 1905. Report on the birds collected in northeastern Siberia by the Jesup North Pacific Expedition, with field notes by the collectors. *Bulletin American Museum of Natural History*, 21: 216–257.

AMADON, D. 1959. The significance of sexual differences in size among birds. *Proceedings of the American Philosophical Society*, 103: 531–536.

AMADON, D. 1978. Remarks on the taxonomy of some Australasian raptors. *Emu*, 78: 115–118.

AMADON, D. 1982. The genera of booted eagles: *Aquila* and relatives. *Journal of the Yamashina Institute of Ornithology*, 14: 108–121.

AMADON, D. & BULL, J. 1988. Hawks and owls of the world: a distributional and taxonomic list. *Proceedings of the Western Foundation of Vertebrate Zoology*, 3: 294–357.

ANDERSON, D. E., RONGSTAD, O. J. & MYTTON, W. R. 1990. Home-range changes in raptors exposed to increased human activity levels in southeastern Colorado. *Wildlife Society Bulletin*, 18: 134–142.

ANDERSON, W. W. 1975. Pole changes keep eagles flying. *Transmission and Distribution*, November: 28–31.

ANDERSSON, M. & NORBERG, R. Å. 1981. Evolution of reversed sexual size dimorphism and role partitioning among predatory birds, with a size scaling of flight performance. *Biological Journal of the Linnean Society*, 15: 105–130.

ANDRINOS, G. E. 1987. L'Aigle Royal en Grèce. In: *L'Aigle Royal en Europe* (Ed. S. Michel), pp.18–22. Actes du Premier Colloque International, Arvieux.

ANTHONY, R. G. & ISAACS, F. B. 1989. Characteristics of Bald Eagle nest sites in Oregon. *Journal of Wildlife Management*, 53: 148–159.

AOYAMA, I., SEKIYAMA, F., OBARA, N., TAMURA, G. & SAKAGUCHI, H. 1988. Breeding biology of a pair of Golden Eagles in the Kitakami Mountains. *Aquila chrysaetos*, 6: 14–23.

ARMSTRONG, E. A. 1958. *The Folklore of Birds.* Collins, London.

ARMSTRONG, A. M. & MATHER, A. S. 1983. Land ownership and land use in the Scottish Highlands. O'Dell Memorial Monograph No. 13. Aberdeen University Department of Geography, Aberdeen.

ARNELL, W. B. 1971. Prey utilization by nesting Golden Eagles *Aquila chrysaetos* in central Utah. M.Sc. thesis. Brigham Young University, Provo, Utah.

ARNOLD, L. W. 1954. The Golden Eagle and its economic status. *U.S. Fish & Wildlife Service Circular* No. 27: 35pp.

ARROYO, B., GARZA, V. & SANSEGUNDO, C. 1986. Ecología del Águila Real *Aquila chrysaetos* en la Sierra de Gredos. *V Congreso Internacional Sobre Rapinas Mediterranieas.* Evora, Portugal.

ARROYO, B., FERREIRO, E. & GARZA, V. 1990. El Águila Real *Aquila chrysaetos* en España: censo, distribución, reproducción y conservación. ICONA, Madrid.

AUSTEN, M. J. W., CADMAN, M. D. & JAMES R. D. 1994. *Ontario Birds at Risk.* Federation of Ontario Naturalists, Long Point Bird Observatory.

AUSTRUY, J. & CUGNASSE, J. 1981. L'Aigle Royal *Aquila chrysaetos* dans le Massif Central. *Nos Oiseaux*, 36: 133–142.

BAHAT, O. 1989. Aspects in the ecology and biodynamics of the Golden Eagle *Aquila chrysaetos homeyeri* in the arid regions of Israel. M.Sc. thesis. Tel-Aviv University, Tel Aviv.

BAHAT, O. 1991. Choice of directional exposure of Golden Eagle nests in the arid areas of Israel. *Israel Journal of Zoology*, 37: 170–171.

BAHAT, O. 1992. Post-fledging movements of Golden Eagles *Aquila chrysaetos* in the Negev desert, Israel, as determined by radio-telemetry. In: *Wildlife Telemetry* (Ed. I. G. Priede & S. M. Swift), pp. 612–621. Ellis Horwood, Chichester.

BAHAT, O. and MENDELSSOHN, H. 1996. The long-term effect of precipitation on the breeding success of Golden Eagles in the Judean and Negev Deserts, Israel. In: *Eagle Studies*, pp. 517–522. WWGBP, Berlin, London and Paris.

BAKER-GABB, D. J. 1982. Asynchronous hatching, fratricide and double clutches in the Marsh Harrier. *Corella*, 6: 83–86.

BAKER-GABB, D. J. 1984 The breeding ecology of twelve species of diurnal raptor in northwestern Victoria. *Australian Wildlife Research*, 10: 145–160.

BARRINGTON, R. M. 1915. The last (?) Irish Golden Eagle. *Irish Naturalist*, 24: 63.

BATES, G. G. 1976. Breeding of sub-adult Golden Eagle. *Bird Study*, 23: 284.

BAXTER, E. V. & RINTOUL, L. J. 1953. *The Birds of Scotland.* Oliver & Boyd, London.

BEECHAM, J. J. & KOCHERT M. N. 1975. Breeding biology of the Golden Eagle in southwestern Idaho. *Wilson Bulletin*, 87: 506–513.

BEEHLER, B. M, PRATT, T. K. & ZIMMERMAN, D. A. 1986. *Birds of New Guinea.* University Press, Princeton.

BELKA, T., SREIBR, O. & VRANA, J. 1990. Some notes on fledging of two Lesser Spotted Eagle *Aquila pomarina* young without human assistance (in Czech). *Buteo*, 5: 49–58.

BENSON, P. C. 1981. Large raptor electrocution and powerpole utilization: a study in six western states. Ph.D. thesis. Brigham Young University. Provo, Utah.

BENT, A. C. 1937. Life histories of North American Birds of Prey. Part 1. *U.S. National Museum Bulletin*, 167: 1–409.

BERGMANIS, U., PETRINS, A. & STRAZDS, M. 1990. Lesser Spotted Eagle in Latvia—numbers, distribution and ecology. *Baltic Birds*, 5: 35–38.

BERGO, G. 1984a. Population size, spacing and age structure of Golden Eagle *Aquila chrysaetos* (L.) in Hordaland, West Norway. *Fauna Norvegica Series C, Cinclus,* 7: 106–108.

BERGO, G. 1984b. Habitat and nest-site features of Golden Eagles *Aquila chrysaetos* (L.) in Hordaland, West Norway. *Fauna Norvegica Series C, Cinclus,* 7: 109–113.

BERGO, G. 1987a. Territorial behaviour of Golden Eagles in Western Norway. *British Birds,* 80: 361–376.

BERGO, G. 1987b. Eagles as predators on livestock and deer. *Fauna Norvegica Series C, Cinclus,* 10: 95–102.

BERGO, G. 1988. Trios in the Golden Eagle *Aquila chrysaetos* (L.). *Fauna Norvegica Series C, Cinclus,* 11: 40–44.

BEZZEL, E. 1994. Situation und Bestand des Steinadlers *Aquila chrysaetos* in Deutschland. *Journal für Ornithologie,* 135: 113–115.

BEZZEL, E. & FÜNFSTÜCK, H-J. 1994. Brutbiologie und Populationsdynamik des Steinadlers *Aquila chrysaetos* im Werdenfelser Land/Oberbayern. *Acta Ornithoecologica,* 3: 5–32.

BIJLEVELD, M. 1974. *Birds of Prey in Europe.* Macmillan, London.

BILDSTEIN, K. 1992. Causes and consequences of reversed sexual size dimorphism in raptors: the head start hypothesis. *Journal of Raptor Research,* 26: 115–123.

BIRKS, H. J. B. 1988. Long-term ecological change in the British uplands. In: *Ecological Change in the Uplands* (Eds. M. B. Usher & D. B. A. Thompson), pp. 37–56. Blackwell Scientific Publications, Oxford.

BLAKERS, M., DAVIES, S. J. J. F. & REILLY, P. N. 1984. *The Atlas of Australian Birds.* University Press, Melbourne.

BLOOM, P. H. & HAWKS, S. J. 1982. Food habits of nesting Golden Eagles in northeast California and northwest Nevada. *Raptor Research,* 16: 110–115.

BLOOM, P. H., SCOTT, J. M., PATTEE, O. H. & SMITH, M. R. 1989. Lead contamination of Golden Eagles *Aquila chrysaetos* within the range of the California Condor *Gymnogyps californianus.* In: *Raptors in the Modern World* (Eds. B.-U. Meyburg & R. D. Chancellor), pp. 481–482. WWGBP, Berlin, London & Paris.

BOAG, D. A. 1977. Summer food habits of Golden Eagles in southwestern Alberta. *Canadian Field Naturalist,* 91: 296–298.

BOEKER, E. L. 1970. Use of aircraft to determine Golden Eagle *Aquila chrysaetos* nesting activity. *Southwestern Naturalist,* 15: 136 137.

BOEKER, E. L. 1974. Status of Golden Eagle surveys in the Western States. *Wildlife Society Bulletin,* 2: 46–49.

BOEKER, E. L. & BOLEN, E. G. 1972. Winter Golden Eagle populations in the southwest. *Journal of Wildlife Management,* 36: 477–484.

BOEKER, E. L. & NICKERSON, P. R. 1975. Raptor electrocutions. *Wildlife Society Bulletin,* 3: 79–81.

BOLEN, E. G. 1975. Eagles and sheep: a viewpoint. *Journal of Range Management,* 28: 11–17.

BORTOLOTTI, G. R. 1984a. Age and sex variation in Golden Eagles. *Journal of Field Ornithology,* 55: 54–66.

BORTOLOTTI, G. R. 1984b. Trap and poison mortality of Golden and Bald Eagles. *Journal of Wildlife Management,* 48: 1173–1179.

BOUCHE, M. 1989. Développment anormal d'un Aiglon *Aquila chrysaetos* dans les Hautes-Alpes en 1986. *Nos Oiseaux,* 40: 48–49.

BOURNE, W. R. P. 1976. Seabirds and pollution. In: *Marine Pollution,* Vol. 6, (Ed. R. Johnson). Academic Press, London.

BOWMAN, T. D., SCHEMPF, P. F. & BERNATOWICZ, J. A. 1995. Bald Eagle survival and population dynamics in Alaska after the Exxon Valdez oil spill. *Journal of Wildlife Management,* 59: 317–324.

BRAZIL, M. A. & HANAWA, S. 1991. The status and distribution of diurnal raptors in Japan. WWGBP *Bulletin,* 4: 175–238.

BRODKORB, P. 1964. Catalogue of fossil birds. Pt. 2. (Anseriformes through Galliformes). *Bulletin of the Florida State Museum*, 8: 195–355.

BROOKE, R. K., GROBLER, M. P. S. I. & STEYN, P. 1972. A study of the migratory eagles *Aquila nipalensis* and *Aquila pomarina* (Aves: Accipitridae) in Southern Africa, with comparative notes on other large raptors. *Occasional Papers National Museum of Rhodesia B*, 5: 61–114.

BROOKER, M. G. 1974 Field observations of the behaviour of the Wedge-tailed Eagle. *Emu*, 74: 39–42.

BROOKER, M. G. & RIDPATH, M. G. 1980. The diet of the Wedge-tailed Eagle *Aquila audax* in Western Australia. *Australian Wildlife Research*, 7: 433–452.

BROWN, C. J. 1991. Declining Martial *Polemaetus bellicosus* and Tawny *Aquila rapax* Eagle populations and causes of mortality on farmlands in central Namibia. *Biological Conservation*, 56: 49–62.

BROWN, D. 1975. A test of randomness of nest spacing. *Wildfowl*, 26: 102–103.

BROWN, L. 1970. *African Birds of prey*. Collins, London.

BROWN, L. 1976. *British Birds of prey*. Collins, London.

BROWN, L. & AMADON, D. 1968. *Eagles, Hawks and Falcons of the World*, 2 Vols. Country Life Books, Feltham.

BROWN, L. H. 1952. On the biology of the large birds of prey of the Embu District, Kenya Colony. *Ibis*, 94: 577–620.

BROWN, L. H. 1953. On the biology of the large birds of prey of the Embu District, Kenya Colony. *Ibis*, 95: 74–114.

BROWN, L. H. 1969. Status and breeding success of Golden Eagles in northwest Sutherland in 1967. *British Birds*, 62: 345–363.

BROWN, L. H. & CADE, T. J. 1972. Age classes and population dynamics of the Bateleur and African Fish Eagle. *Ostrich*, 43: 1–16.

BROWN, L. H. & HOPCRAFT, J. B. D. 1973. Population structure and dynamics in the African Fish Eagle *Haliaeetus vocifer* (Daudin) at Lake Naivasha, Kenya. *East African Wildlife Journal*, 11: 255–269.

BROWN, L. H. & WATSON, A. 1964. The Golden Eagle in relation to its food supply. *Ibis*, 106: 78–100.

BROWN, L. H., GARGETT, V. & STEYN, P. 1977. Breeding success in some African eagles related to theories about sibling aggression and its effects. *Ostrich*, 48: 65–71.

BROWN, L. H., URBAN, E. K. & NEWMAN, K. 1982. *The Birds of Africa*. Vol. 1. Academic Press, London.

BRUCE, A. M., ANDERSON, R. J. & ALLEN, G. T. 1982. Observations of Golden Eagles nesting in western Washington. *Raptor Research*, 16: 132–134.

BRUNS, E. H. 1970. Winter predation of Golden Eagles and Coyotes on Pronghorn Antelopes. *Canadian Field Naturalist*, 84: 301–304.

BUEHLER, D. A., FRASER, J. D., SEEGAR, J. K. D., THERRES, G. D. & BYRD, M. A. 1991. Survival rates and population dynamics of Bald Eagles on Chesapeake Bay. *Journal of Wildlife Management*, 55: 608–613.

BUNDY, G. 1985. Communal roosting by Imperial Eagles. *British Birds*, 78: 108.

CALDERÓN, J., CASTROVIEJO, J., GARCIA, L. & FERRER, M. 1987. El Águila Imperial *Aquila adalberti* en Doñana: alguinos aspectos de su reproduccion. *Alytes*, 5: 47–72.

CALDERÓN, J., CASTROVIEJO, J., GARCIA, L. & FERRER, M. 1988. El Águila Imperial *Aquila adalberti*: dispersion de los jovenes, estructura de edades y mortalidad. *Doñana Acta Vertebrata*, 15: 79–98.

CALLANDER, R. F. & MACKENZIE, N. A. 1991. *The Management of Red Deer in Scotland*. Rural Forum, Perth.

CAMENZIND, F. J. 1968. Nesting ecology and behaviour of the Golden Eagle in west-central Utah. M.Sc. thesis. Brigham Young University, Provo, Utah.

CAMENZIND, F. J. 1969. Nesting ecology and behaviour of the Golden eagle *Aquila chrysaetos* (L). *Brigham Young University Science Bulletin Biological Series*, 10: 4–15.

CAMERON, E. S. 1905. Nesting of the Golden Eagle in Montana. *Auk*, 22: 158–167.

CAMERON, E. S. 1908. Observations on the Golden Eagle in Montana. *Auk*, 25: 251–268.

CARNIE, S. K. 1954. Food habits of Golden Eagles in the coast ranges of California. *Condor*, 56: 3–12.

CHARLET, D. A. & RUST, R. W. 1991. Visitation of high mountain bogs by Golden Eagles in the northern Great Basin. *Journal of Field Ornithology*, 62: 46–52.

CHENG, T. 1976. *Distributional List of Chinese Birds*. Science Press, Peking.

CHEYLAN, G. 1973. Notes sur la compétition entre l'Aigle Royal *Aquila chrysaetos* et l'Aigle de Bonelli *Hieraaetus fasciatus*. *Alauda*, 41: 203–212.

CHEYLAN, G. 1977. La place trophique de l'Aigle de Bonelli *Hieraaetus fasciatus* dans les biocenoses méditerranéennes. *Alauda*, 45: 1–15.

CHRISTENSEN, N. H. 1962. Observationer af fugle og noter om fugletraek i Iraq, 1958. *Dansk Ornithologisk Forenings Tidskrift*, 56: 56–81.

CHRISTENSEN, S. & SORENSEN, U. G. 1989. A review of the migration and wintering of *Aquila pomarina* and *Aquila nipalensis orientalis*. In: *Raptors in the Modern World* (Eds. B.-U. Meyburg & R. D. Chancellor), pp. 139–150. WWGBP, Berlin, London & Paris.

CLARK, W. S. 1992. The taxonomy of Steppe and Tawny Eagles with criteria for separation of museum specimens and live eagles. *Bulletin of British Ornithologists Club*, 112: 150–157.

CLOUET, M. 1981. L'Aigle Royal *Aquila chrysaetos* dans les Pyrénées Francaises. Résultats de 5 ans d'observations. *L'Oiseau et R.F.O.*, 51: 89–100.

CLOUET, M. & BARRAU, C. 1993. L'Aigle Royal *Aquila chrysaetos* dans le Massif du Bale—Ethiopie. *Alauda*, 61: 200–201.

CLOUET, M. & GOAR, J. L. 1981. Eléments de comparaison de deux populations d'Aigle Royal dans le midi de la France: Pyrénées et Languedoc. Rapaces Méditerranéens. *Annales du C.R.O.P.*, 1: 88–91.

CLUTTON-BROCK, T. H. & ALBON, S. D. 1989. *Red Deer in the Highlands*. BSP Professional Books, Oxford.

COLLOPY, M. W. 1983a. A comparison of direct observations and collections of prey remains in determining the diet of Golden Eagles. *Journal of Wildlife Management*, 47: 360–368.

COLLOPY, M. W. 1983b. Foraging behavior and success of Golden Eagles. *Auk*, 100: 747–749.

COLLOPY, M. W. 1984. Parental care and feeding ecology of Golden Eagle nestlings. *Auk*, 101: 753–760.

COLLOPY, M. W. 1986. Food consumption and growth energetics of nestling Golden Eagles. *Wilson Bulletin*, 98: 445–458.

COLLOPY, M. W. & EDWARDS, T. C. 1989. Territory size, activity budget, and role of undulating flight in nesting Golden Eagles. *Journal of Field Ornithologists*, 60: 43–51.

COOKE, A. S. 1973. Shell thinning in avian eggs by environmental pollutants. *Environmental Pollutants*, 4: 85–152.

COOPER, A. B. 1969. Golden Eagle kills red deer calf. *Journal of Zoology*, 158: 215–216.

CORBET, G. B. & HARRIS, S. 1991. *The Handbook of British Mammals*. Blackwell Scientific Publications, Oxford.

CORKHILL, P. 1980. Golden Eagles on Rhum. *Scottish Birds*, 11: 33–42.

CRAIG, T. H. & CRAIG, E. H. 1984. A large concentration of roosting Golden Eagles in southeastern Idaho. *Auk*, 101: 610–613.

CRAIG, T. H., CRAIG, E. H. & POWERS, L. R. 1984. Recent changes in eagle and buteo densities in southeastern Idaho. *Murrelet*, 65: 91–93.

CRAIG, T. H., CONNELLY, J. W., CRAIG, E. H. & PARKER, T. L. 1990. Lead concentrations in Golden and Bald Eagles. *Wilson Bulletin*, 102: 130–133.

CRAMP, S. & SIMMONS, K. E. L. 1980. *The Birds of the Western Palearctic*. Vol 2. University Press, Oxford.

D'ANDRIA, A. 1967. Courtship of a Wedge-tailed Eagle. *Emu,* 67: 55–56.

DARLING, F. F. & BOYD, J. M. 1964. *Natural History in the Highlands and Islands.* Collins, London.

DAVIES, A. 1985. Golden Eagle taking badger cubs. *British Birds,* 78: 592.

DAVIS, P. E. & NEWTON, I. 1981. Population and breeding of Red Kites in Wales over a 30–year period. *Journal of Animal Ecology,* 50: 759–772.

DAVIS, W. B. & GLASS B.P. 1951. Notes on eastern Chinese birds. *Auk,* 68: 86–91.

DEANE, C. D. 1962. Irish Golden Eagles and a link with Scotland. *British Birds,* 55: 272–274.

DEJONGHE, J-F. 1980. Analyse de la migration prénuptiale des rapaces et des cigognes au Cap Bon (Tunisie). *L'Oiseau et R.F.O.,* 50: 125–147.

DEKKER, D. 1985. Hunting behaviour of Golden Eagles *Aquila chrysaetos* migrating in southwestern Alberta. *Canadian Field Naturalist,* 99: 383–385.

DEL HOYO, J., ELLIOTT, A. & SARGATAL, J. (eds) 1994. *Handbook of the Birds of the World. Vol. 2. New World Vultures to Guineafowl.* Lynx Editions, Barcelona.

DELIBES, M. 1978. Ecologia alimenticia del Águila Imperial Iberica *Aquila adalberti* en el Coto Doñana durante la crianza de los pollos. *Doñana Acta Vertebrata,* 5: 35–60.

DELIBES, M., CALDERÓN, J. & HIRALDO, F. 1975. Selección de presa y alimentación en España del Águila Real *Aquila chrysaetos. Ardeola (Special),* 21: 285–303.

DEMENTIEV, G. 1936. Le vol a l'aigle au Turkestan. *L'Oiseau et R.F.O.,* 6: 361–365.

DEMENTIEV, G. 1937. Where eagles work for man. *Zoo Magazine,* 2: 4–9.

DEMENTIEV, G. P. & GLADKOV, N. A. 1966. *Birds of the Soviet Union.* Vol. 1. Israel Programme of Scientific Translations, Jerusalem.

DENNIS, R. 1983. Probable polygyny by Golden Eagle. *British Birds,* 76: 310–311.

DENNIS, R. H., ELLIS, P. M., BROAD, R. A. & LANGSLOW, D. R. 1984. The status of the Golden Eagle in Britain. *British Birds,* 77: 592–607.

DI CASTRI, F., GOODALL, D. W & SPECHT, R. L. 1981. *Ecosystems of the World, Vol 11: Mediterranean-type Shrublands.* Elsevier, Amsterdam.

DIXON, J. B. 1937. The Golden Eagle in San Diego County, California. *Condor,* 39: 49–58.

DONÁZAR, J. A., CEBALLOS, O. & FERNÁNDEZ, C. 1989. Factors influencing the distribution and abundance of seven cliff-nesting raptors: a multivariate study. In: *Raptors in the Modern World* (Eds. B.-U. Meyburg & R.D. Chancellor), pp. 545–552. WWGBP, Berlin, London & Paris.

DUCEY, J. 1992. Bird items and their use in some Omaha indian artifacts. *Nebraska Bird Review,* 60: 154–163.

EAKLE, W. L. & GRUBB, T. G. 1986. Prey remains from Golden Eagle nests in central Arizona. *Western Birds,* 17: 87–89.

EATES K. R. 1937. The distribution of the Greater Spotted Eagle in Sind. *Journal of the Bombay Natural History Society,* 39: 403–405.

EDWARDS, C. C. 1969. Winter behaviour and population dynamics of American eagles in western Utah. Ph.D. thesis. Brigham Young University, Provo, Utah.

EDWARDS, T. C. & COLLOPY, M. W. 1983. Obligate and facultative brood reduction in eagles: an examination of factors that influence fratricide. *Auk,* 100: 630–635.

EDWARDS, T. C. & KOCHERT, M. N. 1986. Use of body weight and length of footpad as predictors of sex in Golden Eagles. *Journal of Field Ornithology,* 57: 317–319.

ELLIOTT, J. E., LANGELIER, K. M., SCHEUHAMMER, A. M., SINCLAIR, P. M. & WHITEHEAD, P. E. 1992. Incidence of lead poisoning in Bald Eagles and lead shot in waterfowl gizzards from British Columbia, 1988–91. *Canadian Wildlife Service Progress Notes No. 200.*

ELLIS, D. H. 1979. Development of behavior in the Golden Eagle. *Wildlife Monographs No. 70.*

ELLIS, D. H. 1986. Extremely tall eagle nests. *National Geographic Research,* 2: 517–519.

ELLIS, D. H. 1992. Talon grappling by Aplomado Falcons and Golden Eagles. *Journal of Raptor Research,* 26: 41.

ELLIS, D. H. & POWERS, L. 1982. Mating behaviour in the Golden Eagle in non-fertilization contexts. *Raptor Research*, 16: 134–136.

EMELEUS, C. H. & GYOPARI, M. C. 1992. *British Tertiary Volcanic Province*. Chapman & Hall, London.

ETCHÉCOPAR, R. D. & HÜE, F. 1964. *Les Oiseaux du Nord de l'Afrique*. Editions Boubée, Paris.

EVANS, I. M. & PIENKOWSKI, M. W. 1991. World status of the Red Kite—a background to the experimental reintroduction to England and Scotland. *British Birds*, 84: 171–187.

EVERETT, M. J. 1971. The Golden Eagle survey in Scotland in 1964–68. *British Birds*, 64: 49–56.

EVERETT, M. J. 1981. Role of male Golden Eagle during incubation. *British Birds*, 74: 309–310.

EWINS, P. J. 1987. Golden Eagles attacking deer and sheep. *Scottish Birds*, 14: 209–210.

FALA, R. A., ANDERSON, A. & WARD, J. P. 1985. Highwall to pole Golden Eagle nest site relocations. *Raptor Research*, 19: 1–7.

FAWCETT, D. & VAN VESSEM, J. 1995. *Lead Poisoning in Waterfowl: International Update Report 1995. JNCC Report No. 252*. Joint Nature Conservation Committee, Peterborough.

FASCE, P. & FACSCE, L. 1984. *L'Aquila Reale in Italia: Ecologia e Conservazione*. Lega Italiana Protezione Uccelli, Serie Scientifica, Parma.

FASCE, P. & FASCE, L. 1987. L'Aigle Royal en Italie. In: *L'Aigle Royal en Europe* (Ed. S. Michel), pp. 23–28. Actes du Premier Colloque International, Arvieux.

FERNÁNDEZ, C. 1987. Seasonal variation in the feeding habits of a pair of Golden Eagles in Navarra. In: *L'Aigle Royal en Europe* (Ed. S. Michel), pp.107–117. Actes du Premier Colloque International, Arvieux.

FERNÁNDEZ, C. 1989. El Águila Real *Aquila chrysaetos* (L.) en Navarra: Utilización del espacio, biología de la reproducción y ecología trófica. Tesis doctoral, Universidad de León, León.

FERNÁNDEZ, C. 1993a. Effect of the viral haemorrhagic pneumonia of the wild rabbit on the diet and breeding success of the Golden Eagle *Aquila chrysaetos* (L.). *Revue Ecologie (Terre Vie)*, 48: 323–329.

FERNÁNDEZ, C. 1993b. Sélection de falaises pour la nidification chez l'Aigle Royal *Aquila chrysaetos*: influence de l'accessibilité et des dérangements humains. *Alauda*, 61: 105–110.

FERNÁNDEZ, C. & CEBALLOS, O. 1990. Uneven sex-ratio of wild rabbits taken by Golden Eagles. *Ornis Scandinavica*, 21: 236–238.

FERRER, M. 1992a. Regulation of the period of postfledging dependence in the Spanish Imperial Eagle *Aquila adalberti*. *Ibis*, 134: 128–133.

FERRER, M. 1992b. Natal dispersal in relation to nutritional condition in Spanish Imperial Eagles. *Ornis Scandinavica*, 23: 104–107.

FERRER, M. 1993a. *El Águila Imperial*. Quercus, Madrid.

FERRER, M. 1993b. Reduction in hunting success and settlement strategies in young Spanish Imperial Eagles. *Animal Behaviour*, 45: 406–408.

FERRER, M. & DE LE COURT, C. 1988. Les Aigles Impérieaux Espagnols menacés d'électrocution. *L'Homme et L'Oiseaux*, 26: 231–236.

FERRER, M. & DE LE COURT, C. 1992. Sex identification in the Spanish Imperial Eagle. *Journal of Field Ornithology*, 63: 359–364.

FERRER, M. & HIRALDO, F. 1992. Man-induced sex-biased mortality in the Spanish Imperial Eagle. *Biological Conservation*, 60: 57–60.

FERRER, M., GARCIA-RODRIGUEZ, T., CARRILLO, J. C. & CASTROVIEJO, J. 1987. Hematocrit and blood chemistry values in captive raptors. *Comparative Biochemistry and Physiology*, 87A: 1123–1127.

FERRER, M., DE LA RIVA, M. & CASTROVIEJO, J. 1991. Electrocution of raptors on power lines in southwestern Spain. *Journal of Field Ornithology*, 62: 181–190.

FEWKES, W. J. 1900. Property rights among the Hopi. *American Anthropologist*, 2: 600–707.

FISCHER, D. L., ELLIS, K. L. & MEESE, R. J. 1984. Raptor habitat selection in Utah. *Raptor Research*, 19: 98–102.

FISCHER, W., ZENKER, D. & BAUMGART, W. 1975. Ein Beitrag zum Bestand und zur Ernährung des Steinadlers *Aquila chrysaetos* af der Balkanhalbinsel. *Beiträge zur Vogelskunde*, 21: 275–287.

FLEMING, R. L. 1988. An east-west Aquila eagle migration in the Himalaya. *Torgos*, 7: 91–99.

FLINT, V. E., BOEHME, R. L., KOSTIN, Y. V. & KUZNETSOV, A. A. 1984. *A Field Guide to Birds of the USSR*. University Press, Princeton.

FRAMARIN, F. 1982. Enquête sur l'Aigle Royal *Aquila chrysaetos* dans le Parc National Grand Paradis. *Nos Oiseaux*, 36: 263–273.

FREMMING, O. R. 1980. Kongeørn i Norge. *Viltrapport*, 12: 1–63.

FRYER, G. 1987. Evidence for the former breeding of the Golden Eagle in Yorkshire. *Naturalist*, 112: 3–7.

FURNESS, R. W., THOMPSON, D. R., LOVE, J. A. & JOHNSTON, J. L. 1989. Pollutant burdens and reproductive success of Golden Eagles *Aquila chrysaetos* exploiting marine and terrestrial food webs in Scotland. In: *Raptors in the Modern World* (Eds. B.-U. Meyburg & R. D. Chancellor), pp. 495–500. WWGBP, Berlin, London & Paris.

GALLAGHER, M. D. & BROWN M. R. 1982. Golden Eagle *Aquila chrysaetos* breeding in Oman, eastern Arabia. *Bulletin of the British Ornithologists Club*, 102: 41–42.

GAMAUF, A. 1991. Greifvögel in Österreich: Popoulationen, Gefähren, Gesetzen. *Mongr. Umweltbundesantes*, 29.

GARCELON, D. K. 1990. Observations of aggressive interactions by Bald Eagles of known age and sex. *Condor*, 92: 532–534.

GARGETT, V. 1970. Black Eagle survey, Rhodes Matopos National Park: a population study, 1964–1968. *Ostrich Supplement*, 8: 397–414.

GARGETT, V. 1975. The spacing of Black Eagles in the Matopos, Rhodesia. *Ostrich*, 46: 1–44.

GARGETT, V. 1977. A 13–Year population study of the Black Eagles in the Matopos, Rhodesia, 1964–1976. *Ostrich*, 48: 17–27.

GARGETT, V. 1990. The Black Eagle—a study. Acorn Books, Randburg.

GARNETT, S. 1987. An Australian record of Gurney's Eagle *Aquila gurneyi*. *Australian Bird Watcher*, 12: 134–135.

GASKELL, P. 1980. *Morvern Transformed: a Highland Parish in the Nineteenth Century.* University Press, Cambridge.

GAULTIER, T. 1985. Diurnal raptors in Tunisia: status and protection. *WWGBP Bulletin*, 2: 61–66.

GÉNSBØL, B. 1987. *Birds of Prey of Britain and Europe*. Collins, London.

GERRARD, J. M., GERRARD, P. N., GERRARD, P. N., BORTOLOTTI, G. R., & DZUS, E. H. 1992. A 24–year study of Bald Eagles on Besnard Lake, Saskatchewan. *Journal of Raptor Research*, 26: 159–166.

GJERSHAUG, J. 1991. Rovfugler. In: *Norges Dyr. Fuglene 1* (Ed. O. Hogstad), p. 191. J. W. Cappelens Forlag, Oslo.

GLADSTONE, S. 1910. *The Birds of Dumfriesshire*. Witherby, London.

GLOTOV, I. N. 1959. Data on the biology of *Aquila clanga* (in Russian). *Trudy Biology Inst., Sibirsk. Otdel, SSSR*, 5: 167–170.

GLUTZ VON BLOTZHEIM, U. N., BAUER, K. M. & BEZZEL, E. 1971. *Handbuch der Vögel Mitteleuropas*. Band 4. Falconiformes. Akademische Verlagsgesellschaft, Frankfurt.

GONZÁLEZ, L. M. & HIRALDO, F. 1988. Organochlorine and heavy metal contamination in the eggs of the Spanish Imperial Eagle *Aquila (heliaca) adalberti* and accompanying changes in eggshell morphology and chemistry. *Environmental Pollution*, 51: 241–258.

GONZÁLEZ, L. M., GONZÁLEZ, J. L., GARZÓN, J., & HEREDIA, B. 1987. Censo y distribucion del Águila Iberica *Aquila (heliaca) adalberti* (Brehm 1861) en España durante el periodo 1981–1986. *Boletín de la Estación Central de Ecología*, 31: 99–109.

GONZÁLEZ, L. M., HIRALDO, F., DELIBES, M. & CALDERÓN, J. 1989. Zoogeographic support for the Spanish Imperial Eagle as a distinct species. *Bulletin of the British Ornithologists Club*, 109: 86–93.

GONZÁLEZ, L. M., BUSTAMANTE, J. & HIRALDO, F. 1990. Factors influencing the present distribution of the Spanish Imperial Eagle *Aquila adalberti*. *Biological Conservation*, 51: 311–319.

GONZÁLEZ, L. M., BUSTAMANTE, J. & HIRALDO, F. 1992. Nesting habitat selection by the Spanish Imperial Eagle *Aquila adalberti*. *Biological Conservation*, 59: 45–50.

GORBAN, I. 1985. Current status of eagles in the western Ukraine. *WWGBP Bulletin*, 2: 28–29.

GORDON, J. E. & SUTHERLAND, D. G. 1993. *Quaternary of Scotland*. Chapman & Hall, London.

GORDON, S. 1927. *Days with the Golden Eagle*. Williams and Norgate, London.

GORDON, S. 1955. *The Golden Eagle: King of Birds*. Collins, London.

GORDON, S. 1971. Oil and the eagle: an unsolved riddle. *Country Life*, December: 1639.

GREGORY, M. 1985. Glider attacked by Golden Eagle. *Scottish Birds*, 13: 230–231.

GRIER, J. W. 1973. Techniques and results of artificial insemination with Golden Eagles. *Raptor Research*, 7: 1–12.

GRUBAČ, B. R. 1988. The Golden Eagle in Southeastern Yugoslavia. *Larus*, 38/39: 95–135.

GRUBAČ, R. 1987. L'Aigle Royal en Macedone. In: *L'Aigle Royal en Europe* (Ed. S. Michel), pp.37–39. Actes du Premier Colloque International, Arvieux.

GRUBB, T. G. & EAKLE, W. L. 1987. Comparative morphology of Bald and Golden Eagle nests in Arizona. *Journal of Wildlife Management*, 51: 744–748.

HAGEN, Y. 1976. Havørn og kongeørn i Norge. *Viltrapport*, 1.

HALLER, H. 1982. Raumorganisation und Dynamik einer Population des Steinadlers *Aquila chrysaetos* in den Zentralalpen. *Der Ornithologische Beobachter*, 79: 163–211.

HALLER, H. 1987. L'Aigle Royal en Suisse. In: *L'Aigle Royal en Europe* (Ed. S. Michel), pp. 52–53. Actes du Premier Colloque International, Arvieux.

HALLER, H. 1994. Der Steinadler *Aquila chrysaetos* als Brutvögel im schweizerischen Alpenvorland: Ausbreitungstendenzen und ihre populationsökologischen Grundlagen. *Der Ornithologische Beobachter*, 91: 237–254.

HALLMANN, B. 1980. *Guidelines for The Conservation of Birds of Prey in Evros*. Typscript. 31pp.

HALLMANN, B. 1985. Status and conservation problems of birds of prey in Greece. In: *Conservation Studies on Raptors* (Eds. I. Newton & R. D. Chancellor), *Technical Publication No. 5*. 55–59. ICBP, Cambridge.

HAMERSTROM, F., RAY, T., WHITE, C. M., & BRAUN, C. E. 1975. Conservation committee report on status of eagles. *Wilson Bulletin*, 87: 140–143.

HARASZTHY, L. & BAGYURA, J. 1993. Protection of birds of prey in Hungary in the last 100 years. *Aquila*, 100: 105–121.

HARLOW, D. L. & BLOOM, P. H. 1989. Buteos and the Golden Eagle. In: *Proceedings of the Western Raptor Management Symposium and Workshop* (Ed. B. G. Pendleton), pp. 102–110. *Scientific and Technical Series No. 12*. National Wildlife Federation, Washington.

HARMATA, A. R. 1982. What is the function of undulating flight display in Golden Eagles? *Raptor Research*, 16: 103–109.

HATLER, D. F. 1974. Foods at a Golden Eagle nest in central Alaska. *Condor,* 76: 356–357.

HECTOR, D. P. 1981. The habitat, diet and foraging behaviour of the Aplomado Falcon *Falco femoralis* (Temminck). M.Sc. thesis. Oklahoma State University.

HEIM DE BALSAC, H. & MAYAUD, N. 1962. Les oiseaux du nord-ouest de l'Afrique. Lechevalier Editions, Paris.

HELBIG, A. J. & WELLS, D. R. 1990. Steppe Eagles in peninsular Malaysia in 1987. *Dutch Birding,* 12: 77–79.

HENNINGER, C., BANDERET, G., BLANC, T. & CANTIN, R. 1987. L'Aigle Royal dans une partie des Pre-Alpes Suisses. In: *L'Aigle Royal en Europe* (Ed. S. Michel), pp. 54–58. Actes du Premier Colloque International, Arvieux.

HERNÁNDEZ, L. M., GONZÁLEZ, M. J., RICO, M. C., FERNÁNDEZ, M. A. & ARANDA, A. 1988. Organochlorine and heavy metal residues in Falconiforme and Ciconiforme eggs (Spain). *Bulletin of Environmental Contamination and Toxicology,* 40: 86–93.

HEWSON, R. 1981. Scavenging of mammal carcases by birds in West Scotland. *Journal of Zoology,* 194: 525–537.

HEWSON, R. 1984. Scavenging and predation upon sheep and lambs in West Scotland. *Journal of Applied Ecology,* 21: 843–868

HEWSON, R. & VERKAIK, A. J. 1981. Body condition and ranging behaviour of blackface hill sheep in relation to lamb survival. *Journal of Applied Ecology,* 18: 401–415.

HICKMAN, G. L. 1972. Aerial determination of Golden Eagle nesting status. *Journal of Wildlife Management,* 36: 1289–1292.

HIGUCHI, Y. & TAKEDA, M. 1983. Survey of Japanese Golden Eagles. *Survey on special birds for protection* (1983): 77–97.

HIRALDO, F., DELIBES, M. & CALDERÓN, J. 1976. Sobre el status taxonomico del Águila Imperial Iberica. *Doñana Acta Vertebrata,* 3: 171–182.

HIRALDO, F., BLANCO, J. C. & BUSTAMANTE, J. 1991. Unspecialized exploitation of small carcasses by birds. *Bird Study,* 38: 200–207.

HOBBIE, J. E. & CADE, T. J. 1962. Observations on the breeding of Golden Eagles at Lake Peters in northern Alaska. *Condor,* 64: 235–237.

HOECHLIN, R. 1976. Development of Golden Eaglets in southern California. *Western Birds,* 7: 137–152.

HOECK, H. N. 1982. Population dynamics, dispersal and genetic isolation in two species of Hyrax (*Heterohyrax brucei* and *Procavia johnstoni*) on habitat islands in the Serengeti. *Zeitschrift fur Tierpsychologie,* 59: 177–210.

HÖGSTRÖM, S. & WISS, L.-E. 1992. Diet of the Golden Eagle *Aquila chrysaetos* (L.) in Gotland, Sweden during the breeding season. *Ornis Fennica,* 69: 39–44.

HOLLOWAY, S. 1996. *The Historical Atlas of Breeding Birds in Britain and Ireland,* 1875–1900. Poyser, London.

HOLTHUIJZEN A. M. A. 1989. *Behaviour and productivity of nesting Prairie Falcons in relation to construction activities at Swan Falls Dam.* Final Report. Idaho Power Co., Boise, Idaho.

HOUSTON, D. & MADDOX, J. G. 1974. Causes of mortality among young Scottish Blackface lambs. *Veterinary Record,* 95: 575.

HOWARD, H. 1947. An ancestral Golden Eagle raises a question in taxonomy. *Auk,* 64: 287–291.

HOWARD, R., MOORE, A. 1991. *A Complete Checklist of the Birds of the World,* 2nd edn. Academic Press, London.

HUBOUX, R. 1987. Contribution à une meilleure connaissance du régime alimentaire de l'Aigle Royal en periode de reproduction pour les Alps de Sud et la Provence. In: *L'Aigle Royal en Europe* (Ed. S. Michel), pp.118–123. Actes du Premier Colloque International, Arvieux.

HUDSON, P. 1992. *Grouse in Space and Time: the Population Biology of a Managed Gamebird.* Game Conservancy, Fordingbridge.

HUEY, L. M. 1962. Comparison of the weight-lifting capacities of a House Finch and a Golden Eagle. *Auk*, 79: 485.

HUSTLER, K. & HOWELLS, W. W. 1986. A population study of Tawny Eagles in the Hwange National Park, Zimbabwe. *Ostrich*, 57: 101–106.

HUSTLER, K. & HOWELLS, W. W. 1989. Habitat preference, breeding success and the effect of primary productivity on Tawny Eagles *Aquila rapax* in the tropics. *Ibis*, 131: 33–40.

IKEDA, Y. & YAMAZAKI, T. 1988. Diseases of Golden Eagles: a review. *Aquila chrysaetos*, 6: 36–40.

IVANOVSKY, V. V. 1990. Birds of prey and ornithological monitoring (in Russian). *Communication of the Baltic Commission for Study of Bird Migration*, 22: 92–101.

JACQUAT, B. 1977. Age remarquable d'un Aigle Royal. *Nos Oiseaux*, 34: 31–35.

JENKINS, A. 1984. Hunting behaviour and success in a pair of Black Eagles. *Ostrich*, 55: 102–103.

JENKINS, M. A. & JOSEPH, R. A. 1984. 1981—An extraordinary year for Golden Eagle 'triplets' in the Central Rocky Mountains. *Raptor Research*, 18: 111–113.

JENSEN, R. A. C. 1972. The Steppe Eagle *Aquila nipalensis* and other termite-eating raptors in South-west Africa. *Madoqua, Series 1*, 5: 73–76.

JOHNSGUARD, P. A. 1990. Hawks, Eagles and Falcons of North America. Washington: Smithsonian Institution Press.

JOHNSON, R. E. 1993. Use of snow as a water source by Golden Eagles in the Great Basin. *Journal of Field Ornithology*, 65: 58–59.

JOHNSTON, J. 1966. *The Eagle in Fact and Fiction*. W. H. Allen & Co, London.

JOLLIE, M. 1947. Plumage changes in the Golden Eagle. *Auk*, 64: 549–576

JOLLIE, M. 1957. Comments on the bird genus *Aquila* and its occurrence in New Guinea and Australia. *Nova Guinea*, 8: 179–181.

JORDANO, P. 1981. Relaciones interespecificas y coexistencia entre el Águila Real *Aquila chrysaetos* y el Águila Perdicera *Hieraaetus fasciatus* en Sierra Morena central. *Ardeola*, 28: 67–87.

KALMBACH, E. R., IMLER, R. H. & ARNOLD, L. W. 1964. *The American Eagles and their Economic Status*. USDI, Fish & Wildlife Service, Washington.

KASPARSON, G. R. 1958. Feeding habits of some diurnal predatory birds in Latvian SSR (in Russian). *Zoologicheskii Zhurnal*, 39: 1389–1396.

KENWARD, R. E. 1978. *Wildlife Radio Tagging*. Academic Press, London.

KERAN, D. 1981. The incidence of man-induced natural mortalities to raptors. *Raptor Research*, 15: 108–112.

KNIGHT, R. L. & ERICKSON, A. W. 1978. Marmots as a food source of Golden Eagles along the Columbia River. *Murrelet*, 59: 28–30.

KNIGHT, R. L. & SKAGEN, S. K. 1988. Effects of recreational disturbance on birds of prey: a review. In: *Proceedings of the Southwest Raptor Management Symposium and Workshop* (Ed. R. L. Glinski *et al.*), pp. 355–359. National Wildlife Federation, Washington D.C.

KNIGHT, R. L., ATHEARN, J. B., BRUEGGEMAN, J. J. & ERICKSON, A. W. 1979. Observations on wintering Bald and Golden Eagles on the Columbia River, Washington. *Murrelet*, 60: 99–105.

KOCHERT, M. N. 1972. Population status and chemical contamination in Golden Eagles in southwestern Idaho. M.Sc. thesis. University of Idaho, Moscow.

KOCHERT, M. N. 1980. Golden Eagle reproduction and population changes in relation to jackrabbit cycles: implications to raptor electrocutions. In: *Proceedings of a workshop on raptors and energy developments* (Eds. R. P. Howard and J. F. Gore), pp. 71–86. USDI, Fish & Wildlife Service, Boise, Idaho.

KOCHERT, M. N. & PELLANT, M. 1986. Multiple use in the Snake River Birds of Prey Area. *Rangelands*, 8: 217–220.

KOCHERT, M. N., MILLSAP, B. A. & STEENHOF, K. 1988. Effects of livestock grazing on raptors with emphasis on the southwestern U.S. In: *Proceedings of the southwest raptor management symposium and workshop* (Ed. R. L. Glinski *et al.*), pp. 325–334. National Wildlife Federation, Washington D.C.

KRÓL, W. 1985. Breeding density of diurnal raptors in the neighbourhood of Susz (Ilawa Lakeland, Poland) in the years 1977–79. *Acta Ornithologica*, 21: 95–114.

KRÓL, W. 1987. L'Aigle Royal en Polagne. In: *L'Aigle Royal en Europe* (Ed. S. Michel), pp. 43–47. Actes du Premier Colloque International, Arvieux.

KROPIL, R. & KORNAN, J. 1990. Interesting case of cainism of Golden Eagle *Aquila chrysaetos* (L.) (in Czech). *Tichodroma*, 3: 181–188.

KRYLOV, D. G. 1965. Character of distribution of birds of prey on Sarydzhazskie syrts in central Tyan Shan (in Russian). *Ornitologija*, 7: 203–208.

KUCHIN, A.P. 1961. Ecology of some raptors between the rivers Biya and Katun (in Russian). *Zoologicheskii Zhurnal*, 40: 730–735.

KULVES, H. 1973. Havsörnens *Haliaeetus albicilla albicilla* L. ekologi på Åland. *Skrifter utgivna av Ålands kultustiftelse nr 9.*

LABUTIN, Y. V., LEONOVITCH, V. V. & VEPRINTSEV, B. N. 1982. The Little Curlew *Numenius minutus* in Siberia. *Ibis*, 124: 302–319.

LAISTAL, O. 1966. Im Tal der Königsadler. In: *Mit den Zugvögeln zum Polarkreis* (Eds. F. Steiniger & I. Steiniger). Landbuck-Verlag GmbH, Hannover.

LANO, A. 1922. Golden Eagle *Aquila chrysaetos* and porcupine. *Auk*, 39: 258–259.

LE FRANC, M. N. & CLARK, W. S. 1983. Working bibliography of the Golden Eagle and the genus *Aquila*. Scientific & Technical Series No. 7. National Wildlife Federation, Washington.

LEITCH, A. F. 1986. *Report on eagle predation on lambs in the Glenelg Area in 1986.* Report to Nature Conservancy Council, Inverness.

LESHAM, Y. 1985. Israel: an international axis of raptor migration. In: *Conservation studies on Raptors* (Ed. I. Newton & R. D. Chancellor), pp. 243–250. *Technical Publication No. 5.* ICBP, Cambridge.

LEVINS, R. 1968. *Evolution in Changing Environments.* University Press, Princeton.

LEOPOLD, A. S. & WOLFE T. O. 1970. Food habits of nesting Wedge-tailed Eagles *Aquila audax* in southeastern Australia. *CSIRO Wildlife Research*, 15: 1–17.

LIKHACHEV, G.N. 1957. Description of nesting of large raptors in a deciduous forest (in Russian). *Trudy 2 Pribalt. Ornithol. Konf.*, pp. 308–336.

LIVERSIDGE, R. 1989. Factors influencing migration of 'wintering' raptors in southern Africa. In: *Raptors in the Modern World* (Ed. B-U. Meyburg & R. D. Chancellor), pp. 151–158. WWGBP, Berlin, London & Paris.

LOBACHEV, V. S. 1960. Data on the biology of *Aquila heliaca* northeast of the Aral Sea (in Russian). *Ornitologija*, 3: 306–314.

LOBACHEV, V. S. 1967. Food of *Aquila heliaca* north-east of the Aral Sea (in Russian). *Ornitologija*, 8: 366–369.

LOCATI, M. 1990. Female Chamois defends kids from eagle attacks. *Mammalia*, 54: 155–156.

LOCKHART, J. M. 1976. The food habits, status and ecology of nesting Golden Eagles in the Trans-Pecos region of Texas. M.Sc. thesis. Ross State University, Alpine, Texas.

LOCKIE, J. D. 1964. The breeding density of the Golden Eagle and Fox in relation to food supply in Wester Ross, Scotland. *Scottish Naturalist*, 71: 67–77.

LOCKIE, J. D. & RATCLIFFE, D. A. 1964. Insecticides and Scottish Golden Eagles. *British Birds*, 57: 89–102.

LOCKIE, J. D. & STEPHEN, D. 1959. Eagles, lambs and land management on Lewis. *Journal of Animal Ecology*, 28: 43–50.

LOCKIE, J. D., RATCLIFFE, D. A. & BALHARRY R. 1969. Breeding success and organochlorine residues in Golden Eagles in West Scotland. *Journal of Applied Ecology*, 6: 381–389.

LOVE, J. A. 1983. *The Return of the Sea Eagle.* University Press, Cambridge.

LOVE, J. A. 1989. *Eagles*. Whittet Books, London.

LUDLOW, F. & KINNEAR, N. B. 1933. A contribution to the ornithology of Chinese Turkestan. Part III. *Ibis Series 13*, 3: 658–694.

MACDONALD, D. 1984a. *The Encyclopaedia of Mammals: 1*. Guild Publishing, London.

MACDONALD, D. 1984b. *The Encyclopaedia of Mammals: 2*. Guild Publishing, London.

MACKAY, R. D. 1988. Gurney's Eagle *Aquila gurneyi* in the Highlands. *Muruk*, 3: 56.

MACKENZIE, O. H. 1928. *A Hundred Years in the Highlands*. Geoffrey Bles, London.

MACNALLY, L. 1964. Some notes on Golden Eagles. *Scottish Birds*, 3: 26–27.

MACPHERSON, H. A. 1892. *A Vertebrate Fauna of Lakeland*. David Douglas, Edinburgh.

MACPHERSON, H. B. 1909. *The Home-life of a Golden Eagle*. Witherby, London.

MAGRINI, M., RAGNI, B. & AMERTANO, L. 1987. L'Aigle Royal dans la partie centrale des Appennins. In: *L'Aigle Royal en Europe* (Ed. S. Michel), pp. 29–32. Actes du Premier Colloque International, Arvieux.

MARCHANT, S. & HIGGINS, P. J. 1993. *Handbook of Australian, New Zealand and Antarctic Birds*, Vol 2. University Press, Oxford.

MARQUISS, M., RATCLIFFE, D. A. & ROXBURGH, R. 1985. The numbers, breeding success and diet of Golden Eagles in southern Scotland in relation to changes in land use. *Biological Conservation*, 33: 1–17.

MARR, N. V. & KNIGHT, R. L. 1983. Food habits of Golden Eagles in eastern Washington. *Murrelet*, 64: 73–77.

MARZLUFF, J. M., SCHUECK, L. S., VEKASY, M., KIMSEY, B. A, MCFADZEN, M., TOWSEND, R. R. & MCKINLEY, J. O. 1994. Influence of military training on the behaviour of raptors in the Snake River Birds of Prey National Conservation Area. In: *Snake River Bird of Prey National Conservation Area—1993 Annual Report* (Ed. K. Steenhof), pp. 40–125. USDI, Boise, Idaho.

MARZLUFF, J. M., SCHUECK, L. S., VEKASY, M., KIMSEY, B. A, MCFADZEN, M., TOWSEND, R. R. & MCKINLEY, J. O. 1995. Influence of military training on the behaviour of raptors in the Snake River Birds of Prey National Conservation Area. In: *Snake River Bird of Prey National Conservation Area—1994 Annual Report* (Ed. K. Steenhof), pp. 41–112. USDI, Boise, Idaho.

MATCHETT, M. R. & O'GARA, B. W. 1987. Methods of controlling Golden Eagle depredation on domestic sheep in southwestern Montana. *Journal of Raptor Research*, 21: 85–94.

MATHER, A. S. 1978. The alleged deterioration in hill grazings in the Scottish Highlands. *Biological Conservation*, 14: 181–194.

MATHIEU, R. 1985. Développement du poussin d'Aigle Royal *Aquila chrysaetos* et determination de l'age dans la nature par l'observation éloignée. *Bièvre*, 7: 71–86.

MATHIEU, R. & CHOISY, J. P. 1982. L'Aigle Royal *Aquila chrysaetos* dans les Alpes Meridionales Francaises de 1964 a 1980. Essai sur la distribution, les effectifs, le régime alimentaire et la reproduction. *Bièvre*, 4: 1–32.

MCGAHAN, J. 1968. Ecology of the Golden Eagle. *Auk*, 85: 1–12.

MCGARIGAL, K., ANTHONY, R. G. & ISAACS, F. B. 1991. Interactions of humans and Bald Eagles on the Columbia River estuary. *Wildlife Monographs No. 115*.

MCVEAN, D. N. & LOCKIE, J. D. 1969. *Ecology and Land Use in Upland Scotland*. University Press, Edinburgh.

MCVEAN, D. N. & RATCLIFFE, D. A. 1962. *Plant Communities of the Scottish Highlands: Monographs of the Nature Conservancy No. 1*. HMSO, London.

MEBS, T. 1964. Zur Biologie und Populationsdynamik des Mäusebussards *Buteo buteo*. *Journal für Ornithologie*, 105: 247–306.

MEINERTZHAGEN, R. 1940. How do larger raptorial birds hunt their prey? *Ibis*, 4: 530–535.

MENGEL, R. M. & WARNER, D. W. 1948. Golden Eagles in Hidalgo, Mexico. *Wilson Bulletin*, 60: 122.

MENKENS, G. E. & ANDERSON, S. H. 1987. Nest site characteristics of a predominantly tree-nesting population of Golden Eagles. *Journal of Field Ornithology*, 58: 22–25.

MERSMANN, T. J., BUEHLER, D. A., FRASER, J. D. & SEEGER, J. K. D. 1992. Assessing bias in studies of Bald Eagle food habits. *Journal of Wildlife Management*, 56: 73–78.

MEYBURG, B-U. 1973. Studies of less familiar birds: 172, Lesser Spotted Eagle. *British Birds*, 66: 439–447.

MEYBURG, B-U. 1974. Sibling aggression and mortality among nestling eagles. *Ibis*, 116: 224–228.

MEYBURG, B-U. 1987. Clutch size, nestling aggression and breeding success of the Spanish Imperial Eagle. *British Birds*, 80: 308–320.

MEYBURG, B-U. & MEYBURG C. 1987. Present status of diurnal birds of prey *Falconiformes* in various countries bordering the Mediterranean. *Richerche Biologia Selvaggina*, 12: 147–152.

MEYBURG, B-U., SCHELLER, W. & MEYBURG, C. 1993. Satelliten-Telemetrie bei eninem juvenilen Schreiadler *Aquila pomarina* auf dem Herbstzug. *Journal für Ornithologie*, 134: 173–179.

MEYBURG, B-U., EICHAKER, X., MEYBURG, C. & PAILLAT, P. 1995a. Migrations of an adult Spotted Eagle tracked by satellite. *British Birds*, 88: 357–361.

MEYBURG, B-U., MIZERA, T., MACIOROWSKI, G., DYLAWERSKI, M. & SMYK, A. 1995b. Juvenile Spotted Eagle apparently killed by Eagle Owl. *British Birds*, 88: 376.

MICHEL, S. 1987a. *L'Aigle Royal Aquila chrysaetos en Europe*. Actes du Premier Colloque International, Arvieux.

MICHEL, S. 1987b. Estimation du nombre de couples d'Aigles Royaux en Europe. In: *L'Aigle Royal en Europe* (Ed. S. Michel), p. 165. Actes du Premier Colloque International, Arvieux.

MICHEV, T., PETROV, T., PROFIROV, L., YANKOV, P. & GAVRAILOV, S. 1989. Distribution and nature-defensive status of the Golden Eagle *Aquila chrysaetos chrysaetos* (L., 1758) in Bulgaria (in Russian). *Bulletin of the Museums of South Bulgaria*, 25: 79–87.

MILLER MUNDY, A. 1996. Riding in the Eagles' Wake. *The Field.* February 1996.

MILLSAP, B. A. & VANA, S. L. 1984. Distribution of wintering Golden Eagles in the eastern United States. *Wilson Bulletin*, 96: 692–701.

MOFFATT, R. E. 1972. Natural pox infection in a Golden Eagle. *Journal of Wildlife Diseases*, 8: 161–162.

MOLLHAGEN, T. R., WILEY, R. W. & PACKARD, R. L. 1972. Prey remains in Golden Eagle nests: Texas and New Mexico. *Journal of Wildlife Management*, 36: 784–792.

MOONEY, N. & HOLDSWORTH, M. 1991. The effects of disturbance on nesting Wedge-tailed Eagles *Aquila audax fleayi* in Tasmania. *Tasforests*, 3: 15–31.

MOORE, J. H. 1986. The ornithology of the Cheyenne religionists. *Plains Anthropologist*, 31: 177–190.

MORNEAU, F., BRODEUR, S., DECARIE, R., CARRIERE, S. & BIRD, D. M. 1994. Abundance and distribution of nesting Golden Eagles in Hudson Bay, Quebec. *Journal of Raptor Research*, 28: 220–225.

MOSHER, J. A. & WHITE, C. M. 1976. Directional exposure of Golden Eagle nests. *Canadian Field Naturalist*, 90: 356–359

MRLÍK, V. & DANKO, S. 1990. Numbers of birds of prey nesting in Czechoslovakia (in Czech). *Sylvia*, 27: 71–78.

MUELLER, H. C. & MEYER, K. 1985. The evolution of reversed sexual dimorphism in size: a comparative analysis of the Falconiformes of the Western Palearctic. In: *Current Ornithology*, Vol. 2 (Ed. R. J. Johnston). Plenum Press, New York.

MURIE, A. 1944. *The Wolves of Mt. McKinley. (Golden Eagle—Chapter 8)*. U.S. Fauna Series No 5, Washington.

MURPHY J. R. 1975. Status of the Golden Eagle in central Utah 1967–1973. *Raptor Research Report*, 3: 91–96.

NAOROJI, R. 1990. Predation by *Aquila* eagles on nestling storks and herons in Keoladeo National Park, Bharatpur. *Journal of the Bombay Natural History Society*, 87: 37–46.

NCC (NATURE CONSERVANCY COUNCIL). 1986. *Nature Conservation and Afforestation in Britain*. NCC, Peterborough.

NELSON, M. W. 1982. Human impacts on Golden Eagles: a positive outlook for the 1980s and 1990s. *Raptor Research*, 16: 97–103.

NELSON, M. W. & NELSON, P. 1977. Power lines and birds of prey. In: *World Conference on Birds of Prey—Report on Proceedings*, (Ed. R. D. Chancellor), pp. 228–242. ICBP, Cambridge.

NETTE, T., BURLES, D. & HOEFS, M. 1984. Observations of Golden Eagle *Aquila chrysaetos* predation on Dall Sheep *Ovis dalli dalli* lambs. *Canadian Field Naturalist*, 98: 252–254.

NEWTON, I. 1979. *Population Ecology of Raptors*. Poyser, Berkhamsted.

NEWTON, I. 1986. *The Sparrowhawk*. Poyser, Carlton.

NEWTON, I. & GALBRAITH, E. A. 1991. Organochlorines and mercury in the eggs of Golden Eagles *Aquila chrysaetos* from Scotland. *Ibis*, 133: 115–120.

NEWTON, I. & MARQUISS, M. 1982. Food, predation and breeding season in Sparrowhawks. *Journal of Zoology*, 197: 221–240.

NEWTON, I., MARQUISS, M., WEIR, D. N. & MOSS, D. 1977. Spacing of Sparrowhawk nesting territories. *Journal of Animal Ecology*, 46: 425–441.

NEWTON, I., WYLLIE, J. & MEARNS, R. 1986. Spacing of Sparrowhawks in relation to food supply. *Journal of Animal Ecology*, 55: 361–370.

NEWTON, I., BOGAN, J. & HAAS, M. B. 1989. Organochlorines and mercury in the eggs of British Peregrines *Falco peregrinus*. *Ibis*, 131: 355–376.

NICHOLSON, E.M. 1957. Golden Eagle *Aquila chrysaetos*. *British Birds*, 50: 131–135.

NIELSEN, B. P. 1969. Further Spring observations on the birds of Gilan, Northern Iran. *Dansk Ornithologisk Forenings Tidsskrift*, 63: 50–73.

NIEMEYER, C. 1977. *Montana Golden Eagle removal and Translocation Project. Final Report.* USDI Fish & Wildlife Service, Billings, Montana.

NILSSON, I. N., NILSSON, S. G. & SYLVEN, M. 1982. Diet choice, resource depression, and the regular nest spacing of birds of prey. *Biological Journal of Linnean Society*, 18: 1–9.

NOVELLETTO, A. & PETRETTI, F. 1980. Ecologia dell'Aquila Reale negli Appennini. *Rivita Italiana di Ornitolgia*, 50: 127–142.

OLENDORFF, R. R. 1975. Population status of large raptors in northeastern Colorado—1970–1972. *Raptor Research Report*, 3: 185–205.

OLENDORFF, R. R., MILLER, A. D. & LEHMAN, R. N. 1981. Suggested practices for raptor protection on power lines: the state of the art in 1981. *Raptor Research Report No. 4.*

OLSEN, D. & MARPLES, T. G. 1992. Alteration of the clutch size of raptors in response to a change in prey availability: evidence from control of a broad-scale rabbit infestation. *Wildlife Research*, 19: 129–135.

OSMOLSKAYA, V. I. 1953. Geographic distribution of birds of prey in the lowlands of Kazakhastan and their significance to the destruction of pest rodents (in Russian). *Trudy Inst. Geograph.*, 54: 219–307.

PAGE, J. L & SEIBERT, D. J. 1973. Inventory of golden eagle nests in Elko County, Nevada. *CAL-NEVA Wildlife*, 1973: 1–8.

PALÁŠTHY, J. & MEYBURG, B-U. 1970. Zur Ernährung des Schreiadlers *Aquila pomarina* in der Ostslowskei unter atypischen klimatischen Bedingungen. *Ornithologische Mitteilungen*, 25: 62–72.

PALMA, L. 1985. The present situation of birds of prey in Portugal. In: *Conservation Studies on Raptors* (Eds. I. Newton & R. D. Chancellor), pp 3–14. *Technical Publication No. 5*. ICBP, Cambridge.

PALMER, R. 1988. *Handbook of North American Birds*, Vol 5. University Press, Yale.

PBRG (PREDATORY BIRD RESEARCH GROUP) 1995. *A pilot Golden Eagle population study in the Altamont Pass Wind Resource Area, California.* University of California, Santa Cruz.

PEETERS, H. J. 1994. Suspected poisoning of Golden Eagles *Aquila chrysaetos* by chlorophacinone. In: *Raptor conservation today* (Eds. B.-U. Meyburg & R.D. Chancellor) pp. 775–776. WWGBP, London.

PERRINS, C. M. & BIRKHEAD, T. R. 1983. *Avian Ecology.* New York: Chapman & Hall.

PHILLIPS, R. L. & BESKE, A. E. 1990. *Distribution and abundance of Golden Eagles and other raptors in Campbell and Converse Counties, Wyoming.* Fish and Wildlife Service Technical Report No. 27. USDI, Washington.

PHILLIPS, R. L., MCENEANEY, T. P. & BESKE, A. E. 1984. Population densities of breeding Golden Eagles in Wyoming. *Wildlife Society Bulletin*, 12: 269–273.

PHILLIPS, R. L., WHEELER, A. H., FORRESTER, N. C., LOCKHART, J. M. & MCENEANEY, T. P. 1990. *Nesting ecology of Golden Eagles and other raptors in southeastern Montana and northern Wyoming.* Fish and Wildlife Technical Report No. 26. USDI, Washington.

PHILLIPS, R. L., CUMMINGS, J. L. & BERRY, J. D. 1991. Response of breeding Golden Eagles to relocation. *Wildlife Society Bulletin*, 19: 430–434.

PINEAU, J. & GIRAUD-AUDINE, M. 1977. Notes sur les oiseaux nicheurs de l'extrême nord-ouest du Maroc: reproduction et movements. *Alauda*, 45: 75–103.

POOLE, A. F. 1989. *Ospreys: a natural and unnatural history.* University Press, Cambridge.

POOLE, K. G. & BROMLEY, R. G. 1988. Interrelationships within a raptor guild in the central Canadian Arctic. *Canadian Journal of Zoology*, 66: 2275–2282.

PORTER, R. F. & BEAMAN, M. A. S. 1983. A résumé of raptor migration in Europe and the Middle East. In: *Conservation Studies on Raptors* (Eds. I. Newton & R. D. Chancellor), pp. 237–242. *Technical Publication No. 5.* ICBP, Cambridge.

PORTER, R. F., WILLIS, I., CHRISTENSEN, S. & NIELSEN, B. P. 1981. *Flight Identification of European Raptors*, 3rd edn. Poyser, Carlton.

POSTOVIT, H. R., GRIER, J. W., LOCKHART, J. M. & TATE, J. 1982. Directed relocation of a Golden Eagle nest site. *Journal of Wildlife Management*, 46: 1045–1048.

POSTUPALSKY, S. 1974. Raptor reproductive success: some problems with methods, criteria and terminology. *Raptor Research Report*, 2: 21–31.

POTOČNÝ, R. 1989. Number and character of the occurrence of the Lesser Spotted Eagle *Aquila pomarina* in the District of Presov in the years of 1988–1990 (in Czech). *Buteo*, 4: 73–78.

PRAKASH, V. 1989. Population and distribution of raptors in Keoladeo National Park, Bharatpur, India. In: *Raptors in the Modern World* (Eds. B-U. Meyburg & R. D. Chancellor), pp 129–137. WWGBP, Berlin, London & Paris.

PRIKLONSKI, S. G. 1960. Food of *Aquila clanga* in River Belaya estuary (in Russian). *Ornitologija*, 3: 174–179.

RAGNI, B., MAGRINI, M. & ARMENTANO, L. 1986. Aspetti della biologia dell'Aquila Reale *Aquila chrysaetos* nell' Appennino umbro-marchigiano. *Avocetta*, 10: 71–85.

RAMOVSKI, S. 1979. Trained eagle saved prisoners in a soviet prison in Siberia from starvation (in Hebrew). *Yidioth Achronoth*: 16 Dec 1979.

RATCLIFFE, D. A. 1962. Breeding density of the Peregrine *Falco peregrinus* and Raven *Corvus corax*. *Ibis*, 104: 13–39.

RATCLIFFE, D. A. 1970. Changes attributable to pesticides in egg breakage frequency and eggshell thickness in some British birds. *Journal of Applied Ecology*, 7: 67–107.

RATCLIFFE, D. A. 1980. *The Peregrine Falcon.* Poyser, Carlton.

RATCLIFFE, D. A. 1990. *Bird Life of Mountain and Upland.* University Press, Cambridge.

RATCLIFFE, D. A. & THOMPSON, D. B. A. 1988. The British uplands: their ecological character and international significance. In: *Ecological Change in the*

Uplands (Eds. M. B. Usher & D. B. A. Thompson), pp. 9–36. Blackwell Scientific Publications, Oxford.

RATCLIFFE, P. R. & ROWE, J. J. 1979. A Golden Eagle *Aquila chrysaetos* kills an infant Roe Deer *Capraeolus capraeolus*. *Journal of Zoology*, 189: 532–535.

RAY, M. S. 1928. Record set of eggs of the Golden Eagle. *Condor*, 30: 250.

REYNOLDS, H. V. 1969. Population status of the Golden Eagle in south-central Montana. M.Sc. thesis. University of Montana, Missoula, Montana.

REYNOLDS, R. T. 1972. Sexual dimorphism in *Accipiter* hawks: a new hypothesis. *Condor*, 74: 191–197.

RICKLEFS, R. E. 1968. Patterns of growth in birds. *Ibis*, 110: 419–451.

RIDPATH, M. G. & BROOKER, M. G. 1986a. The breeding of the Wedge-tailed Eagle *Aquila audax* in relation to its food supply in arid Western Australia. *Ibis*, 128: 177–194.

RIDPATH, M. G. & BROOKER, M. G. 1986b. Age, movements and the management of the Wedge-tailed Eagle *Aquila audax* in arid Western Australia. *Australian Wildlife Research*, 13: 245–260.

RIDPATH, M. G. & BROOKER, M. G. 1987. Sites and spacing of nests as determinants of Wedge-tailed Eagle breeding in arid Western Australia. *Emu*, 8: 143–149.

RITCHIE, R. J. & CURATOLO, J. A. 1982. Notes on Golden Eagle productivity and nest site characteristics, Porcupine River, Alaska, 1979–1982. *Raptor Research*, 16: 123–127.

RODRÍGUEZ-ESTRELLA, R., LLINAS-GUTIÉREZ, J. & CANCINO, J. 1991. New Golden Eagle records from Baja California. *Journal of Raptor Research*, 25: 68–71.

RODWELL, J. S. 1991. *British Plant Communities Volume 2: Mires and Heaths.* University Press, Cambridge.

RODWELL, J. S. 1992. *British Plant Communities Volume 3: Grasslands and Montane Communities.* University Press, Cambridge.

ROWE, E. G. 1947. The breeding biology of *Aquila verreauxi* Lesson. *Ibis*, 89: 387–410 & 576–606.

RSPB & NCC (ROYAL SOCIETY FOR THE PROTECTION OF BIRDS & NATURE CONSERVANCY COUNCIL). 1991. *Death by Design.* RSPB, Sandy.

RUFINO, R., ARAÚJO, A. & ABREU, M. V. 1985. Breeding raptors in Portugal: distribution and population estimates. In: *Conservation Studies on Raptors* (Eds. I. Newton & R. D. Chancellor), pp 15–28. *Technical Publication No. 5.* ICBP, Cambridge.

SANDEMAN, P. W. 1957. The breeding success of Golden Eagles in the southern Grampians. *Scottish Naturalist*, 69: 148–152.

SEMINARA, S., GIARRATANA, S. & FAVARA, R. 1987. L'Aigle Royal en Sicile. In: *L'Aigle Royal en Europe* (Ed. S. Michel), pp.33–36. Actes du Premier Colloque International, Arvieux.

SEVERIN, T. 1991. *In search of Genghis Khan.* Hutchinson, London.

SHARROCK, J. T. R. 1976. *The Atlas of Breeding Birds in Britain and Ireland.* Poyser, Carlton.

SHERRINGTON, P. 1993. Golden Eagle migration in the Front Ranges of the Alberta Rocky Mountains. *Birders Journal*, 2: 195–204.

SHERROD, S. K., WHITE, C. M. & WILLIAMSON, F. S. L. 1977. Biology of the Bald Eagle on Amchitka Island, Alaska. *Living Bird*, 15: 143–182.

SIMEON, D. & CHEYLAN, G. 1985. Conservation strategies for raptors in the south of France. *WWGBP Bulletin*, 2: 113–116.

SIMMONS, R. 1988. Offspring quality and the evolution of cainism. *Ibis*, 130: 339–357.

SIMMONS, R. E. & MENDELSOHN, J. M. 1993. A critical review of cartwheeling flights of raptors. *Ostrich*, 64: 13–24.

SIMMONS, R. E., AVERY, D. M. & AVERY, G. 1991. Biases in diets determined from pellets and remains: correction factors for a mammal and bird-eating raptor. *Journal of Raptor Research*, 25: 63–67.

SINGH, G. 1961. The Eastern Steppe Eagle *Aquila nipalensis nipalensis* on the south col of Everest. *Journal of the Bombay Natural History Society*, 58: 270.

SLÁDEK, J. 1959. Zur Ernährung des Schreiadlers in der Slowakei. *Zoologiské Listy,* 8: 108–113.

SLEVIN, J. R. 1929. A contribution to our knowledge of the nesting habits of the Golden Eagle. *Proceedings of the Californian Academy of Science,* 18: 45–71.

SMEENK, C. 1974. Comparative ecological studies of some East African birds of prey. *Ardea,* 62: 1–97.

SMITH E. C. 1974. Some additional information on birds in Afghanistan. *Ardea,* 62: 226–235.

SMOUT, T.C. 1969. *A History of the Scottish People 1560–1830.* Fontana Press, London.

SNH (SCOTTISH NATURAL HERITAGE). 1994. *Red Deer and the Natural Heritage. SNH Policy Paper.* Scottish Natural Heritage, Edinburgh.

SNOW, C. 1973. *Golden Eagle Aquila chrysaetos. Habitat management series for unique or endangered species.* USDI Bureau of Land Management Tech. Note TN-239.

SNOW, D. W. (Ed.). 1978. *Atlas of Speciation in African Non-passerine Birds.* British Museum, London.

SNYDER, L. L. 1949. On the distribution of the Golden Eagle in eastern Canada. *Canadian Field Naturalist,* 63: 39–41.

SNYDER, N. F. R. & WILEY, J. W. 1976. *Sexual Size Dimorphism in Hawks and Owls of North America.* Ornithological Monographs No. 20. American Ornithologists' Union.

SPECHT R. L. 1979. *Ecosystems of the world, Vol 9A: Heathlands and Related Shrublands.* Elsevier, Amsterdam.

SPOFFORD, W. R. 1964. *The Golden Eagle in the Trans-pecos and Edwards plateau of Texas.* Audubon Conservation Report No. 1.

SPOFFORD, W. R. 1971. The breeding status of the Golden Eagle in the Appalachians. *American Birds,* 25: 3–7.

SRGE (SOCIETY FOR RESEARCH OF GOLDEN EAGLE) 1983. Journal of Society for Research of Golden Eagle. *Aquila chrysaetos No. 1.*

SRGE (SOCIETY FOR RESEARCH OF GOLDEN EAGLE) 1985. Period of breeding in the Japanese Golden Eagle. *Aquila chrysaetos,* 3: 1–8.

SRGE (SOCIETY FOR RESEARCH OF GOLDEN EAGLE) 1988. The list of Golden Eagle specimens in Japan and their measurements. *Aquila chrysaetos,* 6: 1–13.

SRGE (SOCIETY FOR RESEARCH OF GOLDEN EAGLE) 1991. Human impacts on Golden Eagles in Japan. *Aquila chrysaetos,* 8: 1–9.

SRGE (SOCIETY FOR RESEARCH OF GOLDEN EAGLE) 1992. Population and breeding success of the Golden Eagle in Japan (1981–1990). *Aquila chrysaetos,* 9: 1–11.

STAAV, R. 1990. The oldest Golden Eagle so far (in Swedish). *Vår Fågelvärld,* 49: 34.

STEENHOF, K. 1987. Assessing raptor reproductive success and productivity. In: *Raptor Management Techniques Manual* (Eds. B. A. Giron Pendleton, B. A. Millsap, K. W. Cline & D. M. Bird), pp 157–170. *Scientific Technical Series No. 10.* National Wildlife Federation.

STEENHOF, K. & KOCHERT, M. N. 1985. Dietary shifts of sympatric buteos during a prey decline. *Oecologia,* 66: 6–16.

STEENHOF, K. & KOCHERT, M. N. 1988. Dietary responses of three raptor species to changing prey densities in a natural environment. *Journal of Animal Ecology,* 57: 37–48.

STEENHOF, K., KOCHERT, M. N. & DOREMUS, J. H. 1983. Nesting of subadult Golden Eagles in southwestern Idaho. *Auk,* 100: 743–747.

STEENHOF, K., KOCHERT, M. N. & MORITSCH, M. Q. 1984. Dispersal and migration of southwestern Idaho raptors. *Journal of Field Ornithology,* 55: 357–368.

STEYN, P. 1973a. *Eagle Days.* Purnell, Cape Town.

STEYN, P. 1973b. Observations on the Tawny Eagle. *Ostrich,* 44: 1–22.

STEYN, P. 1980. Further observations on the Tawny Eagle. *Ostrich,* 51: 54–55.

STEYN, P. 1982. *Birds of Prey of Southern Africa.* David Philip, Cape Town.

STROUD, D. A., MUDGE, G. P. & PIENKOWSKI, M. W. 1990. *Protecting Internationally Important Bird Sites.* Nature Conservancy Council, Peterborough.

SUKHININ, A. N. 1958. Breeding and feeding of some birds of prey in Badkhyz (in Russian). *Trudy Inst. Zool. An Turkmen. SSR*, 3: 47–118.

SULKAVA, S. & RAJALA, P. 1966. Diet of the Golden Eagle *Aquila chrysaetos* during the nesting period in the Finnish reindeer husbandry area (in Finnish). *Suomen Riista*, 19: 7–19.

SULKAVA, S., HUHTALA, K. & RAJALA, P. 1984. Diet and breeding success of the Golden Eagle in Finland 1958–82. *Annales Zoologici Fennici*, 21: 283–286.

SUMNER, E.L. 1929. Comparative studies in the growth of young raptores. *Condor*, 31: 85–111.

SUTER, G. W. & JONES, J. L. 1981. Criteria for Golden Eagle, Ferruginous Hawk and Prairie Falcon nest site protection. *Raptor Research*, 15: 12–18.

SVEHLIK, J. & MEYBURG, B-U. 1979. Gelegegroße und Bruterfolg des Schreiadlers *Aquila pomarina* und des Kaiseradlers *Aquila heliaca* in den ostslowakishcen Karpaten 1966–1978. *Journal für Ornithologie*, 120: 406–415.

TARBOTON, W. R. 1978. *A Survey of Birds of Prey in the Transvaal. Transvaal Nat. Cons. Div. Progr., Rep. TN 6/4/4/9.*

TARBOTON, W. R. & ALLAN, D. 1984. *The Status and Conservation of Birds of Prey in the Transvaal. Transvaal Museum Monograph 3.*

TERESA, S. 1980. Golden Eagles successfully breeding in subadult plumage. *Raptor Research*, 14: 86–87

THÉVENOT, M., BERGIER, P. & BEAUBRUN, P. 1985. Present distribution and status of raptors in Morocco. In: *Conservation Studies on Raptors* (Eds. I. Newton & R. D. Chancellor), pp 83–101. *Technical Publication No. 5*. ICBP, Cambridge.

THIOLLAY, J.-M. 1977. Distribution saisonaire des rapaces diurnes en Afrique Occidentale. *L'Oiseau et R.F.O.*, 47: 253–285.

THIOLLAY, J.-M. 1989. Distribution and ecology of Palearctic birds of prey wintering in west and central Africa. In: *Raptors in the Modern World* (Eds. B-U. Meyburg & R. D. Chancellor), pp. 95–107. WWGBP, Berlin, London & Paris.

THIOLLAY, J.-M. & DUHAUTOIS, L. 1976. Notes sur les oiseaux du Nord Yemen. *L'Oiseau et R.F.O.*, 46: 261–271.

THIOLLAY, J.-M. & MEYER, J. A. 1978. Densité, taille des territoires et production dans une population d'Aigles Pêcheurs, *Haliaeetus vocifer* (Daudin). *La Terre et la Vie*, 32: 203–219.

THOMPSON, S. P., JOHNSTONE, R. S. & LITTLEFIELD, C. D. 1982. Nesting history of Golden Eagles in Malheur-Harney Lakes Basin, southeastern Oregon. *Raptor Research*, 16: 116–122.

TJERNBERG, M. 1977. Individuell igenkänning av kungsörnar *Aquila chrysaetos* i fält samt rcultat av vinterinventeringar i sydvästra Uppland. *Vår Fågelvärld*, 36: 21–32.

TJERNBERG, M. 1981. Diet of the Golden Eagle *Aquila chrysaetos* during the breeding season in Sweden. *Holarctic Ecology*, 4: 12–19.

TJERNBERG, M. 1983a. Habitat and nest site features of Golden Eagles *Aquila chrysaetos* (L.), in Sweden. *Swedish Wildlife Research*, 12: 131–163.

TJERNBERG, M. 1983b. Prey abundance and reproductive success of the Golden Eagle *Aquila chrysaetos* in Sweden. *Holarctic Ecology*, 6: 17–23.

TJERNBERG, M. 1985. Spacing of Golden Eagle *Aquila chrysaetos* nests in relation to nest site and food availability. *Ibis*, 127: 250–255.

TJERNBERG, M. 1988. Age determination of Golden Eagles *Aquila chrysaetos* (in Swedish). *Vår Fågelvärld*, 47: 321–334.

TJERNBERG, M. 1990. Kungsörnen *Aquila chrysaetos* i Sverige—utbreding, status och hot. *Vår Fågelvärld*, 49: 339–348.

TUCKER, G. M. & HEATH, M. F. 1994. *Birds in Europe: Their Conservation Status. BirdLife Conservation Series No.3*. BirdLife International, Cambridge.

TODD, C. S. 1989. Golden Eagle. In: *Proceedings of Northeast Raptor Management*

Symposium and Workshop (Ed. B. G.Pendleton), pp. 65–70. *Scientific and Technical Series No. 13*. National Wildlife Federation, Washington.

TYUREKHODZHAEV, Z. M. 1973. Influence of *Aquila nipalensis* on population structure and number fluctuations of *Citellus pygmaeus* (in Russian). *Trudy Kazakh. Inst. Zastchity Rastenii*, 12: 69–76.

USSHER, R. J. & WARREN, R. 1900. *The Birds of Ireland*. Gurney and Jackson, London.

VAGLIANO, C. 1981. Contributions au statut des rapaces diurnes et nocturnes nicheurs en Crete. *Rapaces Médeterranéens*, Annales du C.R.O.P., 1: 14–18.

VARSHAVSKI, B. S. 1973. Some landscape-ecological characteristics of feeding of *Buteo rufinus, Aquila heliaca* and *Aquila nipalensis* north of the Aral sea (in Russian). *Bull. MOIP Otdel. Biology*, 78: 30–37.

VARSHAVSKI, S. N. 1968. Feeding of *Aquila chrysaetos* in southwestern Ust-urt (in Russian). *Ornitologija*, 9: 146–149.

VASIĆ, V., GRUBAČ, B., SUŠIĆ, G. & MARINKOVIĆ, S. 1985. The status of birds of prey in Yugoslavia, with particular reference to Macedonia. In: *Conservation Studies on Raptors* (Eds. I. Newton & R. D. Chancellor), pp 45–53. *Technical Publication No. 5*. ICBP, Cambridge.

VERNER, W. 1909. *My life Among the Wild Birds in Spain*. London.

VILLAGE, A. 1990. *The Kestrel*. Poyser, London.

VIROLAINEN, E. & RASSI, P. 1990. Suomen maakotkakannan kehitys 1970–1980 luvuilla. *Lintumies*, 25: 59–65.

VOSKÁR, J., MOSANSKY, A. & PALÁSTHY, J. 1969. Zur Bionomie und Okologischen Verbreitung des Steinadlers *Aquila chrysaetos* (L.) in der Ostslowakei. *Zoologiské Listy*, 18: 39–54.

WALKER, D. G. 1987. Observations on the post-fledging period of the Golden Eagle *Aquila chrysaetos* in England. *Ibis*, 129: 92–96.

WALKER, D. G. 1988. The behaviour and movements of a juvenile Golden Eagle *Aquila chrysaetos* in England in 1986. *Ibis*, 130: 564–565.

WALTER, H. & BOX, E. O. 1983. The Orobiomes of Middle Asia. In: *Temperate deserts and semi-deserts* (Ed. N. E. West), pp. 161–191. *Ecosystems of the world 5*. Elsevier, Amsterdam.

WATERSTON, G. 1959. Golden Eagle with tuberculosis and aspergillosis. *British Birds*, 52: 197–198.

WATSON, A. 1957. The breeding success of Golden Eagles in the north-east Highlands. *Scottish Naturalist*, 69: 153–169.

WATSON, A. 1972. The behaviour of the Ptarmigan. *British Birds*, 65: 6–21 & 93–117.

WATSON, A. & JENKINS D. 1964. Notes on the behaviour of the Red Grouse. *British Birds*, 57: 137–170.

WATSON, A. & ROTHERY, P. 1986 Regularity in spacing of Golden Eagle *Aquila chrysaetos* nests used within years in northeast Scotland. *Ibis*, 128: 406–408.

WATSON, A., PAYNE, S. & RAE, R. 1989. Golden Eagles *Aquila chrysaetos*: land use and food in northeast Scotland. *Ibis*, 131: 336–348.

WATSON, D. 1977. *The Hen Harrier*. Poyser, Berkhamsted.

WATSON, J. 1991. The Golden Eagle and pastoralism across Europe. In: *Birds and Pastoral Agriculture in Europe* (Eds. D. J. Curtis, E. M. Bignal & M. A. Curtis), pp 56–57. Joint Nature Conservation Committee, Peterborough.

WATSON, J. 1992a. Golden Eagle *Aquila chrysaetos* breeding success and afforestation in Argyll. *Bird Study*, 39: 203–206.

WATSON, J. 1992b. Status of the Golden Eagle *Aquila chrysaetos* in Europe. *Bird Conservation International*, 2: 175–183.

WATSON, J. & DENNIS, R. H. 1992. Nest site selection by Golden Eagles *Aquila chrysaetos* in Scotland. *British Birds*, 85: 469–481.

WATSON, J., LEITCH, A. F. & BROAD, R. 1992a. The diet of Sea Eagles *Haliaeetus albicilla* and Golden Eagles *Aquila chrysaetos* in western Scotland. *Ibis*, 133: 27–31.

WATSON, J., RAE, S. R. & STILLMAN R. 1992b. Nesting density and breeding success of Golden Eagles *Aquila chrysaetos* in relation to food supply in Scotland. *Journal of Animal Ecology*, 61: 543–550.

WATSON, J., LEITCH, A. F. & RAE, S. R. 1993. The diet of Golden Eagles *Aquila chrysaetos* in Scotland. *Ibis*, 135: 387–393.

WEIR, D. 1982. Cliff nesting raptors of the Kisaralik River, western Alaska. In: *Raptor Management and Biology in Alaska and Western Canada* (Eds. W. N. Ladd & P. F. Schempf), pp 138–152. U.S. Fish & Wildlife Service, Anchorage.

WEIR, D. 1985. Golden Eagles and lambs in Badenoch, Highland. *Scottish Birds*, 13: 263–267.

WELCH, G. & WELCH, H. 1989. Autumn migration across the Bab-el-Mandeb Straits. In: *Raptors in the Modern World* (Eds. B-U. Meyburg & R. D. Chancellor), pp 123–125. WWGBP, Berlin, London & Paris.

WEST, N. E. 1983. *Ecosystems of the World, Vol 5: Temperate Deserts and Semi-deserts*. Elsevier, Amsterdam.

WHEELER, B. K. & CLARK, W. S. 1995. *A Photographic Guide to North American Raptors*. Academic Press, London.

WILLIAMS, R. D. & COLSON, E. W. 1989. Raptor associations with linear rights-of-way. In: *Proceedings of the Western Raptor Management Symposium and Workshop* (Ed. B. G. Pendleton), pp. 173–192. *Scientific and Technical Series No. 12.* National Wildlife Federation, Washington.

WILSON, G. L. 1928. Hidatsa eagle trapping. *Anthropological Papers of the American Museum of Natural History*, 30: 101–245.

WIMBERGER, P. H. 1984. The use of green plant material in bird nests to avoid ectoparasites. *Auk*, 101: 615–618

WOLFE, L. R. 1950. Notes on the birds of Korea. *Auk*, 67: 433–455.

WOODGERD, W. 1952. Food habits of the Golden Eagle. *Journal of Wildlife Management*, 16: 457–459.

YAMANOI, A. 1984. Food habits of the Golden Eagle in Japan. *Aquila chrysaetos*, 2: 1–6.

ZASTROV, M. 1946. Om Kungsörnens *Aquila chrysaetos* ut bredning och biologi i Estland. *Vår Fågelvärld*, 5: 64–80.

Tables 1–73

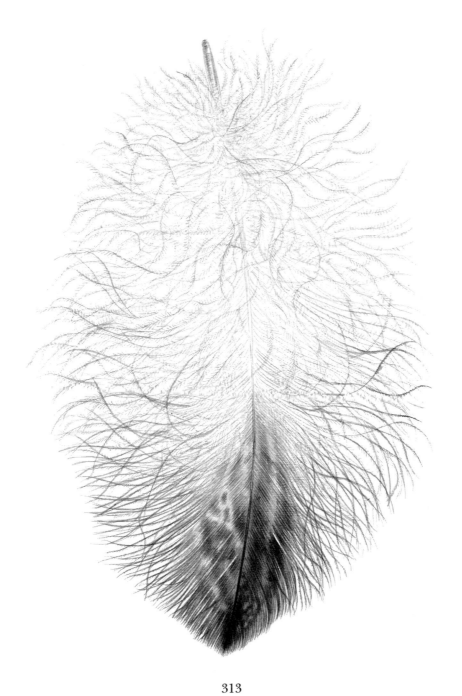

TABLE 1   *Various measurements of Aquila eagles, with data for different subspecies where available*

Species	Subspecies	Wing-span (cm)*	Wing-length Male (mm)†	Wing-length Female (mm)†	Wing-length ratio F/M	Weight Male (g)‡	Weight Female (g)‡	Weight ratio F/M
Lesser Spotted Eagle	A. p. pomarina	150–170	470	490	1.04	1210	1520	1.26
	A. p. hastata		490	500	1.02	–	–	–
Greater Spotted Eagle	A. clanga	160–180	500	530	1.06	1770	2140	1.21
Steppe Eagle	A. n. nipalensis	170–200	570	620	1.09	3260	3950	1.21
	A. n. orientalis		530	570	1.08	2650	3190	1.20
Tawny Eagle	A. r. rapax	170–190	510	530	1.04	1790	1990	1.11
	A. r. belisarius		520	540	1.04	2000	2240	1.12
	A. r. vindhiana		510	530	1.04	–	–	–
Imperial Eagle	A. h. heliaca	180–220	570	610	1.07	2580	3510	1.36
	A. h. adalberti		590	630	1.07	–	–	–
Gurney's Eagle	A. gurneyi	170–190	–	–	–	–	–	–
Golden Eagle	A. c. chrysaetos	200–220	620	670	1.08	3690	5170	1.40
	A. c. homeyeri		590	640	1.08	–	–	–
	A. c. daphanea		640	700	1.09	4050	6350	1.57
	A. c. kamtschatica		640	690	1.08	–	–	–
	A. c. japonica		590	630	1.07	2550	3250	1.27
	A. c. canadensis		610	650	1.07	3480	4910	1.41
Wedge-tailed Eagle	A. a. audax	190–230	600	650	1.08	3100	4050	1.31
	A. a. fleayi		–	–	–	–	–	–
Black Eagle	A. verreauxii	210–240	580	620	1.07	3760	4840	1.29
Average					1.06			1.29

Sources of information: Dementiev & Gladkov (1966); Ali & Ripley (1968); Glutz von Blotzheim *et al.* (1971); Brooke *et al.* (1972); Cramp & Simmons (1980); Bortolotti (1984a); SRGE (1988); Gargett (1990); Marchant & Higgins (1993).

*Wing-span measurements indicate the approximate range for the nominate race.

†Wing-length data are median figures based on various sources, rounded to the nearest 10 mm.

‡Weight data are median figures based on various sources, rounded to the nearest 10 g.

TABLE 2 Variation in size of Golden Eagles of differing sex and age. Data are from Bortolotti (1984a) and refer to the North American race A. c. canadensis

Variable	Age class	Males*			Females*		
		n	Mean ± SD	Range	n	Mean ± SD	Range
Wing length	Adult	23	595.0 ± 15.11	569–619	27	640.4 ± 19.75	601–674
	Immature†	26	585.9 ± 16.63	559–636	31	632.2 ± 16.00	601–665
Tail length	Adult	22	286.5 ± 10.03	267–310	24	307.2 ± 9.69	290–330
	Immature	23	297.7 ± 17.95	269–341	30	322.0 ± 21.09	285–375
Culmen length	Adult	23	40.55 ± 1.44	36.9–43.5	27	44.21 ± 1.66	41.7–47.5
	Immature	26	39.36 ± 1.44	36.2–42.6	31	43.34 ± 1.36	39.9–50.0
Hallux claw length	Adult	23	49.35 ± 1.69	45.9–52.9	26	55.67 ± 2.70	49.8–63.4
	Immature	24	47.75 ± 1.62	44.9–51.3	30	54.01 ± 2.15	49.7–58.2

*All measurements are in millimetres.

†defined by Bortolotti (1984a) as 'young birds having large amounts of white on the rectrices'.

TABLE 3: Size differences (as indicated by female wing-length) and plumage characteristics of Golden Eagle subspecies

Race	Locality (general area)	Size	Female wing-length (mm)	Plumage characteristics
A. c. chrysaetos	NW Europe	Medium	670	Palest race, feathers on nape golden
A. c. homeyeri	SW Europe	Small	640	Dark plumaged, feathers on nape browner than chrysaetos
A. c. daphanea	Central Asia	Large	700	Dark plumaged, feathers on nape intermediate between chrysaetos and homeyeri
A. c. kamtschatica	NE Asia	Large	690	Dark plumaged, feathers on nape rufous-brown
A. c. japonica	Japan & Korea	Small	630	Darkest race, feathers on nape bright rufous
A. c. canadensis	North America	Medium	650	Dark plumaged, feathers on nape bright rufous

TABLE 4 *Summary of key features in 16 ecological regions within the Golden Eagle's world range*

Ecological region	Number*	Topography	Dominant habitats in hunting range	Principal prey of Golden Eagles			Principal ungulates
				Mammals	Birds	Reptiles	
Palearctic							
Arctic fringe of Eurasia	1	Flat	Open woodland and heathland	Mountain Hare	Willow Grouse Ptarmigan		Reindeer
Mountains of northwest Europe	2	Low mountains	Open woodland and grass/heathland	Mountain Hare Rabbit	Red/Willow Grouse Ptarmigan		Reindeer Red Deer Domestic Sheep
Taiga of northeast Europe and Asia	3	Flat	Dense woodland and open peatland	Mountain Hare	Capercaillie Black Grouse		Reindeer Elk
Alpine Mountains of Europe	4	High mountains	Alpine grassland and scree	Alpine Marmot Brown Hare			Roe Deer Chamois
Mountains of the Mediterranean	5	Low mountains	Open woodland and scrub	Rabbit Brown Hare	Partridge spp.	Tortoise spp.	Wild Goat
Deserts of Middle Asia	6	Flat with low mountains	Open scrub and bare ground	Bobak Marmot Large-toothed Suslik		Tortoise spp.	Goitred Gazelle Wild Goat
Alpine Mountains of Central Asia	7	High mountains	Alpine grassland and scrub	Long-tailed Marmot Pika spp.	Snowcock Chukar Partridge		Siberian Ibex Argali Sheep
Mountains of Japan and Korea	8	Low mountains	Woodland scrub and grass/heathland	Japanese Hare	Copper Pheasant	Snake spp.	Japanese Serow
Deserts of North Africa and Arabia	9	Flat with low mountains	Bare ground and scrub		Barbary Partridge	Lizard spp. Tortoise spp.	Barbary Sheep Wild Goat
Nearctic							
Arctic fringe of North America	10	Flat	Open woodland and heathland	Arctic Ground Squirrel Arctic Hare	Willow Grouse (Willow Ptarmigan) Ptarmigan (Rock Ptarmigan)		Reindeer (Caribou)

Mountains of the Pacific northwest	11	High mountains	Open woodland and grass/heathland	Arctic Ground Squirrel, Hoary Marmot, Snowshoe Hare, Columbian Ground Squirrel, Yellow-bellied Marmot	Blue Grouse	Reindeer (Caribou), Dall Sheep, Bighorn Sheep
Taiga of North America	12	Flat	Dense woodland with open peatland	Snowshoe Hare	Spruce Grouse	Reindeer (Caribou), Elk (Moose)
Foothills east of the Rocky Mountains	13	Low mountains	Grassland with scattered woodland	White-tailed Jackrabbit, Richardson's Ground Squirrel, Nuttall's Cottontail, Black-tailed Prairie Dog		Pronghorn Antelope, Mule Deer, Domestic Sheep
Deserts of the Great Basin	14	Flat with low mountains	Open scrub and bare ground	Black-tailed Jackrabbit, Nuttall's Cottontail, Townsend's Ground Squirrel		Pronghorn Antelope, Mule Deer, Domestic Sheep
Mountains of California and Mexico	15	Low mountains	Open woodland, grassland and scrub	Californian Ground Squirrel, Black-tailed Jackrabbit	Yellow-billed Magpie	Black-tailed Deer
Mountains of eastern North America	16	Low mountains	Dense woodland	Snowshoe Hare	Heron spp.	White-tailed Deer

*Typical localities for the 16 ecological regions are indicated by these numbers in Fig. 3.

TABLE 5 *Principal and secondary land uses in the nine intensive study areas in Scotland (see Fig. 6 for location details)*

Study area	Ecological region	Principal land uses	Secondary land uses	Size of area (km²)
A	Inner Hebrides, north	Sheep grazing	Forestry plantation	520
B	Inner Hebrides, south	Sheep grazing Red Deer Forestry plantation		456
C	North Highlands	Red Deer Sheep grazing	Forestry plantation	1095
D	Northwest Highlands	Red Deer Sheep grazing		1146
E	Northwest Highlands	Red Deer	Sheep grazing Forestry plantation	1195
F	West central Highlands	Sheep grazing Red Deer	Forestry plantation	1017
G	Southwest Highlands	Forestry plantation Sheep grazing	Red Deer	1294
H	East Highlands	Red Deer	Red Grouse Forestry plantation	1017
I	East Highlands	Red Deer Sheep grazing	Red Grouse	591

TABLE 6   *Hunting techniques used by Golden Eagles and the circumstances in which the various techniques are most likely to be employed*

Hunting technique	Types of prey and occasions when the technique is likely to be used
High soar with glide attack	Solitary or widely dispersed animals such as hares or grouse, usually living in open habitats.
High soar with vertical stoop	Birds in flight, especially slow-flying and flocking species such as geese.
Contour flight with glide attack	Colonial mammals such as rabbits and marmots, also birds such as grouse when living at high densities; used in areas where topography is broken or where habitat includes a mixture of woodland and open ground.
Glide attack with tail-chase	Active species of birds and mammals when these have been flushed from cover; used in similar habitat to 'Contour Hunting'.
Low flight with slow descent attack	Slow-moving species such as reptiles and mammals such as hedgehogs, also used against potentially dangerous prey such as carnivores; may be used more commonly in woodland habitats.
Low flight with sustained grip attack	Large animals such as young ungulates and also carnivores; tends to be used when other prey is unavailable such as in deep snow cover.
Walk and grab attack	Defenceless prey which cannot be easily flushed; includes young ungulates sheltering in vegetation, under a rock or under a parent.

TABLE 7 *Diet of Golden Eagles (% by number) in nine regions in Scotland during summer*

Prey categories		1	2	3	4	5	6	7	8	9
Mammals (family)										
Erinaceidae	Hedgehogs			0.7			1.1			
Soricidae	Shrews	0.9			0.7		1.1			
Leporidae	Hares/Rabbits	28.6	34.1	46.9	18.2	13.5	10.7	25.5	42.2	24.8
Muridae	Rats/Mice/Voles	7.1	4.7	0.7	10.9	6.8	7.9	6.4	2.5	4.6
Canidae	Foxes/Dogs		1.2		1.5	2.0	2.8	4.3	0.6	2.8
Mustelidae	Weasels/Badgers	1.8		5.6	2.2	2.0	2.3	2.1	2.5	1.8
Cervidae	Deer	5.4	1.2	8.4	15.3	22.3	19.8	14.9	3.7	14.7
Bovidae	Sheep/Goats	26.8	25.9	23.1	16.8	17.6	18.6	23.4	0.6	15.6
Birds (family)										
Procellariidae	Petrels	17.0	11.8	2.1	8.0					
Phalacrcocoracidae	Cormorants						0.6			
Ardeidae	Herons				0.7					
Anatidae	Ducks/Geese			0.7	2.9	2.0	1.7	2.1		2.8
Accipitridae	Hawks/Eagles	0.9								
Falconidae	Falcons					0.7	1.1			
Tetraonidae	Grouse	5.4	8.2	6.3	18.2	25.0	20.3	19.1	47.8	12.8
Phasianidae	Pheasants	1.8			0.4					2.8
Rallidae	Rails			0.7			·			
Charadriidae	Plovers	1.8		2.1	0.7	1.4	1.1			2.8
Scolopacidae	Sandpipers/Snipe		5.9			0.7				
Laridae	Gulls				0.4		2.3			0.9
Columbidae	Pigeons					0.7				4.6
Strigidae	Owls						1.1			
Alaudidae	Larks				0.4		2.3			
Motacillidae	Pipits	0.9	3.5	2.1	0.7	2.0	0.6	2.1		2.8
Turdidae	Thrushes/Chats					0.7				1.8
Corvidae	Crows	1.8	3.5	0.7	1.1	2.0	4.0			4.6
Reptiles (order)										
Ophidia	Snakes				0.4	0.7	0.6			
Amphibians					0.4					
Sample size		112	85	143	274	148	177	47	161	109
Number of nests		26	23	29	29	38	25	16	28	3
Dietary breadth		5.14	4.71	3.47	7.21	5.94	7.25	5.38	2.44	7.43

Regions 1, 2 and 3 are Scottish Islands, 4, 5, 6, 7 and 9 west Scotland and 8 east Scotland (see Fig. 6).

TABLE 8 *Frequency (%) of prey items identified among six prey categories from nine regions in Scotland in summer (May–October) and winter (November–April)*

Region	Season	Prey categories						Sample size
		Deer	Sheep	Lagomorph	Other mammal	Grouse spp.	Miscellaneous	
1	Summer	5.2	25.9	27.6	9.5	5.2	26.7	116
	Winter	20.7	20.7	31.0	10.3	0.0	17.2	29
2	Summer	1.2	25.9	34.1	5.9	8.2	24.7	85
	Winter	9.5	33.3	42.9	4.8	4.8	4.8	21
3	Summer	8.2	22.6	45.9	7.5	6.2	9.6	146
	Winter	14.0	8.0	48.0	10.0	8.0	12.0	50
4	Summer	14.8	16.2	17.6	14.8	17.6	19.0	284
	Winter	30.0	14.4	15.6	7.8	11.1	21.1	90
5	Summer	21.6	17.0	13.1	11.1	24.2	13.1	153
	Winter	32.8	20.3	14.1	10.9	15.6	6.3	64
6	Summer	19.2	18.1	10.4	14.8	19.8	17.6	182
	Winter	27.6	30.6	7.5	12.7	13.4	8.2	134
7	Summer	14.9	23.4	25.5	12.8	19.2	4.3	47
	Winter	19.7	18.0	26.2	13.1	18.0	4.9	61
8	Summer	3.7	0.6	42.0	5.6	47.5	0.6	162
	Winter	9.6	1.9	36.5	7.7	42.3	1.9	52
9	Summer	13.7	14.5	23.1	8.6	12.0	28.2	117
	Winter	–	–	–	–	–	–	–
Total								1793

TABLE 9   *Diet of Golden Eagles (% by number) as reported in 24 studies from continental Europe and Asia*

Prey categories		1	2	3	4	5	6	7	8	9	10	11	12	13	14	15	16	17	18	19	20	21	22	23	24
Mammals (family)																									
Erinaceidae	Hedgehogs				42.5	28.6		0.3											1.5	0.4					
Soricidae	Shrews						0.3																		
Talpidae	Moles/Desmans						0.3					1.2													
Leporidae	Hares/Rabbits	25.8	23.6	20.7	25.6	15.0	20.9	28.8	10.7	6.8	37.4	33.7	52.3	3.5	48.8	39.6	29.7	67.3	63.1	38.5	48.5	66.5	4.7	10.1	49.5
Hystricidae	Porcupines														0.6										
Sciuridae	Squirrels/Marmots	1.0	2.6	0.4	1.4	7.5	0.5	5.8	48.4	68.9	4.0	7.2	3.7	5.3	4.4	6.0				0.8				43.1	0.2
Muridae	Rats/Mice/Voles	2.6	2.7	1.4	0.2	1.5	0.9	0.5		0.7				7.0	0.6	10.7			3.1	2.4	0.9		3.5	11.2	2.8
Gliridae	Dormice										0.5		0.9				0.7	1.0							
Canidae	Foxes/Dogs	0.9	0.7	1.7	0.2	3.0	1.3	5.6	2.3	0.7	4.0	3.6	0.9	4.4	2.5	2.7	13.5					1.2			
Mustelidae	Weasels/Badgers	0.6	0.7	1.8		2.3	1.4	5.8	1.3	1.7	2.5	3.6	10.1	1.8	3.8	6.0		1.0		1.6				0.5	0.8
Viverridae	Genet											1.2													
Felidae	Cats			0.1			0.7	3.2	0.7	0.5	1.0		3.4			1.3							2.4		
Equidae	Horses																						1.2		
Suidae	Pigs						0.3			0.5	1.0			0.9			2.7						2.4		
Cervidae	Deer	9.3		8.2					14.6	2.4	3.5			14.9									5.9		
Bovidae	Sheep/Goats			0.1	1.1		0.1		2.3	5.0	8.1	3.6	3.4	4.4	0.6	0.7	14.9	4.8		0.8			8.2	1.6	0.5
Birds (family)																									
Gaviidae	Divers																								
Ardeidae	Herons		0.2		0.2		0.5																		
Anatidae	Ducks/Geese	5.9	5.8	3.8	15.4	3.0	14.4	0.5				1.2													
Pandionidae	Osprey						0.1																		
Accipitridae	Hawks/Eagles	0.5	0.4	0.5	0.5	1.5	0.5	2.6		1.2	2.0			4.4	1.3				6.2						
Falconidae	Falcons		0.1	0.1					0.3						0.6	1.3		1.0							
Tetraonidae	Grouse	47.6	55.5	54.3	18.1	47.8		8.7	13.6	2.4				15.8											
Phasianidae	Pheasants				0.2	0.8		3.4	1.3	2.4	17.7	13.2	11.9	4.4	20.6	16.1	2.7	8.7	9.2	28.7	24.5	22.8			
Gruidae	Cranes	1.7	5.5	0.7	6.8	2.4																		0.5	17.8
Otididae	Bustards																			0.4					
Haematopodidae	Oystercatchers			0.2																					

	Common name	1	2	3	4	5	6	7	8	9	10	11	12	13	14	15	16	17	18	19	20	21	22	23	24
Burhinidae	Stone Curlews													1.7											
Charadriidae	Plovers			0.2		0.5	0.5																		
Scolopacidae	Sandpipers/Snipe		0.3	1.9	0.8	3.8																			
Laridae	Gulls			1.7			1.1																		
Alcidae	Auks			0.3			0.1																		
Columbidae	Pigeons	0.1		2.6		7.4		0.2	2.0	1.2	0.9		1.3	1.3			1.9	3.1	2.0	0.9	1.2				0.6
Cuculidae	Cuckoos			0.1		0.3													0.4						
Tytonidae	Barn Owls																								0.4
Strigidae	Owls	0.4	0.4	1.4	0.6	2.4		2.4	1.8				0.6												
Picidae	Woodpeckers	0.2	0.2		0.2		0.1												0.8	0.4					
Alaudidae	Larks																								
Motacillidae	Pipits									1.2															
Laniidae	Shrikes		0.1		0.1																				
Turdidae	Thrushes/Chats	1.5	1.3	0.2	0.3	1.1	1.9	7.2	1.8	1.0		3.5	1.3	1.3	8.1		2.9	7.7							0.2
Fringillidae	Finches		0.1													0.7									
Sturnidae	Starlings						4.8										0.4								
Corvidae	Crows	2.0	1.0	3.9		2.0	2.6	9.6	10.8	8.3	7.9	6.3	10.1	2.7		4.8	3.1	9.3	0.9	0.6			1.1	0.3	
Reptiles (order)																									
Chelonia	Tortoises							2.4	5.6		2.5														
Squamata	Lizards									1.2		8.8		3.9		1.5	13.0	12.7	6.0				52.9	31.9	
Ophidia	Snakes	0.2	0.1		0.2	0.5	0.3			2.4	0.9	9.7	3.8	1.3	25.7		2.9	1.5					1.8	11.8	27.5
Amphibians													2.6												
Sample size		3766	1796	2792	645	133	749	378	308	424	198	83	109	114	160	149	74	104	65	247	229	167	85	188	967
Number of nests		>50	>50	105	>8	4	>10	>10	>65	17	6	5	7	>10	5	>7	>10	30	6	3	2	3	19	?	?
Dietary breadth		3.26	2.69	2.87	3.66	6.2	3.38	7.5	3.47	2.06	5.14	6.2	3.23	11.2	3.43	4.69	4.92	2.13	2.38	3.88	3.11	2.01	3.2	3.22	2.83

Source: 1 Sulkava et al. (1984), N Finland; 2 Sulkava et al. (1984), S Finland; 3 Tjernberg (1981), Sweden; 4 Högström & Wiss (1992), Sweden (Gotland); 5 Zastrov (1946), Estonia; 6 Ivanovsky (1990), Belorus; 7 Danko (in litt.), Slovakia; 8 Glutz von Blotzheim et al. (1971), Switzerland; 9 Huboux (1987), France (Alps); 10 Huboux (1987), France (Alps); 11 Austruy & Cugnasse (1981), France (Massif Central); 12 Mathieu & Choisy (1982), France (Alps); 13 Clouet (1981), France (Pyrénées); 14 Novelletto & Petretti (1980), Italy (Apennines); 15 Magrini et al. (1987), Italy (Apennines); 16 Seminara et al. (1987), Italy (Sicily); 17 Fernández (1987), NE Spain; 18 Jordano (1981), Spain (Central); 19 Delibes et al. (1975), NW Spain; 20 Delibes et al. (1975), Spain (Central); 21 Delibes et al. (1975), SW Spain; 22 Grubač (1987), Macedonia; 23 Varshavski (1968), Turkmenia; 24 Yamanoi (1984), Japan.

TABLE 10   *Diet of Golden Eagles (% by number) as reported from 13 studies in North America*

Prey categories		1	2	3	4	5	6	7	8	9	10	11	12	13
Mammals (family)														
Didelphidae	Opossums											0.4		
Talpidae	Moles/Desmans											0.2		
Leporidae	Hares/Rabbits	32.1	0.4	59.1	0.5	69.8	72.7	72.8	2.6	12.8	85.6	28.8	41.2	65.8
Erethizontidae	Porcupines					0.1					0.1			0.1
Chinchillidae	Chinchillas						0.1							
Sciuridae	Squirrels/Marmots		84.2	27.3	84.0	12.1	8.3	4.0	41.8	40.4	4.7	27.8	17.6	19.6
Geomyidae	Pocket Gophers				0.5		0.3			2.1		0.6		0.1
Heteromyidae	Kangaroo Rats						0.2	1.1			0.1			
Muridae	Rats/Mice/Voles	1.9	4.8	6.1	0.5	1.1	1.0	1.1	1.3		0.4	1.4	2.9	0.7
Canidae	Foxes/Dogs								1.6		0.5	0.2	5.9	0.2
Procyonidae	Raccoons											0.4		1.4
Mustelidae	Weasels/Badgers	13.2		1.5	0.5	1.1	0.2			0.2	4.0	8.8	0.4	
Felidae	Cats						0.1		0.3			0.8		
Equidae	Horses													
Cervidae	Deer		3.5		1.0	2.5	0.1		3.9	6.4	0.1	12.7	2.9	
Antilocarpidae	Pronghorns					0.3					0.3			
Bovidae	Sheep/Goats		2.2			0.1			0.3		0.4			6.6
Birds (family)														
	Unidentified													4.0
Podicipedidae	Grebes										0.1			
Ardeidae	Herons								0.3			0.2		
Anatidae	Ducks/Geese	1.9		1.5			0.4		1.6	2.1	1.0	0.4		
Accipitridae	Hawks/Eagles		0.2			0.2		0.7	0.3	2.1		0.8	8.8	
Falconidae	Falcons					0.1	0.2	0.9	0.6		0.1	0.2		

	1	2	3	4	5	6	7	8	9	10	11	12	13
Tetraonidae — Grouse	49.1			10.0	3.1	0.1		14.5	4.3	0.6		0.8	
Phasianidae — Pheasants	3.0				3.1	10.0	6.4	14.2	2.1	2.4			
Rallidae — Rails						0.2				0.4			
Scolopacidae — Sandpipers/Snipe						0.1		0.3		0.1			
Laridae — Gulls			1.5				0.9						2.9
Columbidae — Pigeons				0.1		2.7	0.9	3.5		0.1			2.9
Cuculidae — Cuckoos										0.4			
Tytonidae — Barn Owls						0.2				0.2			
Strigidae — Owls				0.9		0.3	0.9	0.6		0.5	1.4		2.9
Caprimulgidae — Nighthawks						0.1	0.9						
Picidae — Woodpeckers			1.5		0.4			0.6		0.3	0.4		
Alaudidae — Larks							0.9						
Turdidae — Thrushes/Chats						0.1				0.1			
Emberizidae — Buntings			1.7			0.1	0.9	0.6		0.1			
Icteridae — American Blackbirds											1.6		
Sturnidae — Starlings						0.2	0.2						
Corvidae — Crows	1.9		1.5		4.5	1.3	3.1	9.7	10.6	0.2	7.2		2.9
Unidentified					0.4	1.1		1.0	14.9	1.6	5.6		
Reptiles (Order)							4.8						0.6
Ophidia — Snakes													
Fish			1.5			0.2		0.3			3.6		
Sample size	53	60	66	200	980	1297	456	311	47	1154	503	34	993
Number of nests	1	?	17	2	38	28	8	74	2	119	17	7	41
Dietary breadth	2.76	1.4	2.33	1.4	1.97	1.83	1.86	4.35	4.52	1.36	5.3	4.45	2.09

Source: 1 Hatler (1974), Alaska; 2 Murie (1944), Alaska; 3 Ritchie & Curatolo (1982), Alaska; 4 Boag (1977), Alberta; 5 McGahan (1968), Montana; 6 Kochert (1972), Idaho; 7 Collopy (1983a), Idaho; 8 Knight & Erickson (1978), Washington; 9 Eakle & Grubb (1986), Arizona; 10 Bloom & Hawks (1982), Nevada; 11 Carnie (1954), California; 12 Thompson et al. (1982), Oregon; 13 Mollhagen et al. (1972), New Mexico.

TABLE 11   *Diet of Aquila eagles (% by number) as reported from 16 studies in continental Europe and Asia*

Prey categories		Lesser Spotted Eagle			Greater Spotted Eagle				Steppe Eagle				Imperial Eagle				
		1	2	3	4	5	6	7	8	9	10	11	12	13	14	15	16
Mammals (family)																	
Erinaceidae	Hedgehogs												1.9				
Soricidae	Shrews	21.5	14.7			2.1	1.2	5.1						3.5	14.7		
Talpidae	Moles/Desmans			1.3													
Ochotonidae	Pika Hares															2.8	
Leporidae	Hares/Rabbits	7.9	1.3		1.7	1.1	0.3						5.7	7.5	13.8	2.8	39.8
Hystricidae	Porcupines								2.0								
Sciuridae	Squirrels/Marmots				1.7			8.8	6.0	97.0	46.0	80.6	43.8	8.9	29.3	19.4	
Muridae	Rats/Mice/Voles	73.9	50.6	38.7	61.8	52.7	89.1	46.4	88.0	0.6	39.8	9.7	21.5	54.7	34.5	30.6	1.9
Gliridae	Dormice																0.6
Zapodidae	Jumping Mice						1.2										
Dipodidae	Jerboas									0.6	3.5	6.5	0.5	1.6		2.8	
Canidae	Foxes/Dogs												1.9	0.7		8.3	
Mustelidae	Weasels/Badgers		4.5	1.3		1.1				1.2	3.5		4.4	0.2		2.8	
Bovidae	Sheep/Goats												4.4		0.9		
Birds (family)																	
	Unidentified							18.9									
Ardeidae	Herons																0.2
Theskiornithidae	Ibises/Spoonbills																0.2
Anatidae	Ducks/Geese				3.4		1.2					3.2		0.2			30.4
Accipitridae	Hawks/Eagles												3.5	0.2		2.8	
Falconidae	Falcons																0.2
Tetraonidae	Grouse				1.7	3.2	1.5										
Phasianidae	Pheasants	4.5	1.3			29.0	1.5						0.3	0.9		11.1	1.3
Rallidae	Rails					10.7	0.6							2.8	16.4		0.2

Family	Common name	Values (% of diet, across studies)
Otididae	Bustards	0.2
Recurvirostridae	Avocets/Stilts	0.2
Scolopacidae	Sandpipers/Snipe	1.9, 1.3
Pteroclididae	Sandgrouse	1.4
Columbidae	Pigeons	0.8
Tytonidae	Barn Owls	0.2
Strigidae	Owls	0.2
Alaudidae	Larks	1.6, 2.0, 5.1, 1.3
Turdidae	Thrushes/Chats	0.5, 2.7, 1.8, 2.0, 2.3, 1.3, 1.3
Sylviidae	Warblers	0.2
Fringillidae	Finches	1.1
Ploceidae	Sparrows/Weavers	1.1
Corvidae	Crows	4.0, 13.9, 2.1, 0.3, 15.8, 0.3, 2.3, 1.5
Reptiles (order)		
Chelonia	Tortoises	3.1, 2.5
Squamata	Lizards	2.3, 1.8, 10.8, 4.9, 0.9, 0.6, 4.1, 2.7, 12.5
Ophidia	Snakes	0.8, 2.6, 4.3, 2.5, 0.9, 0.9, 27.0
Amphibians		0.2, 0.6, 0.9, 38.7, 6.8
Fish		0.2, 0.3, 0.6

	1	2	3	4	5	6	7	8	9	10	11	12	13	14	15	16
Sample size	88	79	75	178	93	342	317	50	167	113	31	367	426	116	36	477
Dietary breadth	1.78	3.1	3.1	2.19	2.67	1.26	3.47	1.28	1.06	2.68	1.5	3.98	3.04	4.03	5.73	3.56

Source: 1 Palásthy & Meyburg (1970), Slovakia; 2 Sládek (1959), Slovakia; 3 Kasparson (1958), Latvia; 4 Priklonski (1960), Ukraine; 5 Kuchin (1961), Bijsk, Russia; 6 Likhachev (1957), Tula, Russia; 7 Glotov (1959), Novosibirsk, Russia; 8 Sukhinin (1958), Turkmenistan; 9 Tyurekhodzhaev (1973), Kazakhstan; 10 Varshavski (1973), Kazakhstan; 11 Osmolskaya (1953), Kazakhstan; 12 Lobachev (1967), Kazakhstan; 13 Varshavski (1973), Kazakhstan; 14 Osmolskaya (1953), Kazakhstan; 15 Glutz von Blotzheim *et al.* (1971), Kazakhstan; 16 Delibes (1978), Spain.

TABLE 12   *Diet of Aquila Eagles (% by number) as reported from nine studies in Africa*

Prey categories		Tawny Eagle				Black Eagle				
		1	2	3	4	5	6	7	8	9
Mammals (family)										
Erinaceidae	Hedgehogs		1.4		0.5					
Soricidae	Shrews				0.5					
Leporidae	Hares/Rabbits	11.9	17.9	5.0	8.9	0.6		10.7		2.4
Sciuridae	Squirrel/Marmots				1.6	0.1				
Lorisidae	Bushbabies									
Cercopithecidae	Monkeys	2.4			0.5	0.4			7.1	
Pedetidae	Jumping Hares		0.7	0.9	0.5					
Thryonomyidae	Cane Rats					0.1			10.7	
Muridae	Rats/Mice/Voles	4.8	1.4	0.3						
Canidae	Foxes/Dogs		0.7							
Viverridae	Mongooses	7.1	5.7	4.7	6.3	0.1	0.4		7.1	2.4
Procaviidae	Hyraxes			0.3	4.2	98.1	99.1	89.1	53.6	53.7
Suidae	Pigs				1.0					
Bovidae	Antelopes	7.1	7.1	30.0	8.4	0.1	0.4		3.6	
Birds (family)										
	Unidentified							10.9		12.2
Struthionidae	Ostrich			0.6	0.5					
Ardeidae	Herons		1.4							
Scopidae	Hamerkop	2.4								
Anatidae	Ducks/Geese			0.6	0.5					
Accipitridae	Hawks/Eagles			0.3						
Saggitariidae	Secretary Bird	2.4								
Phasianidae	Pheasants	19.4	35.0	16.5	18.4	0.2			3.6	29.3

		1	2	3	4	5	6	7	8	9
Turnicidae	Button Quails									
Otididae	Bustards		0.7	7.1	10.0					
Charadriidae	Plovers	2.4	1.4							
Glareolidae	Coursers			0.9						
Pteroclididae	Sandgrouse			1.5	1.0					3.6
Columbidae	Pigeons	11.9	9.3	0.6						
Psittacidae	Parrots			0.3						
Musophagidae	Turacos			0.6						
Cuculidae	Cuckoos	4.8								
Tytonidae	Barn owls		0.7							
Strigidae	Owls		0.7		0.5					
Caprimulgidae	Nightjars		1.4							
Bucerotidae	Hornbills			5.0	4.2					
Motacillidae	Pipits			0.3						
Laniidae	Shrikes			0.6	0.5					
Ploceidae	Weavers			0.6						
Sturnidae	Starlings		1.4	0.9						
Dicruridae	Drongos			0.3						
Reptiles (order)										
Squamata	Lizards	2.4	2.0	2.0	2.1		0.2			
Ophidia	Snakes	21.4	11.4	20.3	29.5					
Amphibians			1.4		0.5					
Sample size		42	140	340	190	1748	224	55	28	41
Dietary breadth		7.73	5.37	5.82	6.48	1.04	1.02	1.24	3.09	2.56

Source: 1 Steyn (1973a), Zimbabwe; 2 Steyn (1980), Zimbabwe; 3 Smeenk (1974), Kenya; 4 Smeenk (1974), Kenya; 5 Gargett (1990), Zimbabwe; 6 Hoeck (1982), Tanzania; 7 Jenkins (1984), South Africa; 8 Gargett (1990), Zimbabwe; 9 Rowe (1947), Tanzania.

TABLE 13   *Diet of Wedge-tailed Eagles (% by number) as reported from six studies in Australia*

Prey categories		1	2	3	4	5	6
Mammals (family)							
Tachyglossidae	Echidna						3.5
Dasyuridae	Marsupial Carnivores						0.4
Peramelidae	Bandicoots						0.4
Phalangeridae	Brushtails				3.1		14.9
Pseudocheiridae	Ringtail Possums	5.4		0.7	20.1		11.8
Macropodidae	Kangaroos	1.9	25.5	7.7	3.5		13.6
Vombatidae	Wombats						0.9
Vespertilionidae	Vesper Bats				0.4		
Leporidae	Hares/Rabbits	59.6	30.6	20.2	49.9	75.7	24.1
Muridae	Rats/Mice/Voles				0.8		
Canidae	Foxes/Dogs	2.3	3.0	1.4			0.4
Felidae	Cats	0.4	0.5	1.4	0.4	2.2	3.1
Bovidae	Sheep/Goats	10.4	7.6	15.1	4.2	1.1	2.2
Birds (family)	Unidentified	4.6	4.1	3.2	2.3	2.0	
Dromaiidae	Emu			1.4			
Pelecanidae	Pelicans					1.1	
Phalacrocoracidae	Cormorants					1.1	1.3
Ardeidae	Herons						1.3
Theskiornithidae	Ibises				0.8		
Anatidae	Ducks/Geese			4.3	5.8		0.9
Accipitridae	Hawks/Eagles			0.4			0.4
Falconidae	Falcons			1.2			
Phasianidae	Pheasants			0.5	3.1		2.2
Charadriidae	Plovers			0.2			0.4
Laridae	Gulls						0.4
Columbidae	Pigeons			0.6	0.4		
Cacatuidae	Cockatoos			7.4	0.4	5.5	
Psittacidae	Parrots	3.5	4.1	4.3			0.4
Cuculidae	Cuckoos			0.2			
Tytonidae	Barn owls			1.2			
Strigidae	Owls			0.2			
Podargidae	Frogmouths			0.7	0.4		
Alcidinide	Kingfishers				1.2		0.9
Turdidae	Thrushes/Chats				1.2		
Sturnidae	Starlings						1.8
Grallinidae	Magpie Larks			0.2			
Cracticidae	Butcher Birds	3.1	2.1	2.9	0.8	2.2	1.3
Corvidae	Crows	5.4	4.9	9.9	1.2	8.8	0.9
Reptiles (order)							
Squamata	Lizards	3.5	17.6	13.8			9.6
Ophidia	Snakes			0.5			2.7
Sample size		260	369	936	250	91	228
Detary breadth		2.64	4.94	9.05	3.35	1.71	7.87

Source: 1 Leopold & Wolfe (1970), Canberra (ACT); 2 Leopold & Wolfe (1970), New South Wales & Queensland; 3 Brooker & Ridpath (1980), Western Australia; 4 Marchant & Higgins (1993), Victoria; 5 Marchant & Higgins (1993), Victoria; 6 Marchant & Higgins (1993), Tasmania.

TABLE 14   *Dimensions of a sample of Golden Eagle nests from Scotland, Sweden and Arizona. All measurements are in m ± SE where available*

Location	Nest type	Length	± SE	Width	± SE	Depth	± SE	Sample size	Source
Scotland	Cliff	1.33	±0.09	1.06	±0.05	0.79	±0.06	53	Watson (this title)
Sweden	Tree	1.4	N/A	1.4	N/A	1.1	N/A	115	Tjernberg (1983a)
Arizona	Cliff	1.76	±0.13	1.2	±0.12	0.65	±0.15	12	Grubb & Eakle (1987)

TABLE 15   *Number of Golden Eagle pairs using cliff or tree nests in different parts of the range in Scotland in 1982. The range is divided into successive longitudinal bands from west (1) to east (9) as described by Watson & Dennis (1992).*

Nest type	1	2	3	4	5	6	7	8	9
Cliff	45	45	33	49	55	57	53	36	18
Tree	0	0	1	0	0	3	1	3	10
Total	45	45	34	49	55	60	54	39	28

TABLE 16   *The location of Golden Eagle nest sites in western Scotland in relation to cliff height*

	Cliff height in 20-m bands													Total
	1–20	21–40	41–60	61–80	81–100	101–120	121–140	141–160	161–180	181–200	201–220	221–240	241–260	
Number of nests	25	14	9	8	2	1	1	1	1	–	1	–	1	64
Frequency (%)	39.1	21.9	14.1	12.5	3.1	1.6	1.6	1.6	1.6	–	1.6	–	1.6	

TABLE 17　*Mean altitude above sea level (m ± SE) of nest sites of Golden Eagles in different parts of the range in Scotland in 1982. The range is divided into successive longitudinal bands from west (1) to east (9) as described by Watson & Dennis (1992). Also shown is the mean maximum altitude (m ± SE) for a random sample of 10 × 10 km squares within each respective band*

	1	2	3	4	5	6	7	8	9	Total
Mean nest-site elevation (a)	154 ± 15	211 ± 21	208 ± 19	281 ± 18	372 ± 17	442 ± 19	402 ± 17	474 ± 28	460 ± 28	
Mean maximum elevation (b)	345 ± 36	446 ± 45	459 ± 49	640 ± 43	855 ± 37	904 ± 29	844 ± 32	777 ± 42	778 ± 46	
% a/b	44.6	47.3	45.3	43.9	43.5	48.9	47.6	61	59.1	
Number of nests	45	45	34	49	55	60	54	39	28	409

TABLE 18　*Direction of exposure for 407 Golden Eagle nests in Scotland in 1982, recorded in eight compass segments. Also given are exposure directions of hill slopes selected at random from 283 10 × 10 km squares within the nesting range. The exposure direction of 194 climbers' crags in the Scottish Highlands is also given (data from Henty in litt.)*

		Compass segments								Total
		N-NE	NE-E	E-SE	SE-S	S-SW	SW-W	W-NW	NW-N	
Eagle nests	n(%)	100(24.6)	76(18.7)	48(11.8)	32(7.9)	23(5.6)	32(7.9)	35(8.6)	61(15.0)	407
Hill slopes	n(%)	42(14.8)	28(9.9)	39(13.8)	42(14.8)	40(14.1)	34(12.0)	34(12.0)	24(8.5)	283
Climbers' crags	n(%)	69(35.6)	35(18.0)	15(7.7)	16(8.2)	11(5.7)	8(4.1)	8(4.1)	32(16.5)	194

In a χ^2 test for nests *vs* slope the difference is significant ($P<0.001$) but for nests *vs* climbers' crags it is not significant ($P<0.5$).

TABLE 19 *Frequency of Golden Eagle pairs in Scotland in 1982 with different numbers of alternative nest sites*

	Number of alternative nests													Total
	1	2	3	4	5	6	7	8	9	10	11	12	13	
Number of pairs of Golden Eagles	57	92	104	66	39	29	9	5	3	3	3	–	1	411
Frequency (%)	13.9	22.4	25.3	16.1	9.5	7.1	2.2	1.2	0.7	0.7	0.7	–	0.2	

TABLE 20 *Types of nest sites used by different species of Aquila eagles*

Species	Typical habitat	Usual nest-site	Other sites used occasionally	Source
Lesser Spotted Eagle	Woodland	Trees		Meyburg (1973)
Greater Spotted Eagle	Woodland	Trees	Bushes	Cramp & Simmons (1980)
Steppe Eagle (*nipalensis*)	Mountains	Crags	Stoney mounds and ground	Dementiev & Gladkov (1966)
Steppe Eagle (*orientalis*)	Steppe	Ground	Bushes and man-made structures (haystacks)	Cramp & Simmons (1980)
Tawny Eagle	Savanna woodland	Trees	Man-made structures (pylons)	Brown *et al.* (1982)
Imperial Eagle (*heliaca*)	Open woodland and steppe	Trees	Bushes, crags and ground	Dementiev & Gladkov (1966)
Imperial Eagle (*adalberti*)	Open woodland	Trees	Man-made structures (pylons)	Ferrer (1993a)
Gurney's Eagle	Tropical forest and forest savanna	Unknown, but probably trees	–	
Golden Eagle	Mountains and open woodland	Crags and trees	Ground and man-made structures (pylons)	Cramp & Simmons (1980)
Wedge-tailed Eagle	Open woodland	Trees	Bushes, crags and ground	Marchant & Higgins (1993)
Black Eagle	Mountains	Crags	Trees and man-made structures (pylons)	Gargett (1990)

TABLE 21   *Number and frequency of undulating display flights by male and female Golden Eagles in four territories in southwestern Idaho. Flights recorded close to a nest site are given separately from flights which clearly had a territorial function (after Collopy & Edwards, 1989)*

| Site | Sex | Location of undulating display flights | | | |
| | | Nest Site* | | Territorial | |
		n	%	n	%
1	Male	31	30.4	71	69.6
	Female	23	29.1	56	70.9
2	Male	14	27.5	37	72.5
	Female	2	16.7	10	83.3
3	Male	12	52.2	11	47.8
	Female	5	26.3	14	73.7
4	Male	24	33.3	48	66.7
	Female	4	13.3	26	86.7
Totals	Male	81	32.7	167	67.3
	Female	34	24.3	106	75.7

*Undulating displays seen within 400 m of the nest were considered to be associated with the nest site.

TABLE 22 *Dispersion behaviour of* Aquila *eagles during the breeding and non-breeding seasons*

Species	Breeding dispersion behaviour	Non-breeding dispersion behaviour	Sources
Lesser Spotted Eagle	Defends nesting territory Mainly exclusive hunting ranges	Gregarious and nomadic	Cramp & Simmons (1980)
Greater Spotted Eagle	Defends nesting territory Mainly overlapping hunting ranges	Loosely gregarious in Africa Possibly solitary further north	Cramp & Simmons (1980)
Steppe Eagle	Defends nesting territory Mainly overlapping hunting ranges	Highly gregarious and nomadic	Cramp & Simmons (1980)
Tawny Eagle	Defends nesting territory Mainly exclusive hunting ranges	Gregarious and nomadic	Brown *et al.* (1982)
Imperial Eagle	Defends nesting territory Mainly overlapping hunting ranges	Remains on breeding territories in Spain Eastern population more migratory and occurs in small flocks or solitary	Cramp & Simmons (1980)
Gurney's Eagle	Unknown	Unknown	–
Golden Eagle	Defends nesting territory Exclusive hunting territory or overlapping hunting ranges	Most remain on breeding territories High latitude populations migratory and loosely gregarious in winter	Watson (1957) Collopy & Edwards (1989)
Wedge-tailed Eagle	Defends nesting territory Overlapping hunting ranges	Most remain on breeding territories Non-breeders can be gregarious	Marchant & Higgins (1993)
Black Eagle	Defends nesting territory Exclusive hunting territory	Remains on breeding territories Non-breeders nomadic and solitary	Gargett (1990)

TABLE 23   *Distance between nearest neighbours for 159 Golden Eagle nests in nine Scottish Regions. Data are given separately for the west (4W) and east (4E) of Region 4*

Region	Distance in (km)																Number of nests	Average NND (km)	GMASD
	1	2	3	4	5	6	7	8	9	10	11	12	13	14	15	16			
1	4		8	6	5	2		1	1								27	4.6	0.79
2			2	7	4	1	1										15	4.8	0.91
3			6	3	6	2											17	4.7	0.89
4W	2		5	4	2	3		1									17	4.6	0.81
4E								2	2		1		1			1	7	10.8	0.89
5			2	9	11	1	4		2		1						27	5.3	0.93
6	2		10	6		4			2								22	4.2	0.86
7								2	2	2		1	2				9	10.6	0.94
8					2	4	2	3	2						1		14	7.9	0.83
9											2	2					4	12	0.99
Total																	159		

For method of calculating GMASD statistic see Appendix 5.

TABLE 24   *Nearest-neighbour distance (NND) and the GMASD statistic from a range of studies of Golden Eagle nesting dispersion*

Country	Locality	Nests (n)	NND (km)	GMASD	Source
Greece	Evros	18	9.3*	0.89	Hallman (1980)
Israel	Judean desert	11	15.9	0.83	Bahat (1989)
Israel	Negev desert	24	13.1	0.74	Bahat (1989)
Italy	Alps	80	8.6†	0.71	Fasce & Fasce (1984)
Norway	Hordaland	15	16	0.92	Bergo (1984a)
Spain	Navarra	31	11.5	0.89	Fernández (1989)
Sweden	Mountain region	75	10.2	0.84	Tjernberg (1985)
Sweden	Forest region	65	17	0.94	Tjernberg (1985)
Switzerland	Alps	52	8*	0.82	Haller (1982)

*The NND data were measured by me from maps in the source literature.
†The NND data given in the source literature were used to calculate the GMASD statistic.
For method of calculating GMASD statistic see Appendix 5.

TABLE 25   *Details of the nine study areas in Scotland; total area and amount under closed canopy woodland, open water and improved farmland are given (all figures are km².). Ecological Regions are as described in Chapter 4. The amount of suitable hunting ground is total area − (woodland + water + farmland). The number of pairs of Golden Eagles in each area refers to the years 1982–85 except for areas A, B and I for which data were available only for 1985*

Study area	Ecological region	Total area	Closed canopy woodland	Open water	Improved farmland	Suitable hunting ground	Number of pairs of eagles	Density* pairs/ 1000 km² (total area)	Density* pairs/ 1000 km² (suitable area)
A	2	519.5	27.7	2.7	26.4	462.7	15	28.9	32.4
B	3	455.8	44.6	8.3	9.0	393.9	15	32.9	38.1
C	4	1094.8	50.5	19.6	44.1	980.6	15–16	14.6	16.3
D	5	1146.1	34.8	80.3	51.0	980.0	18–19	15.7	18.4
E	5	1195.0	116.8	41.9	40.8	995.5	17	14.2	17.1
F	6	1017.0	145.9	15.4	50.4	805.3	21	20.6	26.1
G	7	1293.8	373.4	44.4	120.9	755.1	14–15	11.6	19.9
H	8	1175.0	99.9	4.9	46.7	1023.5	15	12.8	14.7
I	8	590.9	7.0	12.6	10.4	560.9	6	10.2	10.7

*Nesting density was calculated using number of pairs for 1985.

TABLE 26   *Results of food assessments by line transects in nine Scottish study areas in 1985. All food data are means (± SE) of several transects for each area; data for nesting density were number of pairs per 1000 km² of suitable hunting ground. (Data after Watson et al. 1992b)*

Study area	Number of transect	Length of transects (km)	Live prey (kg/20 km)	Carrion (kg/20 km)	Total food (kg/20 km)	Density (pairs/1000 km²)
A	4	79	27.6 ± 22.0	96.3 ± 40.1	123.6 ± 54.1	32.4
B	5	90	7.2 ± 1.3	67.6 ± 19.5	74.8 ± 20.5	38.1
C	6	112	2.5 ± 0.9	16.8 ± 9.3	19.3 ± 9.3	16.3
D	6	106	3.2 ± 0.8	20.3 ± 10.6	23.6 ± 11.0	18.4
E	5	101	6.7 ± 1.3	17.7 ± 5.8	24.4 ± 4.7	17.1
F	6	116	2.2 ± 0.7	88.9 ± 24.3	91.2 ± 23.9	26.1
G	7	134	5.8 ± 2.3	42.0 ± 19.0	47.8 ± 19.0	19.9
H	5	95	29.3 ± 7.3	5.5 ± 3.4	34.8 ± 6.8	14.7
I	5	88	14.3 ± 1.3	5.8 ± 5.2	20.1 ± 4.3	10.7

TABLE 27 *Golden Eagle nearest neighbour distances (NND) and nesting densities from studies in continental Europe/Asia, Scotland and the United States*

Country	Locality	Source	Pairs (n)	Study area (km²)	NND (Average) (km)	NND (Range) (km)	Area/ pair* (km²)	Area/ pair (Max Density)† (km²)	Density* (pairs/ 1000 km²)	Max Density† (pairs/ 1000 km²)
Belrus	Vitebsk	Ivanovsky (1990)	25	13200	15	–	528	195	1.9	5.1
France	Massif Central	Austruy & Cugnasse (1981)	29	26250	(32.4)	–	(905)	(909)	1.1	(1.1)
France	Massif Central	Austruy & Cugnasse (1981)	14	26250	(53.7)	–	1875	(2500)	0.5	(0.4)
France	High Alps	Mathieu & Choisy (1982)	8	–	8.7	7–10	(137)	66	(7.3)	15.1
France	Low Alps	Mathieu & Choisy (1982)	25	–	9.9	3.5–17	(164)	85	(6.1)	11.8
France	Pyrenees	Clouet (1981)	19	–	10	5–13	(167)	87	(6.0)	11.5
France	Pyrenees	Clouet & Goar (1981)	6	–	14	–	(270)	170	(3.7)	5.9
Greece	Evros	Hallman (1980)	18	4200	9.3	7–15.5	233	75	4.3	13.3
Israel	Judea	Bahat (1989)	11	–	15.9	8.5–22.8	(217)	219	(3.1)	4.6
Israel	Negev	Bahat (1989)	24	–	13.1	6.6–26.4	(250)	149	(4.0)	6.7
Italy	Sardinia	Fasce & Fasce (1984)	5	–	10.4	6–14	(179)	94	(5.6)	10.6
Italy	Apennines	Ragni et al. (1986)	10	3250	18.1	12–29.5	325	284	3.1	3.5
Italy	Apennines	Fasce & Fasce (1984)	8	–	21	–	(500)	382	(2.0)	2.6
Italy	Alps	Fasce & Fasce (1984)	80	–	8.6	3–19	(135)	64	(7.4)	15.6
Italy	Alps	Framarin (1982)	11	1000	(6.6)	–	91	(38)	11	(26.3)
Norway	Hordaland	Bergo (1984a)	15	–	16	10–20.5	(333)	222	(3.0)	4.5
Russia	Tien Shan	Krylov (1965)	6	–	9	5–13	(143)	70	(7.0)	14.3
Spain	Gedros	Arroyo et al. (1986)	16	2000	6.5	3.4–14.7	125	37	8	27
Spain	Navarra	Fernandez (1989)	31	6613	11.5	–	213	115	4.7	8.7
Sweden	Mountain	Tjernberg (1985)	63	–	10.2	4–19	(172)	90	(5.8)	11.1
Sweden	Forest	Tjernberg (1985)	62	–	17	8–25	(357)	251	(2.8)	4
Sweden	Gotland	Tjernberg (1985)	9	–	15.8	11–21	(323)	216	(3.1)	4.6
Switzerland	Alps	Haller (1982)	52	5565	8	4–18	107	56	9.3	17.9
Scotland	W Highlands	Lockie (1964)	13	900	(5.5)	–	69	(26)	14.5	(38.4)
Scotland	E Highlands	Watson & Rothery (1986)	15	677	5.4	4.3–8.2	45	25	22.2	40
Scotland	E Highlands	Watson & Rothery (1986)	17	677	4.6	3–8.4	40	18	25	55.6
Scotland	E Highlands	Watson & Rothery (1986)	15	834	5.8	4.1–11.3	56	29	17.9	34.5

Scotland	Region 1	Watson (this title)	28	1400	4.6	2–9	50	18	20	55.6
Scotland	Region 2	Watson (this title)	19	950	4.8	3–7	50	20	20	50
Scotland	Region 3	Watson (this title)	19	800	4.7	3–6	42	19	23.8	52.6
Scotland	Region 4w	Watson (this title)	17	1350	4.6	2–8	79	18	12.7	55.6
Scotland	Region 4e	Watson (this title)	7	1600	10.8	8–16	229	105	4.4	9.5
Scotland	Region 5	Watson (this title)	27	1550	5.3	3–7	57	24	17.5	41.7
Scotland	Region 6	Watson (this title)	24	1050	4.2	2–6	44	15	22.7	65.4
Scotland	Region 7	Watson (this title)	9	1500	10.6	8–13	167	97	5.9	10.3
Scotland	Region 8	Watson (this title)	14	1600	7.9	5–15	114	54	8.8	18.5
USA	Alaska	McIntyre *in litt.*	59	5500	5.4	2–14	93	25	10.8	39.5
USA	Alaska	Weir (1982)	12	–	4.8	–	(57)	20	(17.6)	50
USA	California	Dixon (1937)	27	2520	(6.7)	–	93	(39)	10.8	(25.6)
USA	Colorado	Olendorff (1975)	12	2598	(12.0)	–	217	(125)	4.6	(8.0)
USA	Idaho	Kochert (1972)	39	3388	5.2	0.8–22.7	87	23	11.5	43.5
USA	Montana	Reynolds (1969)	23	3263	(9.0)	–	142	(70)	7	(14.2)
USA	Nevada	Page & Seibert (197?)	88	22083	(13.2)	–	251	(152)	4	(6.6)
USA	Utah	Camenzind (1968)	14	1399	(7.0)	–	100	(43)	10	(23.1)
USA	Utah	Edwards (1969)	24	2858	(8.0)	–	119	(55)	8.4	(18.2)
USA	Wyoming	Phillips et al. (1984)	37	2074	4.9	–	73	21	13.7	47.6
USA	Wyoming	Phillips et al. (1984)	29	1753	5.4	–	60	25	16.7	40
USA	Wyoming	Phillips et al. (1984)	120	7115	5.8	–	59	29	17	34.5
USA	Wyoming	Phillips et al. (1984)	13	749	5.2	–	58	23	17.2	43.5
USA	Wyoming	Phillips et al. (1984)	16	1425	8.2	–	89	58	11.2	17.2
USA	Wyoming	Phillips et al. (1984)	12	881	7.5	–	73	49	13.7	20.4
USA	Wyoming	Phillips et al. (1984)	18	1321	7.1	–	73	44	13.7	22.7
USA	Wyoming	Phillips et al. (1984)	15	622	4.1	–	41	15	24.4	66.7
USA	Wyoming	Phillips et al. (1984)	9	414	3.1	–	46	8	21.7	125
USA	Wyoming	Phillips et al. (1984)	13	598	3.6	–	46	11	21.7	90.9
USA	Wyoming	Phillips et al. (1984)	23	787	3.4	–	34	10	29.4	100
USA	Wyoming	Phillips et al. (1984)	15	1026	4.9	–	68	21	14.7	47.6

Note: Figures in brackets have been calculated using the regression equation in Fig. 27.

*These data refer to actual density as calculated from the number of pairs in a study area of known size.

†These data refer to maximum theoretical density calculated from known average nearest neighbour distances (see Appendix 5 for details).

TABLE 28 *Number of adult and juvenile/immature Golden Eagle sightings during January–March in western Scotland (Regions 6 and 4 + 5 combined) over the years 1982–85. Each sighting represents a contact with one bird on a particular day. If the same individual was seen on several occasions on the same day it was counted only once. Most sightings were within the study areas C, D and F*

Region	Year	Adult	Juvenile/immature	Total	%(Juv & Imm)/Total
6	1982	52	8	60	13.3
6	1983	49	6	55	10.9
6	1984	37	6	43	14.0
6	1985	25	3	28	7.1
4 + 5	1982–1985	46	6	52	11.5
Total		209	29	238	Av. 12.2

Juv: juvenile; Imm: immature.

TABLE 29 *Population estimates of Golden Eagles and current trends in 29 European countries and four of the large Mediterranean islands*

Location	Estimated population size (Number of breeding pairs)	Trend*	Source
1 Albania	40–50	U	Michel (1987)
2 Andorra	3	S	Tucker & Heath (1994)
3 Austria	200–250	I	Gamauf (1991)
4 Belarus	30–40	D	V. Ivanovsky (*in litt.*)
5 Bulgaria	130–140	U	Michev *et al.* (1989)
6 Corsica	29–35	S	Thibault (pers. comm.)
7 Crete	10	U	Vagliano (1981)
8 Croatia	100–150	S	Tucker & Heath (1994)
9 England	1–2	S	RSPB (*in litt.*)
10 Estonia	25–30	S	T. Randla (*in litt.*)
11 Finland	220	I	Virolainen & Rassi (1990)
12 France (except Corsica)	250	S	Michel (1987)
13 Germany	48–50	I	Bezzel (1994)
14 Greece (except Crete)	150–200	D	Andrinos (1987)
15 Hungary	2	I	Tucker & Heath (1994)
16 Italy (except Sicily, Sardinia)	250–339	U	Fasce & Fasce (1987)
17 Latvia	10	U	T. Randla (*in litt.*)
18 Liechtenstein	1–2	S	Tucker & Heath (1994)
19 Macedonia	100	D	Vasič *et al.* (1985)
20 Norway	700–1000	S	Gjershaug (1991)
21 Poland	15	D	Król (1987)
22 Portugal	15–20	D	Rufino et al. (1985)
23 Romania	28–30	D	L. Kalaber (*in litt.*)
24 Russia	200–400	S	Tucker & Heath (1994)
25 Sardinia	30–38	U	Fasce & Fasce (1987)
26 Scotland	420–425	S	Dennis *et al.* (1984)
27 Sicily	13	D	Seminara *et al.* (1987)
28 Slovakia	50	S	Mrlík & Danko (1990)
29 Slovenia	10–25	S	Tucker & Heath (1994)
30 Spain	1192–1265	S	Arroyo *et al.* (1990)
31 Sweden	600	S	Tjernberg (1990)
32 Switzerland	200–250	S	Haller (1987)
33 Ukraine	5–6	U	Gorban (1985)
Total	5077–6030		

*S, stable; I, increasing; D, decreasing; U, unknown.

TABLE 30   *Population estimates of Golden Eagles in each of five biogeographic regions across Europe. A brief description of the ecological character of each region, as this relates to Golden Eagles, is given*

Biogeographic region	Population estimate (pairs of Golden Eagles)	Ecological character
Northwest Mountains	1880	Nesting at or above treeline, on cliffs or trees; main food is grouse (*Tetraonidae*) and hares/rabbits (*Leporidae*).
East Baltic Lowlands	810	Only strictly lowland (<200 m above sea level) population in Europe; exclusively tree-nesting. Food mainly avian and varied.
West Mediterranean Mountains	1470	Nesting below tree-line in arid landscapes, mainly on cliffs. Main food is partridge (*Alectoris*) and hare (*Lepus*).
Alpine Mountains	840	Nesting in cliffs at high altitude; generally hunting above the natural tree-line. Food usually includes high % of marmots (*Marmota*).
Balkan Mountains	600	Mainly cliff-nesting; hunting below natural tree-line. Tortoises (*Testudinidae*) usually form high % of diet.
Total	5600	

TABLE 31   *Estimates of wintering Golden Eagle numbers in the western United States (after Olendorff et al. 1981)*

State	Area of suitable habitat (square miles)*	Eagles per 100 square miles†	Total eagles
Arizona	96 800	0.9	871
California	95 200	5.3	5046
Colorado	73 000	9.7	7081
Idaho	41 800	6.7	2801
Kansas	8200	7.2	590
Montana	110 400	11.9	13 138
Nebraska	7700	7.2	554
Nevada	88 400	5.3	4685
New Mexico	103 400	8.5	8789
North Dakota	10 600	2.1	223
Oregon	43 600	0.9	392
South Dakota	15 400	7.2	1109
Texas	93 600	1.7	1591
Utah	72 200	8.3	5993
Washington	34 100	0.9	307
Wyoming	78 300	12.9	10 072
Total	972 700		63 242

*Original data given by Olendorff *et al.* (1981) in square miles.
†Eagle data from a wide range of sources acknowledged in the original paper.

TABLE 32   *Status and trends in Golden Eagle populations in nine states in the western USA (data are from Harlow & Bloom 1989)*

State	Trend*	Statewide estimate of breeding pairs	Total known territories 1977–86
California	D	500	U
Oregon	U	U	506
Washington	U	U	190
Idaho	U	U	156
Utah	I	U	U
Nevada	S	1200	430
Wyoming	I	3381	804
Montana	I	U	50
Colorado	S	500–600	500

*S, stable; D, declining; I, increasing; U, unreported/unknown.

TABLE 33   *Population estimates and trends in* Aquila *eagles in Europe*

Species	Estimates of breeding pairs	Trend	Source
Lesser Spotted Eagle	6700–9500	Mainly stable	Tucker & Heath (1994)
Greater Spotted Eagle	860–1100	Decreasing throughout	Tucker & Heath (1994)
Steppe Eagle	15 000–25 000	Decreasing throughout	Tucker & Heath (1994)
Imperial Eagle (*heliaca*)	320–570	Mainly decreasing	Tucker & Heath (1994)
Imperial Eagle (*adalberti*)	150–169	Increasing	Tucker & Heath (1994)
Golden Eagle	5000–6000	Mainly stable	Watson (this title)

TABLE 34 *Changes in the numbers of nesting pairs of Eastern Imperial Eagles in Hungary from 1977–1993, and in the numbers of young fledged (data are from Haraszthy & Bagyura 1993)*

Year	Number of known nesting pairs	Number of young fledged
1977	7	5
1978	4	6
1979	5	4
1980	10	7
1981	13	5
1982	10	6
1983	12	3
1984	15	8
1985	14	11
1986	17	16
1987	19	13
1988	21	13
1989	26	18
1990	29	30
1991	28	30
1992	30	34
1993	35	27
1994	37	19
1995	37	36

The increase in the Hungarian population of Imperial Eagles is against the trend in other east European countries. This has been achieved by a programme of nest protection, provision of artificial nests and reintroduction of the European Ground Squirrel, an important food of Imperial Eagles.

TABLE 35 *Frequency of occurrence (% of all contacts) of various types of behaviour in Golden Eagles during successive months of the year. Data are from western Scotland and pooled from observations made over 13 years*

Month	Behaviour				Number of contacts*
	High soaring	Undulating display	Nest building	Mating	
October	19	3	4	0	56
November	33	6	7	0	48
December	59	11	6	0	86
January	55	22	9	2	121
February	57	15	10	5	139
March	41	18	9	7	144
April	29	11	5	1	88
May	24	6	1	0	99
June	19	0	0	0	59
July	9	3	1	0	66
August	10	0	0	0	49
September	11	4	1	0	60
Total					1015

*A contact is defined as a sighting of a single eagle, or pair of eagles (see text).

TABLE 36   *A selection of breeding statistics for Aquila eagles*

Species	Clutch size	Egg size (mm)	Egg weight (g)	Incubation period (days)	Fledging period (days)	Replacement clutches	Source
Lesser Spotted Eagle	2 (1–3)	64 × 52	79	38–41	50–60	Not recorded	Glutz von Blotzheim et al. (1971)
Greater Spotted Eagle	2 (1–3)	68 × 54	110	42–44	60–65	Rare	Glutz von Blotzheim et al. (1971)
Steppe Eagle	2 (1–3)*	69 × 54	115	(45)§	(60–70)§	Rare	Glutz von Blotzheim et al. (1971)
Tawny Eagle	2 (1–3)	70 × 54	122	42–44	75–85	Rare	Steyn (1973a); Cramp & Simmons (1980)
Imperial Eagle	3 (1–4)	73 × 57	132	43	70–80	Rare	Ferrer (1993a); Meyburg (1987)
Gurney's Eagle	Unknown	Unknown	Unknown	Unknown	Unknown	Unknown	–
Golden Eagle	2 (1–3)†	75 × 59	145	43–45	70–80	Rare	Cramp & Simmons (1980)
Wedge-tailed Eagle	2 (1–3)†	73 × 59	137	42–44	75–85	Rare	Ridpath & Brooker (1986a)
Black Eagle	2 (1–2)‡	77 × 58	140	45	85–95	Rare	Gargett (1990)

*Exceptional clutches of 4 and 5 recorded (Agafanov et al. 1957).

†Exceptional clutches of 4 recorded (Ray, 1928; Marchant & Higgins, 1993).

‡Exceptional clutches of 3 recorded (Gargett, 1990).

§These figures need to be checked, the fledging period seems short and the incubation period a little long.

TABLE 37   *Median egg-laying date for Golden Eagles at different latitudes*

Locality	Latitude (deg. N)	Median laying date	Source
Oman	21	3 December	Gallagher & Brown (1982)
SW Morocco	27	15 January	Heim de Balsac & Mayaud (1962)
Israel	31	22 January	Bahat (1989)
Atlas Mountains, Morocco	33	15 February	Heim de Balsac & Mayaud (1962)
Japan	37	4 February	SRGE (1985)
California, USA	36	20 February	Dixon (1937)
South Spain	36	23 February	Watson, unpublished data
Utah, USA	40	3 March	Camenzind (1969)
Central Spain	42	14 March	Fernández (1989)
Idaho, USA	43	27 February	Beecham & Kochert (1975)
Montana, USA	44	15 March	Phillips & Beske (1990)
Kyzyl Kum, South Russia	45	7 March	Dementiev & Gladkov (1966)
Alps, France	45	17 March	Mathieu (1985)
Tien Shan Mountains, Russia	47	22 March	Dementiev & Gladkov (1966)
Belorus	54	20 March	Ivanovsky (*in litt.*)
West Russia	55	9 April	Dementiev & Gladkov (1966)
Hudson Bay, Canada	56	17 April	Morneau *et al.* (1994)
Scotland	57	25 March	Watson, this title
Central Alaska, USA	63	14 April	McIntyre, *in litt.*
Arctic Russia	65	1 May	Dementiev & Gladkov (1966)
Lapland, Russia	67	25 April	Dementiev & Gladkov (1966)
Arctic Canada	68	21 April	Poole & Bromley (1988)
Arctic Alaska, USA	69	7 May	Hobbie & Cade (1962)

TABLE 38   *Golden Eagle clutch size from various parts of the world*

	Locality	Date	Sample size	C1 (%)	C2 (%)	C3 (%)	Mean	Source
A	Scotland	1840–1900	147	7	86	7	1.99	J. Love, *in litt.*
B	Scotland	1900–50	156	7	90	3	1.95	J. Love, *in litt.*
C	Scotland	Pre-1950	82	18	72	10	1.92	Gordon (1955)
D	Scotland	Post-1970	197	16	82	2	1.86	Watson, this title
E	Spain	1875–1975	42	7	91	3	1.95	Delibes *et al.* (1975)
F	Finland	Pre-1970	125	10	85	5	1.95	Glutz von Blotzheim *et al.* (1971)
G	Switzerland	Pre-1970	26	12	88	0	1.88	Glutz von Blotzheim *et al.* (1971)
H	Morocco	Pre-1960	48	17	77	6	1.90	Heim de Balsac & Mayaud (1962)
I	California, USA	*circa* 1920	21	19	67	14	1.95	Slevin (1929)
J	Idaho, USA	1969–71	89	8	76	16	2.08	Beecham & Kochert (1975)
K	Montana, USA	1964–5	20	5	80	15	2.10	McGahan (1968)
L	Utah, USA	1967–8	23	13	83	4	1.91	Camenzind (1969)

Differences in the frequency of different clutch sizes were tested using χ^2.
Clutch size for Scotland post-1970 was significantly lower than for the periods 1840–1900 and 1900–50 (A *vs* D; $P<0.01$: B *vs* D; $P<0.01$).
Clutch size for Scotland post-1970 was significantly less than for Idaho, USA (D *vs* J; $P<0.001$).

TABLE 39   *Golden Eagle clutch size in the west and east Highlands of Scotland (post–1970)*

Locality	Date	Sample size	C1 (%)	C2 (%)	C3 (%)	Mean
West Highlands	post–1970	144	19	80	1	1.82
East Highlands	post–1970	53	8	87	5	1.98

Differences in the frequency of different clutch sizes were tested using χ^2.
Clutch size in west Highlands was significantly lower than east Highlands ($P<0.05$).

TABLE 40   *Frequency of Golden Eagle pairs which did not lay in three study areas in Scotland. For each area, figures are means ± SE from 5 years of observation*

Locality	Pairs not laying each year (% ± SE)	Years in which observations were made	Total number of pairs checked each year
West Highlands, Scotland*	25.5 ± 3.31	1982–86	15–18
West Highlands, Scotland†	25.6 ± 3.21	1982–86	18–20
East Highlands, Scotland‡	13.5 ± 1.95	1982–86	13–15

*Study area C (see Chapter 4, Fig. 6).
†Study area F (see Chapter 4, Fig. 6).
‡Study area H (see Chapter 4, Fig. 6).

TABLE 41   *The sequence of plumage development and other changes in nestling Golden Eagles. (After Sumner 1929; Hoechlin 1976; Ellis 1979; and Mathieu 1985)*

Age (days)	Plumage development and other physical changes
1 5	Chicks covered in dense, off-white 'pre-pennae' down; egg-tooth present; talons flesh-coloured, feet and cere pale yellowish-flesh
5–15	Off-white down progressively replaced by snow-white 'pre-plumulae' down; egg-tooth present; talons grey; feet and cere pale yellow
15–25	Primary, secondary, scapular and tail feathers begin to grow in their sheaths; egg-tooth lost around 20–25 days
25–30	First signs of primary, secondary, scapular and tail feathers emerging from their sheaths; talons black; feet and cere bright lemon-yellow
30–35	First signs of greater coverts emerging from sheaths
35–40	Chicks have roughly equal amounts of dark contour feathers and white down visible on back and wings
40–45	Dark contour feathers more prevalent than white down on back and wings; underparts still predominantly down covered
45–50	Predominance of dark contour feathers on upperside and underside but head and neck still conspicuously down-covered
50–55	Emergence of dark contour feathers on head; feet now darker yellow than cere
55–60	Preponderance of dark contour feathers on head; some down still visible
60–70	Little down visible anywhere; white band at base of tail becoming conspicuous
70–80	Little further change except continued growth of flight feathers; plumes on head take on rich auburn colour

TABLE 42   *Number and biomass of prey deliveries by male and female Golden Eagles in relation to week of chick rearing. Data are from four nests observed in Idaho, USA during two breeding seasons by Collopy (1984)*

Week of chick rearing	Number of daylight hours observed	Mean (± SE) number of prey deliveries per 15-h day		Mean (± SE) biomass (g) of prey delivered per 15-h day	
		Male	Female	Male	Female
1	67	1.4 ± 0.38	0.1 ± 0.13	1251 ± 426.5	7 ± 6.5
2	103	1.2 ± 0.43	0.3 ± 0.19	750 ± 15.6	26 ± 16.9
3	119	0.7 ± 0.27	0.6 ± 0.37	503 ± 295.8	309 ± 166.9
4	134	1.3 ± 0.41	0.0	1137 ± 372.8	0
5	158	1.1 ± 0.36	0.6 ± 0.27	714 ± 262.7	216 ± 149.2
6	121	1.6 ± 0.46	0.8 ± 0.31	1184 ± 303.8	268 ± 178.6
7	145	1.3 ± 0.25	1.0 ± 0.38	1317 ± 556.7	902 ± 313.2
8	122	1.5 ± 0.27	1.5 ± 0.33	1140 ± 260.8	845 ± 242.2
9	134	0.9 ± 0.23	0.8 ± 0.31	968 ± 359.3	801 ± 315.2
10	145	1.0 ± 0.27	0.5 ± 0.27	1331 ± 500.6	482 ± 276.2
Overall	1248	1.2 ± 0.28	0.6 ± 0.44	1030 ± 284.6	387 ± 270.0

TABLE 43   *The nature of 'cainism' in species of* Aquila *eagles and aspects of their ecology*

Species	Cainism*	Breeding distribution	Migratory behaviour
Lesser Spotted Eagle	Obligate	Temperate	Long-range migrant
Greater Spotted Eagle	Facultative	Temperate/subtemperate	Medium-range migrant
Steppe Eagle†	Facultative	Temperate	Long-range migrant
Tawny Eagle	Obligate	Tropical/subtropical	Mainly resident
Imperial Eagle	Facultative	Temperate/subtemperate	Medium-range migrant
Golden Eagle	Facultative	Temperate	Mainly resident
Wedge-tailed Eagle	Facultative	Subtemperate	Mainly resident
Black Eagle	Obligate	Tropical	Mainly resident

*Based on information in Simmons (1988). See text for definitions of 'obligate' and 'facultative'.
†Ian Newton (*in litt.*) has pointed out that the two races of Steppe Eagle have quite different migratory behaviour. It would be interesting to know whether they differ in the type of cainism.

TABLE 44 *Frequency of fledged broods of 1 and 2 chicks among Golden Eagles over a 10-year period in two Regions of Scotland*

Area	Fledged 1		Fledged 2		Total successful broods
	n	(%)	n	(%)	
Skye (Region 2, Fig. 6)	113	(80)	28	(20)	141
West central Highlands (Region 6, Fig. 6)	54	(96)	2	(4)	56

These two Regions are less than 30 km apart and yet there is a significant difference in the frequency of 1 and 2 chick broods ($\chi^2 = 8.24$; $P < 0.01$).

Birds on Skye would be classed as 'facultative cainists' and those in the West Central Highlands as 'obligate cainists' according to Simmons (1988).

The key difference between the two localities is the amount of food available during the breeding season, with appreciably more in Skye (see Chapter 15).

Breeding density of Golden Eagles is not appreciably different between the two Regions (see Chapter 9).

TABLE 45 *The proportion of subadults in the Golden Eagle nesting population in relation to jackrabbit density, and eagle winter populations. Data are from Idaho (after Steenhof et al. 1983)*

Year	Percentage of nesting pairs with subadults	Jackrabbit density (n/100 km²)	Winter density of Golden Eagles (n/1000 km²)	
			Adult	Subadult
1970	4	–	–	–
1971	3	8980	–	–
1972	0	–	–	–
1973	5	1769	32	33
1974	6	1434	22	10
1975	0	1099	17	8
1976	6	1319	23	8
1977	3	1911	19	1
1978	6	2131	18	4
1979	9	3690	16	5
1980	13	4798	9	7
1981	3	5786	22	19

The incidence of subadult nesting was not correlated with either density of wintering subadults ($r = -0.15$, $P = 0.667$) or with jackrabbit abundance ($r = 0.10$, $P = 0.787$).

There was an inverse correlation between subadult nesting and winter adult density ($r = -0.63$, $P = 0.069$).

TABLE 46   *Biomass of live prey detected on line transects and breeding success of Golden Eagles in nine study areas in Scotland. Work was carried out in six areas (C,D,E,F,G,H) in 4 years (1982–85) and in three areas (A,B,I) in one year only (1985)*

Study area*	Year	Number of transects done	Length of transects (km)	Live prey (kg/20 km ± SE)	Fledged young per territorial pair (± SE)	Number of pairs of golden eagles
C	1982	9	162	5.8 ± 2.7	0.72 ± 0.12	15
C	1983	9	164	4.2 ± 0.9	0.56 ± 0.15	15
C	1984	4	77	2.5 ± 0.9	0.39 ± 0.11	15
C	1985	6	112	2.5 ± 0.9	0.42 ± 0.12	16
D	1982	3	53	3.0 ± 0.8	0.67 ± 0.16	18
D	1983	7	136	3.3 ± 0.9	0.44 ± 0.15	18
D	1984	6	111	4.1 ± 1.1	0.50 ± 0.14	19
D	1985	6	106	3.2 ± 0.8	0.56 ± 0.17	18
E	1982	0	–	–	0.65 ± 0.17	17
E	1983	4	82	8.9 ± 2.4	0.47 ± 0.17	17
E	1984	9	177	7.9 ± 0.9	0.88 ± 0.19	17
E	1985	5	101	6.7 ± 1.3	0.53 ± 0.19	17
F	1982	8	163	2.4 ± 0.8	0.38 ± 0.13	21
F	1983	8	171	2.6 ± 1.0	0.19 ± 0.09	21
F	1984	6	106	1.5 ± 0.5	0.24 ± 0.10	21
F	1985	6	116	2.2 ± 0.7	0.29 ± 0.10	21
G	1982	0	–	–	0.63 ± 0.18	14
G	1983	5	112	7.6 ± 2.5	0.61 ± 0.18	15
G	1984	5	98	5.0 ± 1.4	0.56 ± 0.17	15
G	1985	7	134	5.8 ± 2.3	0.67 ± 0.18	15
H	1982	2	37	24.6 ± 3.1	1.00 ± 0.22	16
H	1983	4	71	27.3 ± 9.7	0.60 ± 0.19	15
H	1984	7	137	17.1 ± 6.3	0.60 ± 0.19	15
H	1985	5	95	29.3 ± 7.3	0.69 ± 0.24	14
A	1985	4	79	27.6 ± 22.0	0.57 ± 0.17	15
B	1985	5	90	7.2 ± 1.3	0.60 ± 0.13	15
I	1985	5	88	14.3 ± 1.3	0.80 ± 0.20	6

*See Fig. 6.

TABLE 47 Breeding success among Golden Eagles in different years in three study areas in Scotland

Study area*	Year	Number of pairs of territorial eagles	Number (and %) of pairs laying eggs		Number (and %) of pairs with fledged young		Total number of fledged young	Mean number of fledged young per pair
			n	%	n	%	n	
F	1982	20	17	85.0	7	35.0	8	0.40
F	1983	20	13	65.0	4	20.0	4	0.20
F	1984	20	15	75.0	5	25.0	5	0.25
F	1985	20	15	75.0	6	30.0	6	0.30
F	1986	18	13	72.2	3	16.7	3	0.17
F	1987	18	11	61.1	5	27.8	6	0.33
F	1988	15	9	60.0	6	40.0	6	0.40
F	1989	16	10	62.5	7	43.8	7	0.44
F	1990	15	12	80.0	6	40.0	6	0.40
F	1991	18	14	77.8	7	38.9	7	0.39
10-year mean				71.4		31.7		0.33
A	1982	28	22	78.6	15	53.6	16	0.57
A	1983	19	18	94.7	9	47.4	9	0.47
A	1984	27	20	74.1	15	55.6	17	0.63
A	1985	30	20	66.7	15	50.0	17	0.57
A	1986	30	22	73.3	10	33.3	13	0.43
A	1987	30	25	83.3	15	50.0	16	0.53
A	1988	30	26	86.7	15	50.0	21	0.70
A	1989	29	23	79.3	19	65.5	25	0.86
A	1990	29	22	75.9	15	51.7	20	0.69
A	1991	28	22	78.6	13	46.4	15	0.54
10-year mean				79.1		50.3		0.60
H	1982	15	13	86.7	10	66.7	16	1.07
H	1983	15	13	86.7	7	46.7	9	0.60
H	1984	15	13	86.7	7	46.7	9	0.60
H	1985	13	12	92.3	6	46.2	9	0.69
H	1986	15	12	80.0	8	53.3	9	0.60
H	1987	13	11	84.6	8	61.5	12	0.92
H	1988	14	12	85.7	7	50.0	12	0.86
H	1989	13	12	92.3	11	84.6	15	1.15
8-year mean				86.9		57.0		0.81

*See Fig. 6 for locations; data for area A refer to a substantially larger area than that used in the food supply work (Table 46).

TABLE 48   *Summary breeding data for 16 pairs of Golden Eagles in central Utah (1967–73), and state of jackrabbit cycle (after Murphy 1975)*

Year	Fledged young per territorial pair	Fledged young per successful pair	State of Jackrabbit cycle
1967*	0.56	1.80	Numbers moderately low
1968	0.87	1.40	Numbers increasing
1969	1.06	1.89	Peak numbers
1970	1.00	1.60	Numbers declining
1971	0.62	1.67	Numbers declining
1972	0.44	1.17	Numbers declining
1973	0.31	1.25	Numbers very low

*1967 breeding data were incomplete.

TABLE 49   *Annual differences in the breeding success of Golden Eagles before (1982–89) and after (1990–92) VHP†. Data are from Navarra in northern Spain (after Fernández 1993a).*

Year	Number of pairs	Percentage of laying pairs	Percentage of successful pairs	Number of fledglings per successful pair	Number of fledglings per pair
1982	7	71	57	1.50	0.86
1983	8	75	75	1.16	0.88
1984	10	80	50	1.20	0.60
1985	12	83	58	1.29	0.75
1986	12	92	83	1.30	1.08
1987	12	75	50	1.33	0.75
1988	11	82	46	1.40	0.64
1989	14	100	57	1.33	0.79
Before VHP	86	84	59	1.29	0.77
1990	15	60	27	1.25	0.33
1991	15	67	40	1.17	0.47
1992	15	73	27	1.25	0.33
After VHP	45	67	31	1.21	0.38

†VHP (viral haemorrhagic pneumonia) is a new epizootic disease affecting rabbits in the Mediterranean.

TABLE 50   *Frequency of different clutch-sizes among Steppe Eagles in spring 1955 (after Agafanov et al. 1957)*

Clutch size	Number of clutches	Percentage of clutches
1	22	21.8
2	30	29.7
3	37	36.6
4	10	9.9
5*	2	2.0
Total	101	

*These are the only documented C5 in an *Aquila* eagle. See text for explanation.

TABLE 51   *Frequency of prey deliveries to a Golden Eagle nest under different weather conditions. Data are from a nest in Japan observed throughout the nestling period (after Aoyama et al. 1988)*

Weather conditions	Number of prey deliveries per day										Total days
	0		1		2		3		4		
	n	%	n	%	n	%	n	%	n	%	
Fine	16	33.3	16	33.3	13	27.1	1	2.1	2	4.2	48
Cloudy	8	33.3	8	33.3	6	25	1	4.2	1	4.2	24
Snow/Rain	7	87.5	1	12.5	0	–	0	–	0	–	8

In statistical analysis, birds were significantly more likely to bring in no food on days with snow/rain than on fine/cloudy days ($\chi^2 = 8.90$, $P < 0.01$).

TABLE 52   *Breeding success figures from a range of Golden Eagle studies in Scotland, continental Europe and the United States.* Dietary breadth figures are from Tables 7, 9 and 10*

Country	Location	Fledged young per territorial pair	Dietary breadth	Source
Scotland	Region 2	0.60	4.71	Watson (this title)
Scotland	Region 3	0.45	3.47	Watson (this title)
Scotland	Region 4	0.52	7.21	Watson (this title)
Scotland	Region 5	0.59	5.94	Watson (this title)
Scotland	Region 6	0.33	7.25	Watson (this title)
Scotland	Region 7	0.62	5.38	Watson (this title)
Scotland	Region 8	0.81	2.44	Watson (this title)
Scotland	Region 9	0.23	7.43	Watson (this title)
Belorus		1.10	3.38	Ivanovsky (1990)
France	Alps	0.76	3.23	Mathieu & Choisy (1982)
France	Alps	0.45	2.06	Huboux (1987)
France	Alps	0.30	5.14	Huboux (1987)
France	Pyrénées	0.48	11.20	Clouet (1981)
Italy	Apennines	0.61	3.43	Novelletto & Petretti (1980)
Italy	Apennines	0.58	4.69	Magrini et al. (1987)
Macedonia		1.00	3.20	Grubač (1987)
Slovakia		0.55	7.50	Danko (in litt.)
Spain	Navarra	0.75	2.13	Fernández (1987)
Sweden		0.70	2.69	Tjernberg (1983a)
United States	Alaska	1.50	2.33	Ritchie & Curatolo (1982)
United States	Alaska	1.60	1.40	Murie (1944)
United States	Idaho	1.15	1.83	Kochert (1972)
United States	Washington	0.50	4.35	Knight & Erickson (1978)
United States	Arizona	1.08	4.45	Thompson et al. (1982)

TABLE 53   *Frequency of Golden Eagle recoveries in Scotland* at different distances from place of ringing. Data are given separately for birds recovered <18 months old and older*

Age at recovery	Distance between ringing and recovery location (km)						Average distance moved (km)	Total birds recovered
	1–30	*31–60*	*61–90*	*91–120*	*120–150*	*>150*		
<18 months, n (%)	8 (31)	5 (19)	6 (23)	4 (15)	2 (8)	1 (4)	63	26
>18 months, n (%)	5 (56)	2 (22)	2 (22)	0 (–)	0 (–)	0 (–)	36	9
Total								35

*Includes one bird ringed and recovered in England.
In statistical analysis (Mann–Whitney U-test) the difference between the two age groups is close to significance. $U = 154$, $n_1 = 9$, $n_2 = 26$, $P = 0.07$.

TABLE 54   *Ring recoveries and wing-marker sightings of Golden Eagles at different distances from the place of marking. Data are from southern Idaho, USA and after Steenhof et al. (1984)*

Type of mark	Distance between recovery location and natal site (km)				Total
	<100	*100–300*	*300–1000*	*>1000*	
Ring n (%)	41 (77)	10 (19)	2 (4)	0 (–)	53
Wing-marker n (%)	114 (77)	18 (12)	14 (10)	1 (1)	147
Total					200

TABLE 55   *Numbers of Golden Eagles counted migrating over the Mount Lorette area, Alberta in spring and autumn 1992–95 (after Sherrington, 1993, and in litt)*

1992*		1993		1994		1995	
Spring	*Autumn*	*Spring*	*Autumn*	*Spring*	*Autumn*	*Spring*	*Autumn*
386	2043	4140	4599	4213	3836	4143	3703

*Coverage in 1992 was less complete than in later years.

TABLE 56   *Differences in migration behaviour among the* Aquila *eagles*

Species	Migratory behaviour
Lesser Spotted Eagle	Intercontinental migrant
Greater Spotted Eagle	Partial migrant over moderate distances
Steppe Eagle	Eastern race is probably a partial migrant over moderate distances
	Western race is an inter continental migrant
Tawny Eagle	Mainly resident, some populations may be intra-African migrants
Imperial Eagle	Eastern race is a partial migrant over moderate distances
	Spanish race is mainly resident
Gurney's Eagle	Unknown but presumably resident
Golden Eagle	Mainly resident, some northern populations are long-range migrants
Wedge-tailed Eagle	Mainly resident
Black Eagle	Mainly resident

Sources of information; Cramp & Simmons (1980); Brown *et al.* (1982); Gargett (1990); Marchant & Higgins (1993).

TABLE 57   *Numbers of Lesser Spotted and Steppe Eagles counted on autumn migration at various localities in the Middle East. Counts of more than 1000 birds have been rounded to the nearest 1000*

Species	Bosphorous* 13 Aug–8 Oct 1971	Eastern Black Sea* 17 Aug–10 Oct 1976	Suez† 24 Sep–5 Nov 1981	Eilat† 24 Sep–29 Nov 1980	Bab-el-Mandeb‡ 15 Oct–1 Nov 1985
Lesser Spotted Eagle	19 000	740	22 000	–	–
Steppe Eagle	–	270	65 000	24 000	61 000

*from data given in Newton (1979).
†From data given in Christensen & Sorensen (1989).
‡From data in Welch & Welch (1989).

TABLE 58   *Estimated adult survival rate, and average adult life expectancy among Golden Eagles and other large eagles*

Species	Locality	Estimated adult survival	Average adult life expectancy* (years)	Source
Golden Eagle	Germany	0.92	12	Bezzel & Fünfstück (1994)
Golden Eagle	Western Scotland	0.975	39.5	Nellist & Crane (*in litt.*)
Spanish Imperial Eagle	Spain	0.936–0.972	15.1–34.6	Ferrer (1993a)
Bald Eagle	Alaska	0.95	19.5	Sherrod *et al.* (1977)
Bald Eagle	Saskatchewan	0.92–0.94	12–16.1	Gerrard *et al.* (1992)
Bald Eagle	Alaska	0.88	7.8	Bowman *et al.* (1995)

*Calculated from the equation $(2 - m)/2m$ where m is the annual adult mortality rate as a fraction of unity (Perrins & Birkhead 1983).

TABLE 59   *Causes of death among Golden Eagles in Britain*

Source	Period		Shooting and trapping	Poisoning	Electrocution	Collision with wires	Unspecified trauma	Disease	Other	Unknown or unreported	Total
						Cause of death					
BTO*	1957–93	n (%)	6 (18)	3 (9)	0 (–)	6 (18)	0 (–)	1 (3)	2 (6)	16 (47)	34
SASA†	1980–95	n (%)	8 (10)	29 (36)	2 (2)	0 (–)	10 (12)	1 (1)	0 (–)	31 (38)	81
ITE‡	1963–95	n (%)	4 (21)	3 (16)	1 (5)	2 (11)	1 (5)	1 (5)	2 (11)	5 (26)	19

*Information taken from British Trust for Ornithology ringing recovery forms. Five birds caught in crow traps and allegedly released by the finder are included under 'shooting and trapping'.

†Information provided by K. Hunter (*in litt.*) from Golden Eagles submitted for post-mortem analysis to the Scottish Agricultural Science Agency, Edinburgh, Scotland.

‡Information provided by L. Dale (*in litt.*) from Golden Eagles submitted for post-mortem analysis to the Institute of Terrestrial Ecology, Monks Wood, England.

Note 1. Some of the birds included under BTO may also be included under either SASA or ITE. All birds in SASA and ITE samples are definitely different.

Note 2. Birds recorded as dead from 'other' causes included individuals believed to have drowned, and birds probably killed by other eagles.

Note 3. In some cases the report stated 'trauma – probably shot' and these birds are included in the shot column.

Note 4. Nestling eagles have been excluded from all data sets.

TABLE 60   *Cause of death among Golden Eagles as reported in one study in Spain and three studies in North America*

Location	Period		Shooting	Trapping	Poisoning	Electrocution	Unspecified trauma	Disease	Other	Unknown	Total
						Cause of death					
Spain*	1980–90	n (%)	157 (59)	21 (8)	14 (5)	57 (21)	0 (–)	0 (–)	0 (–)	17 (6)	266
Idaho, USA†	1970–71	n (%)	5 (16)	0 (–)	0 (–)	9 (29)	8 (26)	3 (10)	0 (–)	6 (19)	31
North America‡	?	n (%)	8 (6)	16 (11)	11 (8)	0 (–)	2 (1)	0 (–)	1 (1)	105 (73)	143
North America§	?	n (%)	9 (25)	3 (8)	0 (–)	0 (–)	0 (–)	0 (–)	6 (17)	18 (50)	36

*From data in Arroyo *et al.* (1990).

†From data in Kochert (1972)

‡From data in Bortolotti (1984b). Note that this information was taken from museum skins and for many there was no record of cause of death.

§From data in Table 4 in Keran (1981). Note that birds placed in the 'natural' mortality category by Keran are included above under 'unknown'.

TABLE 61 *Exceptional levels of organochlorine and mercury contamination in a Golden Eagle from the island of Lewis, Scotland. Data from Newton & Galbraith (1991) who described this bird as 'the most contaminated raptor they had ever examined'. The source of this contamination was seabirds, mainly Fulmars, on which the eagle was known to feed*

	HEOD	DDE	PCBs	Mercury
Concentration in liver (ppm)	59	182	447	76

TABLE 62 *Numbers of Golden Eagles shot from aircraft by a single operator in Texas during six winters in the 1940s (after Spofford 1964)*

Year	Number of Golden Eagles shot
1941–42	657
1942–43	667
1943–44	1008
1944–45	800
1945–46	867
1946–47	819
Total	4818

TABLE 63 *Level of human disturbance at nest sites of 335 pairs of Golden Eagles in Scotland in 1982, together with fledging success (after Watson & Dennis 1992)*

Level of disturbance*	Number of young fledged					Total	(%)
	0	(%)	1	2	(% 1 + 2)		
Low	109	(46)	107	20	(54)	236	(70)
Moderate	52	(74)	14	4	(26)	70	(21)
Severe	27	(93)	2	0	(7)	29	(9)

*During the 1982 national survey, observers subjectively classified the level of disturbance at Golden Eagle nests as follows.

Low: no evidence of human disturbance in 1982, nor in the recent past (defined as the previous 5–10 years).

Moderate: some evidence of human disturbance by hill-walkers, or occasional evidence of visits by egg-collectors either in 1982 or in the recent past.

Severe: evidence of use of poisons within the home range, killing of adult eagles, destruction of nest contents, or persistent egg-collecting in 1982 and/or in the recent past.

TABLE 64   *The number of Golden Eagle nests subjected to different levels of disturbance in differen parts of Scotland. Data are from 335 nests for 1982 and the range is divided into longitudinal bands from west (1) to east (9) across the Highlands. See Watson & Dennis (1992) for definition of the bands. Disturbance criteria are explained under Table 62*

Level of disturbance	1	2	3	4	5	(%1–5)	6	7	8	9	(%6–9)
Low	21	23	21	32	42	(74)	44	28	13	12	(66)
Moderate	10	7	2	15	9	(23)	8	9	7	3	(18)
Severe	2	2	0	1	0	(3)	0	4	13	7	(16)
Total	33	32	23	48	51		52	41	33	22	

In statistical analysis, severe disturbance was higher in bands 6–9 than in bands 1–5, $\chi^2 = 19.16$, $P<0.001$.

TABLE 65   *The incidence of breeding failure among Golden Eagles, and the number of nests fledging 1 and 2 young in Scotland in 1982. Data are for 348 nests classified as easy, moderate or difficult in terms of accessibility by people*

Accessibility*	Failed (%)	Number of young fledged			Total
		1	2	(% 1 + 2)	
Easy	47 (69)	15	6	(31)	68
Moderate	73 (55)	47	13	(45)	133
Difficult	73 (50)	66	8	(50)	147

*Accessibility was classified subjectively by observers in 1982 as follows:

Easy: nest site could be reached safely without the aid of a rope.

Moderate: a rope was advisable for safety but not judged essential.

Difficult: it was physically impossible to reach the nest site without the aid of a rope.

In statistical analysis, sites that were 'easy' of access were more likely to fail than 'difficult' sites $\chi = 7.14$, $P<0.01$.

TABLE 66   *Breeding success of Golden Eagles in western Scotland in the 1960s, in relation to dieldrin levels in eggs (after Lockie et al. 1969)*

Period	Number of nests with eggs	Percentage of nests that fledged young	Mean dieldrin level (ppm)	Number of eggs analysed
1963–65	39	31	0.86	48
1966–68	69	45	0.34	23

Differences in dieldrin residues between the two periods were significant. Mann–Whitney U-test: $U = 279$, $n_1 = 23$, $n_2 = 48$, $P = 0.0004$.

TABLE 67   *Organochlorine levels (ppm) and shell-indices in Golden Eagle eggs from different periods and regions in Scotland. For organochlorines the figures show the geometric means (and range within one geometric standard error), while for shell-indices the figures show the arithmetic standard error (after Newton & Galbraith 1991)*

	West Highland (coastal)			West Highland (inland)			East Highland (inland)		
	1963–70	1971–80	1981–86	1963–70	1971–80	1981–86	1963–70	1971–80	1981–86
n	24	33	23	37	40	34	8	11	15
DDE	0.483	0.300	0.316	0.146	0.183	0.072	0.095	0.054	0.032
	(0.371–0.630)	(0.240–0.375)	(0.228–0.436)	(0.114–0.186)	(0.163–0.205)	(0.058–0.090)	(0.066–0.135)	(0.042–0.070)	(0.022–0.047)
HEOD	0.463	0.0969	0.068	0.178	0.062	0.066	0.037	0.023	0.035
	(0.364–0.590)	(0.080–0.117)	(0.041–0.078)	(0.135–0.235)	(0.053–0.072)	(0.053–0.083)	(0.027–0.049)	(0.018–0.029)	(0.026–0.047)
PCB	–	1.220	1.527	–	0.674	1.454	–	0.151	0.443
		(0.951–1.565)	(1.061–2.198)		(0.577–0.788)	(1.232–1.718)		(0.102–0.224)	(0.261–0.753)
Shell-index	–	3.028 ± 0.069	2.990 ± 0.092	–	3.055 ± 0.043	3.120 ± 0.065	–	2.932 ± 0.066	3.255 ± 0.043

Pre-1947 (pre-DDT), the mean shell-index in western Scotland was 3.146 ± 0.035, and in eastern Scotland 3.164 ± 0.032 (Ratcliffe, 1970). In 1951–65, the mean shell index for western scotland was 2.834 ± 0.034 ($n = 27$) (Ratcliffe, 1970). This was significantly lower than the 1971–80 coastal mean given above ($t_{58} = 2.14$. $P<0.05$), and than the 1971–80 western mean given above ($t_{65} = 3.32$, $P<0.01$).

TABLE 68 *Number of Golden Eagles reported electrocuted at power poles in the western United States in 1972 and 1973 (after Boeker & Nickerson 1975)*

State	1972	1973
California	3	3
Colorado	–	6
Idaho	14	16
Kansas	–	6
Missouri	–	1
Montana	4	20
Nevada	25	34
New Mexico	4	10
North Dakota	1	–
Oregon	9	2
South Dakota	6	2
Texas	1	1
Utah	66	14
Washington	1	–
Total	134	115

TABLE 69 *Sex differences in nestlings, in adult mortality, and in the use of perches by Spanish Imperial Eagles (after Ferrer & Hiraldo (1991)*

	Males		Females	
	n	(%)	n	(%)
Nestlings	22	(48)	24	(52)
Mortality				
Electrocution	7	(22)	25	(78)
Other causes	15	(47)	17	(53)
Electrocution				
Inside Doñana	4	(22)	14	(78)
Outside Doñana	3	(21)	11	(79)
Perches used				
Pylons	32	(54)	27	(46)
Other perches	358	(60)	242	(40)

The sex ratio on leaving the nest was not significantly diferent from 1:1 ($\chi^2 = 0.086$, $P = 0.77$).

There was a significant difference between the sexes in mortality due to electrocution ($\chi^2 = 10.1$, $P = 0.001$).

There was no significant difference in the choice of perches (pylons *vs* others) between the sexes.

TABLE 70   *Number of young fledged by four pairs of Golden Eagles in Galloway, southwest Scotland over 10 years (1974–83). Also shown is the per cent of open ground below 305 m that had been afforested by 1979 within 2.5 km of roosting places in each territory (after Marquiss et al. 1985)*

	Territory			
	A	B	C	D
Breeding success (young fledged per pair over 10 years)	0.0	0.1	0.3	0.8
Per cent ground below 305 m afforested by 1979	90.4	84.5	30.9	33.6

TABLE 71   *Extract from game books showing numbers of grouse shot on one estate in the West Highlands of Scotland in the late nineteenth century (after Gaskell 1980)*

Year	Number of grouse shot each year (includes Black and Red Grouse)
1886	519
1887	514
1888	619
1889	951
1890	1042
1891	1268
1892	512
1893	674
1894	258
1895	434
Average per year	679

This is an area I know well, and where the average number of Red Grouse seen on a 20-km walk is now fewer than five birds. There are now virtually no Black Grouse in the area.

TABLE 72   *The range of threats experienced by Aquila eagles. Serious and/or widespread threats are indicated by (++), more localized threats by (+). Where a particular type of threat is probably unimportant it is indicated by (−).*

Species*	Type of threat						Comment†
	Shooting and trapping	Poisoning	Unintentional disturbance	Pesticides and pollutants	Electrocution and collisions	Land use change	
Lesser Spotted Eagle	++	−	+	−	−	+	Large numbers shot in Syria and Lebanon on migration. Habitat loss through agricultural improvement.
Greater Spotted Eagle	+	−	+	−	−	++	Drainage of wetlands in nesting area.
Steppe Eagle	+	+	+		++	++	Agricultural development of steppe habitat. Large numbers found dead under power lines in Russia.
Tawny Eagle	−	+	−		−	+	Susceptible to poisoning. Loss of habitat through intensification of farming in southern Africa.
Imperial Eagle	++	+	+	+	++	++	Shooting of birds on migration in the Middle East. Electrocution in Spain. Loss of Habitat throughout.
Golden Eagle	++	++	+	+	+	++	Shooting of birds in southern Europe. Poisoning in various countries. Habitat change in various countries.
Wedge-tailed Eagle	++	+	+	−	−	++	Persecution and logging in Tasmania. Frequently shot in mainland Australia.
Black Eagle	+	−	−	−	−	+	Persecuted in parts of southern Africa. Overgrazing by stock has reduced wild prey in places.

*No information available on Gurney's Eagle, although it is likely to be threatened by habitat change.

†Based on information in Marchant & Higgins (1993); del Hoyo et al. (1994); Tucker & Heath (1994). Additional information from Gargett (1990); Ferrer (1993a); Brown (1991); Mooney & Holdsworth (1991).

TABLE 73   *Names of Golden Eagles in various (mainly European) languages*

Language	Name
Bashahr*	Dhungoorish
Chamba*	Mūriāri
Bulgarian	Skalen orel
Croatian	Suri orao
Czech	Orla skalni
Dutch	Steenarend
English	Golden eagle
French	Aigle royal
Finnish	Maakotka
Gaelic (Irish)	Iolar
Gaelic (Scots)	Iolaire
German	Steinadler
Greek	Χρυσαετός
Hungarian	Szirti sas
Italian	Aquila reale
Japanese	イヌワツ
Lithuanian	Kilnieji ereli
Norwegian	Kongeørn
Polish	Orzeł przedni
Portuguese	Águia real
Russian	**Беркут**
Slovene	Planinski orel
Spanish	Águila real
Swedish	Kungsörn
Welsh	Eryri

*Languages spoken in northern India.

Index